Eva Hausbacher, Elena Huber, Julia Hargaßner (eds.)

Fashion, Consumption and Everyday Culture in the Soviet Union between 1945 and 1985

DIE WELT DER SLAVEN
SAMMELBÄNDE · СБОРНИКИ

Herausgegeben von
Peter Rehder (München) und Igor Smirnov (Konstanz)

Band 54

2014
Verlag Otto Sagner
München – Berlin – Washington/D.C.

Fashion, Consumption and Everyday Culture in the Soviet Union between 1945 and 1985

Edited by

Eva Hausbacher
Elena Huber
Julia Hargaßner

2014
Verlag Otto Sagner
München – Berlin – Washington/D.C.

Gedruckt mit freundlicher Unterstützung
des Austrian Science Fund (FWF)

Bibliografische Information der Deutschen Nationalbibliothek
Die Deutsche Nationalbibliothek verzeichnet diese Publikation in der
Deutschen Nationalbibliografie; detaillierte bibliografische Daten
sind im Internet über http://dnb.d-nb.de abrufbar

Vignette:
Ausschnitt aus einem Schnittbogen aus der Beilage zur Zeitschrift *Rabotnica* 1971, Nr. 1.

ISBN 978-3-86688-522-6; e-Book 978-3-86688-523-3

Heßstr. 39/41 – D-80798 München *** Friedrichstr. 200 – D-10117 Berlin
1532 T Street NW – Washington/D.C. 20009, USA
Telefon +49(0)8954218–107; Telefax +49(0)8954218–216
»Verlag Otto Sagner« ist ein Imprint der Kubon & Sagner GmbH
Die Auslieferung für die USA übernimmt die Kubon & Sagner Inc., Washington/D.C.

Druck und Bindung: Strauss GmbH, D-69509 Mörlenbach

Gedruckt auf alterungsbeständigem Papier

INHALTSVERZEICHNIS

Mode und Kunst

VORWORT

„Dem Studium der Mode sind offensichtlich keine Grenzen mehr gesetzt“, konstatieren Gertrud Lehnert, Alicia Kühl und Katja Weise in der Einleitung des Readers *„Modetheorie. Klassische Texte aus vier Jahrhunderten“* (2014). Ausgehend von Großbritannien und den USA, wo Fashion Studies mittlerweile fixer Bestandteil an den Universitäten sind, ist auch in Russland Fashion Theorie[1] zu einem wichtigen Feld im wissenschaftlichen Diskurs geworden. Seit einigen Jahren sind diese Entwicklungen auch im deutschsprachigen Raum, wo Kleidermode lange Zeit als Phänomen der Oberfläche und des Alltäglich-Trivialen eine negative wissenschaftliche Reputation hatte, wahrnehmbar. Auch hier hat Modeforschung als interdisziplinär verhandelter Gegenstand seit den 1990er Jahren Konjunktur.[2] Der vorliegende Band, der die Beiträge der Tagung *Fashion, Consumption and Everyday Culture in the Soviet Union between 1945 and 1985* versammelt, die von 24. bis 26 Oktober 2013 am Fachbereich Slawistik der Universität Salzburg stattgefunden hat, versteht sich als Baustein dieses Forschungsfeldes in den Fächern der Slawistischen Kulturwissenschaft sowie der Osteuropastudien.

Die Tagung wurde im Rahmen eines mehrjährigen Forschungsprojekts am Fachbereich Slawistik ausgerichtet, in dem Fragen nach den gesellschaftlichen Transformationen in der Sowjetunion von der Tauwetterperiode bis zur Perestrojka anhand der Untersuchung der Veränderungen in der Kleidermode verhandelt werden.[3] Mitte der 1950er Jahre lässt sich ein Wendepunkt in der sowjetischen Konsumpolitik feststellen, der mit politischen und sozialen Verschiebungen und Erneuerungen verbunden war. Ausgehend von der Rolle der materiellen Kultur im Spannungsfeld zwischen sowjetischem Dresscode und individuell hergestellter Kleidung und ihrer sozialen und kulturellen Bedeutung fokussiert das Projekt den Zusammenhang zwischen dem Konsum und seiner Legitimation einerseits und dem Staat und den gesellschaftlichen Machtbeziehungen andererseits. Dieser Zugang eröffnet nicht nur neue Perspektiven für die Analyse der gesellschaftlichen, ökonomischen und politischen Entwicklungen und Umbrüche der späten Sowjetunion, sondern ermöglicht zudem, die Bedeutungen dieser Prozesse für die (De-)Stabilisierung der Herrschaftsstrukturen zu verstehen und neue Facetten des alltäglichen Lebens zu entdecken, die Verhaltensmuster der Sowjetbürger, wie individuelle Aneignungs- und Abgrenzungsprozesse veranschaulichen und ihre Sehnsüchte und Bedürfnisse sichtbar werden lassen.

Die von unterschiedlichen Disziplinen und Forschungskontexten ausgehenden Beiträge des vorliegenden Sammelbandes verbindet der gemeinsame Ansatz, die Alltags- und Gesellschaftsgeschichte der Sowjetunion aus der Perspektive der materiellen Kultur zu betrachten und deren Auswirkungen auf das soziale und kulturelle Leben auszuloten. Im Zentrum steht dabei die Frage, wie sich Form, Sinn und Gebrauch von Alltagsdingen unter besonderen politischen, wirtschaftlichen und gesellschaftlichen Bedingungen transformieren. Der zentrale

---

[1] Die Zeitschrift *Teorija mody* wurde im Jahr 2006 gegründet. Wurden anfänglich viele Beiträge aus *Fashion Theory: The Journal of Dress, Body & Culture* nachgedruckt, so ist mittlerweile die russische Forschungslandschaft zum Thema so angewachsen, dass die Verlagsarbeit auf die Buchreihe *Bibliotheka žurnala «Teorija mody»* (2010) erweitert wurde. Zahlreiche Konferenzen, öffentliche Vorlesungen und Studienlehrgänge, die sich mit der Mode als Kulturphänomen interdisziplinär beschäftigen, zeigen, dass sich Mode als Forschungsbereich auch in Russland etabliert hat.

[2] Vgl. WEHINGER, B. 2002. Modisch/ Mode. In: Barck, K. (Hrsg.). *Ästhetische Grundbegriffe: historisches Wörterbuch in sieben Bänden.* Stuttgart 2002, 168 – 183

[3] Das aus Mitteln des Austrian Science Fund (FWF) geförderte *Projekt „Needle and thread. Transformations in Soviet dress and changes in values in the Soviet Union as an example of individual clothing production (1953-1985)”* mit einer Laufzeit von drei Jahren wird am Fachbereich Slawistik der Universität Salzburg unter der Leitung von Univ.Prof. Dr. Eva Hausbacher und der Mitarbeit von Dr. Elena Huber und Mag. Julia Hargaßner durchgeführt.

Untersuchungsfokus aller Beiträge ist die Kleidermode, wie sie sich in der Sowjetunion zwischen 1945 und 1985 entwickelt hat, einerseits im Bereich der individuellen, d.h. zu Hause, bei einer Schneiderin oder in einem Atelier hergestellten Kleidung, andererseits auch in dem der offiziell propagierten Modewelt. In den unterschiedlichen Kontextualisierungen von Mode- und Kleidungsforschung, Frauen- und Geschlechterforschung sowie den Forschungen zur Konsumgeschichte werden Fragen nach den, insbesondere in Differenzsetzung zu „westlichen" Trends feststellbaren Besonderheiten im Bereich der sowjetischen Kleidermode zwischen Nachkriegszeit und Perestrojka, ebenso wie nach politischen, ökonomischen, ideologischen und kulturellen Gegebenheiten und Normvorstellungen, die zu dieser Entwicklung beigetragen haben, verhandelt. Darüber hinaus wird in den Beiträgen aus unterschiedlichen Perspektiven untersucht, inwiefern die individuelle Herstellung der Kleidung eine Veränderung im alltäglichen Bekleidungsverhalten der sowjetischen Frau ermöglicht und damit zur Herausbildung einer neuen Konsumentin und schließlich zur Transformierung gesellschaftlicher Normen beigetragen hat, welche Rolle dafür westliche „Vorbilder" spielten und ab wann und wie es zu derartigen Individualisierungsprozessen gekommen ist.

Die Beiträge des Bandes sind in drei Bereiche gruppiert:[4] Im ersten Abschnitt finden sich unter dem Titel „Sozialistische Mode" jene Aufsätze, die in die Geschichte und Diskurse der sowjetischen Kleidermode einführen und einen fundierten Überblick über die sowjetische Konsumkultur und deren Erforschung geben. Mit „Mode und Gesellschaft" ist der zweite und längste Abschnitt betitelt, der jene Beiträge versammelt, die aus sozial- und kulturwissenschaftlicher Perspektive Phänomene der Ökonomie und des Handels, alltagskulturelle Gegebenheiten und genderspezifische Aspekte des untersuchten Zeitraums ausleuchten. Im dritten Abschnitt schließlich sind unter dem Kapitelnamen „Mode und Kunst" jene Aufsätze gereiht, die die vielseitigen Wechselwirkungen von literarischen und filmischen Kleiderdiskursen mit den realen Gegebenheiten jener Zeit, wie sie aus heutiger Sicht rekonstruierbar sind, nachgehen.

Die vierzehn Beiträge des vorliegenden Bandes sind auf Deutsch, Englisch und Russisch verfasst, was die Edition des Buches aufgrund der Unterschiede in den wissenschaftlichen Traditionen zu einem anspruchsvollen Unternehmen gemacht hat. Unsere Vereinheitlichung betrifft in erster Linie die bibliographischen Regeln, nicht jedoch die Transliterationssysteme des jeweiligen Sprachraums.

Wir danken allen Autorinnen, die mit ihren Vorträgen, Diskussionen und Aufsätzen zum Gelingen dieses Sammelbandes beigetragen haben. Sowohl die Durchführung der Tagung als auch die Drucklegung des Tagungsbandes wurde aus Mitteln des Austrian Science Fund (FWF) finanziert, bei dem sich die Herausgeberinnen für die großzügige Förderung bedanken. Darüber hinaus gilt unser Dank dem Fachbereich Slawistik der Universität Salzburg, der das Projekt beheimatet und in den verschiedenen Phasen seiner Realisierung tatkräftig unterstützt, insbesondere Frau Gertraud Hatheyer.

Salzburg im November 2014 — Eva Hausbacher, Elena Huber, Julia Hargaßner

[4] Am Ende jedes Beitrags findet sich eine kurze englischsprachige Zusammenfassung.

MYTH AND REALITY: Five-Year Plans and Socialist Fashion

DJURDJA BARTLETT, LONDON

Introduction

Following the Bolshevik revolution in 1917, Russia went through a series of very different socialist practices, from the initial Leninist period, through the New Economic Policy (NEP) and its reintroduction of semi-capitalism in the 1920s,[1] to Stalinism which economically and politically centralized the country and isolated it from the West, and then to a new political turn introduced by Nikita Khrushchev in the 1950s, which attempted to abandon Stalinist isolationism and modernize the Soviet Union. As his reforms failed, Khrushchev was in 1964 succeeded by Leonid Brezhnev, resulting in a political and economic stagnation of the country. From the mid-1980s a new leader, Mikhail Gorbachev, proposed a set of radical reforms, which eventually led to the dismantling of socialist Russia in 1991. During this historical period of seventy-four years, the official relationship towards the phenomenon of fashion kept changing.[2] Fashion became a despised activity immediately after 1917, and continued to be ideologically distrusted throughout these various political and social shifts, since it originated in the West and was part of the rejected bourgeois cultural and commercial heritage. In early-1920s Russia, the Constructivists embodied Bolshevik anxieties concerning dress as a carrier of status and gender differences. Relying on the aesthetics of utopian abstractionism, they envisioned a total change in dress, advocating functionality, modesty, and simple geometrical lines.

While such initial attempts at utopia had rejected fashion, it received official approval in the Stalinist Soviet Union from the mid-1930s on. The phenomenon of socialist official fashion developed within a highly centralized system and its Five-Year Plans, which were introduced as a part of the Stalinist industrialization drive, designed to raise technical and organizational levels of the backward Russian textile and clothing industries. Born in the *Dom modelei* 'House of Prototypes'[3] in Moscow in 1935, socialist official fashion marked a return to concepts of traditional luxury, elegance and femininity within Stalinist mythical culture.[4] The ideological imposition of conventionally elegant, feminine dress took place amidst the terrible deprivations of everyday life that had begun with the introduction of the Five-Year Plans and subsequently accompanied the Soviet industrialization.[5] Yet the birth of socialist fashion was not disturbed by real-life changes, fashion trends or the laws of the market. Strongly promoted

---

[1] The New Economic Policy (NEP) was established in 1921, with a Council of People's Commissars' decree that legalized private trade in a desperate attempt to improve the supply of basic goods in a country exhausted by political and social disturbances following the revolution and the civil war (1918–1921).

[2] For an overview of the history of various guises of socialist fashion, in both the Soviet Union and five other ex-socialist countries (East Germany, Czechoslovakia, Hungary, Poland and Yugoslavia), see: BARTLETT 2004, BARTLETT 2010.

[3] 'Dom modelei' is often translated as the 'House of Fashion', but a more accurate translation, the 'House of Prototypes', already points to its main task: to design and produce prototypes of dresses, to be, ideally, reproduced into mass clothing in textile factories all over the country.

[4] For an overview of the concept and practices of Stalinist mythical culture, see: FITZPATRICK 1993, GLATZER 2002, CLARK 2000.

[5] For an overview on shortages in everyday life during the 1930s, see: FITZPATRICK 1993, LEBINA 1999, OSOKINA 2001.

through magazines, films, newsreels and theatre, it developed into a timeless, luxurious and unique phenomenon of its own. It was characterized by pastiche aesthetics and by selective borrowing from both the most traditional expressions of western opulence and the national ethnic heritage. Consequently, the 1930s socialist official fashion abandoned the Constructivist modernist geometry and embraced the paradigms of Socialist Realism.[6]

Socialist official fashion developed a new aesthetic during the Khrushchev period. In contrast to the Stalinist preference for grandness and preciousness, a new style, socialist good taste, was characterized by simple and moderate lines. While the former promoted an outdated concept of luxury, the latter was tied up with the socialist concept of modesty. Although the concept of modesty was officially promoted, and luxury was supposed to be banished along with Stalinism, the old-fashioned concept of luxury was never abandoned. Those timeless grandiose dresses were welcomed by the ruling bureaucracy, as they implied that changes within fashion production were not needed. The field of fashion production could not be organized on different principles to those on which the whole system was organized. Till the end of socialism, the *ODMO* 'All-Union House of Prototypes' and its regional branches imposed trends on textile and clothing companies, which, due to the hierarchical levels of decision-making, caused delays in promoting new styles, and also diluted their quality.

Just as in Stalinist times, socialist official fashion from the late 1950s on had little to do with everyday reality. It was an ideological construct, a discourse channelled through the stateowned media, and exclusively presented at domestic exhibitions and fashion shows, socialist fashion congresses and international trade fairs. As official fashion was unaffected by the poor quality of clothes in the shops, women were compelled to use a whole range of informal channels, from the officially illegal services of a seamstress, to the black market and networks of connections to obtain desired dresses in their everyday life. While the state-owned ateliers also offered custom-made clothes, their quality differed. The existence of Do-It-Yourself columns in women's magazines, which were regularly accompanied by paper patterns, additionally linked the fantasy world with the dysfunctional socialist consumer reality. All these state-supported or informally run activities resulted in another specific socialist sartorial phenomenon, everyday fashion. While socialist official fashion was set in the country's slow master narrative, everyday fashion was embedded in an unofficial modernity which ran in parallel with the official modernity, and became increasingly more important from the late 1950s on. In contrast to slow-moving official fashion and its fears of change, everyday fashion recognized change and individual expression in dress.

In order to explore these two particular sartorial phenomena – socialist official fashion and everyday fashion – in their economic, social and cultural surroundings, this paper scrutinizes the socialist concept of time, the changes in social stratification, the official reconceptualizations of gender, state ownership, central planning and central fashion institutions, as well as Do-It-Yourself practices, and various modes of consumption within a controlled market, along with the relevant media through which these concepts and practices were mediated.

Socialist Official Fashion

British *Vogue* reported in 1945 on a five-day-long fashion show at the Moscow *Dom modelei* showing 1,100 outfits, from which it was claimed 325 were chosen for mass production on the basis of "attractiveness, usefulness, and their possibilities for mass manufacture" (ALDRIDGE 1945: 49). The deputy Commissar of Light Industry, A. I. Rybakov, stated that each outfit was to be made in five sizes and five different colours. Nonetheless, the English report-

[6] Socialist Realism was initially advocated by a Stalinist ideologue, Andrei Zhdanov, at the First Congress of Soviet Writers in 1934, and subsequently introduced as the official aesthetics.

er could not understand the criteria of the professional jury: "A lot of trimming was hand embroidery, excellently worked and perfectly finished. I was surprised to see this embroidery accepted for mass production" (ibid). The reporter was confused as this lavish fashion show was embedded in the field of socialist official fashion, which considerably differed from its western counterpart. While western fashion operates in the field of commerce in which privately owned companies compete for their slice of the market by launching ever-new trends each season, socialist fashion was informed by state ownership, central planning and a limited market. But, these burdensome facts only encouraged its flights of fantasy, such as pledges that handicraft embellishments could be mass-produced.

This fashion show took place immediately after the end of World War Two, but the phenomenon of socialist official fashion goes back to the mid-1930s. It was born in the Stalinist Soviet Union, and survived till the end of the 1980s. Stalinism replaced the early Bolshevik attempts at constructing a radically new and utopian society by the rapid industrialization of the country. At the same time, Stalinism translated the difficult Soviet reality into an ideal mythical image which was disconnected from the hardships of everyday life. Sheila Fitzpatrick recognized two Stalinist realities as 'life as it is' and 'life as it is becoming' (FITZPATRICK 1993: 219-227). Defining the myth as a depoliticized speech, Roland Barthes stressed that myth is always about eternalizing the present and not about transforming it. Revolution itself therefore excludes myth and its Left versions suffer from encompassing only a narrow range of political notions:

> "The left-wing myth never reaches the immense field of human relationships, the very vast surface of 'insignificant' ideology. Everyday life is inaccessible to it [...]. Statistically myth is on the right. There, it is essential; well fed, sleek, expansive, garrulous, it invents itself ceaselessly. It takes hold of everything, all aspects of the law, of morality, of aesthetics, of diplomacy, of household equipment, of literature, of entertainment." (BARTHES 1976: 147–149)

Leaving behind the early Bolshevik revolutionary ideals, Stalinist hasty industrialization of the country was accompanied by the equally hasty production of its mythical images. The media promoted a whole new world populated with new objects, from smart cars to gramophones, pianos, decorative lampshades, opulent curtains, perfumes, cosmetics, furs, ladies' hats and elegant dresses.[7] Traditional western luxuries were de-rooted from their natural commercial habitat, only to be given a new representational role within a new Stalinist mass culture. Once transferred into the Stalinist context they were perceived as democratic and progressive goods, an appropriate part of the new cultured life-style.[8] This move from the paradigms of the so-called high culture to the paradigms of the so-called low culture happened precisely because Stalinism wanted to engage the masses in its project. As it could not in everyday life deliver on its promises of a new enchanting existence and the glamorous dresses that fitted it, its media – from dailies to weeklies, illustrated magazines, newsreels and films – provided a desired reality. Fashion became one of the new Stalinist rituals which were carefully re-coded from traditional western patterns. A new cultured person was supposed to be well behaved and take special care of her or his appearance.

In this context, the symbolic importance of smart dress only grew within the Stalinist mythical culture. In 1935, its physical existence was officially confirmed with the opening of

---

[7] Jukka Gronow states that the Soviet Union of the 1930s was a unique historical case as almost all its material culture was invented and created from nothing, and launched from the highest level of administration (GRONOW 2003: 7–8).

[8] For an overview of the Stalinist cultured trade, see: HESSLER 2000, while the concept of *kul'turnost'* 'culturedness' is discussed in DUNHAM 1990, KELLY and VOLKOV 1998.

the *Dom modelei* 'House of Prototypes' in Moscow. The established fashion designer, Nadezhda Makarova, who started her career under Nadezhda Lamanova's guidance, was its first director, while Lamanova was appointed as its artistic consultant.[9] So, in contrast to the Constructivists such as Varvara Stepanova, who had encouraged change but did not allow space for fashion, Stalinism released a space for socialist fashion with the opening of the *Dom modelei*, but stopped short of change by insisting on the concept of timelessness in dress. Generally, myth and fashion share very little. While fashion is a modernist, fast-changing phenomenon immersed in everyday reality, myth is conservative, traditional and preserves the status quo. Their relationship to the past is also different. Fashion depends on the past in order to progress towards the future. As Ulrich Lehmann argued, fashion "[...] requires quotation to rewrite its own history" (LEHMANN 1999: 308). However, fashion grabs its quotations from the past erratically and unpredictably. In contrast, myth is "an instrument for the obliteration of time" (LÉVI-STRAUSS 1986: 16). It "needs time only in order to deny it", as it "unfolds in a temporal dimension ... [which] ... overcomes the contradiction between historical, enacted time, and a permanent constant" (ibid: 15-16). In this context, myth is unrelated to the historical concept of time in which the phenomenon of fashion is set.[10]

Unlike Bolshevism, which attempted to expel history from its new world and enforce immediate change, Stalinism imposed an aesthetics that was greatly indebted to pre-modernist times. It incorporated different layers, from Russian medieval history to Hollywood glamour, gluing these disparate historical phenomena together in its new official aesthetics, Socialist Realism.[11] Moreover, as observed by Evgeny Dobrenko, Socialist Realism was not a mere aesthetics but a machine for the production of socialism:

> "Socialist Realism is a *highly* aestheticized culture, a radically transformed world. [...] Aesthetics did not beautify reality, it was reality. By contrast, all reality *outside* of Socialist Realism was but the wilderness of everyday life, waiting to be rendered fit to be read and interpreted. [...] 'Hiding' or 'glossing over' truth, portraying it through representative types, 'romanticizing' it, and the like are *merely mechanisms of aestheticization*. To aestheticize is to re-create the world, to transform it 'according to the laws of beauty and harmony'." (DOBRENKO 2007: 4)

Embedding it in its mythical culture, Stalinism imposed an over-decorated style on its ideal dress, which matched the main characteristics of the aesthetics of Socialist Realism: grandness, classicism, uniqueness and preciousness. Embellished with ethnic motifs, socialist fashion re-introduced opulence, decoration and femininity, which held a wide appeal for the masses. Moreover, Stalinist fashion was supposed to emanate a domestic, Soviet glamour rather than being of western or of avant-garde origin. Although it copied technically superior cuts and a traditional concept of luxury from the West,[12] socialist official fashion aesthetically distanced itself from its western counterpart by its frequent quotations from the Russian sartorial heritage. Jean Baudrillard claimed that modern fashion is not guided by the timeless and archaic principle of discrimination but instead by the mobile and promiscuous principle of distinction:

---

[9] All the names, from designers to cutters, sample makers and the members of the Artistic Board, were listed in the editorial of the first issue of the journal *Dom modelei* (1936), in order to demonstrate the importance of the new institution and the new role of fashion at the time.

[10] In his *Mythologies*, Roland Barthes further develops Levi-Strauss's concept of myth, by analyzing it as a de-historicizing mechanism in1950s' France.

[11] For an overview of Socialist Realism see BAKSTEIN 1993, DOBRENKO 2007, HELLER 1997

[12] For example, in 1938 the Leningrad fashion journal *Modeli plat'ia* 'Models of Dresses' reproduced its fashion drawings from the professional tailors' journals *Le Tailleur de Luxe*, *Costumes Manteaux* and *Le Grand Tailleur* (see also GRONOW 2003: 96–97).

> "Fashion relates to the transcendent, modern, mobile, exoteric universe of looking and representation. It arises from a caprice of the desire for forms, from an aesthetic and political desire for distinction – the signs of fashion are also distinctive, and operate according to a code which is the universal code of fashion, thus entering into the concept of modern subjectivity, opposing the archaic, timeless, discriminatory rigor of ornament. Fashion [...] results fundamentally from a process of confusion and promiscuity of all possible forms. These same forms that were ceremonial have fallen into the system of fashion; we mustn't, however, confuse them." (BAUDRILLARD 1990: 178)

Yet the ethnic motif, an archaic and discriminatory ornament *par excellence*, fulfilled the socialist ideas of fashion and beauty. Writing in 1937 on the initial results of the *Dom modelei*, one of its designers, Anna Blank,[13] advocated that the Soviet style in dress should be achieved by exploring museum ethnic dress collections, by visiting related exhibitions, as well as by examining relevant literature in order to grasp cuts, colours and embroideries as expressed in the national cultures of the peoples inhabiting the Soviet Union. Everything was to be mastered, and subsequently applied on contemporary garments with the purpose of making them not only Soviet but also beautiful and functional (BLANK 1937: 29). Subsequently a magazine, *Zhurnal mod* 'Fashion Journal', begun in 1945, published from its very beginning many drawings and photographs of dresses adorned with ethnic motifs. In 1961, the journal *Dekorativnoe iskusstvo SSSR* 'Decorative Art of the USSR' addressed the topic of national motifs in dress: "We are often asked how justifiable it is to use old national motifs in a contemporary dress. Does this result in an archaic dress?" (MARKOVA 1961: 44). The question was a rhetorical one. The article went on to validate this practice by claiming that Soviet women deserved not only a practical but also a beautiful dress, and that Soviet artists of dress, in order to fulfil these two criteria, relied on the rich reservoir of national art. However, literal copies of the sarafan or peasant blouse were not appropriate. Instead, the uses of traditional national dress should take into account the contemporary life patterns of Soviet people and be applied discreetly, such as embellishing the neckline of a dress, adorning its sleeves or decorating the lower part of the skirt (ibid: 46). When, a year later, the magazine *Soviet Union* interviewed Valentina Ivanova, Head of Design at the Leningrad *Dom modelei*, she equally emphasized: "Folk art is a never-ending source of inspiration. Lines taken from the Russian shirt, or the design of Ukrainian embroidery, the metal ornaments so popular in the Soviet Baltic Republics, are all adaptable to modern dress." (LEONOV 1962: 45)[14]

The ethnic remained an aesthetic staple in official fashion throughout the socialist period,[15] and continued to be an ideologically informed quotation.[16] Initially, the Bolsheviks frowned on western fashion and its opulence and chose the ethnic as the least confrontational type of decoration, and, later, such decoration perfectly suited Stalinist isolationism and its idea of

---

[13] In the years 1944-1948, Anna Blank was chief artistic director (*glavnyi khudozhestvennyi rukovoditel'*) of the Moscow *Dom modeli*, and once the *Obshchesoiuznyi Dom modelei* 'All-Union House of Prototypes' was established in 1949, she became its first chief artistic director, remaining until 1958.

[14] The magazine *Soviet Union* was a propaganda monthly, promoting socialist achievements, from heavy and light industries to science, agriculture and life-style. Apart from Russian, it was published in fifteen languages, including English, French, German, Spanish, Hungarian, Chinese, and Hindu, and was meant mainly for foreign markets.

[15] In an article in 1967, G. Gorina praises G. Gorovitz, whose dress 'Metelitsa' was inspired by a traditional Russian song of the same name, I. Cepkina who designed the outfit 'Russkaia zima' and T. Kuchinskaia and T. Osmerkina, designers of the dress 'Pskovitianka', inspired by the costumes in Nikolai Rimsky-Korsakov's opera set in the time of Ivan the Terrible (GORINA 1967: 9).

[16] Nadezhda Makarova, Lamanova's best-known pupil and first artistic director of the *Dom modelei* in 1935, argues in an article written in 1961 that national dress of the peoples populating the Soviet territory was a boundless source of inspiration for Soviet artists of dress and for designers all over the world (*Dekorativnoe iskusstvo* 1961, 6: 39–40).

uniqueness. Furthermore, even when ethnic motifs embellished hippy-style dresses or fashionable mini dresses in the 1960s, socialist attempts at fashionability were mediated through national traditions.[17] Slava Zaitsev craved western fashion and tried hard to keep up with the latest trends, but became well-known at home and abroad only after his 1965 collection, 'Russian Series'. At home, his designs were appreciated because their quotations privileged Russian historical imagery over western fashions, meaning that they did not capitulate to the western concept of rapid change. On the other hand, the West liked his style because it fulfilled the western preconceptions of an exotic, far-away culture, and indeed his dresses travelled the world from Canada to Japan, France, Italy and Yugoslavia, from 1965 to 1976.[18] Even at the very end of socialism, in 1989, *Zhurnal mod* reported that a group of models, all clad in Liudmila Aristova's artistic, red-coloured interpretations of the sarafan, caused a sensation on the catwalk of the Tallinn Fashion Festival and secured her an award.[19]

An opulent dress adorned with ethnic-inspired decoration was a mythical object *par excellence* within the socialist official fashion narrative, as the lavishness of the ethnic motif visually fulfilled the myth's aesthetic criteria, while simultaneously conforming to its principle of timelessness. But socialist fashion adopted yet another relevant paradigm of Socialist Realism: its appreciation of the classical. Turning away from fashionability, socialist fashion embarked on its search for an eternal style. This trend likewise started in the mid-1930s. The cover of the first issue of the journal *Dom modelei*, published in 1936, shrank the Stalinist grandiose aesthetic from its monumental architectural forms into a small drawing showing a group of women in ancient Greek-style robes sewing clothes, trying out their shapes on each other, and arranging them on a tailor's dummy. This search for classic forms related to the aesthetics of Socialist Realism and its fascination with the heritage of classical aesthetics. As Leonid Heller stated: "[...] the very idea of a classic depends on classification, on judgments of normativity, on categorization – thus was the doctrine of Socialist Realism formulated through debates about norms and categories" (HELLER 1997: 55). A new professional magazine, *Shveinaia promyshlennost'* 'Clothing Industry', appeared in 1929, and throughout the 1930s published numerous discussions and advice on the techniques of impeccable cut and perfect execution of outfits in order to enable Soviet industry to produce its own timeless classics. Ideally, copied from the West and flawlessly mastered in all their complex technical details, they were supposed to protect socialist fashion from future changes.

Offering potential solutions concerning the industrialization of clothing manufacture, *Shveinaia promyshlennost'* invariably favoured the scientific approach to the problems of industrial dress production, while ignoring fashionable and artistic dress. Its early promoter was perceptual psychologist Sof'ia Beliaeva-Ekzempliarskaia who, at the beginning of the 1930s, published a series of articles on the rational application of colour in clothing.[20] Published in 1934, her manual on *Dress Design according to the Laws of Visual Perception* analyzed various theories of form and their application to dress in a serious scientific manner. The unquestionable reliance on science in both utopianism and totalitarianism was guided, as Frédéric Rouvillois stated, by the ideal of perfection:

> "Perfection constitutes the very essence of the utopian project: it is to be an acquired perfection that can be always improved upon and must be defended at all times to en-

[17] See for example: "Fashionable Embroidery". *Zhurnal mod* 4, Winter 1966–1967, and "Exporting Soviet Fashion", in: *Zhurnal mod* 1967 2.

[18] After western media nicknamed him 'Red Dior' in the mid-1960s, Zaitsev was not allowed to travel to the West for twenty years, but continued to be the most respected fashion designer at home, and his dresses continued to represent Soviet fashion (Interview with Slava Zaitsev, Moscow, June 2004).

[19] Krasnyi sarafan. In: *Zhurnal mod* 1989 5.

[20] The articles were published in *Shveinaia promyshlennost'* 1932 4–5: 42–48, 1932 6–7: 5-10, 1932 8–9: 4–13, 1932 8–9: 24–36.

> sure its longevity, eternity being the principal corollary of perfection. Totalitarian doctrines follow suit: they too want to put an end to adversity, and to history. [...] Totalitarianism, like utopia, purports to have triumphed over the anguish of time and the accidents of history." (ROUVILLOIS 2000: 322)

In its approach to science, Stalinism adopted the earlier Constructivist fascination with technology. Yet, while in the utopian Bolshevik vision science served ethical and social ideals, in the Stalinist world science symbolized industrial and homogenized progress.

By enrolling science in its service, Stalinism was not only interested in physically triumphing over the reality that it was so rapidly producing, but also in symbolically separating the process of production from its preferred final products. The former belonged to the gruelling everyday while a number of selected products, such as splendid dress prototypes, were promptly transferred to the Stalinist mythical reality. Additionally, science was emphasized over the supposed irrationality of western fashion, and a scientific approach to design and production of dress continued throughout the socialist period. In 1962, *Soviet Union* reported how a contemporary scientist and his team developed a perfect technique for cutting cloth and making clothes by applying the nineteenth-century invention of the distinguished Russian mathematician Pafnutii Chebyshev:

> "Starting out from Chebyshev formulas for the patterns of a sphere, cylinder and cone, a team of researchers headed by Docent Alexander Savostitsky, of Moscow, has worked out a new method of designing garments. You do not have to know higher mathematics to use this simple and reliable method which does away with allowances and tucks and other approximations. What is more, it reduces the number of seams, simplifies tailoring and paves the way for automation." (DOLDOBANOV 1962: 34)

The article further stated that the Moscow textile factory Thaelmann had already achieved the most satisfying results by applying the new method in its mass production. Moreover, these outfits were supposedly more elegant, fitted better, and retained their original shape longer. The new method also secured significant savings in fabric, allegedly 1500 yards of cloth in the manufacture of a single model over the course of a year (ibid.).

Synthetic fabrics were perceived as the ultimate socialist materials – technological, modern, scientific, aesthetic, and able to satisfy consumer demands. The development of new man-made fabrics was constantly connected to socialist progress. A research proper in the field of chemistry covering polymeric materials, including fibre-forming polymers, had already started in the 1930s, but Kapron, the first synthetic fabric to be utilized in the textile industry, was launched only in 1949.[21] Initially, it was made in a single factory, Klinvolokno, so products incorporating it were rare and treasured, consequently lingering in the mythical world of socialist official fashion rather than in the local textile shops. Kapron's early mythical status was confirmed by an advertisement published by the Ministry of Light Industry in 1952. On that poster, a beautiful, carefully made-up woman, clothed in a delicate white morning robe, holds in her hand a Kapron stocking as if it were a very precious object. Promoted by the Ministry, instead of by its producer or retailer, this nylon stocking was more important as a mythical transmitter of Stalinist policies on luxury and femininity than as a real product.[22]

---

[21] For an overview of synthetic fibre production in the USSR, see: MURAV'EV and MIKHAILOV 1977.

[22] The practice of glossy advertisements being launched from government departments was common from the mid-1930s on, with the Ministry of Light Industry in charge of clothing and fashion accessories, among other products, and the Ministry of Food covering not only food and drink but also cosmetics and perfume. Designed by Viktor Pimenov in 1952, this specific Kapron poster has been reproduced in: SNOPKOV, A. et al. 2001. *Ruskii reklamnyi plakat.* Moskva.

The subsequent development of technologically advanced synthetic fabrics continued to perpetuate the symbiotic relationship between science and myth. In line with the Soviet space successes, a new synthetic fabric was named Kosmos in the late 1960s. Covering in an article the relationship between traditional Russian textiles and fashionable dress, G. Gorina linked Kosmos's shiny, low-relief texture to the unevenly woven Russian ethnic fabrics (GORINA 1967: 10). Yet, the photography that accompanied her article – of an evening suit designed by N. Tokareva from the *VIAlegprom* 'All-Union Institute for Light Industry Goods'[23] and sewn from Kosmos – showed that it was more in tune with the contemporary western trend for shimmering fabrics, such as lurex, than with any textile from the reservoir of the national sartorial heritage. Gorina claimed many more examples of ethnic influences in the contemporary Soviet textile design. She related the tightly knotted surface (*faktura*)[24] of a fashionable bouclé fabric to coarsely woven cloth traditionally used for ethnic skirts and over-garments, such as the *ponëva*. Equally, contemporary jacquard patterns were favourably compared to intricate ethnic embroidered motifs, while the fashionable uses of contrasting bright colours were also traced back to Russian sartorial history (GORINA 1967: 8). Gorina argued that popular art and Soviet dress design shared the same principle: unity of the functional and the aesthetic (GORINA 1967: 9).

All these concepts – the frequent uses of the ethnic as a socialist attempt at an original aesthetic, the striving towards the classic and the perfect, the preference for the scientific over the fashionable – had already been introduced in the *Dom modelei* in the mid-1930s, and continued to inform Soviet dress design. Equally, an ideal dress that would fulfil all these criteria was already produced in its design studio, yet only as a perfect prototype. In its first issue, the journal *Dom modelei* claimed that a new institution had already designed 4,297 original outfits between October 1935 and July 1936, and that these prototypes were being reproduced as mass clothing in textile factories from Moscow to Ukraine, Byelorussia, Georgia, and Azerbaijan.[25] According to Anna Blank, making highly artistic samples of dresses to be consequently mass-produced by textile factories was indeed the main task of the *Dom modelei* from its very beginning (BLANK 1937: 28). However, the newly mechanized industry, still struggling with weak organization, a meagre supply of raw materials, and low quality of fabrics, could not live up to the ideals imposed by the Stalinist myth.

Due to the terrible devastation of the country during the war, the mythical space that accommodated representational images only widened in the immediate post-war period. At the same time, the centralized economic model strengthened, as the powerful bureaucracy established under Stalinism continued to govern the industry through an over-centralized system informed by consecutive Five-Year Plans.[26] In 1949, the existing Moscow *Dom modelei* was transformed into the central *Obshchesoiuznyi Dom modelei* 'All-Union House of Prototypes', (ODMO), while the establishment of regional *Dom modelei* completed the centralized, hierarchical model of Soviet dress design.[27] The Leningrad *Dom modelei*, founded in 1945, deliv-

[23] Established in 1958, and embedded within the highly bureaucratized Ministry of Light Industry, the *VIAlegprom* acted through a highly organized structure, consisting of many sections, such as wool, silk, cotton, linen, fur, man-made fabrics, weaving, knitting, fashion accessories and professional clothes. In 1989, *VIAlegprom* changed its name to the *Centre for Fashion of USSR*, but its structure and mode of operating stayed the same.

[24] Introduced by the Constructivists in their search for transparency in the new arts at the beginning of the 1920s, the concept of 'faktura' referred to the material aspect of the surface.

[25] Editorial in the journal *Dom modelei* 1936 1.

[26] The first two Plans in the post-war period the Fourth Five-Year Plan (1945–1951) and the Fifth-Five Year Plan (1951–1955) – emphasized the development of heavy industry and transportation. The Sixth Five-Year Plan which started in 1956 was eventually abandoned in 1957 and turned into a new Seven-Year Plan, which focused on chemical industry and rise of consumer goods.

[27] Simultaneously, the regional Moscow *Dom modelei* was established in the line with the institution of other regional *Dom modelei*.

ered five hundred prototypes to Leningrad factories in its first year, and 1,500 prototypes in 1954.[28] The *Dom modelei* in the city of Gor'kii, founded in 1949, provided prototypes for fifty factories in three neighbouring republics (KHLUSTOVA 1954: 16). The media, such as *Zhurnal mod* 'Fashion Magazine' and *Modeli sezona* 'Models of the Season', continued to report on the activities of the various *Dom modelei* throughout the socialist period. The names of the designers were usually quoted and attributed to the particular *Dom modelei* which employed them, contributing to a certain credibility for the outfits.

The physical existence of these dress institutions and their designers provided an element of reality, but socialist official fashion did not exist in the real world. It inhabited the limitless mythical space introduced under Stalinism. The ideal dress prototype eventually shared not only its aesthetics but also its ontological status with Socialist Realism. Its perfect beauty on a magazine page or on the film screen conjured up a life that did not exist. Mikhail Epshtein argued that the ideological production of reality had played a key role in Russian history, and that in Soviet times this practice was taken even further. For him, all the "signs of new reality", from Stalin's massive hydroelectric plant to Khrushchev's agricultural reform and Brezhnev's numerous autobiographies: "[...] were actually pure ideological simulations of reality. This artificial reality was intended to demonstrate the superiority of ideas over simple facts" (EPSHTEIN 1995: 194). Epshtein's statement gets close to Michel Foucault's idea of productive power. Foucault argued that the effects of power should not be described in negative terms. He abandoned the idea of power that 'excludes', 'represses', 'censors', 'abstracts', 'masks', or 'conceals' and insisted that, in fact, power produced reality, its objects and rituals of truth (FOUCAULT 1991: 194). The socialist official fashion maintained its mythical status, precisely because the Stalinist ruling bureaucracy interiorized the logic of mythical perfection in its vigorous attempts to present Stalinist reality as the best possible world. Successive governments carefully nurtured the existing system, increasingly employing more and more staff on the creative, technical and administrative levels. The magazine *Soviet Union* boasted in 1963 that the *VIAlegprom* 'All-Union Institute for Light Industry Goods' had "a large staff of artists, designers, fabric experts, engineers and planners, and that its activities were impressive": "Last year these arbiters of fashion discussed 32,709 models, ranging from fabrics and knitted goods to buttons, bracelets and hair-combs. Of these, 17,867 were recommended for production. The Institute also prepared 12,530 albums and 1,652 sample books containing 2,710,000 different patterns and sent them out to factories and fashion houses (GORIN 1963:46)".[29] Equally, the All-Union *Dom modelei* employed more than sixty designers in the mid-1960s, including those working in its special experimental atelier and those designing prototype collections for industry.

Already in 1937, T. Frolova from the Dress Laboratory of the Factory N 1 within the *Mosbel'e* Trust,[30] argued that the beautiful prototypes which arrived from the *Dom modelei* could not be mass-produced, claiming, among other things, that their cuts were too complicated and that their production would incur a huge waste of fabric (FROLOVA 1937: 30-31). She suggested that the designers from the *Dom modelei* should get closer to production, and learn about its possibilities and requirements (ibid.).[31] But, the practice of making a hand-embellished

---

[28] CGA SPb. F. 2071. Op. 8. D. 426. L.I., quoted in LEBINA and CHISTIKOV 2003: 204. In 1962, the journal *Soviet Union* stated that the Leningrad *Dom modelei* designed 2500 prototypes in the previous year, claiming that nearly all of them were accepted for mass production (LEONOV 1962: 44).

[29] While *VIAlegprom* and the ODMO competed against each other, their tasks overlapped. The ODMO was more dedicated to fashion design, while the VIAlegprom was more closely connected to the textile and clothing industries.

[30] All Russian textile and clothing firms were nationalized by decree in 1918, and organized in ten trusts.

[31] Pointing towards the disjunction between the central *Dom modelei* and the dress laboratories within textile factories, Frolova's article was published as a critical response to Anna Blank's praise of the activities of the *Dom modelei*, in the same issue of *Shveinaia promyshlennost'*.

representational dress, and presenting it as an appropriate prototype for subsequent mass production, had started even earlier.[32] From the mid-1920s, when it became clear that socialist industry was incapable of producing any decent clothes, Nadezhda Lamanova's artistic custom-made outfits decorated with ethnic motifs were appropriated as prototypes for mass production and promoted by the Bolshevik regime.[33] Lamanova's pupils Nadezhda Makarova and Fekla Gorelenkova had mastered the couture technique of making a perfect, bespoke outfit while working in Lamanova's fashion house in the pre-revolutionary period. Both Makarova and Gorelenkova were incorporated in the *Dom modelei* in 1935, and Gorelenkova continued to work at the central dress institution through its subsequent transformations even in the mid-1950s,[34] while her colleague Anna Blank, who already in 1937 strongly supported both artistic prototype and reliance on the ethnic (BLANK 1937: 28–30), became the first artistic director of the All-Union *Dom modelei*, remaining there until 1958.

While both these sartorial practices – bespoke garments and hand-made embellishment – belong to the world of haute couture, the Soviets, for various reasons, continually relied on them in their attempts to invent new socialist dress. In a hastily improvised Bolshevik counter-attack on the NEP luxury, Anatolii Lunacharskii supported Lamanova in the 1920s, while, in the 1930s, couture-style exclusivity corresponded perfectly to the Stalinist representational needs, and nicely fitted into its mythical culture. Despite the Khrushchev regime's opposition to the Stalinist myth, the timeless Stalinist aesthetics and its culture of sartorial prototype had already become firmly embedded in the All-Union *Dom modelei* and its regional branches by the 1950s. In this sense, Khrushchev's re-conceptualization of culture and its objects in line with earlier Constructivist ideas, his attempts at economic reforms and his political opening towards the West had little effect on socialist official fashion. The newly established contacts with the West nevertheless helped to turn a permanent fascination with western couture into a direct rapport between socialist official fashion and Paris fashion, initially manifested through a highly advertised and well-attended Christian Dior fashion show in Moscow in 1959, and later fostered through the activities of the Special Bureau of Artistic Construction, *special'noe khudozhestvenno-konstruktorskoe byro, (SKhKB)*, led by Alla Levashova.[35]

The practice of an unachievable prototype was occasionally challenged in the media. In 1964, L. Kramarenko declared fashion designed in Paris couture houses unachievable and stated that Dior's models could never be mass-produced. The author suggested that socialist dress should oppose fashion's seasonal changes by relying on the national sartorial heritage, and argued that the planned economy could not deal with "new fashion lines", but instead

---

[32] By 'representational dress' I mean a dress which is produced only for the purpose of representing an abstract ideological concept.

[33] Nadezhda Lamanova had opened her fashion salon in Moscow in 1885. By the 1910s, she employed two hundred seamstresses, supplying haute couture dresses to her rich and sophisticated clientele which included gentry and famous actresses. She lost her fashion house in the aftermath of the Revolution, but, unlike other pre-revolutionary fashion designers, offered her superb expertise on dress-making to the Bolsheviks. Designed with the help of her colleagues Evgeniia Pribyl'skaia, Vera Mukhina, Aleksandra Ėkster and Nadezhda Makarova, Lamanova's western-style dresses, decorated with skilfully re-interpreted ethnic motifs, represented the Moscow branch of the Craftsmen association, *Moskunst* at the International Exhibition of Decorative Arts in Paris in 1925.

[34] See, for example, the fashion shoot presenting luxurious evening wear in the ODMO's sumptuous headquarters on Kuznetskii most in Moscow, with Gorelenkova's silk dress in the foreground (*Zhurnal mod* 1956 1: 27). On Gorelenkova, see also BLANK. A. F. 1973. O Fekle Antonovne Gorelenkovoi. In: *Zhurnal mod* 1973 3.

[35] When Dior presented his collection in Moscow in 1959, Alla Levashova, who worked at the time at the All-Union *Dom modelei*, was able to establish contacts with the house of Dior. In 1965, as head of the SKhKB, Levashova led the official Soviet delegation on a visit to the haute couture houses of Christian Dior and Jacques Griffe, and to some well-known French textile companies. Another member of the delegation was L.K. Efremova, who had also been a designer at the All-Union *Dom modelei*, and later became chief fashion designer at the SKhKB. For a detailed account of these visits see ZAKHAROVA 2005.

needed standardization in order to produce mass clothing (KRAMARENKO 1964: 21). But easier access to information about current western fashion trends brought a change, if not in the functioning of the system, then certainly in the aesthetics of socialist official fashion. While it had also been responsive to western fashion during the period of the1930s to the1950s, socialist fashion, at that time, did not borrow fashionable looks from the West but preferred its classical, timeless expressions.[36] In contrast, the 1960s' politically supported opening towards the West was accompanied by the appearance of a new group of professionally educated designers, such as Slava Zaitsev, Tamara Mokeeva, Tat'iana Os'merkina and Galina Gagarina. They entered the field of Soviet official fashion, after graduating from the Moscow Textile Institute, and their modernist designs started to appear frequently in the media, announced as the ODMO's outfits.[37] Employed in its special experimental atelier, they enjoyed relative creative freedom and perks such as access to western magazines.[38]

As a result, prototypes produced by these increasingly better informed designers were not only perfectly executed but also reflected contemporary western fashion trends. Promoted in the pages of *Zhurnal mod*, *Modeli sezona* and the annual publication *Moda stran socializma* 'Fashion of the Socialist Countries',[39] their designs – from miniskirts and dresses with geometrical lines in the late 1960s to the bohemian style of the 1970s and wide-shouldered jackets in the mid-1980s – clearly showed that the ODMO practitioners and their colleagues from the regional *Dom modelei* visually caught up with western fashion.[40] However, these ideological shifts towards fashionability in the later socialist period did not mean that socialist official fashion and textile factories suddenly started to produce fashionable goods, and that the supply in the shops became more varied. Socialist official fashion was neither about fashion, nor about clothes. It was always simply a discourse, with little bearing on reality. As the agents who mediated between socialist official fashion and western fashion, the fashion designers within the various *Dom modelei* were unable to initiate a process which would have changed the ontological status of socialist official fashion. Even when Gorbachev's Perestroika tried to introduce changes in the design and production of socialist fashion, those attempts failed, due both to the power of bureaucracy and to the fear of change that could not be controlled that had been built into the socialist system from the 1930s. Polished and fashionable outfits presented in the late 1980s on the covers of *Zhurnal mod* and *Modeli sezona* were still only the prototypes arriving to the magazines' professionally equipped photography studio from the ODMO, while still never reaching the shops.

---

[36] Quite in line with Stalinist practice of selective borrowing from the West, Anna Blank rejected 'mechanical copying of western fashion' but supported learning from it through critical exploration (BLANK 1937: 30).

[37] Following in the footsteps of the 1920s schools VKhUTEMAS and VKhUTEIN, the Textile Institute was established in 1929. Initially, it educated only textile engineers, gradually incorporating textile design during the 1930s, and introducing the study of fashion design only in the late 1950s (Interview with the Dean of the Textile Institute, Tat'iana Kozlova, Moscow, June 2004).

[38] In an interview, Slava Zaitsev told me that he was very satisfied when he could get hold of western fashion magazines, and stressed that he always shared his information with all the other colleagues at the special experimental atelier, for whom he conducted seminars on Dior, Givenchy, Balenciaga and Cardin (Interview, Moscow, June 2004).

[39] The special annual magazine *Moda stran socializma* 'Fashion of the Socialist Countries', started in 1959 and, published in Moscow, covered the socialist fashion congresses till they ended in 1990. Published in a circulation of a few hundred thousand, and distributed throughout the participating countries for free, the magazine served as a propaganda tool for socialist fashion. Its contents consisted only of fashion images covering the socialist fashion congresses.

[40] See, for example: a collective photography with the modernist outfits of geometrical lines by S. Zaitsev, L. Telegina, G. Mepen, L. Pavlova (*Zhurnal mod* 1967 1); Iulia Denisova's space-style suit (*Zhurnal mod* 1968 1); G. Mepen's white, Courrèges-inspired suits and dresses in the photography accompanying an article on his work (MONAKHOVA. L. "Khudozhnik-model'er G. Mepen". In: *Dekorativnoe iskusstvo* 1966 12, 31–32).

The designers had a crucial role in promoting not only the official aesthetics, but in perpetually applying it to representational dresses instead of to those that could have been adequate for industrial production. The ODMO's special experimental atelier was in charge of delivering these exquisite dresses for domestic and foreign fashion shows, as well as for socialist fashion congresses. The latter was the most important annual parade of socialist official fashion.[41] Starting modestly as a contest in dress culture in 1950, the event grew ever more ambitious once the Soviet Union started to participate in 1953, and soon afterwards imposed its official timeless aesthetics and its culture of prototype. Although from 1957 their full name was International Fashion Congress, those events presented only the collections created within the central dress institutions of each socialist country. Travelling between annual socialist fashion congresses, domestic fairs, the Leipzig International Fairs, and lavish presentations in the West, these prototype collections produced a new sartorial reality which differed markedly from the everyday dress which could be found in local shops. The 1961 international fashion show in Leipzig included the Soviet Union, East Germany, Poland, Hungary, Holland, Sweden and France. Engaging all the participants, its finale revealed the highest representational level of the socialist sartorial ambitions, as their extravagant outfits were in sharp contrast to the smart yet wearable clothes of their commercially minded western counterparts.[42]

The representational activities of socialist official fashion only intensified with Khrushchev's emphasis on light industry, when, again, too-ambitious plans could not be fulfilled in everyday life. The popular weekly *Ogonek* boasted in 1959 that in the first year of a new Seven-Year Plan, the *Trekhgornaiia* textile factory in Moscow managed to provide Soviet consumers with an additional four million meters of textiles, and that, during the same year, its artists offered three hundred new textile designs (FRIDLIAND, UZLIAN 1959: 25). Even more significantly, Soviet textiles and clothes were regularly displayed at the Manezh, Moscow's central exhibition hall. As reported in the *Dekorativnoe iskusstvo*, the 1961 All-Union textile exhibition presented the achievements of the first two years of the Seven-Year Plan through thirty thousand samples of textiles, dresses, threads and carpets provided by two hundred and fifty domestic factories and scientific laboratories (ALEKSEEVA 1961: 7). The report stressed that the display caused huge interest among the general public and suggested that such exhibitions should regularly be organized in order to help resolve complex aesthetic and production issues (ibid: 10). Portraying the same exhibition for international audiences, the *Soviet Union* stated: "Muscovites have got used to seeing interesting shows at their Central Exhibition Hall. These have included a review of Soviet fine arts, a Czech glass exhibition, a display of hundreds of new architectural designs and the work of folk craftsmen. Now, as the *Economic Gazette* modestly put it, the textile workers have a show".[43]

Relying on its exclusive prototype collections, socialist official fashion also ventured beyond its borders, daring to display its aesthetics in a safe environment of international exhibitions and trade fairs. Replicas of Sputniks I and II commanded the huge Soviet pavilion at the

---

[41] Annual dress contests between the socialist countries started in 1950, with only Czechoslovakia and East Germany taking part in the first two, and Hungary joining in 1952. The Soviet Union joined the fourth dress contest held in Prague in 1953, competing with Czechoslovakia, Hungary and East Germany, while Poland and Romania were invited as observers. The event changed its name to the 'International Fashion Congress' in Moscow in 1957, and these annual gatherings, moving from one socialist capital to another, lasted till 1990.

[42] See the image accompanying the article covering this fashion show (DONSKAIA, A. 1961. Pokaz mod v Leiptsige. In: *Zhurnal mod* 1961 3: 14).

[43] N.N. "9,000,000,000 Yards", *Soviet Union,* 1961 133, 46–49, 47. The review also reported on the excellent reception of this exhibition in domestic media, with, for example, the dailies *Izvestiia* and *Pravda* calling it "Fabric Parade" and "World of Fabrics" respectively. According to the media, the following *Manezh* exhibition, with its display of nine thousand samples of consumer goods, showed even greater achievements of Soviet light industry: an increase of 23 million pairs of leather footwear and 22 million items of knitwear in one year (N.N. 1962. Beauty, Comfort, Simplicity – for All. In: *Soviet Union* 1962: 32–35).

Brussels World Exhibition in 1958, but fashion was not neglected. Yet, in contrast to the Soviet cutting-edge technological achievements, fashion was represented by a conventionally elegant collection of dresses and ensembles embellished with ethnic decorations.[44] A decade later, the Soviets dared to compete with western fashion trends, at least in a festival context. Organized by the *ODMO* in 1967, the International Fashion Festival presented the latest East European and western collections, including those by the leading Paris couture houses of Chanel and Christian Dior. The jury acknowledged Chanel's presentation as the best current trend, but the Grand Prix was awarded to Tat'iana Os'merkina from the ODMO for her long red dress, resembling a sarafan, and called *Russia.* The festival was intended to demonstrate that the socialist system had caught up with the West in fashion, but the centralized way of proposing and approving fashion trends did not change. In order to present their unified vision at the Moscow International Fashion Festival, the socialist countries had met beforehand at their own fashion congress in the Bulgarian city of Varna. *Zhurnal mod* commented on their presentations on the catwalk of the Moscow International Fashion Festival: "The SEV countries presented very integral collections, which reflected fashion trends for 1968. East Germany, Romania, Hungary, Poland, Soviet Union and Czechoslovakia presented collections using the principles laid down at the last meeting in Varna".[45] Displays of beautiful clothes at the exhibitions perfectly suited their ontological status. Equally, lavish dress on the catwalk of the highly choreographed fashion shows was a purely ideological product, just another element of fashion as myth rather than fashion as an everyday commodity.

The role of the journals, such as *Modeli Sezona* and *Zhurnal mod,* was crucial in the promotion of socialist official fashion. The former was started in the late 1930s in order to present dresses designed by the then newly-founded *Dom modelei,* while the latter, published by the Ministry of Light Industry from 1945, also maintained the sartorial reproduction of the Stalinist myth, by only ever depicting prototypes from the various *Dom modelei.* During its first decade, *Zhurnal mod* hardly contained any text, accompanying page after page of alluring fashion photography and attractive drawings, apart from the title and technical descriptions of each outfit. In fact, already in the 1930s, *Modeli sezona* strongly relied on the art of fashion drawing. Its illustrations of sumptuous evening dresses barely differed from the outfits designed by the leading 1930s Hollywood designer Adrian. On the other hand, similar to the Hollywood film machinery, the Soviet film industry produced at that time an illusionary, much more interesting world in comparison to the real one. The role of films such as Grigorii Aleksandrov's "*Tsirk*" 'The Circus' (1936) and "*Svetlyi put*'" 'The Radiant Path' (1940), and their famous star, Liubov' Orlova, was to embellish the everyday through costumes fitting a new, home-grown Soviet glamour. Orlova cultivated a glamorous appearance off the screen as well, fulfilling Stalinist efforts to offer role models to the Soviet masses. In that sense, Orlova was a marketable commodity, just as the Hollywood stars of the contemporary period. The difference was that she was not marketing specific fashion brands or particular cosmetic goods, but the socialist project itself.[46]

Furthermore, presented in the pages of magazines or materialized as smart prototypes at exhibitions or on cinema screens, mythical objects suited the increasingly centralized and bureaucratized industrial systems. As Roland Barthes observed: "[...] it [is] necessary to distinguish in clothes between the synchronic or systematic level and the diachronic or processive level. Once again, as with language, the major problem here is that of putting together, in a

---

[44] See for example A. Kozlova's ensemble presented in Brussels, consisting of a lady-like grey afternoon coat, accompanied by a purple dress embellished with picturesque embroidery below the nipped-in waist (*Zhurnal mod* 1958 2: 29).

[45] N.N. 1968. Editorial. In: *Zhurnal mod,* 1968 2.

[46] For an overview on Soviet film costumes in the 1920s-1930s, see: BARTLETT, D. "Stars on Screen and Red Carpet". In: Beumers, B. (ed.). *A Companion to Russian Cinema.* Wiley-Blackwell (forthcoming).

truly dialectical snapshot, the link between the system and process" (BARTHES 2006: 10–11). Once the immobilization of Bolshevik change in the Stalinist myth disabled the link between system and process in socialist fashion, socialist official fashion preferred the synchronic, systematic level over the diachronic, processive level. In the end, the concept and practice of a sartorial prototype suited not only the over-centralized socialist economies, but also an ontological fear of change within a slow socialist master narrative. In that context, a sartorial prototype turned into a paradoxical example of frozen fashion.

Everyday Fashion

The escape into myth prevented the development of a new space in which a new socialist dress could be positioned and consumed. As Henry Lefebvre argued: "The revolution that does not produce a new space has not realized its full potential; indeed it has failed in that it has not changed life itself, but has merely changed ideological superstructures, institutions or political apparatuses" (LEFEBVRE 1991: 54). A designated space for the phenomenon that I call everyday fashion did not exist in the official narrative, so it embedded itself in semi-official, informal or even illegal areas of Soviet everyday life. Such spaces increasingly grew from the late 1950s on, due to Khrushchev's opening to the West, which soon turned into a race in everyday culture between the Soviet Union and the West. While Khrushchev inherited Stalin's middle classes, he tried to reshape them to fit his vision of the new modern society. He also needed a wider participation of Soviet citizenry in his project: firstly to support his radically new political turn, and, secondly, to entrust them with public performances of middle class rituals, in order to compete more convincingly with the West. Observing the political and social changes in the socialist countries in the 1960s, Ken Jowitt argued that the relationship between the regime and society was changing from domination through terror to domination informed by symbolic manipulation (JOWITT 1992: 99–100). This was a more efficient and smarter form of domination, and politically it indicated that "the Party recognized the need to address the imbalances between the regime and society" (ibid). In place of open repression, the regime bought the loyalty of its middle classes with material rewards, while, simultaneously, imposing the new propriety rules on its members. In contrast to the privileged highest strata of Nomenklatura, whose members clandestinely enjoyed expensive status symbols,[47] the new middle classes were publicly encouraged to move into the socialist sartorial version of prettiness and cosiness.

A tacit deal can be traced between Khrushchev's regime and its nascent middle classes, through which consumption and fashion practices were legitimized.[48] Furthermore, this deal gave the middle classes visibility, so they urgently needed civilian clothes. As the new aesthetics of their dress had to be decided quickly, promoted through the media and applied in everyday life, socialism was forced to borrow its new official dress style from the reservoir of bourgeois culture, just as Stalinism had done. In contrast to the Stalinist preference for lavish excesses, the socialist official discourse now appropriated a much quieter stylistic expression: good taste. While Stalinist taste had a highly representational role, socialist good taste provided a guide to everyday life by merging proletarian style with petit-bourgeois 'good taste'.

---

[47] For an overview on the Soviet most privileged social strata, Nomenklatura, see VOSLENSKY 1984.

[48] Vera Dunham detects the Big Deal between Stalin and the members of the various social strata loyal to his project, from Stakhanovites to the managerial and technical intelligentsia, and claims that they were apolitical, uncritical, upwardly mobile and acquisitive (DUNHAM 1990: 13–17). Furthermore, Dunham states that Stalin's regime was not held together simply by pure terror (ibid: 13). Ken Jowitt analyses a tacit deal between the new middle classes and the Soviet regime during the 1960s (JOWITT 1992). Accordingly, Khrushchev's political deal with his middle classes was supported by the economic preferences set down in the 1959 Seven-Year Plan, and tirelessly promoted in the contemporary media. See also Millar's observations on Brezhnev's 'little deal' (MILLAR 1988).

Their mutual characteristics, such as modesty, blandness, appropriateness and comfort contributed towards its aesthetics, but socialist good taste also incorporated two new categories – prettiness and elegance. At the end of the 1950s, those categories were needed to soften the asceticism of proletarian style. Socialist good taste was an ideal medium to filter, neutralize and slow down fashion changes, and to offer safe sartorial choices to those who were new to the sophisticated rituals of dressing up. In that sense, a luxurious dress fulfilled the representational role of socialist fashion, while a modest but pretty dress was the perfect choice for the members of the socialist middle classes in their everyday life.

Generally, there are significant differences between changing fashions and 'good taste' in western dress, mainly related to the latter's aesthetic neutrality and its slower changes.[49] Regarding the concept of time, socialist good taste had similar characteristics. Both versions of 'good taste', petit bourgeois and socialist, were almost immutable, and equally scared of unpredictability and individuality. The socialist regimes reserved for themselves the right eventually to change dress standards. In that way, they introduced a slow movement in socialist fashion meant for their middle classes, but always within their master narrative of modesty, simplicity and appropriateness. Petit-bourgeois sartorial codes were ready-made and could be used immediately, but the reasons why socialism adopted the petit-bourgeois style, and not some other version, were also rooted in socialist poverty, lost traditions of dress making, and the previous rejection of past fashion styles. Smoothly blending proletarian asceticism and petit-bourgeois prettiness, socialist good taste was the agency through which fashion was eventually reintroduced as a legitimate practice in the Soviet Union.

Along with the concept of socialist good taste, an official re-conceptualization of gender was also channelled through women's magazines, advice manuals and etiquette books from the late 1950s on. In contrast to both the 1920s austere Bolshevik woman and the 1930s Stalinist mythical Superwoman, a new ideal woman connected the old puritanical idea of modesty with new categories such as prettiness and elegance.[50] Advice on appropriate dress and proper behaviour insisted that only simplicity is tasteful and beautiful. The rules were straightforward: shoes and handbags should match, more than three colours should never be used in an outfit, the shape of your hat should take into account the shape of your face, look lovely but do not over-dress. Carefully composed and often repeated, this new guidance demonstrated the process through which proletarian sartorial asceticism was carefully recoded into a controlled version of femininity. There were clear boundaries between the categories of appropriateness and inappropriateness, and no transgression was allowed. The woman could be pretty but not sexy. She could be adorned but not to excess.[51] Inner beauty was more appreciated than its exterior version.

In order to promote its new style and its new female ideal, Khrushchev's regime did not rely on the elitist media. The perfectly executed dresses and luxurious eveningwear, paraded at the socialist fashion congresses and promoted on the pages of *Modeli sezona* and *Zhurnal mod*,[52] belonged to a completely different world from the one shared by the millions of Soviet

---

[49] Ted Polhemus and Lynn Procter (1978) argue that any "good taste" in western clothes, ranging from the upper class to the middle class or the petit-bourgeois version, is an anti-fashion statement.

[50] Different notions of womanhood accompanied Soviet socialism from the very beginning. The dramatic difference between the concepts of the utopian Bolshevik woman and the over-decorated NEP woman demonstrated the huge schism within the Soviet social body throughout the 1920s. Within the Stalinist petitbourgeoisification of society during the mid-1930s, the New Woman was transformed into a Superwoman, with displaying femininity and other attributes of traditional womanhood added to the list of her duties.

[51] See for example SEMENOVA, E. Ukrasheniia? Da, no v mery. In: *Rabotnitsa* 1959 2: 32.

[52] For example, *Zhurnal mod* filled its January 1958 issue with a luxurious photo presentation of the 8th Moscow Socialist Fashion Congress. In contrast, *Rabotnitsa* covered the event with a short text, and a few small drawings of dresses from the congress (N.N. 1957. Mezhdunarodnyi congress mody. In: *Rabotnitsa* 1957 7: 28–29).

women. So the new official aesthetic which united modesty with prettiness was advocated through the mass women's magazines, such as *Rabotnitsa* 'Working Woman', and popular picture weeklies, such as *Ogonek*. While reporting on a fashion show at the Riga *Dom modelei*, *Ogonek* enthusiastically praised clothes and their designers but nevertheless commented that there was a thick stone wall between the *Dom modelei* and the shops, as well as another wall of misunderstanding between consumers and the *Dom modelei* (KHRABROVA 1960: 15). While the article ended with an enthusiastic statement that the activities of the Riga *Dom modelei* were breaking down those walls, the existing problems were equally clearly exposed (ibid.: 16). Similarly close to Soviet reality, *Rabotnitsa* was quietly allowed to raise issues about the current ready-to-wear production, as well as to offer practical advice on making and repairing your own clothes. In the mid-1960s, the magazine regularly interviewed designers from the *ODMO* about new trends,[53] but also discreetly acknowledged that the style and quality of clothes offered in the shops were still very poor. The designer-correspondent E. Semenova shared with her readers a story about how her clever young neighbour bought a ready-made dress, and, being very unhappy with its poor quality and standardized style, embellished the dress herself.[54] In an article published in the same issue, *Rabotnitsa* reminded women that dresses made from brocade and velvet belonged to evening wear and were not an appropriate sartorial work code. The same article also condemned another widespread women's habit: arriving at work without make-up and wearing hair curlers, only to perform their beauty routines in public. And while modesty in dress was expected at the work place, a controlled tidiness of a simple functional dress, instead of an old stained house-robe, was the new recommended look for the home.[55]

The drive to educate citizens in the socialist culture of dress had already started with the editorial of the first issue of *Zhurnal mod*, which acknowledged that the magazine had a duty to educate its readers into a taste for beautiful dresses and in the culture of commodities.[56] Nevertheless, educational efforts only intensified once the opening towards the West started, as the phenomenon of fashion, and its seasonal changes, became the most sensitive issue for fashion magazines and books on fashion. In her book *Thoughts on Beauty and Taste* (1962), Olga Rusanova insists that Soviet fashion designers should educate the masses in beauty and taste. Armed with adequate knowledge, the citizens would learn to say 'no' to the latest fashion crazes with which they were being bombarded from the West. Along these lines, fashion's eternal staple, the 'little black dress', fulfilled the new socialist criteria of prettiness, femininity, simplicity and, even, democracy. In her book *On the Culture of Dress* Ljudmila Efremova calls it a universal outfit, and offers a drawing with three options for the same dress. The office version is accompanied by a pretty blouse with dots and a wide belt, a short smart jacket completes a leisurely walking variant, while the smartest version, adorned with pearls, stole and black gloves, is meant for the theatre. *Rabotnitsa* suggests its readership should accessorize a little black dress with different details, such as a lace collar and cuffs, a silk blouse with a ruffle, a tiny fur detail or a white collar.[57]

These details were not only supposed to embellish the little black dress; they also pointed towards its versatility and functionality. Furthermore, the socialist fashion media's attention to detail had economic reasons. As observed by Roland Barthes:

[53] The representatives of the *ODMO* would usually stress that fashion was not about to change in the new season see N.N. Nashe interv'iu. In: *Rabotnitsa*, 1966 1: 29.

[54] Semenova, E. 1963. Kak odevat'sia i doma. In: *Rabotnitsa* August 1963.

[55] Semenova, E. 1963. Na rabote. In: *Rabotnitsa* August 1963.

[56] N.N. The Editorial. In: *Zhurnal mod* 1945 1.

[57] N.N. 1963. Vashe chernoe plat'e. In: *Rabotnitsa* 1963 7: 31.

> "The rhetoric of the detail seems to take on an increasing extension, and the stake it has in doing so is an economic one: by becoming a mass value (through its magazines, if not through its boutiques), Fashion must elaborate meanings whose fabrication does not appear costly; this is the case of the 'detail': one detail is enough to transform what is outside meaning into meaning, what is unfashionable into Fashion, and yet a 'detail' is not expensive; by this particular semantic technique, Fashion departs from the luxurious and seems to enter into a clothing practice accessible to modest budgets; but at the same time, sublimated under the name find, this same low-priced detail participates in the dignity of the idea: likewise free, likewise glorious, the detail consecrates a democracy of budgets while respecting an aristocracy of tastes." (BARTHES 1990: 243)

In their more popular versions, western women's magazines also relied on the power of detail, but the semantic value of the so-called 'little nothing that changes everything' was even stronger in the socialist fashion media's efforts to make its female readership happy, while politically depending on the ideological dictate of the day, and economically being limited by the Soviet planned economy.

Indeed, the Five-Year Plans caused permanent problems in the production of mass clothing, as the powerful bureaucracy established under Stalinism governed the industry through a rigid and hierarchical structure, and, subsequently, determined the functioning of the field of fashion up to the end of socialism. With their activities informed by the hierarchical principle, textile factories did not respond to their customers' desires, but to their superiors, from whom they were given both supplies and orders to fulfil their plan. If an enterprise could not obtain the required quantity or quality of raw material, or some essential component was unavailable, production would not stop as the plan had to be fulfilled. The production process would continue by the mechanism of substitutions, which affected the quality of products.[58] After a series of substitutions, of either fabric or detail, the look and quality of the dress that would reach the shop floor in order to be reproduced into a hundred thousand copies had little in common with the fashion drawing or with the prototype that had arrived at the textile company from the central *Dom modelei*.

Although they could have easily been mass produced, unlike the prototypes of extravagant dresses made from luxurious fabrics, the 1960s simple and functional dresses never appeared in the shops in the required quantity or quality. Why did modest dresses, in keeping with the new form of minimalist socialist modernity, not materialize in the Soviet Union, regardless of the huge politically imposed campaign and its appealing aesthetics which acknowledged prettiness and elegance? Dress was just one element in Khrushchev's process of the de-Stalinization of the fine arts, applied arts and everyday objects, which embraced architecture, furniture, kitchen appliances and clothes. He planned to leave Stalinist over-decorativeness behind, as the space age was supposed to be served by an uncomplicated and practical style in dress, which would be easy to manufacture on a mass scale. Yet, while Khrushchev's political project to weaken ideological pressures was welcomed by the intelligentsia and by artists,[59] his project to reconstruct Soviet industry failed.[60]

---

[58] For an overview of the principles that guided socialist economy, see KORNAI 1990.

[59] His political efforts exhausted themselves in the mass magazines and specialized applied arts magazines, such as *Dekorativnoe iskusstvo SSSR* 'Applied Art of the USSR', which in the late 1950s and 1960s dedicated many pages to rehabilitate and reintroduce the 1920s Avant-garde, especially the Constructivists, whose work and ideas were completely abandoned during the Stalinist times.

[60] Moshe Levin states that the "cult of Stalin" was exchanged by the "cult of the state", and that bureaucracy had turned the Party into its own "ruling servant". Levin calls the Soviet system "bureaucratic absolutism" and argues that Khrushchev's project failed because the radical changes that he planned did not suit the ruling bureaucracy (LEVIN 1995: 204–208).

Apart from the mass-manufacture of clothes by large state companies, the only other officially recognized type of dress production was offered by the state-owned fashion ateliers. They appeared in the mid-1930s, serving only privileged social groups, from the praised "shock-workers" to the highest echelons of the bureaucracy. From the 1950s the fashion ateliers increased in number, offering custom-made clothes and accessories to all categories of citizens in order to make up for the poor quality and limited variety of sizes of mass-manufactured clothes.[61] All fashion ateliers were officially the same, but there was a significant difference between the elitist ateliers and those that served the average customer. Although the latter also provided custom-made outfits, the quality of their service was often very low, with an inadequate choice of fabrics. Fighting rudeness and poor service in the state-owned fashion ateliers, *Rabotnitsa* demanded: "Let Fashion Enter the Atelier!"[62] Although they charged higher prices and were supposed to create custom-made dresses, the state-owned ateliers adopted the inefficient practices of industrial production, even borrowing the brigade technique from mass production.[63]

For many Soviet women therefore, the discreet service provided by a skilful seamstress was the most important tactic in their efforts to dress smartly and challenge socialist cultural isolationism. Such relationships were widespread, but both the client and the seamstress had to be careful, as the institution of self-employment was not legally recognized. However, the discreet army of small dressmakers acted as unrecognized *couturières* by relying on their skills and the occasional old copy of a western fashion magazine. Used by both professional seamstresses and women who made their own clothes, paper patterns played a special role in the field of everyday fashion. Started as supplements to fashion and women's magazines, including *Rabotnitsa*, already in the 1920s, paper patterns became ever more important, once the official aesthetics of socialist good taste began to encourage women to be pretty and feminine in their everyday life. Moreover, Lidiia Orlova, a fashion and interiors editor of *Rabotnitsa*, succeeded in making ubiquitous paper patterns more reliable and attractive to her readers by obtaining in 1978 permission from the German magazine *Burda* to use its paper patterns.[64] Like advice columns, paper patterns served a dual role: to disseminate western fashion trends that were being gradually acknowledged, but also to control the process of dissemination. While they both helped to resolve the clash between dreams of the latest trends and socialist dysfunctional consumerist reality, the former hinted that the dreams could be achieved by self-provision.

Paper patterns provided templates for desirable dresses without any obligation on the regime to deliver them, but they nevertheless facilitated women's desire for prettiness, because they offered only slightly more of what was in any case allowed. As they were unable to buy dresses complying with the officially promoted aesthetics in the shops, women achieved the approved ideal in Do-It-Yourself versions. Moreover, this practice allowed for some difference, such as an individual play with colour or use of an unusual fabric. Since the authorities discreetly acknowledged both the necessary and symbolic roles of Do-It-Yourself dress, the

[61] In 1975, for example, the state spent 34 million roubles on repairs in Moscow alone, due to the bad quality of industrially produced clothes (for an overview see GERASIMOVA and CHUIKINA 2004).

[62] N.N. 1960. Pustite modu v atel'e! In: *Rabotnitsa* 1960 10: 26–27.

[63] One article in the book about the activities of the Moscow ateliers describes in detail the military-style division of labour in the production of each outfit. After the order for an outfit was accepted, different workers dealt with its different parts in a mechanically organized process, which left no space for creativity or for the real acknowledgement of the customer's individual desires (MALININA 1958).

[64] Lidiia Orlova shared with me her experiences about her editorship of *Rabotnitsa* in the period 1970–1986. She introduced more pages on fashion, and started to present fashion through fashion editorials. Showing an independent spirit, Orlova wrote to Mrs Burda asking her for permission to print their paper patterns, and finally obtained the permission for free. By the end of her period in *Rabotnitsa* the circulation of the magazine reached 26 million (Interview, Moscow, June 2004).

choice of fabrics for home dressmaking was more varied than fabrics used for mass-produced clothes.[65] On the other hand, the aesthetics of socialist good taste was so strongly promoted through the media that women interiorized its rules on moderation in smartness and prettiness. The conventional concept of femininity was never questioned or challenged by women in Soviet Russia, as they were too busy struggling with the regime to let them indulge in the rites of traditional womanhood.[66] It could be said that the appropriation of pretty and feminine expressions of western fashion was informed both by the cultural isolation to which women were exposed and by their limited material resources.

Conclusion

Distinguishing between two socialist sartorial fashion phenomena – socialist official fashion and everyday fashion – this paper argues that they were embedded in different spheres of Soviet society and served by different concepts of time. In its official version fashion was embedded in the socialist mythical reality, both as a part of the centralized economy and its five-year plans, and as an image of conventional yet unachievable elegance, obeying in this sense the aesthetics of Socialist Realism. Moreover, such bureaucratic over-centralization was not only in line with the prevailing economic model, but also demonstrated the socialist fear of change and discontinuity of time. Preferring the synchronic, systematic level over the diachronic, processive level, subsequent regimes attempted to control and tame fashion trends through centralized systems of clothes production and distribution. But the very existence of socialist official fashion, manifested through the regimes' huge efforts to maintain it through the All-Union *Dom modelei* and its regional branches, and to promote it through their women's magazines,[67] showed the socialist system's deep anxieties about the phenomenon of fashion. In the end, all the distortions that would haunt socialist fashion till the very end of socialism were already inscribed in the first embodiment of socialist fashion conceived in the *Dom modelei* in the mid-1930s: various hierarchically imposed levels of decision making, an obsession with science, a confused relationship with western fashion, a lack of tradition and experience, a misrepresentation of an ideal prototype as an average mass-produced garment, and an isolationism relying on the ethnic heritage. Privileges for the few and clothes shortages persisted, as the state continued to act as an allocator of goods in an inefficient centrally organized field of fashion production.

In contrast, everyday fashion was partially embedded in an unofficial modernity that ran in parallel with the official modernity, and became increasingly more important from the late 1950s on. The weakening of ideological pressures, following Khrushchev's rise to power, also promoted a new official aesthetics – socialist good taste, which united socialist ideals of modesty and simplicity with two 'bourgeois' categories, prettiness and elegance. The new official style was accompanied by a reconceptualization of gender, which promoted conventional femininity, presenting a new, softer, and sophisticated face of socialism against the backdrop of the Cold War. Moreover, both socialist good taste and a new female ideal re-

---

[65] See for example a collage matching new colourful, patterned fabrics with drawings of fashionable dresses (N.N. Novye tkani. In: *Rabotnitsa* 1957 5).

[66] The repressed socialist market was unable to deal with diversified and changing images of femininity, while in the West the post-war woman and notions of femininity were socially articulated in the context of advanced consumer economies. For an overview see NOLAN, M. 2003. Consuming America, Producing Gender. In: Laurence Moore R., Vaudagna, M. (ed.). *The American Century in Europe*. Ithaca., 243–261, CARTER, E. 1997. *How German Is She*. Ann Arbor., ROSS, K. 1996. *Fast Cars, Clean Bodies: Decolonization and the Reordering of French Culture*. Cambridge.

[67] See picture 1: Photograph from the Soviet magazine *Sovetskaia zhenshchina* in 1946, No 2

sponded to the need to dress up the new middle classes and gratify their increasing interest in fashion.

Everyday fashion existed in a fluid space in which the official, the informal and the illegal were equally present. It could be obtained at state ateliers which offered custom-made dresses, acquired through the prohibited services of a seamstress, or sewn by oneself. In contrast to the concept of timelessness which defined socialist official fashion, everyday fashion acknowledged change and was served by a faster flow of time. However, fashionability had been controlled and tamed, unless fashionable dresses were produced in an unofficial arena. Everyday fashion nevertheless showed the ongoing negotiations between the Soviet regimes and their female population, especially expressed through the regular advice columns, which acknowledged the interest in fashion but communicated to their readership that their fashion dreams could be achieved by Do-It-Yourself. Furthermore, socialist official fashion was served by the elitist magazines, while everyday fashion was either dealt with in the popular media or informed by western fashion magazines.

Summary

This paper argues that in its official version fashion was embedded in the socialist mythical reality, both as a part of the centralized economies and their five-year plans, and as an image of conventional yet unachievable elegance, obeying in this sense the aesthetics of socialist realism. The paper claims that such bureaucratic overcentralization was not only in line with the prevailing economic model, but also demonstrated the socialist fear of change and discontinuity of time. Preferring the synchronic, systematic level over the diachronic, processive level, the Soviet authorities attempted to control and tame fashion trends through centralized systems of clothes production and distribution. The paper situates everyday fashion in a fluid space in which the official, the informal and the illegal were equally present. It could be obtained at state ateliers, acquired through the prohibited services of a seamstress, or sewn by oneself. In contrast to the concept of timelessness, which defined socialist official fashion, everyday fashion acknowledged change and was served by a faster flow of time.

References

ALDRIDGE, D. 1945. Radio report: First Russian Fashion. In: *Vogue* 7: 48–9.

ALEKSEEVA, V. 1961. Govorit tekstil'. In: *Dekorativnoe iskusstvo* 4, 7–11.

BAKSHTEIN, J. 1993. Notes on the origin of socialist realist iconography. In: Banks, M. (ed.). *Aesthetic Arsenal: Soviet Realism under Stalin.* New York. 1993, 47–60.

BARTHES, R. 1976. *Mythologies.* London.

BARTHES, R. 1990. *The Fashion System.* Berkeley.

BARTHES, R. 2006. *The Language of Fashion.* Oxford.

BARTLETT, D. 2004. Let Them Wear Beige: the petit-bourgeois world of official socialist dress. In: *Fashion Theory* 2, 127–64.

BARTLETT, D. 2010. *FashionEast: The Spectre that Haunted Socialism.* Cambridge.

BAUDRILLARD J. 1990. *Fatal Strategies.* New York.

BLANK, A. 1937. Nekotorye itogi raboty Doma modelei. In: *Shveinaia promyshlennost'* 4, 28–30.

BELIAEVA-EKZEMPLIARSKAIA, S. 1996 (1934). *Modelirovanie odezhdy po zakonam zritel'nogo vospriiatiia.* Moskva.

CLARK, K. 2000. *The Soviet Novel: History as Ritual.* Bloomington.

DOBRENKO, E. 2007. *Political Economy of Socialist Realism.* New Haven.

DOLDOBANOV, G. 1962. Formulas and Fashions. In: *Soviet Union* 154, 34–35.

DUNHAM, V. S. 1990. *In Stalin's time: Middleclass values in Soviet fiction.* Durham.

EFREMOVA, L. 1960. *O kul'ture odezhdy.* Moskva.

EPSHTEIN, M. N. 1995. *After the Future: the Paradoxes of Postmodernism and Contemporary Russian Culture.* Amherst.

FITZPATRICK, S. 1993. *The Cultural Front: Power and culture in revolutionary Russia.* Ithaca, London.

FOUCAULT, M. 1991. *Discipline and Punish.* London.

FRIDLIAND, S., UZLIAN, A. 1959. Trista novyh risunkov. In: *Ogonek* 15, 24–27.

FROLOVA, T. 1937. Dom modelei priblizit' k proizvodstvu. In: *Shveinaia promyshlennost'* 4, 30–31.

GERASIMOVA E., CHUIKINA, S. 2004. Obshchestvo remonta. In: *NZ* 34 (electronic version).
GLATZER ROSENTHAL, B. 2002. *New Myth, New World: From Nietzsche to Stalin.* University Park.
GORIN, V. 1963. Comfort, Simplicity and Economy. In: *Soviet Union* 160, 46–47.
GORINA, G. 1967. Tradicii v modnom kostiume. In: *Dekorativnoe iskusstvo SSSR* 3, 7–10.
GRONOW, J. 2003. *Caviar with Champagne: Common luxury and the ideals of the good life in Stalin's Russia.* Oxford.
HELLER, L. 1997. A world of prettiness. In: Lahusen T., Dobrenko E. (ed.) *Socialist Realism Without Shores.* Durham 1997, 51–75.
HESSLER, J. 2000. Cultured Trade: The Stalinist turn towards consumerism. In: Fitzpatrick S. (ed.) *Stalinism: New directions.* London 2000, 182–209.
JOWITT, K. 1992. *New World Disorder: the Leninist extinction.* Berkeley.
KELLY, C., VOLKOV, V. 1998. Directed Desires: Kul'turnost' and consumption. In: Kelly C., Shepherd D. (ed.). *Constructing Russian Culture in the Age of Revolution, 1881-1940.* Oxford 1998, 291–313.
KHLUSTOVA, N. 1954. U khudozhnikov model'erov g. Gorkogo. In: *Zhurnal Mod* 4, 16.
KHRABROVA, N. 1960. V poiskakh krasivogo, udobnogo. In: *Ogonek* 10, 15–16.
KORNAI, J. 1990. *Vision and Reality, Market and State: contradictions and dilemmas revisited.* Budapest.
KRAMARENKO, L. 1964. Ob iskusstve odezhdy. In: *Dekorativnoe iskusstvo* 5, 16–21.
LEBINA. N. B., CHISTIKOV, A. N. 2003. *Obyvatel' i reformy.* St Peterburg.
LEBINA, N.B. 1999. *Povsednevnaia zhizn' sovetskogo goroda, 1920-1930 gody.* Sankt-Peterburg.
LEFEBVRE, H. 1991. *The Production of Space.* Oxford.
LEHMANN, U. 1999. Tigersprung: Fashioning history. In: *Fashion Theory* 3, 297–322.
LEONOV, L. 1962. Fashions for Fun and Pleasure. In: *Soviet Union* 143, 44–45.
LÉVI-STRAUSS, C. 1986. *The Raw and the Cooked.* Harmondsworth, Middlesex.
MALININA; N. I. 1958. Organizatsiia izgotovleniia legkogo zhenskogo plat'ia brigadnym metodom. In: N.N. *Krasivaia odezhda: iz opyta raboty mosk. atel'e.* Moskva 1958, 10–29.
MARKOVA, S., 1961, Nacional'nye motivy v odezhde. In: *Dekorativnoe iskusstvo SSSR* 6, 44–48.
MILLAR, J. R. 1988. The Little Deal: Brezhnev's contribution to acquisitive socialism. In: Thompson T.L., Sheldon R.R. (ed.). *Soviet Society and Culture: essays in honor of Vera S. Dunham.* Boulder 1988, 3–19.
MURAV'EV, V.K., MIKHAILOV, P. V. 1977. History of synthetic Fibre Production in the USSR. In: *Fibre Chemistry* 2, 116–119 (originally published in: *Khimicheskie volokna*, March–April 1977 2, 11–13).
OSOKINA, E. A. 2001. *Our Daily Bread: socialist distribution and the art of survival in Stalin's Russia, 1927-1941.* Armonk, New York.
POLHEMUS, T., PROCTER, L. 1978. *Fashion and anti-fashion.* London.
ROUVILLOIS, F. 2000. Utopia and totalitarianism. In: Schaer R., Claeys G., Tower Sargent L. (ed.). *Utopia: the search for the ideal society in the western world.* New York 2000, 316–31.
RUSANOVA, O. 1962. *Razdum'ia o krasote i vkuse* . Moskva.
VOSLENSKY, M. 1984. *Nomenklatura: anatomy of the Soviet ruling class.* London.
ZAKHAROVA, L. 2005. Kazhdoi sovetskoi zhenshchine – plat'e ot Diora! (Frantsuzskoe vliianie v sovetskoi mode 1950-1960-kh godov). In: *Sotsial'naia istoriia: Ezhegodnik 2004*, 339–367.

Periodicals:

Dekorativnoe iskusstvo SSSR 'Decorative Art of the USSR', 1950s–1980s.
Moda stran socializma 'Fashion of the Socialist Countries' (annual publication), 1959–2000.
Modeli sezona 'Prototypes of the Seasons' (fashion biannual), 1938–1989.
Ogonek 'Little Flame' (illustrated weekly), 1950s–1970s.
Rabotnitsa 'Working Woman' (women's weekly), 1929–1989.
Shveinaia promyshlennost' 'Clothing Industry', the 1930s.
Soviet Union (monthly), 1950s-1980s.
Zhurnal mod 'Fashion Journal' (fashion monthly), 1945-1989.

CONSUMPTION / CULTURE / COMMUNISM: The Significance of Terminology or Some Realities and Myths of Socialist Consumption

ULRIKE GOLDSCHWEER, BOCHUM

1. Introduction

"Soviet culture of consumption sounds paradoxical to those who associate culture with civilized manners and consumption with abundance of goods and service." (GRONOW 2011: 251) This is the first sentence of Jukka Gronow's entry on socialist consumption published in the first volume of the *"Encyclopedia of Consumer Culture"* (2011), intentionally suggesting a Western-naive point of view and thus illustrating the popular image of socialist societies as being ineffective with regard to consumerist and, implicitly, cultural prosperity.

The main purpose of my paper is, therefore, in the first place to draw attention to the fact, that the terminology of the conceptual field of consumption is for the most part contaminated with the idea of the superiority of market economy, thus making ideologically neutral discussions of the subject virtually impossible. After that I would like to point out some myths and realities of socialist consumption.

Consumption can be regarded as an everyday phenomenon concerning the handling of and the attitude towards things, including the acquisition, the use and wasting of consumer goods, the practices and discourses of usage as well as questions of product design. In modern consumer societies, it serves as the most important means of the creation and maintainance of personal and cultural identity.

The English term *consumption* – as well as its derivatives such as *consumerism, consumer society, consumer culture* – is anything but ideologically neutral; on the contrary, it implies a thoroughly Western point of view, equating the freedom of choice from a great variety of products supplied by market economy with democratic values. Socialist consumption, in contrast, is from this point of view associated with notions of shortages and the state-organized distribution and allocation of goods. This holds true for the German equivalents of this terms, too. Although the collapse of socialist economies 25 years ago seems to give evidence of this point of view, we have to be careful not to confuse shortages of certain commodities with the absence of consumerist practices at all. The terminology in the field of consumption theory, thus, tends to reflect the perspective of the so-called winner of the Cold War; the specifically socialist practices, circumstances, and values of consumption are either ignored, or characterized as a deviation from the norm of market economy. In this way, the failure of socialist economy as a postulate seems to be confirmed retrospectively[1]. Russian terminology, on the other hand, shows a peculiar mixture of traditional Marxist and newly adopted Western connotations.

In the field of the culturological study of socialist consumption a specialized terminology could be helpful, that takes into account the specific premises and assumptions of socialist or communist societies. It should bear in mind ideas such as, the Utopian idea of communist affluence, or the rationalist image of human behaviour, the postulates of communist morality, or, of course, the everyday experience of shortages as part of a particular form of consumer culture, generating specific consumer practices. Such a terminology also has to reflect the fact, that the availability of commodities and the promise of prosperity in the near future

[1] Cf. my discussion of the topic in GOLDSCHWEER 2013.

became a crucial point of securing the system's stability. Since such a terminology is still a desideratum, we have to choose our word very carefully in order to avoid to be terminologically trapped from both sides.

Without claiming to be exhaustive, the following terminological examples from various sources are meant to confirm and substantiate my point of view.

2. Consumption – Society – Culture: A Question of Terminology

The ideological relativity of terms such as consumption and culture is in fact crucial for the perception of a conceptual field that confronts us with a wide range of concepts and terms of different theoretical, historical, cultural, and ideological provenience. The translation of these terms into different languages (here: in German, English and Russian) reveals even more nuances in meaning. Whereas in the English language, the terminological field seems to be extremely differentiated and may have influenced the German terminology as well, the translation of these terms into Russian reveals another multitude of ideological and historical differences, resulting from the ambivalence of a still virulent marxist terminology on one hand, and only recently adopted market economy concepts on the other. In the following chapter I would like to highlight some of the most important difficulties and misunderstandings.

2.1. Konsum / Consumption / Potreblenie

First of all, I would like to introduce the economic, social, cultural and even aesthetic perspectives of consumption as a multidisciplinary concept, in which ideological prepositions seem to be virtually absent. From this point of view, the term (at least in German and English) seems to be fairly objective. This can be illustrated by quoting from the introduction of one of the most important studies in this field, the "*Europäische Konsumgeschichte*" (*European History of Consumption*), published in 1997, but nevertheless still influential. In the introductory article by Hannes Siegrist the term *Konsumieren* 'consumption' is defined as follows:

> "In a most general sense, consumption means the buying, using, and wasting of commodities; including the discourses, emotions, relations, rituals, and forms of sociability and socialisation involved. Consumption research traditionally concentrates on certain areas, such as product design, the supply of commodities and services, the availability of particular goods, the reasons, decisions and intentions of buying, the significance of owning and using, the places and temporal structures of using, the fulfilment of physical, emotional, cultural, and social needs and, finally, the discourse about consumption itself." (SIEGRIST 1997: 16-17)[2]

[2] „In einem allgemeinsten Sinne wird hier unter Konsumieren das Kaufen, das Gebrauchen und Verbrauchen/ Verzehren von Waren verstanden; eingeschlossen in dieses Verständnis sind die damit in Zusammenhang stehenden Diskurse, Emotionen, Beziehungen, Rituale und Formen der Geselligkeit und Vergesellschaftung. Die Konsumforschung konzentriert sich traditionell auf ausgewählte Bereiche wie Produktgestaltung, Angebot, Vertrieb und Verkauf von [...] Gütern sowie [...] Dienstleistungen. Sie blickt auf die Zugänglichkeit bestimmter Güter, auf die Motive, Entscheidungen und Ziele des Kaufens, die Bedeutung des Habens und Verbrauchens bzw. Benutzens der Waren, auf die Orte, wo Verbrauch stattfindet, die zeitliche Strukturierung, die Erfüllung von physischen, emotionalen, kulturellen und sozialen Bedürfnissen und letztlich auf die Diskurse über den Konsum." All translations are mine (if not indicated otherwise), UG.

In a footnote, he adds: "In the social and cultural sphere consumption is a homogenizing force, but it is associated with differentiation and protest, too." (SIEGRIST 1997: 17, footnote 11).[3]

This extensive definition is the result of a long theoretical tradition, starting with a negative interpretation of consumption as the annihilation of the starting product, which gave way to more positive economic interpretations only in the 18th century, declaring consumption to be the original aim of production and thus one of the most important factors of economic growth (MERKEL 1999: 19ff.). [4] A cultural component is added to this concept not before the end of the 19th century (MERKEL 1999: 20-21).[5] The 20th century witnesses the rise of consumerism and the consumer society especially in Western Europe and the United States, a fact that has influenced our image of consumption until today. In the second half of the 20th century the number of interpretations, that are critical of consumerism as a morally corrupting and destructive force, increases (MERKEL 1999: 19ff.)[6]. The consumerist excess becomes part of the so-called postmodern condition as well.[7]

The Soviet interpretation of the term *consumption* 'potreblenie' is, of course, ideologically determined by the writings of Karl Marx. The most prominent factor, documented extensively in all three editions of the "*Bol'šaja Sovetskaja Ėnciklopedija*" (*Great Soviet Encyclopedia*),[8] seems to be the differentiation between *productive* 'proizvodstvennoe' und *non-productive*, i.e. *personal*, 'ličnoe', forms of consumption, as well as the emphasis on the interdependence between production and consumption. In class conflict the two forms of consumption turn out to be antagonistic forces at the expense of the working proletariat creating a surplus value, consumed parasitically by the capitalist bourgeoisie. In contrast, socialist societies as a rule manage to achieve a perfect balance of these forces, creating a kind of communist consumer paradise:

> "Для социализма характерно планомерное неуклонное повышение уровня П[отребления] трудящихся и улучшение его структуры на основе развития и совершенствования социалистического производства и роста производительности общественного труда ([...]). Основным способом распределения фонда личного П. выступает распределение по труду, однако с развитием общественного производства в П. трудящихся возрастает доля материальных и духовных благ, получаемых ими через общественные фонды потребления."[9] (MAJER 1975: 437-438)

---

[3] „Konsum homogenisiert sozial und kulturell, er verbindet sich aber ebenso mit Differenzierung und Protest."

[4] According to Adam Smith, cf. (MERKEL 1999: 19).

[5] Merkel refers here to Thorstein Veblens *Theory of the Leisure Class* (1899).

[6] MERKEL refers here to the "*Hidden Persuaders*" by Vance Packard or the Idea of the "Konsumterror" by Adorno and Horkheimer,

[7] It is very interesting how at the beginning of the eighties of the 20th century Postmodernism was directly linked with consumerism, cf. the following quotation from Fokkemas account of postmodernist literature: "The Postmodernist code can be linked to a particular way and view of life, common in the Western world, including part of Latin America. The literary preference for nonselection coincides with an 'embarras du choix' offered by luxurious living conditions, which enable many people to have numerous options. The Postmodernist appeal to the imagination is out of place in the world of Ivan Denisovič or in the People's Republic of China. [...] The Postmodernist code has clearly its geographical and sociological limitations." (FOKKEMA 1983: 55).

[8] First edition (*БСЭ* 1926-1947): (N.N. 1940: 573-576); second edition (*БСЭ* 1949-1958): (MAJER 1955: 292-295); third edition (*БСЭ* 1969-1978): (MAJER 1975: 437-430).

[9] "The systematic and steadfast increase of the standards of consumption of the working class and the improvement of its structures based upon the development and perfection of socialist production and the growth of the productivity of social labour is a characteristic trait of socialism. ([...]) A constitutive means for the allocation of goods for personal consumption is the allocation according to labour; but together with the growth

This idea, of course, is part of the Utopian ideal of communist affluence: As a result of the abolishment of private property, the difference between the rich and the poor was expected to disappear. Instead of consumption, non-alienated work was meant to determine the workers' life; consumption would restrict itself to the essentials – in accordance with the notorious slogan: Each according to his ability, to each according to his needs (Cf. MARX 1875: 21). The socially distinctive dimension of consumption would disappear as well (MERKEL 1999: 16-17). The rationalization of needs (!) and of production would save natural ressources and raise productivity, leading to an abundance of commodities which would cause prices to fall, until money as a means of exchange would disappear as well (MERKEL 1999: 51). The goal was a communist society of affluence, meaning in fact a society with utterly rationalized needs.

Modern Russian definitions (if we take for instance the Russian *"Wikipedia")*[10] tend to avoid such ideological implications and – like their Western counterparts – cover economic, social and cultural aspects as well.

2.2. Consumer Society / Konsumgesellschaft / Obščestvo potreblenija

Whereas *consumption* (as well as *Konsum* or even *potreblenie* in a modern interpretation of the word) seems to be a fairly neutral, but multidisciplinary concept, most derivations of the word obviously seem to rest on ideological assumptions and prejudices.

This applies, for instance, to the idea of a *consumer society* (or – in German – *Konsumgesellschaft*), a concept describing societies, creating and maintaining their identities mostly through consumption. Its most important features according to John Brewer are the following:

- the "free choice" from a "broad range of goods",
- the development of "communication systems" about and by consumer goods (for instance, the development of advertising as a cultural practice),
- the development of "spheres of taste, fashion, and style",
- the "emphasis on spare time instead of work, and on consumption instead of production"
- the emergence of the consumer as a scientific category, and
- a kind of typical "ambivalence" concerning consumption, referring to a growing contradiction between the consumerist desires and the social responsibility of the individual (BREWER 1997: 51-57).

It seems to be quite evident, that this definition has nothing in common with the ideals of socialist economy – where in fact the priority is given to production, and aspects such as "free choice" and a "broad range of goods", advertising as a prevailing strategy of consumer communication or even notions of fashion and style cannot be regarded as typical traits.

But it also becomes clear, that the entire idea of a "consumer society" is deeply rooted in Western thought, for socialist consumption is excluded from it completely, or as Hannes Siegrist has put it:

> "Western European consumer society and culture is based upon a specific mixture of European and American goods and values, trends of design and taste, practices and mentalities, institutions and strategies. It has developed in a competition with Eastern

---

of social productivity the part of the workers' consumption of goods and services, provided by social pools of consumption, increases."

[10] Cf. Wikipedia: Потребление. I deliberately chose the Wikipedia here as a source, because I take it to be an appropriate medium for discussions about a terminology in flux.

European consumer society, that is regarded as a state controlled communist economy, characterized by shortages, provisioning, and command." (SIEGRIST 1997: 19f.)[11]

Although Siegrist chose the term "Eastern consumer society", its specifics are excluded from this definition: Even the fact that socialist economy was conceptualized as a countermodel to early capitalism (and not the other way round), seems to be ignored at all. Ina Merkel criticizes in her "*Konsumgeschichte der DDR*", that the Western idea, "[...] that mass consumption brings about democracy as well as a sovereign and mature consumer, who is able to choose from a variety of consumer goods as well as from a variety of political parties" is taken for granted and serves as the justification of a feeling of superiority (MERKEL 1999: 20)[12]. The consumers' freedom of choice obviously is equated with democratic values: "[...] one aspect of consumption – namely acquisition – is generalized and regarded as the decisive factor in the assessment of a whole society model" (MERKEL 1999, 24). The particular socialist forms of designing, acquiring, using and wasting goods, of communication by and about things, of the creation of identity as well as the cultural imprint of the socialist consumer are deliberately excluded from this perspective. The Western provenience of this term is further proved by the fact, that the term *obščestvo potreblenija* is virtually missing in the Russian encyclopedias; in the "*Wikipedia*" the term is obviously regarded as a concept associated with Western economy (cf. WIKIPEDIA: ОБЩЕСТВО ПОТРЕБЛЕНИЯ).

This raises the question, if the identification of socialist societies as consumer societies could be acceptable or reasonable at all. It is, primarily, a question of definition. David Crowley and Susan Reid, for instance, have argued recently (*"Pleasures of Socialism"*, 2010), that socialist societies have to be regarded as "mass consumer societies" from the 1950s on, when consumption started to become an important means of constructing identity (CROWLEY, REID 2010: 9). From this point of view, the opposition of a Western consumer society and an Eastern society of shortages proves to be a relic of the Cold War rhetorical framework (serving as a kind of "socialist Other", as it were) (CROWLEY, REID 2010: 12). Socialist consumption apparently became a kind of supplement (in a Derridaen sense of the word)[13] of the normative Western consumer society, who obviously needed to define socialist consumption as an economy of shortages to assure itself of its own normative qualities. The colonialisation of the socialist consumer societies by Western practices in post-socialist times may be very well justified by this conceptualisation, too.

2.3. Consumerism / Konsumismus / Potrebitel'stvo

Another popular term in this field is *consumerism*. The current debate about its significance for the understanding of modern societies seems to oscillate between two extremes, namely

---

11 „Die westeuropäische Konsumgesellschaft und Konsumkultur beruht auf einer spezifischen Mischung europäischer und amerikanischer Güter und Werte, Design- und Geschmacksrichtungen, Praktiken und Mentalitäten, Institutionen und Strategien. Sie entwickelte sich in Konkurrenz und Abgrenzung zur osteuropäischen Konsumgesellschaft, die sie als kommunistische Mangel-, Versorgungs-, Kommando- und Staatswirtschaft bezeichnet hat."

12 „Dabei speist sich das Überlegenheitsgefühl der westlichen Industrienationen gegenüber den osteuropäischen Mangelgesellschaften aus der Vorstellung, die breite Auswahl an Konsumgütern verschaffe den Individuen die Mittel, sich von anderen sozial und kulturell zu unterscheiden. Dabei wird sich zugute gehalten, daß der Massenkonsum die Demokratisierung der Gesellschaft bewirke und einen souveränen und mündigen Konsumenten hervorbringe, der seine Wahl unter einer Vielfalt von Konsumgütern treffen kann, was in seiner Bedeutung mit dem politischen Wahlverhalten gleichgesetzt wird."

13 Cf. „Das Supplement ist ein unwesentlicher Zusatz, der zu etwas hinzugefügt wird, was schon in sich vollständig ist; aber das Supplement wird hinzugefügt, um zu vervollständigen, um in dem, was eigentlich als vollständig galt, einen Mangel zu kompensieren." (CULLER 1999: 114).

between the idea of an ethically responsible consumerism as a positive force promising prosperity and wealth for all on the one hand and a thoroughly critical approach on the other.

While in the German concept with its – not very frequently used – terms *Konsumismus*, *Konsumerismus* or *Konsumentismus*[14] critical attitudes prevail, the English concept tends to cover both extremes and includes positive as well as negative connotations. In the positive interpretation of the term, the consumer is envisioned as an informed participant of a market place that ensures economic justice and fairness; consumerism therefore includes all efforts supporting the consumers' interests including product information and consumer protection. Critical interpretations equate consumerism with materialism with all its negative implications ranging from selfishness to irresponsibility. Consumerism is accused of being a lifestyle, "which destroys individuality and harms society"; an attitude often associated with the anti-globalization movement (Cf. *Consumerism*). The term *ethical consumerism* underlines the consumers' responsibility "to influence labour and environmental practices in faraway places"; a highly controversial concept, though:

> "Critics see ethical consumerism as a dangerous marketization of ethics whereby the values of wealthy consumers 'go global', unfairly constraining the freedom of others. These critics charge that consumerist movements in advanced countries are too quick to equate their preferences with the best interest of the labourers and environmental concerns on whose behalf they purport to act. Underpinning the practice of ethical consumerism is thus the presumption that consumption, a process driven by the global distribution of wealth, can serve as an effective surrogate for other, more traditional forms of democratic representation, such as voting." (ENCYCLOPAEDIA BRITANNICA: ETHICAL CONSUMERISM)

In Soviet dictionaries such as the *"Slovar' po ėtike"* (*Dictionary of Ethics*, 1981) the Russian term *potrebitel'stvo* – just like *obščestvo potreblenija* – is closely associated with Western (capitalist) consumerism in its critical interpretation. *Potrebitel'stvo* is presented as a moral category synonymous with, for instance, hedonism. Capitalist consumerist societies are thus in danger to loose their moral standards in favour of an individualistic and conformist pursuit of absolute pleasure. Socialist consumption is presented as an alternative, morally superior form:

> "В условиях социализма ориентация всего хозяйственного и социокультурного развития на рост народного потребления не только не обусловливает духа П., но, напротив, создает предпосылки развертывания способностей личности, ее всестороннего совершенствования, т. е. вырабатывает подлинную альтернативу П. Высокий уровень потребления не служит здесь критерием ценности личности, средством социального утверждения и продвижения. Кроме того, в социалистических странах последовательно осуществляется процесс выравнивания уровней потребления населения на основе принципов социальной справедливости." (N.N. 1981, unnumbered)[15]

---

[14] „Konsumismus, auch Konsumerismus oder Konsumentismus (von lat. *consumere* – verbrauchen), ist ein übersteigertes Konsumverhalten zum Zweck der gesellschaftlichen Distinktion oder des Strebens nach Identität, Lebenssinn und Glück. Der Begriff wird zumeist in kritischer Absicht verwendet." (Cf. Konsumismus).

[15] "Under socialist conditions the orientation of the whole economical, social and cultural development towards the increase of public consumption does not only escape the spirit of consumerism, but, on the contrary, lays the foundations for the free development and accomplishment of individual capabilities, that is, it represents a true alternative for consumerism. High standards of consumption are not meant to be a criterion for the evaluation of a personality, or a means of social acknowledgement and advancement. Besides, in socialist

Obvious forms of consumerism in socialist countries are characterized as petit bourgeois relics of capitalism: "Отдельные проявления потребительского подхода к жизни, побуждаемые мещанскими устремлениями к материальному благополучию [...] являются формой пережитков капитализма в сознании и поведении людей." (N.N. 1981, unnumbered).[16]

The dangers of the demoralizing influence of consumerism are admonished of:

> "Потребительский подход влечет за собой снижение моральной ответственности, равнодушие к исполнению гражданских обязанностей, прямые или скрытые нарушения нравственных норм. Использование несоциалистических способов удовлетворения потребительских желаний оказывает деморализующее влияние на окружающих. Проявления П. возникают в связи с тем, что быстрый рост потребления не всегда сопровождается повышением идейно-нравственного и культурного уровня людей. Осуждая все виды П., коммунистическая нравственность, социалистический образ жизни предполагают формирование способности к рациональному потреблению и к сознательному противостоянию вещепоклонничеству."[17] (N.N. 1981, unnumbered)

2.4. Konsumkultur / Consumer Culture / Consumer Culture Theory / Potrebitel'skaja kul'tura / Kul'tura potreblenija

In the light of the ideological premises of the consumer society concept discussed above, Ina Merkel suggests the term *consumer culture* as an ideologically "more neutral" alternative:

> "Consumer culture expresses itself immediately in a perceptible form in the relationship between the individuals of a community and the regionally specific accumulation of objects at one's disposal on the market as consumer goods (bartering included). Consumer culture includes all forms of acquisition as well as of use – in a practical and in a symbolic sense of the word." (MERKEL 1999: 28)[18]

In this definition, *consumer culture* seems to be a synonyme of *consumption* in its multidisciplinary version, with a slight emphasis on the "cultural" aspects. However, this alluring idea proves to be misleading: A closer inspection of the conceptual field of the term also shows a substantial lack of clarity.

---

countries, a process of balancing consumption standards according to the principles of social justice can be observed."

[16] "Particular consumerist phenomena, incited by a petit bourgeois ambition for material wealth as an end in itself are in fact forms of capitalist remnants in the conscience and behaviour of some people."

[17] "The consumerist approach results in a decline of moral responsibility, in the indifference towards the civil duties, and the open or hidden destruction of ethical norms. The use of non-socialist means to satisfy consumerist desires proves to be a demoralising influence on the social environment. Consumerist phenomena emerge from the fact, that the rapid growth of consumption isn't always accompanied by an adequate increase of a person's intellectual, moral, and cultural standards. Condemning all forms of consumerism, the communist morality and the socialist way of life further the ability for rationalist consumption and for the conscious resistence to 'commodity fetishism'." This definition can be found nearly unaltered in the online-edition of the "Slovar' po ètike" (2010) Slovar'po ètike . The term *kommunističeskaja nravstvennost'*, i.e. 'communist morali-ty' is discussed by FIELD 2007.

[18] „Konsumkultur findet ihren unmittelbar sinnlichen Ausdruck in dem Verhältnis, das die Individuen einer Gesellschaft zu der historisch und regional je spezifischen Ansammlung von Gegenständen eingehen, die als Gebrauchswerte / Waren / Konsumgüter auf dem Markt (auch Tausch) erscheinen und ihnen zum Erwerb, Gebrauch und Verbrauch zur Verfügung stehen. Konsumkultur umfasst die Formen des Erwerbs von Gegenständen ebenso wie ihren praktisch-aneignenden und symbolisch-kommunikativen Gebrauch."

The English term *consumer culture* seems to be especially problematic. In the introduction of the "*Encyclopedia of Consumer Culture*" (2011) it is defined as "a generic set of practices in which the consumption of goods and services seems to take on ever-expanding significance in contemporary societies", reflecting "the growing visibility and importance of consumption – of how goods and services are acquired, used, wasted, and desired – and concerns about the ways in which it is organized, experienced, and understood in the everyday lives of people in rich and poor societies". (SOUTHERTON 2011: xxix)

Further investigations reveal a connotation with the "relationship between people and material goods", that can be investigated from "the perspective of a variety of disciplines"; consumer culture is regarded as "a social arrangement in which the buying and selling of goods and services is not only a predominant activity of everyday life but also an important arbiter of social organization, significance, and meaning" (JRANK ENCYCLOPEDIA: CONSUMER CULTURE).[19]

On the other hand, however, the term *consumer culture theory* also implies a marketing dimension. It refers to an informal group of researchers, describing their aims on their website as follows:

> "This approach basically considers consumption and its involved behavioral choices and practices as social and cultural phenomena – as opposed to psychological or purely economic phenomena. CCT, in the words of one of the summarizing articles about the field, 'refers to a family of theoretical perspectives that address the dynamic relationship between consumer actions, the marketplace, and cultural meanings'." (CONSUMER CULTURE THEORY WEBSITE)

Whereas this approach, of course, may be very interesting and useful referring to marketing theory and practice, it adds another complication to understanding the term *consumer culture* as ideologically neutral. On the contrary, for our conceptual field, it implies another colonialisation of the term *consumer culture* by a Western point of view.

Finally, even the Russian variants of the concept, namely *potrebitel'skaja kul'tura*, used for instance by Ol'ga Gurova (2005 and 2006), and its apparent synonyme *kul'tura potreblenija* prove to be more "neutral" only at the first glance. We have to keep in mind, that in Russian and especially Soviet Culture the term *kul'tura* has its own implications and associations. Especially *kul'tura potreblenija* is strongly associated with the paternalistic idea of the education of the cultivated socialist consumer, as suggested by the following article from the *"Bol'šaja Sovetskaja Ėnciklopedija"* (*БСЭ* 1969-1978) about *reklama* 'advertising':

> "Реклама через систему массовой информации охватывает подавляющее большинство членов «общества потребления», способствует всё большему отчуждению личности. [...] Реклама широко используется для пропаганды западного, в частности американского, образа жизни, буржуазной идеологии. [...] В социалистических странах Реклама, осуществляемая планомерно, отличается

[19] Full citation: "There are many definitions of consumer culture. To begin, consumer culture should not be confused with two of its attributes: consumerism and materialism. [...] While one might readily think that materialism is a good synonym for consumerism, materialism, at least as it is defined here, only covers a part of consumerism. Namely, materialism deals only with the social value of material goods. Consumer culture, which subsumes both consumerism and materialism, has been studied from the perspective of a variety of disciplines, including communication, cultural studies, theology, sociology, psychology, marketing, anthropology, and philosophy. Regardless of the disciplinary approach, a central feature of consumer culture is the relationship between people and material goods. Generically, consumer culture is a social arrangement in which the buying and selling of goods and services is not only a predominant activity of everyday life but also an important arbiter of social organization, significance, and meaning."

> правдивостью. Она стимулирует спрос, способствует формированию новых общественных потребностей, повышению культуры потребления, развитию социалистической экономики и культуры."[20] (KANEVSKIJ 1975: 611-612)

As we see here, next to product information, *povyšenie kul'tury potreblenija* 'the enhancement of the culture of the consumer' is named as one of the basic intentions of socialist advertising. In this context, the notorious stalinist *kul'turnost'*-campain of the 1930-s comes into mind, when "cultivated trade" was on the agenda as well (MERKEL 1999: 214, HESSLER 2004: 198ff., RANDALL 2008). From this point of view, the term *kul'tura potreblenija* doesn't only connote a variety of consumer practices, but a paternalistic approach as well.

2.5. Towards a De-ideologization of Terminology

Apparently, there is no ideologically neutral term. In fact, the terminological framework of consumption at least in English and German – tends to produce a kind of short circuit, resulting in the affirmation of the *a priori* stated superiority of market economy.

Whereas terms such as *socialist consumer society*, *socialist consumer culture(s)* or *socialist consumerism* at first glance emphasize socialist forms of consumption as a fact, a closer look reveals, that the subtext of the terminology bears the risk of misunderstanding, that is of implicitly denouncing socialist consumption as an aberration or defective deviance from the norm of its Western counterpart, affirming that it was bound to fail from the very beginning. From my point of view, only the term *socialist consumption* has proved to be a virtually objective concept covering various aspects, that is, a specific form of a consumer *society* (constructing and maintaining its identity through consumption) as well as a specific consumer *culture* (with values, strategies, and practices of its own, embedded in a broader cultural framework). Terms such as *consumerism* with its ambivalent and partly morally subversive subtext seems to be mostly inadequate to describe the socialist consumer situation.

Only if we face these nuances of meaning, we will be able to perceive the socialist consumers and their practices from a multi-disciplinary perspective in all its dimensions of identity construction as an alternative form of consumption and as a part of a broader cultural formation as well.

In research and when describing all forms of socialist consumption, however, we have to be as specific as possible. David Crowley and Susan Reid have pointed out:

> "To understand socialist modernity better we need to investigate the specificity of socialist consumerism. This requires a more dynamic understanding of the relations of shortage to entitlement, of need to want, and of necessity to luxury. Except in the most abject circumstances, 'shortage' is a relative, cultural ascribed, historically contingent term. We must, then, be historically specific. Against what norm or horizon of expectations were shortages, as experienced in the Eastern Bloc societies, defined? Where, when, and how did people acquire their sense of what constituted 'normal' entitlements to leisure and consumer goods? What role was played by the awareness of lifestyles in the West or, for that matter, other parts of the Bloc? What impact did travel and tourism, both within the Bloc and through the 'Iron Curtain' have on ordinary expectations of

---

[20] "By means of a system of mass information, advertising captures the overwhelming majority of the 'consumer society' and furthers the alienation of personality. [...] Advertising is employed mostly for the propagation of a Western, especially American way of life and of bourgeois ideology. [...] In socialist countries, advertising, as a methodical operation, is characterized by its truthfulness. It stimulates demand, enables the formation of new social needs, the advancement of the niveau of the culture of consumption, and the development of the socialist economy and culture."

life? What were the social and political effects of periodic attempts to introduce 'market socialism' and make the economy more responsive to consumer demand? And what new needs and entitlements were produced by attempts to manage social expectations through the introduction of rational consumption norms at different places in the history of the Bloc?" (CROWLEY, REID 2010: 17)

3. Practices and Myths of Socialist Consumption

In the second part of this paper, I would like highlight some typical features as well as some myths and realities of socialist consumption. In doing so, I would like to stress again, that any socialist consumer society and culture is based upon the Utopian ideal of a communist consumer paradise of affluence, arising inevitably out of socialist production practices, as discussed above. As we know well, this state of abundance has never been achieved; however, on a historical plane, we may discern certain periods of different consumer policies. As suggested by Ol'ga Gurova, whereas the 1920-s can be characterized by an ideology of paramilitary ascetism, in the 1930-s a turn to the propagation of luxury took place, that was replaced by a more consistent consumer orientation after 1953 (GUROVA 2005 and 2006). In fact during all periods, shortages must be regarded as an important factor of everyday life, for socialist economy produced a wide range of inner contradictions. Consumers had to cope with these contradictions while at the same time internalizing its assumptions and presuppositions, producing thus further contradictory attitudes and practices.

3.1. Coping with Shortages: Socialist Consumer Strategies

First of all, instead of repeating the discussion about the manifold reasons for the failure of the communist consumer Utopia in detail I would rather like to concentrate on the inner contradictions socialist consumer policies produced (RANDALL 2008: 4, HESSLER 2004: 20ff., MERL 1997), and on the nontheless contradictory practices developed as a consequence of this by the Soviet consumers.

In fact, the persistence of the Utopian ideal seems to be one of the main problems. In this regard, the rationalist consumer ideal has to be mentioned in the first place, an ideal, that proved by and large as being identical with the Utopian ideal of the communist "New man" (Cf. ZALKIND 1928). This ideal didn't meet the reality of consumers and their needs and even less their ever growing desires furthered by consumer oriented policies on the one hand and foreign – socialist and non-socialist – examples on the other.

Describing Soviet consumer policies during the period from 1918 up to 1953, Julie Hessler has proposed two modes of action, resulting in "cyclical patterns of 'crisis' and 'recovery'" (HESSLER 2004: 5-9), that is a pattern of consumer policies vacillating between an ideal of "normalcy" including Utopian postulates (that couldn't be abandoned) and – sometimes – consumerist promises (that couldn't be kept) (Cf. also CROWLEY, REID 2010: 22), and inconsistent ad-hoc-actions in emergency, if something went wrong. The NĖP (New Economic Policy) after the Civil war, when market economy structures were implemented to prevent an economical breakdown of the country, is one example for such an emergency turnaround in trade policy. I think this concept can be applied to later periods, too. After 1953, consumer orientation, meant as a force to stabilize the system, fell, so to say, prey to its counterpart, namely to unfulfilled consumer desires as a force challenging and destabilizing the political system (MERL 1997: 206ff.). Ad-hoc-actions resulted, for instance, in the toleration of a more or less corrupt parallel economy, and in various forms of privilege, that conflicted with the moral implications of socialist consumption such as equality and justice.[21]

[21] A very illustrative example is the system of 'Beriozka'-Shops, as portrayed by Ivanova (2013).

The irrational price policies making some goods very cheap, and others very expensive without fully covering the costs (cf. MERL 1997: 214), is a telling example that must be mentioned in this context. They were the result of the Utopian dogma of ever falling prices, that made every departure from it look like a form of treason.

A product design dictated by mass production and a contradictory semi-rationalist, semi-neobourgeois ideal of taste, that did not really meet the Soviet consumers' desires, can be added to the list, too. The concept of a modest "Soviet taste" (GUROVA 2005: 126 und 2006: 95) was refreshed in the 1960s with an apparently clear intention to regulate "irrational consumer behaviour" (GUROVA 2006: 95 quotes BUCHLI 2000: 139) that mostly women and adolescents were suspected of (REID 2002).

On the consumers' part the contradictions resulted in particular "strategies of acquisition", which often made the situation even worse. Ina Merkel lists the following strategies as being "in conformity with the system": queuing, looking around and searching, do-it-yourself and private import. As "illegal" practices she adds: hoarding, smuggling, bribery, and even stealing (MERKEL 1999: 277). Julie Hessler very vividly describes such practices as "crisis modes of consumption" including, for instance "hoarding and queuing", "baggery" (that is buying and reselling in private, for instance, on a flea market), and "self-provisionment" as early as 1918 (HESSLER 2004: 38ff.) and traces them up to 1953. Obviously, they may be observed in later periods as well. She identifies the accompanying strategies of justification of such illegal practices as a kind of "survivalist consensus" (HESSLER 2004: 273 and 279). These practices, of course, conflicted with the high ethical standards, postulated by the communist morality (cf. FIELD 2007).[22] Apart from that, even the communication in trade was affected by these contradictions: whereas the shop assistant, who since the *kul'turnost'*-campaigns of the mid-1930s was meant to educate the client to make *kul'turnyj* 'cultivated' and rational consumer choices, often took advantage of her position (in accordance with the elsewhere tolerated idea of privilege), she also was the first to be blamed, if something went wrong (MERKEL 1999: 171ff.). To sum up, these contradictory policies and strategies are suitable to illustrate some of the symptomatic features of the socialist *consumer society* on the one hand (shortages and deficiencies), and of a specific socialist *consumer culture* (survivalist consensus, strategies of coping with shortages) on the other.

3.2. The "Socialist Thing"

One of the most interesting aspects of socialist consumption is the character of the relationship between the socialist consumer and the socialist thing. As early as in 1925 Boris Arvatov postulated to bridge the gap between the human being and the thing, that is between the sphere of proletarian production and the everyday sphere of consumption:

> "The construction of proletarian culture, that is, of a culture consciously organized by the working class, requires the elimination of that rupture between Things [sic] and people that characterized bourgeois society. [...] Proletarian society will not know this dualism of things either in practice or in consciousness. To the contrary, this society will be ideologically imbued with the deepest sense of Things. [...] Everyday life [byt] consists of the fixed, skeletal forms of existence [bytie]. The transformation of everyday-life-creation [bytotvorchestvo], in which changes in byt will move in organic, constant, and flexible step with changes in bytie, will lead, in effect, to the liquidation of the everyday as a specific sphere of social life – so long as the process of dissolving

[22] "Communist morality [...] required political loyalty, hard work, and the proper conduct of privat life" (FIELD 2007, 5). Field analyses this concept with regard to sex, love, marriage, and child rearing, but I think, it may be attributed to other aspects of everyday life as well.

> class barriers continues. This makes perfect sense: the concept of the everyday was formed in opposition to the concept of labor, just as the concept of consumer activity was formed in opposition to that of productive activity, and the concept of social stasis was formed in opposition to the concept of social dynamism. Such divisions were possible only on the basis of the class-technical differentiation that characterized the capitalist system, with its administrative top brass standing above production. In proletarian society, and even more in socialist society, where production will directly form all aspects of human activity, the static everyday life of consumption will become impossible." (ARVATOV 1925; English translation: ARVATOV/KIAER 1997: 121)[23]

From this point of view the consumption of the socialist thing is directly linked with production. In her article *"Ot tovara k tovarišču. K ėstetike nerynočnogo predmeta"* ("*From commodities to comrades: Towards the aesthetics of the thing not for the market*", 2005) Ekaterina Degot' tries to specify the nature of the "socialist thing" further. Throughout her article, she proves to be very aware of terminology. In contexts, where capitalist economical structures are concerned, the Russian terms *potrebitel'stvo* and *potreblenie* are replaced by *konsjumerizm* (e.g. DEGOT' 2005: 201) and *konsumpcija* (e.g. DEGOT' 2005: 208). Her starting point, however, is the idea of the "total subjectivisation" of the thing discussed above, declaring it to be one of the most important postulates of the Utopian goal to eliminate the fetish character of commodities: "Отрицая разделение на субъектов и объекты, советское общество провозглашало тотальную субъектность, равенство всех перед всеми, включая женщин, детей и вещи."[24] (DEGOT' 2005: 206)

The typical properties of the Soviet thing can be described as follows: First of all it is a thing, that is determined by essence, not by appearance – it is free from the pressure of the bourgeois market and honestly displays, what it is designed for:

> "Родченко мечтает о новом предмете, который отвечал бы не капиталистическому, но социалистическому способу производства. Такой предмет, по его мысли, избавлен от гнета буржуазного рынка и связанного с ним постоянного лживого показывания. Он честно говорит о том, для чего предназначен."[25] (DEGOT' 2005: 202)

Its essence consists of the "substance of work" in itself, not of its fashionable appearance:

> "Советский предмет – это овеществленная сущность, а не модная видимость, и сущностью этой должна являться сама субстанция труда. Капитализм отчуждает труд в пустых знаках-товарах, которыми пролетарий не владеет, но при социализме труд должен остаться неотчужденным, сохранить свой творческий потенциал. Именно поэтому советские вещи – в идеальном своем, редко выдерживаемом варианте – противятся эстетике «товарного вида» и переходят прямиком к сути дела: теплые штаны греют, макароны питают, зенитные установки стреляют. Немодный, ни во что не упакованный, бесформенный с точки зрения товарной эстетики, предмет воплощает ненарушенную сущность; его заметная многотрудность, запечатленное в нем усилие (неловкость, неглад-

---

[23] For a survey about Arvatov and his concept of the "socialist thing", see KIAER 1997 and 2005: 271-286. Italics are mine, UG.

[24] "Denying the difference between subjects and objects, Soviet society proclaimed the total subjectivity, the equality of all, women, children, and things included."

[25] "Rodčenko dreams of a new thing, that corresponds not with capitalist, but socialist ways of production. Such a thing, so his idea, would be free from the pressure of the bourgeois market and its false juggleries. It honestly tells, what it has been designed for."

кость, несовершенство вещи) есть песнь о труде – песнь, которая считает своим долгом быть правдивой."[26] (DEGOT' 2005: 203)

In addition it informs about the values of its maker – with properties ("warm, friendly, honest, true, modest") normally ascribed to persons:

> "В нем проявлены не коммерческие ценности, а ценности труда и человеческого братства. Теплый, дружественный, не озабоченный своим внешним обликом, честный, правдивый, скромный... Не человеческий ли идеал здесь описан? Почему же в таком случае предмет, этими качествами обладающий – допустим, теплые байковые панталоны — кажется неэстетичным?"[27] (DEGOT' 2005: 202)

Finally, it is not the mass produced thing of poor quality, but in fact the individual, customized, homemade thing:

> "Это предмет, максимально приспособленный к реальному потребителю: ушитые в боках платья; разношенные туфли; электросчетчик, переделанный так, что крутится в обратную сторону; радиоприемник, настроенный исключительно на «Голос Америки». А в особенности – все сделанное дома, будь то варенье с пенкой, свитера ручной вязки или собственно ручносбитые книжные полки. Значительную долю советских редметов составляли вещи переделанные, к чему призывали и чему учили многочисленные тогдашние журналы (например, «Наука и жизнь»), из которых можно было узнать, что полезного можно сделать из старой шины и негодной зубной щетки. Такие вещи прежде всего нестандартные, личные, а следовательно, субъектные. Именно такие вещи, а вовсе не абстрактные новые изделия советской промышленности, составляли повседневную бытовую среду жителя СССР. [...] Советская цивилизация, таким образом, вопреки штампам времен холодной войны, – это не унификация и не стандарт, а, напротив, индивидуальное отступление от стандарта. Это вовсе не коммунальность, а напротив, огромный примат частного над общественным, при, впрочем, большой их взаимозависимости. Советская экономика, равно как и культура, может быть понята только как комплекс официальной и неофициальной частей. Ужасное качество изделий советской консервной промышленности своей оборотной сто-роной имело высочайшее искусство домашних огурцезасольщиков."[28] (DEGOT' 2005: 205)

---

[26] "The Soviet thing represents essence reified instead of a fashionable appearance, making the substance of work itself visible. Capitalism alienates work to empty commodity-signs, which a proletarian doesn't make sense of, but in socialism work has to stay non-alienated, and keep its creative potential. Because of that Soviet things – in their ideal, lasting variant – are opposed to the 'aesthetics of commodity appearance' and come straight to the inner essence: trousers are for keeping warm, maccharoni are for nurturing, cannons are for shooting. The nonfashionable, not packaged in any way, from an aesthetic perspective amorphous thing represents the undisturbed essence, the visible traces of work and labour (the clumsiness, crudeness, and imperfection of things) represent a song about work, a song, that wants to be true."

[27] "Instead of commercial values, it reveals the values of work and of human brotherhood. Warm, friendly, not caring about its outer appearance, honest, true, modest... is it not a human ideal that is described here? But why should a thing with these properties – for instance, warm flanell pants – appear as unaesthetic?"

[28] "It's a thing, that is maximally customized according to the needs of a really existing consumer: the dress, topstitched at the sides; the worn out shoes; the electricity meter, modified to run backwards; the radio receiver, that is modified to receive exclusively the 'Voice of America'. And the point is, that all this is made at home: the jam, the hand-knitted sweater or the do-it-yourself- bookshelves. A great deal of Soviet things were customized in a way suggested by one of the many magazines of that time (e.g. 'Science and Life'), where one could learn about useful things made out of a used tyre or a worn-out toothbrush. Such things were not standardised, but

This characterization of the socialist thing as individual, customized or home-made reminds us of the strategies of acquisition mentioned above. Consumption and especially the act of acquisition in itself is characterized by efforts, that cannot be compared with Western shopping practices, and that should be regarded – as already discussed above – as an important part of a socialist consumer culture. The idea of a differentiation between an official and a non-official part of socialist consumption appears to be very alluring as well, for it stresses the continuity of cultural formations regarded as a whole.

3.3. The Communist Consumer Paradise in Retrospective

The idea of the subjectivization of things, stressed by the efforts of acquisition and of the customizing process, also corresponds with typical testimonies of a specific "sustainability" of socialist consumption such as the following quotation from the "*Encyclopedia of Consumer Culture*":

> "In spite of all its deficiencies, the socialist consumer culture is often represented in the accounts of primarily the elderly as a time of solidarity and a more respectful relationship between consumers and things, subjects and objects. Since there was no market economy-based cycle of fashions and quick obsolescence, there was less waste [...]. Thus, people were either consciously or unconsciously 'sustainable' in their everyday consumption practices, and today's consumer culture is, to a certain extent, shaped by sometimes nostalgic recollections of the socialist times." (KELLER 2011: 342)

Retrospective testimonies of the socialist past are – just like any recollection – in danger to fall prey to nostalgia: negative experiences are superimposed by positive emotions provided by, for instance, childhood or youth recollections. Although consumer goods apparently play an important role in these recollections, a blending of reality and myth seems to be very likely. In her study about the consumer culture in the GDR, Ina Merkel came to interesting conclusions concerning the category "Usage and significance" (Gebrauch und Bedeutung) of consumerist practices (MERKEL 1999: 301ff.)[29] In order to investigate the cultural imprint of the specific practices of socialist consumer culture, in several interviews she asked, what kind of objects were kept or discarded after the fall of the Iron Curtain, and why (MERKEL 1998: 357-397). The answers in fact suggest a strong tendency to associate the socialist object rather with practical qualities such as durability, than with an attractive appearance. In addition, there are several sources of the emotional commitment to things: either the troubles of acquisition (including the act of making or customizing things by oneself), or the high price, one had to pay for the object, or the link of the object with certain, emotionally important phases in life (youth, marriage, new home) or with members of the same generation. Thus, the keeping or discarding of a certain object has to be justified by reasonable motivations: for instance, it has been discarded because it was broken, or it has been kept, because it is still working; its practical or aesthetic qualities are qualified as convincing, especially in comparison to new objects of Western origin that have proved to be disappointing. Concerning the

---

personalised and hence subjective. These things, and not the new products provided by Soviet industries, determined the everyday life of the residents of the Soviet Union. [...] Soviet civilization – in contrast to the Cold War cliché – was not a state of unification and standardisation. It wasn't at all meant to further the collective, but the primacy of the personal over the social. Just like Soviet culture, Soviet economy can only be conceived as a complex of an official and a non-official part. The horrible quality of the Soviet industry of canned food generated the fine art of salting cucumbers."

[29] "Usage and significance" is the third category next to "Production and need" (Produktion und Bedürfnis, 35ff.) and "Trade and distribution" (HANDELN UND VERTEILEN, 169ff.)

typical East German attitude of "Ostalgia" (i.e. nostalgia for the East) Merkel discerns a couple of motivations or types (cf. MERKEL 1998: 397-409):

- a longing for seemingly lost everyday experiences such as tastes, colours and forms (MERKEL 1998: 401);
- a form of self-irony (intellectual distance combined with emotional closeness, MERKEL 1998: 398), that includes effects of estrangement and acts of de-demonisation (MERKEL 1998: 407);
- a defence strategy against cultural devaluation and against the politicization of objects accompanied by the feeling of being errantly exposed to Western inspection (MERKEL 1998: 406);
- a form of musealisation and a gesture of inspection ("Gebärde der Besichtigung", MERKEL 1998: 408); people feel like recovering their own identity by rescuing a lost product culture from the garbage bin (MERKEL 1998: 409)
- and, of course, an act of commercialisation of all those strategies by coining an artificial sense of community from the outside.

From this point of view, sustainability seems to be a very ambivalent concept of socialist consumption. The entire idea of the sustainable, durable and modest thing of the socialist past (and of the poor quality of the "capitalist thing" due to its exposition to the laws of the market) far too conspiciously echoes the idea of a modest "Soviet taste" and of a morally superior non-consumerist alternative; it may be likewise the result of a kind of internalized propaganda. It also reflects an emotional commitment that in retrospective easily transforms into a positive myth mollifying the recollection of the hardships of socialist consumption.[30]

4. Conclusion

In summary, I would like to stress once more the significance of terminology. I hope, I succeeded in showing – without claiming to be exhaustive – how a terminology deeply rooted in either market economy on the one hand or marxist theory on the other influences the connotations of terms and simultaneously the interpretation of cultural practices. Socialist consumption may be regarded as a source of a particular identity, that in accordance with the economical circumstances produces particular practices and traditions. The utilization of an unreflected or inadequate terminology bears the risk of misunderstanding such practices by projecting false assumptions onto the phenomenon in question.

The ambivalence of the Utopian idea of communist affluence and the inner contradictions of its realisation obviously produced a type of consumer, who was able to internalize the propagandistic idea of the superior qualities of Soviet commodities according to the principles of "Soviet taste" (in retrospective often misinterpreted as a particular form of sustainability), and to develop at the same time a whole range of otherwise morally disputable strategies to cope with shortages and growing desires. The Socialist consumer, thus, didn't *a priori* require a broad range of goods, but a good deal of creativity, as the discussion of the qualities of the "socialist thing" by Ekaterina Degot' and the research works of Julie Hessler, Ina Merkel and others have shown vividly.

Summary

The paper explores the significance of terminology in the research of socialist consumer practices. Socialist consumption may be regarded as a source of a particular identity, that in accordance with the economical circumstances produces particular practices and traditions. The utilization of an unreflected or inadequate

[30] Similar observations can be made on web platforms such as "*Enciklopedija našego detstva*", "*Vaš god roždenija, 1922-91*", and "*Muzej 20-j vek*", all of which belong to a a kind of "Born in the USSR"-type of nostalgic websites.

terminology bears the risk of misunderstanding such practices by projecting false assumptions onto the phenomenon in question. From this point of view, a couple of myths and realities of socialist consumption are discussed, including the idea of communist affluence, the Soviet consumers' strategies of coping with shortages, the concept of the "socialist thing", and – last but not least – the idea of a particular socialist sustainability.

Bibliography

ARVATOV, B. 1925. Alltag und Kultur des Dings. In: Hennig, A. (ed.): *Über die Dinge: Texte der russischen Avantgarde*. Hamburg 2010, 307-327.

ARVATOV, B., KIAER, C. 1997. Everyday Culture and the Culture of the Thing (Toward the Formulation of the Question). In: *October* 81, 119-128.

BREWER, J. 1997. Was können wir aus der Geschichte der frühen Neuzeit für die moderne Konsumgeschichte lernen? In: Siegrist, H. et al. (ed.). *Europäische Konsumgeschichte. Zur Gesellschafts- und Kulturgeschichte des Konsums (18. bis 20. Jahrhundert)*. Frankfurt (Main), New York 1997, 52-74.

BUCHLI, V. 2000. *An Archeology of Socialism*. Oxford.

CROWLEY, D., REID, S.E. 2010. Introduction. Pleasures in Socialism? In: Crowley, D., Reid, S.E. (ed.): *Pleasures in socialism. Leisure and luxury in the Eastern Bloc*. Evanston, Ill 2010, 3-51.

CULLER, J. D. 1999. *Dekonstruktion. Derrida und die poststrukturalistische Literaturtheorie*. Reinbek.

DEGOT', E. 2005. От товара к товарищу. К эстетике нерыночного предмета. In: *Логос* 5 (50), 201-210. http://www.ruthenia.ru/logos/number/50/14.pdf (25.02.2014)

FIELD, D. A. 2007. *Private life and communist morality in Khrushchev's Russia*. New York.

FOKKEMA, D. W. 1983. *Literary History, Modernism, and Postmodernism*. Amsterdam, Philadelphia.

GOLDSCHWEER, U. 2013. Frau und Konsum: Genderaspekte der sowjetischen Konsumkultur. In: Norhejl, R. et al. (ed.). *Genderdiskurse und nationale Identität in Russland. Sowjetische und postsowjetische Zeit*. München, Berlin, Washington, 181-196.

GRONOW, J. 2003. *Caviar with champagne. Common luxury and the ideals of the good life in Stalin's Russia*. Oxford.

GRONOW, J. 2011. Consumer Culture in the USSR. In: Southerton, D. (ed.): *Encyclopedia of Consumer Culture* (Vol. 1). Thousand Oaks CA 2011, 251-256.

GUROVA, O. 2005. Идеология потребления в советском обществе. In: *Социологический журнал* 4. http://www.isras.ru/files/File/Sociologymagazin/Socmag_04_2005/06_Gurova.pdf (13.03.2014)

GUROVA, O. 2006. Ideology of consumption in Soviet Union: From Asceticism to the Legitimating of Consumer goods. In: *Anthropology of East Europe Review*, 24:2, 91-98. http://scholarworks.iu.edu/ journals/index.php/aeer/article/view/237 (13.03.2014)

HESSLER, J. 2004. *A social history of Soviet trade. Trade policy, retail practices, and consumption 1917-1953*. Princeton.

IVANOVA, A. 2013. Shopping in *Beriozka*: Consumer Society in the Soviet Union. In: *Zeithistorische Forschungen/Studies in Contemporary History*, 10:2, o.P. http://www.zeithistorische-forschungen.de/ 16126041-Ivanova-2-2013 (09.05.2014)

KANEVSKIJ, E.M. 1975. Реклама. In: *Большая Советская Энциклопедия*, изд. 3, т. 21 Москва, 611-612. http://bse.sci-lib.com/article096325.html bzw. http://slovari.yandex.ru/~книги/БСЭ/ Реклама (12.02.2014).

KELLER, M. 2011. Consumption in Postsocialist Societies: Eastern Europe. In: Southerton, D. (ed.): *Encyclopedia of Consumer Culture* (Vol. 1). Thousand Oaks CA, 341-345.

KELLY, C., VOLKOV, V. 1998. Directed Desires: Kul'turnost' and Consumption. In: Kelly, C., Shepherd, D. (ed.): *Constructing Russian culture in the age of revolution: 1881-1940*. Oxford 1998, 291-313.

KIAER, C. 1997. Boris Arvatovs Socialist Objects. In: *October* 81, 105-118.

KIAER, C. 2005. *Imagine No Posessions. The Socialist Objects of Russian Constructivism*. Cambridge, Mass, London.

MAJER, V.F. 1955. Потребление. In: *Большая Советская Энциклопедия*, изд. 2, т. 34 (Москва 1949-1958), 292-295. http://bse2.ru/book_view.jsp?idn=030299&page=292&format=html (12.02.2014).

MAJER, V.F. 1975. Потребление. In: *Большая Советская Энциклопедия*, изд. 3, т. 34, Москва 1969-1978, 437-430. http://slovari.yandex.ru/~книги/БСЭ/Потребление/ (12.02.2014).

MARX, K. 1875. Kritik des Gothaer Programms. In: Marx, K., Engels,F.: *Werke*, Band 19, Berlin/DDR ^{4}1973, 13-32. http://www.mlwerke.de/me/me19/me19_013.htm (04.08.2014).

MERKEL, I. 1999. *Utopie und Bedürfnis. Die Geschichte der Konsumkultur in der DDR.* Köln, Weimar, Wien.

MERKEL, I. 2010. Luxury in Socialism: An Absurd Proposition? In: Crowley, D., Reid, S.E. (ed.): *Pleasures in socialism. Leisure and luxury in the Eastern Bloc.* Evanston, Ill 2010, 53-70.

MERL, S. 1997. Staat und Konsum in der Zentralverwaltungswirtschaft. Rußland und die ostmitteleuropäischen Länder. In: Siegrist, H. et al. (ed.). *Europäische Konsumgeschichte. Zur Gesellschafts- und Kulturgeschichte des Konsums (18. bis 20. Jahrhundert).* Frankfurt (Main), New York 1997, 205-241.

N.N. 1940. Потребление. In: *Большая Советская Энциклопедия*, изд. 1, т. 46 (Moskva 1926-1947), 573-547.

N.N. 1981. Потребительство. In: И. Кон (ed.). Словарь по этике. Москва 1981. http://terme.ru/dictionary/522/word/potrebitelstvo#a5 (Национальная философская энциклопедия, 27.1.2014).

RANDALL, A. E. 2004. Legitimizing Soviet Trade: Gender and Feminization of the Retail Workforce in the Soviet 1930s. In: *Journal of Social History* 37 4, 965-990.

RANDALL, A. E. 2008. *The Soviet Dream World of Retail Trade and Consumption in the 1930s.* Basingstoke.

REID, S. E. 2002. Cold War in the Kitchen: Gender and the De-Stalinization of Consumer Taste in the Soviet Union under Chruščev. In: *Slavic Review* 61:2, 211-252.

SIEGRIST, H. 1997. Konsum, Kultur und Gesellschaft im modernen Europa. In: Siegrist, H. et al. (ed.). *Europäische Konsumgeschichte. Zur Gesellschafts- und Kulturgeschichte des Konsums (18. bis 20. Jahrhundert).* Frankfurt (Main)/ New York 1997, 13-31.

SOUTHERTON, D. 2011. Introduction. In: Southerton, D. (ed.). *Encyclopedia of Consumer Culture* (Vol. 1). Thousand Oaks CA, xxix-xxxiv.

VOLKOV, V. 2000. The Concept of *kul'turnost'*: notes on the Stalinist civilizing process. In: Fitzpatrick, S. (ed.): *Stalinism. New Directions.* London und New York 2000, 210-230.

ZALKIND, A. 1928. Die Psychologie des Menschen der Zukunft. In: Groys, B., Hagemeister, M. (ed.). *Die Neue Menschheit. Biopolitische Utopien zu Beginn des 20. Jahrhunderts.* Frankfurt (Main) 2005, 608-689.

Internet ressources

Consumer Culture Theory Website. http://www.consumerculturetheory.org (24.07.2013)

Encyclopaedia Britannica: Ethical consumerism. http://www.britannica.com/ (27.01.2014)

Ėnciklopedija našego detstva: Энциклопедия нашего детства. http://www.76-82.ru/ (04.08.2014).

Jrank Encyclopedia: Consumer Culture. http://encyclopedia.jrank.org/articles/pages/6480/Consumer-Culture.html (24.07.2013)

Muzej „20-j vek“: Музей «20-й век». Мы с СССР. Ностальгия по прошлому и нашему детству. http://20th.su/ (04.08.2014).

Vaš god roždenija: Ваш год рождения, 1922-91. http://22-91.ru/ (04.08.2014).

Slovar' po ėtike 2010: Словарь по этике. http://moralphilosophy.ru/pg/potrebitel%27stvo.htm (04.08. 2014).

Wikipedia: Consumer Culture Theory. http://en.wikipedia.org/wiki/Consumer_culture_theory (24.07. 2013)

Wikipedia: Consumerism. http://en.wikipedia.org/wiki/Consumerism (24.07.2013)

Wikipedia: Konsumismus. http://de.wikipedia.org/wiki/Konsumismus (24.07.2013)

Wikipedia: Общество потребления. http://ru.wikipedia.org/wiki/Общество_потребления (14.10. 2013)

Wikipedia: Потребление. http://ru.wikipedia.org/wiki/ Потребление (06.08.2014)

ЭТОТ МНОГОЛИКИЙ МИР МОДЫ
Образец позднесоветского дискурса моды

КАТАРИНА КЛИНГСАЙС, ВЕНА

Дискурс и жизнь

Советская реальность на всем своем протяжении формировалась под аккомпанементом текстовых и визуальных комментариев партийных и государственных органов. В 1982 году вышла в свет книга под названием *«Этот многоликий мир моды»*, авторство которой принадлежит никому другому, как знаменитому модельеру Вячеславу Зайцеву (ЗАЙЦЕВ 1982). До конца советской эры оставалось еще девять лет, но об этом тогда еще не подозревал никто.

В настоящей статье книга Вячеслава Зайцева рассматривается как образец позднесоветского официального дискурса моды. «Дискурс» при этом рассматривается как социальная практика языкового производства и интерпретации, происходящая в определенном социальном контексте (см. FAIRCLOUGH 1989: 25). Соответственно, книга Зайцева, с одной стороны, является продуктом своего времени и его реальных условий, и при этом вписывается в своеобразную традицию. В сталинскую эпоху, программные тексты советских идеологов к реальности имели «весьма опосредованное отношение», как продемонстрировал Е. Добренко на примере «Политэкономии», «перво[го] и главно[го] советско[го] учебник[а] политической экономики» (ДОБРЕНКО 2007: 24) . Зато, по словам автора, «описанные там люди и отношения име[ли] прямое отношение к советскому искусству» (ДОБРЕНКО 2007: 25-26). Добренко резюмирует, что главным элементом производства Советского Союза являлось не производство вещей, а изображений, которые реальность не репрезентировали, а заменили. Цитируя Мераба Мамардашвили, Добренко заключает, что «власть в стране держ[ал]ась "господством *изображений*, заменяющих собой то, что они изображают"» (ДОБРЕНКО 2007: 41). Т. Круглова описывает это обс-тоятельство следующим образом: «Реальное обладание результатом практических действий отождествляется с планированием, проектом этого результата. Составление бесконечных программ, принятие постановлений, написание директивных документов о том, каким должно быть произведение искусства, выполняет те же функции, что и сами практические действия или конкретные художественные тексты.» (КРУГЛОВА 2005: 53-54) Конечно, когда вышла книга Зайцева, эпоха «соцреализма» была позади, но отголоски его отношения к реальности еще ощутимы. Всё это не значит, что тексты и «соцреализма», и подобные книги Зайцева, остались без эффекта в реальности. Об этом свидетельствуют высказывания респондентов интервью, проведённых автором этой статьи в период с 2004 по 2011 гг. в разных крупных российских городах. В них с удивительной настойчивостью воспроизводились максимы советской этики и эстетики внешнего вида, распространённых именно в этих советских текстах (см. KLINGSEIS 2010).

Итак, в данной статье, на примере книги Вячеслава Зайцева, будет рассмотрен образец официального дискурса моды начала 1980-х годов. Ввиду того, что советская потребительская реальность является главным предметом настоящего сборника, социальный контекст выпуска книги Зайцева здесь будет намечен только в некоторых штрихах. Затем будет описана дискурсивная предыстория книги, её темы и аргументации. А вторая половина статьи будет посвящена подробному анализу самого текста Зайцева: как в её темах и аргументациях отражается реальность начала 1980-х годов? Каким образом эти темы преподносятся читателям? С помощью каких прагмалингвистических и риторических средств это осуществляется? Автор данной статьи постарается установить какую бы то ни было опосредованную связь между текстурой этой книги и реальной жизнью потребителей моды данной эпохи.

Потребительские возможности в ранние 1980-е годы

Языковые и неязыковые элементы социального мира являются взаимоконститутивными, хотя не сводимыми друг к другу (см. Chouliaraki, Fairclough 2010: 1215). Исходя из этой предпосылки, обратим внимание на неязыковые элементы мира, в котором вышла книга Зайцева. Она вышла в тот момент, когда «[...] неспособность советской централизованной экономики удовлетворить хотя бы до некоторой степени потребности населения (прежде всего женщин) в одежде заставляла ответственных за планирование, производителей, а также тех, кто рекламировал эту продукцию, занимать оборонительную позицию по отношению к проникающим с запада сведениям и образам в непростой борьбе за эту важную гендерно дифференцированную область культурной семиотики» пишет Риндисбахер (Риндисбахер 2011), указывая на то обстоятельство, что «советские лидеры прекрасно отдавали себе отчет в идеологической и семиотической функции моды».

К этому времени советские потребители уже успели стать придирчивыми. В период правления Генерального Секретаря Л. Брежнева и Председателя Совета Министров А. Косыгина были предприняты весьма серьезные усилия по улучшению снабжения насе-ления привлекательными потребительскими товарами (см. Chernyshova 2013). В 1965 году была запущена «косыгинская реформа» (Chernyshova 2013: 22), которая, между прочими мерами предусматривала установить «прямую связь» между предприятиями и торговыми распределителями для лучшей ориентации на потребительские желания (Chernyshova 2013: 25), а также возможность предприятий сохранить большую часть прибыли на предприятии для использования их на дополнительные вознаграждения рабочих и в других социальных целях (Chernyshova 2013: 24). Это ощутимо улучшило финансовые возможности населения и по словам Чернышовой привело к тому, что данная пятилетка (1966-1970) оказалась «самым успешным периодом для советского производства потребительских товаров» (Chernyshova 2013: 28; перев. с англ. КК). И хотя реформа была прекращена несколько лет спустя, население успело развить новые ожидания к предложению бытовых товаров и одежды, а государственные и партийные де-ятели поняли, что оправдание этих ожиданий имеет первый приоритет, пишет Чернышова. Она и упоминает о том, что приближался 1980 год, к которому Хрущев в свое время обещал наступление коммунизма, тем самим оставив своему преемнику нелегкое нас-ледство. Тем не менее, «косыгинская реформа» была проведена непоследовательно и в конце концов была отменена.

Население страны к этому времени уже привыкло к новому уровню потребления, объясняет Чернышова. В этой новой для них ситуации государственным и партийным деятелям очень кстати пришли нефтяные и газовые месторождения, открытые в 1973 году в Западной Сибири, которые позволили советскому правительству в повышенной мере ввозить в страну зарубежные товары. Это была не обязательно одежда и обувь из других социалистических стран, импортировалась британская, французская, итальянская одежда и обувь, и даже югославская мебель (см. Chernyshova 2013: 31). Это дало возможность той части населения, никогда не бывавшей за рубежом, сравнивать советскую продукцию с иностранной. Результатом было сравнение, которое далеко не всегда было решено в поль-зу первой (см. Chernyshova 2013: 33). К тому же, относительная обеспеченность граждан в 1970-е годы привела к такому явлению, когда многие родители, в юности сами испытавшие лишения войны и послевоенного времени, обнаруживая «расслабленное отношение к потреблению среди молодежи», нередко поддерживали его, стараясь активно снабжать своих детей модной одеждой и другими желаемыми, престижными, дефи-цитными предметами, часто пренебрегая своими собственными потребностями. Этот факт в свою очередь вызвал горячие дискуссий в СМИ (см. Chernyshova 2013: 124).

Мода в дискурсе и культурной политике СССР

При чтении книги Зайцева следует иметь в виду её дискурсивную предысторию, ведь она является прямым звеном в длинной цепи программных текстов этой традиции. Однако, она была написана в то время, когда в отличие от сталинской эпохи стало все труднее ограждать общество от иностранных влияний и мод, последние регулярно обсуждались и в СМИ, и в к ней относящейся специальной литературе. Замену советской реальности идеальными изображениями предвосхищенного светлого будущего, о которой писал Е.Добренко, стало все труднее осуществлять ввиду проникающих реальных предметов, товаров из-за рубежа, где в воображении граждан эта «будущая реальность» якобы уже существовала (правда, воображения этой другой реальности ей соответствовали весьма условно, но об этом знали немногие). Соответственно, именно *интернационализация* оказалась одной из обсуждаемых тем в книге Зайцева.

На протяжении всего советского периода власть рассматривала внешний вид граждан как «символический ресурс» (Гурова 2008: 41), которым она, начиная с этапа «формирования нового человека» в первое десятилетие после революции до «со-ревнования систем» в послевоенные десятилетия и вплоть до конца советской эры, стремилась активно пользоваться. За все это время практики потребления одежных това-ров среди граждан сопровождались официальными публикациями, посвященными их бытовым практикам ухода за телом и оформления внешнего вида. О.Гурова в своей книге о нижнем белье в СССР представила интересную хронологию менявшихся в течение десятилетий тем и аргументаций советского дискурса о теле и внешнем виде. Соответственно этой хронологии, основной темой воспитательного дискурса первого послереволюционного десятилетия оказалась «гигиена» (Гурова 2008: 42), в рамках которой обсуждались «простейшие культурные навыки» (Гурова 2008, 43). Автори-тетными «говорящими» в относящихся текстах, по словам Гуровой, были «врачи», «доктора» или «профессора» (Гурова 2008: 45). В этом дискурсе большевистская концепция красоты, как аргументирует автор, была противопоставлена «мещанской псевдороскоши» (Гурова 2008: 50). В то же время художники-авангардисты этого первого послереволюционного десятилетия, включая таких «конструкторов моды», как Александру Экстер, Любовь Попову или Варвару Степанову, видели цель своей деятельности в «эстетической трансформации жизни», причем не столько жизни инди-видуума, сколько народа как целого (см. Гурова 2008: 52).

Уже в начале 1930-х гг. в культурной политике наблюдалась четкая перемена, которая в общественном дискурсе отражалась как «переориентация на вопросы красоты и культуры». «Прагматическое содержание концепции культурности [...] включало следо-вание моде, умение пользоваться ножом и вилкой, знание литературы и музыки» (Гурова 2008: 55) и в отличие от предыдущего лейтмотива, «культурность» рассма-тривалась не столько как качество народного тела, сколько как индивидуальная практика. Изменение курса в культурной политике, а соответственно и в общественном дискурсе, позволяло легитимировать уступки, сделанные Сталиным советскому «среднему классу» (см. Гурова 2008: 57), которому в обмен за поддержку своей политики он был вынужден предоставить определенные «потребительские блага». Соответственно, во второй поло-вине 1930-х годов изменилось и официальное отношение к потреблению: в дискурсе возникает даже сам термин «потребитель». К тому же появились фразы типа «будет пользоваться успехом у потребителя» или «согласно требованиям потребителя» (Гурова 2008: 62). На это время, кстати, приходится и основание первых «Домов моделей», задача которых по приказу партии состояла в том, чтобы «создать новые функциональные формы костюма для нового трудящегося человека» (Щипакина 2009: 29).

В военные годы о моде перестали говорить. Как пишет Щипакина, в это время «легкая промышленность работала почти исключительно на армию. Люди одевались либо в военную форму, либо в "трофейную" одежду, либо донашивали довоенные вещи» (Щипакина 2009: 29-30). Начиная с 1950-х годов, дискурс тела и внешнего вида делает новый поворот. Как аргументирует Гурова, «потребление стало потенциальной политической силой в конкуренции между Советским Союзом и Западом» (Гурова 2008: 65), с которым Советский Союз «начал восстанавливать экономические и культурные связи». Этот период отмечается многочисленными контактами с западной культурой: Международным фестивалем молодежи и студентов (1957), Московским кинофестивалем 1959 года, Международным конгрессом мод (1961) и многими другими. Все эти мероприятия «сопровожда[лись] широкими дискуссиями в официальных источниках – женских журналах и брошюрах, посвященных [...] моде, красоте, вкусу», темам, которые «легитимир[овались] как необходимые составляющие стиля жизни и облика советского человека» (см. Гурова 2008: 65-66).

Лейтмотивом же официального дискурса с 1950-х по 1980-е годы было «воспитание хорошего вкуса» (см. Гурова 2008; см. также Klingseis 2010). Ему было посвящено множество книг и журнальных статей, выходящих в свет вплоть до конца советской эры. Об этом свидетельствуют одни лишь названия таких публикаций, как «*Воспитание Вкуса*» (Жуков 1954), «*Раздумья о красоте и вкусе*» (Русанова 1961); «*Красота, вкус, экономика*» (Казаринова 1985) или «*Мода, кумиры и собственное "Я"*» (Бастрыкин 1988). Акценты в этих текстах были поставлены по-разному, как покажут приведенные ниже цитаты. В одно время акцент был сделан на «индивидуальность стиля» против нивелирующего эффекта моды, в другое время мода равняется с «мещанством». То он ставится на «потреблении», то на «молодежной антимоде», а то и на «статусе» и «состо-ятельности», тем самым отражая дискуссии своего времени.

Почти во всех официальных текстах послевоенной эры «мода» остается явлением амбивалентным. До самого конца советской эры авторы подчеркивают нетождественность «моды» с «красотой» и «хорошим вкусом»:

> «Многим женщинам кажется, что понятие красоты неотделимо от понятия моды. Это – неверное представление. Оно неверно уже потому, что каждая женщина имеет свои, отличные от других, характер, рост, фигуру, цвет волос, цвет глаз, оттенок кожи, особенности движений, и потому естественно, что не может одна и та же мода быть одинаково хороша для худых и полных, маленьких и высоких, тихих и экспансивных, молодых и старых. Мне кажется, что слепое подражание "за-граничной" моде, влияние которой иногда переносится к нам с Запада, нивелирует индивидуальность вкуса, парализует у женщин чувство "самостильности" и часто прививает ложное понятие о красивом и уродливом.» (Жуков 1954: 170)

Почти все тексты о моде подразумевают, что мода что-то «западное», чуждое советскому обществу. Это положение – отголосок советского отношения к вещам, сформулированного в ранний советский период художественным авангардом. Так, например, Александр Родченко написал в письме Варваре Степановой из Парижа в 1925-м году: «здесь дешево отчасти потому, что плохой материал, ибо им важно дешево купить, модно ходить, а как новая мода, опять новое покупать.» (цит. по Деготь 2000: 10) «Советский предмет, резюмирует Деготь советскую установку, это овеществленная сущ-ность, а не модная видимость, и сущностью этой должна являться сама субстанция труда. Капитализм отчуждает труд в пустых знаках-товарах, которыми пролетарий не владеет, но при социализме труд должен остаться неотчужденным, сохранить свой творческий потенциал. [...] Немодный, ни во что не упакованный, бесформенный с точки зрения товарной эстетики, предмет воплощает ненарушенную сущность; его заметная много-трудность, запечатленное в нем усилие (неловкость, негладкость, несовершенство вещи) есть песнь о труде – песнь, которая считает своим долгом быть правдивой.» (Деготь 2000: 11) На следы такой концепции вещи мы еще натолкнемся, когда речь пойдет о «само-деятельном творчестве», занимавшем важное место в советском дискурсе о моде. Кстати, в сегодняшней перспективе постконсюмерского отрезвления, вызванного огромными эко-логическими проблемами нашей планеты, советская концепция вещей звучит крайне актуальной.

В следующей цитате начала 1960-х годов мода представляется как явление истинно мещанское:

> «Мода рассчитана на обывателя, человека с мещанской психологией. Мещанин – это верноподданный всего отжившего, старого, всякой рутины, цепляющийся за общепризнанные "непререкаемые" авторитеты, всю жизнь сознательно идущий в шо-рах. "Мещанство – проклятие мира, – писал Горький, – оно пожирает личность изнутри, как червь опустошает плод. [...]" Не имея своего вкуса, то есть того, чем руководствоваться, мещанин гонится за тем, что ему подсунули, ибо он верно-подданный, более того – раб вещи! Совершенно естественно, что он верноподданный и моды!» (Русанова 1961: 68-69)

С. Бойм в своей книге о советских общих местах очертила судьбу понятия «мещанство», которое по ее словам пренебрегалось и «дореволюционной интеллигенцией» как «ложный народный дух», и «послереволюционной», по взглядам которой «оно предает идеал революционного пролетариата»:

> «В 1920-е годы борьба с мещанством велась как большевиками, так и художниками, и писателями авангарда. Кампания борьбы с домашним хламом объявила гражданскую войну слоникам, граммофонам, комодам, фикусам, желтым канарейкам и прочим буржуазным элементам. Маяковский, как известно, призывал “свернуть головы“ желтым канарейкам мещанства. Борьба с мещанством затихает на некоторое время в 1930-е годы, когда многие из бывших борцов кончили жизнь самоубийством, были сосланы или перевели разговор на другие темы.» (Бойм 2002: 95)

Если «[в] конце 1940-х – начале 1950-х», как пишет Бойм, «кампания по борьбе с космополитизмом повторила многие лозунги борьбы с мещанством», то «[в] 1960-е годы конфликт между интеллигенцией и мещанством слегка видоизменяется: теперь это битва романтиков и мещан. Образ романтиков 60-х во многом перекликается с революционными романтиками 20-х». (Бойм 2002: 98) Понятие «мещанство» фигурирует и в книге Зайцева 1982 года.

Интересный социологический текст о моде как системе социального общения вышел в свет в 1974 году, в период усиленного импорта иностранных потребительских товаров на основе повышенных нефтяных экспортов. Там находится и следующая апология моды:

> «В наше время иногда сталкиваемся с фактами резко негативного отношения старшего поколения к новым образцам моды. В газетах появляются заметки о ретивых администраторах, которые изгоняют из театра девушек, пришедших на спектакль в брючном костюме, лишают стипендии учащихся техникума, которые носят волосы ниже мочки уха, в некоторых институтах издаются приказы об обязательном бритье подбородков у мужской части студенчества и т.п. Надо прямо сказать, что за скрытой формой борьбы против моды в действительности всегда обнаруживается борьба за другую моду, чаще всего ту, которая господствовала в период молодости данного администрирующего индивида. Борьба против моды имеет историю даже большую, чем сама мода. [...] элементы борьбы с ней появляются еще в античные времена, когда древние греки – мужчины и даже воины носили юбки, а брюки считались символом варварства и дикости.» (Петров 1974: 22)

В приведенном ниже тексте из монографии В.И. Казариновой, вышедшей в свет через три года после книги Зайцева, в 1985-м году, возникает термин, которого у Зайцева еще нет – «культура потребления», причем «разумного»:

> «На июньском (1983 г.) Пленуме ЦК КПСС отмечалось, что понятие „повышение уровня жизни“ нельзя трактовать упрощенно, имея в виду лишь рост доходов населения и производство предметов потребления. Социальный аспект этого понятия гораздо шире и богаче. Тут и постоянный рост сознательности и культуры людей, включая культуру быта, поведения, и то, что называется культурой разумного потребления.» (Казаринова 1985: 5)

А в следующей ниже выдержке из текста 1988 года авторами используется аргументация, которая тоже отсутствует в текстах предыдущих периодов:

> «Буржуазные средства массовой информации, ведущие фирмы, рекламируя товары, формы проведения досуга, старательно подчеркивают их связь со статусом, подстегивая в людях стремление приблизиться к стандартам состоятельной элиты, подняться на более высокую ступень социальной лестницы. Но перераспределение общественного богатства происходит по-прежнему в пользу имущих.» (Бастрыкин/Ширяев 1988: 19)

Связь моды с финансовым состоянием и социальным статусом носящего, которая, следуя этой аргументации, устанавливается западными СМИ, в книге Зайцева 1982-го года еще отсутствует. Но не удивляет, что такая аргументация возникает во второй половине 1980-х годов, в эру так называемой «комсомольской экономики», возникновения «предприятий и фирм, создаваемых под эгидой комсомольских организаций и оказавшихся (как стало очевидным впоследствии) важнейшим компонентом нарождавшегося российского бизнеса» (Крыштановская 2002: 6). Короче говоря, тема накопления состояния и демонстрации своего статуса через модные зарубежные товары стала очень актуальной.

Ханс Риндисбахер указывает еще на одно своеобразное явление дискурса этого позднесоветского периода, а именно на издание журнала *Новые товары*, ежемесячного информационного бюллетеня, издаваемого Министерством легкой промышленности и впервые появившегося в эпоху Хрущева в 1957-м году. «[Ж]урнал “Новые товары” неизменно давал широкий обзор потребительских товаров», пишет Риндисбахер, в нем «обезоруживающе открыто демонстрир[овались] недостатки системы». К тому же, «[н]а протяжении долгих лет (вплоть до 1995-го года) в журнале уделялось значительное вни-мание моде, обуви, одежде и парфюмерии. Постоянными, в частности, были рубрики “*Женская мода*”, посвященная советской одежде», но была и рубрика «*Из иностранных журналов мод*», где советской читательнице несколько десятилетий подряд предо-ставлялась возможность прямого сравнения, продолжает автор. Причину такого подхода со стороны власти Риндисбахер видит в том, что изображения иностранных мод должны были быть «источником вдохновения (а не раздражения читательниц тем, что им было недоступно). Подробные описания одежды служили едва ли не призывом попробовать сшить ее самостоятельно», в этом, как считает автор, власть усмотрела способ снять с на-селения чувство напряжения от постоянного дефицита модных товаров. (см. Риндисбахер 2011)

В поздние 1970-е и ранние 1980-е годы, пишет Чернышова, в обсуждении актуальных тем в СМИ доминировали читатели молодого возраста, присылавшие в редакции газет и журналов письма спорных содержаний на темы моды и потребления. «Потребление и мир товаров стали определяющей эру темой: как будто маргинальная группа *стиляг* вдруг стала главной тенденцией молодежной культуры». (Chernyshova 2013: 128)

Монография Зайцева как образец позднесоветского официального дискурса потребления и моды

Книга самого известного и в Советском Союзе, и за рубежом художника-модельера Вячеслава Зайцева оказалась звеном в длинной цепи советских публикаций на тему моды. Как известно, Зайцев работал в знаменитом Московском Доме моделей на Кузнецком мосту 14, основанном в 1944 году и реорганизованном в 1948 году в Общесоюзный дом моделей (см. Щипакина 2009: 34), расцвет которого пришелся на 1960-1980-е годы. Зайцев, родившийся в 1938-м году, проработал там с 1965-го по 1978-й год худо-жественным руководителем Экспериментально-методического цеха, а в 1978 году перешел на самостоятельную творческую и педагогическую работу, как пишет Щипакина. По информации его официального сайта [1] Зайцев в 1979 году начал работать в системе служ-бы сбыта на фабрике № 19 индпошива, которая потом переросла в Московский Дом Моды, президентом которого он становится в 1982 году. Зайцев был удостоен Гран-При на Всемирном фестивале моды в Москве в 1967 году, он является носителем советских орденов и ему было присвоено почетное звание «*Народный художник РФ*». Коллекции дизайнерских коллективов Московского Дома моделей, которым он руководил, были показаны в Канаде, Японии, Франции, Италии и Югославии. В 2007 году он был избран действительным членом Российской Академии художеств (см. Щипакина 2009: 73). Кроме того, Зайцев в разные времена являлся ведущим популярной телепрограммы «*Модный приговор*».

---

[1] http://www.zaitsev.info/

Темы и аргументации книги

Посмотрим, какие темы доминируют в дискурсе о моде 1982 года. Оглавление книги на этот вопрос не даёт удовлетворительного ответа:

Обратимся к ним по очереди, постараемся расшифровать метафоры и определить, какие темы скрываются за ними:

1. *Гордиевы узлы моды.* Эта глава является предисловием книги, в ней автор обращает внимание на сложность феномена моды: мода как явление эстетическое (*этот мир [моды] беспощаден для эстетически неокрепших людей*); мода как явление этическое (о *взаимосвязи человека с миром вещей*; призвание *одежды [...] воспитывать [...] чувство прекрасного*); мода как предмет интереса разных научных дисциплин (кроме искус-ствоведения и моделирования она являлась предметом для анализа в области философии, психологии, социологии и политики); мода как дух времени (мода как *отражение исторических эпох общества* и *образ наших мыслей*); мода как явление, требующее профессиональной помощи, а именно модельера.

2. *Звенья одной цепи.* В этой главе речь идет о цепочке производства одежды, начиная от задумки модельера до готовых нарядов, продающихся в магазине. Но заметим, что в книге представляется идеальная версия этой «цепи», что подтвердится при прочтении следующих глав:

> «Любой дом моделей – и в Советском Союзе, и за рубежом – это большой творческий коллектив. За каждой моделью стоит труд сотен, а то и тысяч людей. Сегодня, в эпоху широкой демократизации одежды, функции домов моделей корен-ным образом изменились. Мода на поток ... Нет ли в этом сочетании чего-то унизи-тельного, принижающего работу художника-модельера, низводящего его до уровня ремесленника? Я считаю – нет!» (Зайцев 1982: 6)

Характерная черта этой книги заключается в том, что часто остается непонятным тот факт, о какой *моде* идет речь – советской или зарубежной? Какие дома моделей упоминает автор – советские или зарубежные? На самом деле, в этой книге мода представляется с одной стороны как одна, мировая, с другой стороны делается принципиальное различие между модой западной и модой советской. О подобной неопределенности речь пойдет ниже.

Интересно и обозначение дизайнера как *художника-модельера.* Оно указывает на то, что мода в советском обществе с самого начала истолковывается не как легкомысленный и фривольный каприз, а как *составляющая культуры*, которой занимались и занимаются серьезные специально обученные этому профессионалы, художники. Соответственно серьезен был и процесс разработки моды:

> «Весной каждого года на обсуждение авторитетного жюри, членами которого являются представители Министерства легкой промышленности СССР, худо-жественные руководители всех ведущих домов моделей, выносятся разработки ос-новных направлений моды на два года вперед.» (Зайцев 1982: 7)

3. *«Дети – цветы» и деловые люди.* Под данным заголовком рассматривается опасное влияние «западной антимоды, порожденной стихийным протестом молодого поколения против обезличивающего "общества потребления"» и узурпированной «оборотистыми дельцами» (Зайцев 1982: 13), ставшей «составной частью буржуазной массовой культуры» (Зайцев 1982: 15). Угроза видится в «нивелировании», будь то «национальных особенностей» или «индивидуальности» и «неповторимого облика» (Зайцев 1982: 19). Вызвано это «нивелирование» по данной аргументации «интернационализацией» моды вообще (Зайцев 1982: 9) и огромной популярностью «джинсов», в частности.

> «Их отказ от моды салонов и буржуазных кварталов означал желание противопоставить себя прогнившему капиталистическому обществу, побуждающему покупать и уничтожать предметы человеческого труда до того, как они стали непригодными для употребления. [...] Они верно указали на язвы, разъедающие сердца и души людей. И все же за пределы чисто внешнего, во многом показного протеста они выйти не сумели, не смогли найти выход из лабиринтов буржуазного индивидуализма.» (Зайцев 1982: 12)

4. *О «болезнях роста».* В ответ на угрозу *антимоды,* глава освещает проблему *воспитания* молодежи в рамках социалистической этики внешнего вида ввиду *интернационализации* моды. Метафора *болезни роста* отсылает одновременно к трём темам: во-первых, к «тем прошлым подходам ко "всему модному"», которыми «стремление одеваться современно ассоциировалось с мещанским образом жизни» [советскими шестидесятниками, КК] (Зайцев 1982: 27), во-вторых, к незрелому отношению к моде молодых модников/модниц, и, в-третьих, к состоянию «отечественной легкой про-мышленности», которая страдает «болезнью роста», так как оказывается не готовой к «молодежному буму» так же, как и модельеры (Зайцев 1982: 21):

> «[...] отечественная легкая промышленность оказалась не на высоте. До сей поры молодежное моделирование мало занимало [...] умы [социологов, педагогов, модельеров, промышленников], и юношам и девушкам предлагали всё те же "взрослые" образцы, совершенно не подходящие их характеру и стилю жизни.» (Зайцев 1982: 21)

Усложняют «болезни роста необыкновенные сложности [...] овладеть секретами моды» (Зайцев 1982: 27), которые заключаются в том, что в обращении с модой человек проявляет свой характер (Зайцев 1982: 27); что попытки его одеваться «по картинке» из журнала тщетны (Зайцев 1982: 27-28); что «обаяние» возникает из «сдержанного» внеш-него вида (Зайцев 1982: 28); и наконец в том, что «классическое» лучше «экстра-вагантного» (Зайцев 1982: 28).

5. *Эти злополучные «но»*. Глава продолжает тему молодежной моды, подчеркивая значимость обеспечения молодежи модной одеждой как вклад в *пропаганду социалистического образа жизни*. Аргументируется это следующим образом:

> «Воспитывать молодежь, игнорируя пусть не главные, не основные вопросы, это значит впоследствии проиграть и в чем-то главном, основном. Молодости свойственно пробовать и ошибаться. Это период поисков своего образа, стиля, отношения к жизни. [...] А мода, умение одеваться – в данном случае момент далеко не последний. Это в ГДР понимают очень хорошо. Недаром на X съезде Союза свободной немецкой молодежи было четко заявлено в отчетном докладе: создание молодежной моды – задача пропаганды социалистического образа жизни, она важна для формирования личности молодого человека.» (Зайцев 1982: 42)

6. *В поисках идеала*. В этой главе представляется очерк истории мировой моды как единого глобального целого, в котором советский подход как будто представляет перелом. Этот перелом заключается в сенсационном советском проекте сделать моду, проектированную художниками, а доступную всем слоям населения, в то время как от кутюр до этого был доступен только аристократам и, впоследствии, буржуазным элитам. Глава *«В поисках идеала»* отсылает читателя как к истории моды в глобальном масштабе, так и к советскому *поиску идеала*, завершившегося в дизайнерской моде как товара широкого потребления:

> «Впервые в истории художники-модельеры обратились к народным массам, заказчиками, потребителями домов моделей стали сотни [в государстве, насчи-тывающем 180 миллионов граждан!] рабочих и крестьян, граждан нового мира.» (Зайцев 1982: 59)

7. *Период «междувластия»*. Предметом обсуждения этой главы является прекращение *диктатуры* модельеров на Западе после 1968 года с одной стороны и разработка социалистической концепции моды с другой, согласно которой модельеры обращаются к широким слоям населения. Но к какому периоду конкретно относится *период "между-властия"*, не совсем понятно.

> «Социалистическая концепция моды отличается от западной принципиальным образом. Коллекции домов моделей в капиталистических странах продолжают оставаться элитарными. [Буржуазная мода] лишена демократичности. [...] Это мода для узкого круга, а не для широких слоев общества. Советская же мода для всех и для каждого. [...] Куда сложнее придумать такую одежду, которая была бы и практичной, и удобной, и в то же время желанной, гармонирующей с внешностью. В этом, собственно, и заключается творческое кредо и формула успеха советской школы моделирования.» (Зайцев 1982: 66)

Советская же мода для всех и для каждого, а на самом деле её просто нет. Вот, кстати, прекрасный пример отголоска соцреалистического дискурса, изображения которого заменяли то, что изображали (см. выше).

8. *Второе рождение народного костюма*. Глава затрагивает роль традиционных народных костюмов в современном моделировании. Связь с предыдущей главой заклю-чается в

том, что в фольклоре для советской моды усматривается возможность найти «свои пути», «непроторенные» (ЗАЙЦЕВ 1982: 66).

> «Колдовская сила русского народного костюма так велика, что, однажды заглянув в эту сокровищницу и осознав ее связи с обычаями, обрядами, с древнейшими истоками русской культуры, когда магическое значение вещей, изображений превра-щалось в эстетическое, уже не можешь оторваться от нее, - пишет известный в нашей стране знаток и тонкий ценитель национальной одежды Мария Николаевна Мер-цалова.» (ЗАЙЦЕВ 1982: 68-69)

Этим очерчен круг тем и связанных с ними ключевых аргументаций и понятий, определявших дискурс моды в начале 1980-х годов. Речь уже давно не о «гигиене» и «культурности», а к вопросу «мещанства» и заботе о «хорошем вкусе» присоединились другие темы: «западная антимода», «западная молодежная мода», и неспособность ни советской легкой промышленности, ни советских модельеров, предложить советской молодежи «свою», «советскую» альтернативу. Но так прямо, конечно, об этом не гово-рится. В какой форме тогда в 1982 году советским читателям представились *гордиевы узлы моды*? Как мы сейчас увидим, языковые стратегии их презентации не тривиальны и включают большой дополнительный смысловой потенциал. В них отражается вся слож-ность взаимоотношений советской власти со своими гражданами.

Инженерия текста: три «автора»

Одна из особенностей данной книги состоит в том, что Вячеслав Зайцев проявляет в ней своеобразную ментальную тройственность: то его тон – это тон одушевленного художника-модельера, но не редко он вдруг меняется внутри одного только параграфа, и Зайцев приобретает тон брюзгливого моралиста, причем уже в следующем параграфе он может обращаться к читателю в деловом тоне эксперта, социолога культуры.

> «Весной каждого года на обсуждение авторитетного жюри, членами которого являются представители Министерства легкой промышленности СССР, худо-жественные руководители всех ведущих домов моделей, выносятся разработки ос-новных направлений моды на два года вперед. [...] Для всего коллектива это очень волнующие дни, ибо от вердикта жюри зависит судьба многомесячной работы. И не только Дома моделей. Ведь в процессе подготовки коллекции художники уже учитывают предложения и пожелания текстильщиков, обувщиков, кожевников. Дом моделей представляет новую моду целиком, в полном ее объеме – от шляпы до чулок.» (ЗАЙЦЕВ 1982: 7)

«Голос художника-модельера» можно определить по специальным профессиональным темам, по соответствующей терминологии, обозначающей относительно узкую область работы и примыкающие к ней остальные сферы деятельности, по фрагментам относительных к художественной сфере аргументациям[2] (см. LUMER 1990). В конце концов, «го-

---

[2] Автор здесь исходит из «практической аргументационной теории» К. Лумера (LUMER 1990). Опираясь на теорию речевых актов, Лумер интересуется «аргументационным действием» повседневной и научной коммуникации (ср. LUMER 1990: 22-25). Цель «повседневной аргументации» состоит в демонстрации убедительности суждения (LUMER 1990: 319). В быту, мы чаще всего аргументами «обосновываем» какое-либо

лос художника-модельера» можно определить по оценкам, эксплицитным и имплицитным, по переданным им творческим переживаниям, которыми он стремится поражать читателя (жюри – *авторитетный*, дома моделей – *ведущие*, дни – *волнующие*), а также по своим эстетическим суждениям как эксперта. Из суммы всех этих элементов появляется «голос художника-модельера», члена упомянутого им коллектива, и в свою очередь читатель ощущает, как с этим коллективом *художник-модельер* переживает ожидание решения *судьбы многомесячной работы.*

В качестве примера ниже обсуждается вопрос собственно дизайнерский, причем болезненный:

> «Особенности современной моды таковы, что сейчас не может быть мелочей в одежде. Все одинаково важно и достойно внимания художника. И именно художнику по костюму отводится роль организатора ансамбля.» (Зайцев 1982: 8)

Тема *деталей*, кстати, поднимается не случайно, ведь в то время как для модельера детали не мелочь, именно они часто получали отрицательную оценку со стороны ответственных лиц на швейных фабриках, так как внедрение их в производство требовало дополнительного времени, а зачастую и дополнительного оборудования. Поэтому неудивительно, что вопрос деталей волнует художника-модельера.

В следующем параграфе, Зайцев развёртывает другую аргументацию, по-видимому, тоже художественную. А на самом деле она воспроизводит стандартную позицию официального советского дискурса о моде, что мода, якобы, приводит к однообразности, лишая людей индивидуальности и освобождая их от необходимости собственного эстетического решения.

> «Унификация нашего быта оправданно беспокоит многих. И не случайно, футурологи и писатели-фантасты в своих произведениях, словно в предостережение человеку нынешнему, нередко рисуют мир будущего как серый, безликий мегаполис, совершенно одинаковый от Тибета до Гренландии.[...] вызывается интерна-ционализация одежды, как и других сторон нашего быта, чисто объективными при-чинами. Ведь в постоянном соперничестве различных направлений и тенденций неизбежно побеждает то, что более всего отвечает требованиям нашей сложной, наполненной движением жизни.» (Зайцев 1982: 9)

Аргументация того, что *интернационализация одежды* приводит к *унификации*, а *унификация* имплицирует *серый, безликий мегаполис, совершенно одинаковый от Тибета до Гренландии*, вряд ли исходит из уст или принадлежит перу человека искусства. А если еще как-то мыслим дизайнер, придерживающийся такого взгляда, то слова и обороты, такие как *оправданно беспокоит, предостережение, объективными причинами, пос-тоянном соперничестве, побеждает* совсем не характерны для художника-модельера. Это явно нехудожественный дискурс. Назовём его «голосом идеолога».

В следующей цитате разные «голоса» Зайцева проявляются на примере его резко меняющихся взглядов на джинсы. Сначала он выступает восторженным их сторонником, говорящим «голосом художника-модельера»:

действие, или точнее: аргументируем в поддержку определенного тезиса о каком-либо действии, аргументирует Лумер (см. Lumer 1990: 366).

> «Как бы то ни было, джинсы прочно завоевали симпатии и вошли в гардероб нашего современника. [...] Влияние даже не только джинсов, столько джинсового стиля огромно. Джинсы еще носят, но рядом с ними вскоре появились сафари. Иная ткань, другой цвет, а покрой брюк тот же. Многие детали, найденные модельерами в джинсовом стиле, перешли в стиль сафари.» (Зайцев 1982: 18)

А в следующей вырезке он как будто изменил свое мнение и звучит скорее как «идеолог»:

> «Став общепринятой модой, джинсы [...] превратились в своего рода униформу, подавляющую всякое проявление вкуса. [...] Известно, что всякая новая мода лучше старой. Красивее, удобнее. Но не в том случае, когда мы теряем в аккуратности, корректности своей одежды.» (Зайцев 1982: 19)

«Голос идеолога» отличается присутствием главных составляющих советской культурной стратегии «воспитания вкуса» (см. Захарова 2007; Жуков 1954; Klingseis 2010), выдвигающей в письме Зайцева («голосом идеолога») на передний план *аккуратность* и *корректность,* никак не являющиеся категориями «художника-мо-дельера».

В конце концов, в этой книге можно различить еще один «голос». Назовем его «голосом социолога культуры». Он не всегда четко отличный от «голоса художника-модельера», но все-таки заслуживает обсуждения. Его характерные черты заключаются в его социологических и социо-исторических аргументациях, которыми он отличается от чисто «эстетических», «художественных» с одной стороны, и от моральных аргументаций «идеолога», с другой:

> «С помощью каких предметов поведали бы мы потомкам о нашей жизни? Не о той жизни, в которой грохочут стройки, шумят станки, а о той, где по улицам ходят красивые девушки, где группы ребят в обязательных джинсах и разноцветных майках с непременными транзисторами, где есть Большой театр и серьезная публика в строгих вечерних костюмах.» (Зайцев 1982: 5)

И еще пример «голоса социолога культуры»:

> «Развитие моды, как и развитие истории, [...] идет по спирали. И каждый новый виток этой спирали обогащает нас чем-то новым: дает новые идеи, новые формы, новые материалы, дает, наконец, самое главное – новое отношение к одежде.» (Зайцев 1982: 49)

В наличии разных «голосов» в смысле аргументаций и оценок в одной книге нет ничего необыкновенного, если автор указывает на их противоречивость, аргументирует превосходство одного мнения над другим или эксплицитно указывает на амбивалентность какого-либо явления. Но в данной книге этого не происходит. Именно это обстоятельство и производит впечатление о «шизофрении» автора, который резко меняет свои взгляды на одну и ту же вещь.

Противоречивость текста в концептуальном, фактическом и оценочном планах

Впечатление о «шизофрении автора» усиливается еще и тем, что в тексте сосуществуют концептуальные рассуждения, явно противоречащие друг другу, но никак не опосредованные автором. Вернемся еще раз к выше процитированному теоретическому изложению развития моды «голосом социолога культуры» и сравним его со следующим изложением – причем на одной и той же странице (!):

> «Мода – это вариации хорошо забытого старого: И если рассматривать фиговый лист Евы как первое открытие в моде, то не следует удивляться, что модельерам из года в год становится труднее изобретать «последний крик» и наряжать женщин в подобные новинки.» (Зайцев 1982: 49)

Если в первом изложении развития моды имплицитная оценка самой моды положительная и отношение к ней серьезно (*обогащает; дает [...] самое главное – новое отношение к одежде*), то во втором отношение к моде чуть ли не цинично, о чём свидетельствует не только пренебрежительная лексика, указывающая на несерьёзность моды (*«последний крик», наряжать,* и не просто *новинки,* а *подобные новинки*). Но цинизм возникает и из того, что этим высказыванием все последующие в истории изобретения моды ставятся в один ряд с *фиговым листом Евы,* коннотирующим здесь ничто другое, как пресловутый «фривольный женский пол». Зайцев как будто сначала выдвигает вполне серьёзную теорию моды, а на той же странице над ней издевается.

Рассмотрим еще один пример противоречий этой книги, но в этот раз не на концептуальном, а на содержательно-фактическом уровне. Выше было изложена *цепь* производства одежды в Советском Союзе, начиная с эскизов моделей художниками-модельерами Общесоюзного дома моделей одежды (Зайцев 1982: 5-6), их обсуждения и отбора экспертами вплоть до появления моделей на улицах, причем было замечено, что «главную оценку даст последнее, но самое важное звено этой цепочки – покупатель» (Зайцев 1982: 11). Эта последняя мысль сформулирована следующим образом:

> «Модель поступила в магазин. И если она пользуется успехом, если на улицах появились люди в новых костюмах, пальто и плащах, то тогда и можно сказать, что цепочка замкнулась и работа коллектива Дома моделей успешно завершена.» (Зайцев 1982: 11)

Правда, рисуется эта картина в условных придаточных предложениях (*если она пользуется успехом, если на улицах появились люди в новых костюмах*), но в воображении читателя *цепочка замкнулась* на самом деле, и в его голове возникает представление об элегантных, модных людях, прогуливающихся на улицах города в *новых костюмах, пальто и плащах.* Противопоставим процитированной выдержке следующие слова «художника-модельера» из пятой главы *Эти злополучные "но"*:

> «Двадцать лет жизни я отдал профессии художника-модельера, но, по существу, сделал очень мало: ведь не так часто я вижу на улицах людей, одетых в мои модели. [...] Если раньше мне часто задавали вопрос, где можно купить ту или иную модель, то спрашивать об этом сегодня как-то не считают нужным. Я вдруг почувствовал, что мне стало стыдно произносить слово "мода".» (Зайцев 1982: 45)

Поражающий эффект этого высказывания возникает из-за того, что такие фрагменты текста никак не вступают в «диалог» друг с другом, автором не принимается ни малейшего усилия разрешить очевидное противоречие.

Концептуальная неопределённость

Круглова в своей книге говорит о «тавтологии» соцреалистического дискурса, который делает вид «диалектичности мышления», якобы включая перспективу «Другого» в коммуникацию, а на самом деле его «отменяя».

> «Главное, что является основой такой коммуникативной ситуации, в которой все понятно и все неопределенно одновременно, – отмена Другого. Другой в тота-литарном сознании присутствует только как враг или объект бесконечной эксплуатации, то есть отношения с ним выстраиваются за пределами диалоговой ситуации. Мир абсурда возникает в результате повторения того же самого, там невозможно рождение нового, иного, другого. Но тавтология в соцреалистическом дискурсе скрыта, неочевидна. На поверхности дискурса мы имеем дело с риторикой "диалектичности" мышления, языка, искусства, что, казалось бы, должно предполагать изначальную разность позиций.» (Круглова 2005: 52)

Именно это происходит и в книге Зайцева. Следим за процессом на примере двух терминов – *«антимода»* и *«авангардисты моды»*:
Термин *«антимода»* вводится в 3-ей главе – *"Дети-цветы" и деловые люди*:

> «Как это ни парадоксально, значительное большинство идей и новых форм в последнее время родилось отнюдь не в домах моделей, а на улицах городов. Профессиональные создатели моды неожиданно столкнулись с весьма мощной конкуренцией со стороны непрофессионалов – самодеятельных художников движе-ния протеста, создавших течение, получившее название «антимода», объединившее различные тенденции, которые не входят в границы моды, существуют вне, помимо ее и даже наперекор ей.» (Зайцев 1982: 11)

«Антимода» обсуждается «голосом социолога культуры», в нейтральном тоне эксперта, без оценки. В следующей, 4-й главе – *О «болезнях роста» – антимода* опять возникает в самом введении главы, причем здесь слышится голос то ли «художника-модельера», то ли опять-таки «социолога культуры»:

> «Антимода» оказывала и продолжает оказывать немалое влияние на развитие моделирования. И это естественно, ибо художник-модельер, к какой бы школе он ни принадлежал, неизбежно вынужден, чтобы не потерять то, что именуется пульсом времени, внимательно вглядываться в происходящие вокруг него процессы, щедро черпать новые идеи из самых различных источников, в том числе и из самодеятельного творчества.» (Зайцев 1982: 20)

Оценка *«антимоды»* в этой выдержке не эксплицитна, но всё-таки присутствует. Тот факт, что *художник-модельер [...] неизбежно вынужден [...] внимательно вглядываться в нее*, не то, что придает высказыванию отрицательный оттенок, но, по крайней мере, вызывает его ожидание. Это связано с отрицательными коннотациями *неизбежно* и *вынужден*. В то же время, речь здесь идет о *самодеятельном творчестве*, которое возни-кает в роли текстуального синонима *«антимоды»*. А *самодеятельное творчество*, как мы заметим ниже, в официальном советском дискурсе моды всегда оценивается однозначно положительно. Чей этот «голос», нельзя сказать с уверенностью. Но в следующем выс-казывании уже точно услышим «голос идеолога»: Было бы недальновидно отказываться от предложений антимоды лишь потому, что она перечеркивает сложившиеся каноны моды официальной. (Зайцев 1982: 20)

Имплицитная оценка *«антимоды»* - отрицательная. Ведь на самом деле здесь говорится, что, собственно говоря, от *«антимоды»* нужно было бы *отказываться…* Хорошо ли то, что *она перечеркивает сложившиеся каноны моды официальной*, или плохо, читателю не открывается. Во всяком случае, речь здесь идет о западной *«анти-моде»*, ведь *«антимода»* представляется как феномен *протестного движения* против капитализма 1968-го года. В то же время, термин «*самодеятельное творчество»* одноз-начно происходит из советского дискурса, где оценивается положительно, а в про-цитированном тексте пользуется и как синоним *«антимоды»*. Такой процедурой стира-ются границы понятийных содержаний. Посмотрим дальше:

> «И в одежде наших соотечественников можно без труда обнаружить ее [антимоды] вли-яние. В этом, как я считаю, нет ничего страшного. Как справедливо отмечает известный советский искусствовед, доктор философских наук В. И. Толстых, тот факт, что мини-юбки, как некогда и узкие брюки, пришли к нам с Запада, еще ни о чем – хорошем или дурном – не говорит.» (Зайцев 1982: 20)

В пресуппозиции этой аргументации *«антимода»* опять и однозначно является феноменом «западным», иначе аргумент ad verecundiam В.И. Толстых не мог бы служить подкреплением суждения *нет ничего страшного* в том, что *в одежде наших соотечественников можно без труда обнаружить "антимоды"*, чем он призван служить. Читатель же этой аргументацией готовится к *страшному* – и его ожидание сбудется.

В дальнейшем в главе *О «болезнях роста* еще раз появляется термин *«самодеятельное творчество»*, но в этот раз речь однозначно идет о советской практике, описанной в «письме студента Ю.Титова из Кемерово» (Зайцев 1982: 25). Темой, в центре которой стоит это *письмо*, является правильное обращение с *модой*, причем здесь речь вдруг идет о *молодежной моде*, а уже не об *«антимоде»*. Но ассоциативная связь, конечно, уже установлена через термин *«самодеятельное творчество»*, который употребляется для *западной антимоды*, и для практики студента Ю. Титова из Кемерово. Итак, в этом письме нам приводится пример настоящей, однозначно хорошей советской версии *«антимоды»*, т.е. самодеятельной молодежной моды. Студент Титов в своем письме Зайцеву упрекает себя в «почти болезненном стремлении к оригинальности», из-за чего «время от времени [...] попал в число так называемых "авангардистов", встречал косые, насмешливые взгляды и чувствовал: что-то упускаю». Тогда-то он решился на самодеятельность: «Сел и придумал для себя свитер. Затем пошел в ателье и заказал его» (Зайцев 1982: 26).

Термин же *«антимода»*, определившийся в 3-й главе *"Дети-цветы" и деловые люди* «идеями [...] самодеятельных художников протестного движения» (Зайцев 1982: 11), к концу 4-й главы *О "болезнях роста"* возникает снова и в этот раз получает однозначно отрицательную оценку, представляя собой моду «Битлзов, панков, идолов», которых «формируют те, кто заинтересован в том, чтобы массы жили, мыслили, действовали в строго определенных и выгодных буржуазии рамках». Читателю объясняется, что для того, «чтобы образ дошел до потребителя, он должен быть пропущен через “синтезаторы” буржуазной культуры. Именно через них была пущена на поток “антимода”, порожденная движением хиппи. Именно так вышли на орбиту шоу-бизнеса те же “Битлз”, сыгравшие в свое время роль “парней с ливерпульских рабочих окраин”» (Зайцев 1982: 34).

«Антимода», результат творчества «самодеятельных художников движения протеста» (Зайцев 1982: 11), в книге Зайцева служит всего лишь отрицательным фоном единственного легитимного ответа на «каноны моды официальной» (Зайцев 1982: 20) – *«самодеятельное творчество»* советской молодежи.

На примере *«авангардистов моды»* рассмотрим еще один подход к *гордиевому узлу* моды. При этом подходе смещается фокус обсуждаемого понятия с одного значения на другой (см. Круглова 2005: 34), вплоть до полной отмены одного содержания другим. Данным способом отменяются различия между непримиримыми понятиями, отрицается их противоположность, а «в результате [этого] происходит взаимообескровливание и взаимоопустощение» противоречивых и взаимоисключающих понятий. «Борьба противоположностей заканчивается обоюдной деидентификацией (десемантизацией), потерей предметных признаков». (Круглова 2005: 54)

Проследим за таким процессом в книге Зайцева: вводится термин, определяется его понятийное содержание, оценивается (это может произойти эксплицитно или имплицитно). В дальнейшем данный термин употребляется в разных аргументациях и, в конце концов, подра-зумевает совершенно другое, чем он обозначал первоначально. Вме-сте с этим обычно и меняется оценка означаемого соответственным термином, который при этом остался тем же. Читатель при таком подходе остается в растерянности: о чем на самом деле идет речь? И хорошая ли обсуждаемая вещь или плохая? Решить ему данные вопросы с помощью книги Зайцева будет сложно.

> «[Авангардисты], как правило, люди ищущие, пытающиеся выглядеть не так, как другие. Мода для них средство выражения своей индивидуальности. [...] Авангардисты – это прежде всего новаторы, люди, на которых модельеры могут как бы опробовать жизненность своих идей и предложений.» (Зайцев 1982: 25)

Первое определение в выше приведенной цитате скорее всего принадлежит «голосу идеолога», на что указывают *люди ищущие* и их стремление *выражать свою индивидуальность* – все это штампы воспитательного советского дискурса красоты и внешнего вида. Они отнюдь не являются терминами «социолога культуры» или «художника-модельера». Им, скорее всего, принадлежит второе определение – экспертное, ставящее акцент на культурной функции *авангардиста* в модном процессе быть *новатором.* Итак, стремление *выглядеть не так, как другие* в СССР всегда встречалось с подозрением и может считаться имплицитно отрицательной оценкой, в то время как *выразить свою индивидуальность* благосклонно противопоставлялось стремлению *слепо следить за модой* и может считаться положительной оценкой. Имплицитно положительной оценкой является и речь о *новаторстве авангардистов* и их полезной роли в модном процессе. Итого, оценка *авангардистов* до этого момента в тексте, хоть и неоднозначная, всё же скорее положительная, чем отрицательная.

Правда, быть *модным*, а уж тем более быть «*авангардистом моды*» риск, схожий с хождением по острию ножа. Так, студент Титов первым делом сетует на тот факт, что при всей вездесущности моды *не каждому удается быть модным [...] и при этом не изменять чувству меры.* А следующий абзац из письма Титова окончательно вводит читателя в недоумение:

> «Моим сверстникам обидно слышать критические замечания в адрес «авангардистов» моды. Конечно, есть такие люди, для которых стремление идти в ногу с модой превращается в главную цель жизни. Но ведь таких не так уж много. Да и появляются они лишь потому, что наша промышленность пока что не может предложить молодежи широкий выбор современной одежды... [...] Во все времена новое принималось со «скрипом», [...] Но если это новое действительно красиво, оно докажет свою жизнеспособность, привьется, станет общепризнанным.» (Зайцев 1982: 26)

Если те, *для которых стремление идти в ногу с модой превращается в главную цель жизни* - те же самые «*авангардисты*», то, по понятиям «идеолога», «*авангардисты*», безусловно, представляют явление плачевное. Но тут же для них появляется неожиданное оправдание в недостатках *нашей промышленности.* И к тому же, то *новое*, за которым так охотно гонят «*авангардисты*», может оказаться и *действительно красивым.*

Дальше следует резюме Зайцева (говорящего «голосом идеолога»):

> «Я специально привел это письмо почти целиком, чтобы продемонстрировать суть мировоззрения «авангардистов». Они люди творческие и поэтому не только перенимают наимоднейшие линии и силуэты, но и, как студент Ю.Титов, сами пытаются выдумывать и творить. Нужно ли с такими бороться? Нет и еще раз нет!» (Зайцев 1982: 26)

Что же случилось? Оценка *«авангардистов»* при прочтении письма студента Титова перемещалась по шкале от амбивалентной, но скорее положительной, через амби-валентную, но скорее отрицательную, до эксплицитно и однозначно положительной. Происходит это в силу того, что в процессе написания этого длинного письма фунда-ментально и безмолвно изменилось определение *«авангардистов моды»*: от «новаторов, людей, на которых модельеры могут как бы опробовать жизненность своих идей и предложений» через тех, для кого «стремление идти в ногу с модой превращается в главную цель жизни» вплоть до тех, кто «не только перенимают наимоднейшие линии и силуэты, но, как студент Ю.Титов, сами пытаются выдумывать и творить» (Зайцев 1982: 25-26).

Иными словами, *«авангардисты»* исходя из последнего примера отнюдь не те, кем они были в примере первом. Прочитав эти аргументации, читатель уже никак не в состоянии понять, положительный ли, в конце концов, герой *«авангардист»* или отрицательный? Он и не сразу понимает, что речь на самом деле идет о двух разных типах людей, так как меняется понятийное содержание самого термина *«авангардист»*.

Производство подтекста посредством условного наклонения и отрицания

Использование лингвистических средств, таких как условное наклонение в длинном ряду высказываний в изъявительном наклонении могут произвести у реципиента эффект восприятия прочитанного или услышанного фактом. Если посмотреть на выше процитированный пример из книги: «Модель поступила в магазин. И если она пользуется успехом, если на улицах появились люди в новых костюмах, пальто и плащах, то тогда и можно сказать, что цепочка замкнулась и работа коллектива Дома моделей успешно завершена» (Зайцев 1982: 11), то становится видным, что слово *если* легко может усколь-знуть от внимания читателя и оставить в его воображении людей в элегантной дизай-нерской одежде. А только через 44 страницы читатель узнает, что на самом деле цепочка очень редко замыкается, из-за чего модельеру даже стыдно произносить слово *мода*.

Похожая лингвистическая манипуляция воображением наблюдается, например, в следующей формулировке: «Такое творческое содружество [модельера, текстильщиков, обувщиков, кожевников] позволяет создать ансамбль одежды, то есть то единство художественного решения, к которому, в конечном счете стремится моделирование.» (Зайцев 1982: 7). Остается нерешаемым вопрос, все лишь *позволяет* или действительно создает *ансамбль* это *творческое содружество*? А на памяти у реципиента точно остается *ансамбль одежды* [...] *единство художественного решения*. Как пишет Е. Добренко, «стоит [...] иметь в виду, что [...] огромное производство образов, которое занимает весь советский медиум, начинает определять не только политическое бессознательное, но и всю сферу воображаемого. Спустя годы для новых поколений все эти образы возвращаются "правдой": люди уже видят мир *таким*. Соцреализм производил не "ложь", но *образы социализма*, которые через восприятие возвращаются *реальностью*, а именно – *социализмом*» (Добренко 2007: 29). Правда, воображение поколения, подрастающего после выхода в свет книги Зайцева, питали уже другие образы.

А вот еще один вариант игры с воображением реципиентов - вызывание воображения через отрицание: «В этом, как я считаю, **нет ничего** страшного» (Зайцев 1982: 20) *Страшное – страшное – страшное* заражает воображение реципиента. В чем же оно заключается? А ведь в том, что ***в одежде наших соотечественников можно без труда обнаружить влияние западной "антимоды"***. Опытный реципиент невольно воспринимает прочитанное через культурный фрейм предыдущих времен, когда к западной одежде на советском человеке относились однозначно с подозрением.

Это значит, что отрицание работает только при условии, что производитель текста предполагает, что его «идеальный читатель» обладает определенными «знаниями (ментальными схемами)» касательно определенной данной тематики (см. Pagano 1994: 258). Иначе, отрицание высказывания вызвало бы у реципиента вопрос, а почему же *влияние западной "антимоды" в одежде наших соотечественников* может быть страшным или нестрашным? Ведь вполне мыслимы контексты, где видимость ино-странного влияния воспринимается с равнодушием или с восторгом. В этом случае отрицание ее *страшности* не имело бы никакого смысла. Отрицания имплицитных утверждений (имплицитное утверждение: *страшно*) тем же особенно интересны, что они обнаруживают такие элементы дискурса, которые иначе, то есть при положительном выражении смысла, не возникали бы в тексте (см. Pagano 1994: 253). В тот же момент, когда выражается отрицание какой-либо пропозиции, производитель текста проецирует мир, в котором то, что им отрицается, воспринимается как приемлемое, действительное, положенное. Проецируется мир, в котором предполагается, что производитель текста и его читатели соглашаются с отрицаемой в актуальном тексте пропозицией (см. Pagano 1994: 256). Только со ссылкой на этот разделяемый автором и читателем в каком-то другом (может и прошлом) мире вид, процитированное высказывание может восприниматься читателем в порядке «нормальных» высказываний. «Автор не может отрицать любое пред-положение, а только такие, которые убедительны или приемлемы в контексте данной интеракции». (Pagano 1994: 254)

С помощью отрицаний в рассмотренном тексте воспроизводятся смыслы, которые в дискурсе 1982-го года очевидно вступают в конфликт с «духом времени». Поэтому они и вводятся в отрицаемом виде, но, тем не менее, накликаются. Имея в виду эти соображения, прочитаем отрицаемые суждения текста и обратим внимание на подтекст, выступающий из прочитанного. Для визуализации процесса, отрицаемые импликации отмечены подчеркиванием, а лингвистическая реализация отрицания жирным шрифтом:

> «Как справедливо отмечает известный советский искусствовед, доктор философских наук В. И. Толстых, тот факт, что мини-юбки, как некогда и узкие брюки, пришли к нам с Запада, **еще ни о чем** – хорошем или дурном – **не говорит**.» (Зайцев 1982: 20)
>
> «В.И. Толстых соглашается с мнением, что **ничего** худого, ущемляющего национальные или иные чувства в подобном заимствовании [образцов западных модельеров] **нет**, [...].» (Зайцев 1982: 20)
>
> «Питательной среды для проникновения в общественное сознание буржуазной идеологии **не** существовало [поэтому только внешняя сторона этого движения была принята].» (Зайцев 1982: 21)
>
> «[...] не следует винить моду там, где очевидны прорехи эстетического и нравственного воспитания, не стоит путать причину и следствие. И конечно, **нельзя** бороться с модными поветриями, устраивая, как это делалось, иногда рейды против длинноволосых ребят в расклешенных брюках. Такими методами **никому и никого** еще **не** удавалось убедить и перевоспитать.» (Зайцев 1982: 22)
>
> «Отнюдь **не** запрещать **нужно** короткие и слишком длинные, на чьей-то взгляд, юбки, расклешенные или, наоборот, зауженные брюки, [...] (Зайцев 1982: 25)
>
> Бороться с модой, пусть даже чересчур вызывающей, **бессмысленно**. В самом деле, если каждый из нас вспомнит отношение к очередной новой модной волне, то на память наверняка придут и те, кто **безуспешно** пытался грудью встать на пути этой «стихии».» (Зайцев 1982: 25)
>
> «Речь идет вовсе **не** о стилягах, **не** о так называемых "центровых", для которых любая зарубежная тряпка была предметом мечты и целью жизни. Авангардисты – это прежде всего новаторы [...].» (Зайцев 1982: 25)
>
> «Думаю, **не** надо страшиться "налетов" моды. Опасаться следует другого – неподготовленности к восприятию нового, заведомо негативного к нему [восприятию нового] отношения, морализаторства, которое, как известно, **никого не убеждает**.» (Зайцев 1982: 29)

Вся очевидная толерантность к моде перечеркивается в момент ее утверждения воинственной семантикой слов, с которыми *мода* формирует словосочетания, такие как *мода вызывающая, модные поветрия, налет моды* и так далее. Часто в отрицаемых высказываниях и предвосхищаются ожидаемые реакции читателей или выражаются предположения об их склонностях или желаниях:

> «**Нет, никто не** призывает вас плыть по течению и подчинять свои вкусы мнению окружающих. Пожалуйста, будьте модными, будьте элегантными, но постарайтесь, чтобы ваши попытки **не** привели к крикливости в одежде, к ненужной экстравагантности.» (Зайцев 1982: 30)

> «Есть ли в этом [в том, что в 60-е годы [...] женщины садились на жесточайшую диету, чтобы хоть немного приблизиться к господствовавшему в этот период идеалу – английской манекенщице Твигги, "девушке-тростинке"] **что-то негативное**? Думается, что **нет**.» (Зайцев 1982: 32)

В выше приведенном примере проецируется «негативность» определенной практики (диеты с целью приблизиться Твигги), которая в следующем предложении отрицается. То же самое относится к следующим ниже примерам: «**Нет ничего** крамольного в стремлении быть похожим на популярный образ. Но вы можете легко утратить свое "я" в погоне за ним и превратиться в идолопоклонника. (Зайцев 1982: 32)

Последний же пример как-то не вписывается в установленный ряд тем, что место потенциально *плохого, крамольного* или *осуждаемого* неожиданно занимает практика, по опыту советских читателей безоговорочно удобряемая авторитетами. Советский юмор!: «**Нет ничего** плохого в стремлении быть похожим на прославленных людей нашего общества ["легендар-ных героев минувших войн и выдающихся деятелей науки, известных спортсменов и космонавтов"].» (Зайцев 1982: 35)

Прочитав все высказывания, отмеченные курсивом, мы понимаем, что перед нами возникает «мир», резко отличающийся от эксплицитного мира текста, в котором действует снисхождение и осуждается нетерпимость прошлых времен.

Вслед за Пагано, можно задаться вопросом, что «у производителя текста на уме, что его побудило употребить способ отрицания, почему то или другое утверждение должно быть имплицитным в данной ситуации, и почему именно способ отрицания соответствует данному контексту, в котором оно возникает?» (Pagano 1994: 253) Подтекст, созданный таким образом, говорит нам о том, что этот имплицитный «мир» за углом.

Диалогизация

Круглова замечает по отношению к советской публицистике, что «"диалог" превращается в ведущий жанр, в котором журналист и читатель становятся попеременными и как бы равноправными источниками информации [см. письмо студента Титова и другие примеры в книге Зайцева!], замыкая информационную цепь» (Круглова 2005: 35, ссылаясь на Л. Геллер 2000: 167) Автор в этой связи говорит об «олитературивании, противоречащ[ем]функциональности публицистических жанров» (Круглова 2005: 35, ссылаясь на Л. Геллер 2000: 167).

В тексте Зайцева учет суждений других тоже является отличительной чертой, но при этом обнаруживается, что к этому способу аргументации Зайцев прибегает особенно в тех случаях, когда их содержание – по меркам традиционных советских установок – считается спорным или оспоримым с точки зрения официальной культурной политики. Ниже приводятся два примера этого подхода, но их в тексте много.

Из письма Андрея Лопатина из Томска:

> «Наконец-то понятие "модный" вытеснило такое глубоко укоренившееся понятие, как "добротный". "Модный" сегодня стало одним из критериев оценки человека.» (Зайцев 1982: 36)
>
> «Московская учительница Зинаида Николаевна Кулакова верно заметила: «В тех школах, где учителя не знают меры, где строжайше запрещают всё модное, эффект часто получается как раз обратный – иные самые послушные, самые образцовые де-

> вочки через месяц после окончания школы становятся буквально неузнаваемыми, будто спешат объесться после долгого поста.» (Зайцев 1982: 22)

Содержание такого порядка Зайцев редко передает сам. То же самое относится к открытой критике:

> «[...] писал студент Харьковского автомобильно-дорожного института Э.Алексян: «На страницах наших газет и журналов было немало критических выступлений в адрес легкой промышленности, поэтому не хочу повторяться. Пора уже сделать решительные шаги в этом направлении, пора выйти из "тиши кабинетов" и заглянуть в жизнь!» [...] Не могу не согласиться с авторами писем: несмотря на то, что наша одежда по физико-механическим показателям и добротности [...] превышает показатели импортных изделий, она все же уступает в художественном оформлении и в качестве отделки. И здесь нам еще многое предстоит сделать.» (Зайцев 1982: 37)

Заключение

В книге Зайцева отражаются все изложенные в введении противоречия ранних восьмидесятых и непосредственно предыдущих лет: неготовность или невозможность пра-вящих лиц основательно реформировать легкую промышленность в ситуации, когда потребители за счет влияния образов и товаров из западных стран давно успели развить повышенные требования к товарам широкого потребления, в том числе и к одежде. Кроме того, в ней отражается осознание государственными и партийными деятелями большого значения высококачественного потребления как преимущества в «соревновании систем». Соответственно, в ней возникают и те полумеры по реформированию производства и распределения потребительских товаров, предпринятые в рамках несостоявшейся «косыгинской реформы». Отражается восприятие молодежью «западной антимоды» и амбивалентное официальное отношение государственных и партийных деятелей к ней, косвенный взгляд на пример ГДР и другие социалистические страны, где производство модной, т.е. в данном случае, молодежной, одежды в маленьких количествах уже было реальностью. Отражается и, в конце концов, попытка государственных и партийных деятелей всё-таки отстоять советскую идеологию потребления. Короче говоря, в про-тиворечиях текста отражаются вполне реальные противоречия позднесоветского общества. Странность текста заключается в том, что эти противоречия никак не обсуждаются по правилам рациональной аргументации, которая потребовала бы от автора так же, как от читателя, занимать ту или иную позицию. Но этого нет, противоречивые изображения действительности, противоречивые теоретические положения и противоречивые оценки мирно сосуществуют в книге. Это создает странную неопределенность относительно ее смысла. В этом и состоит «соцреалистическое» наследие книги Зайцева. Круглова, ссылаясь на Клода Лефорт, указывает на роль «неопределенности и пустых мест для осуществления проекта тоталитарной власти: "Место я называю пустым, потому что никакой индивид или группа не соприсущи ему: это понятие неизобразимого места не изнутри и не снаружи, это понятие чисто символической инстанции в смысле, что она более нелокализуема в рамках реального"» (цит. по Кругловой 2005: 27-28). Иными сло-вами, с такими учениями никто не мог идентифицироваться, им можно было только «ритуально подчиняться». Автор аргументирует, что отсутствие логики текстов ком-пенсировалось их «ритуализированностью»: «простое повторение "снимает" необ-ходимость логического обоснования». (Круглова 2005: 30)

Что касается конструкции «автора» и «читателя» и их взаимоотношений в этой книге, то конечно, у неискушенного наблюдателя могут возникать вопросы: каким представляется «читатель», которому в ярких красках рисуют мир, о котором тот знает, что его нет, и на глазах у которого несколько страниц дальше откровенно критикуется реально существующий мир именно за отсутствие у него этой яркости? Каким представляется читатель, которого приводят в замешательство семантическими фокусами, незаметно подменяя в течение развертывания текста одно содержание термина другим? Каким представляется «читатель», которому подспудно грозят ссылкой на времена, когда гонялись за людьми, выделяющиеся из толпы своей яркой одеждой, в то время как в книге эксплицитно практики этих времен осуждаются?
Начнем с реальных читателей такого типа официальных текстов: ими являлись, прежде всего, комсомольские вожди и учителя, которые обсуждали подобные вопросы с учениками и студентами на так называемых «тематических вечерах»[3]. Взаимоотношение же реальных авторов и читателей было условленным культурой соцреализма, в которой у каждого была своя роль. Играя свою роль комсомольского вождя или учителя, человек делал вид, что всё в диапазоне нормального: «на уровне советской повседневности происходило приспособление к этой ситуации в таком явлении, как "двойное мышление". [...] самым загадочным концептом советской культуры и искусства является и неимоверная логика, которая многими вненаходимыми адресатами воспринимается как *абсурдная.* Абсурд можно трактовать как свидетельство неограниченной силы тоталитарного общества. [...] Речь идет о том, что советский человек был приучен – самым способом своего бытия – забывать о логике, о здравом смысле, о "практическом разуме" и ориентировался на идеи и понятия, которые исключают друг друга». (Круглова 2005: 22)

Из описанного взаимоотношения автора и читателя, которые не связаны правилами рациональной коммуникации, возникает еще одна характерная черта книги, вписывающая её в традицию соцреалистического дискурса, а именно неопределенность своих позиций и оценок. Она также описывается как отличительная черта текстов соцреализма: «[в]ласть постоянно создает обстановку неопределенности и обещает избавить население от страха перед ней. Таким образом, *система воспроизводит ситуацию непредсказуемости,* негарантированности, порождает тем самым состояние постоянного страха и одно-временно создает иллюзию преодоления неопределенности». (Круглова 2005: 28) Своими неопределенными подспудными угрозами, книга Зайцева является достойным пред-ставителем и наследником соцреалистического дискурса.

И, в конце концов, книга вписывается в традицию советского дискурса своей ритуальной критикой, подменяющей реальное улучшение обстоятельств жизни его периодическим осуждением.

Что касается эффектов таких текстов, то они, безусловно, имели свое действие на умы. Ведь, по словам Чернышовой, о неэффективности официальной пропаганды сетовали не только партийные деятели, но и простые граждане, среди них и молодые люди, которым казалось, что комсомол не положенным образом отстаивал социалистическое отношение к вещам по отношению к капиталистическому вещизму (см. Chernyshova 2013: 129).

---

[3] Благодарю за эту информацию Юлию Градскову.

Summary

The article provides an analysis of a book on fashion dated 1982, the author of which is nobody else but the famous Soviet fashion designer Viacheslav Zaitsev. It brings into focus the linguistic "workmanship" of the text, which reveals typical features of a long tradition of soviet programmatic discourse. At the same time, the article strives to contextualise the book in the historical environment which it reflects: the Soviet authorities' plight in view of the appeal of Western fashionable clothing reaching the Soviet Union by various channels, while the domestic clothing industry is strangled by a clumsy bureaucratic apparatus and thus unable to produce apparel meeting young people's requirements. In its topics and arguments, Zaitsev's book reflects the challenge this situation posed to Soviet cultural politics in terms of competition between socialist and capitalist models of society, even more so as the irresistible appeal capitalist fashions exerted on Soviet youngsters conveyed attitudes not consistent with Soviet ethics.

Библиография

CHOULIARAKI, L., FAIRCLOUGH, N.2010. Critical Discourse Analysis in Organizational Studies: Towards an Integrationist Methodology. In: *Journal of Management Studies* 47, 6 September 2010, 1213–1218, http://onlinelibrary.wiley.com/doi/10.1111/j.1467-6486.2009.00883.x/abstract (11.10.2014).

CHERNYSHOVA, N. 2013. *Soviet Consumer Culture in the Brezhnev Era*. London, New York.

FAIRCLOUGH, N. 1989. *Language and Power*. New York.

FAIRCLOUGH, N. 1995. *Critical Discourse Analysis. The Critical Study of Language*. Longman.

KLINGSEIS, K. 2010. Der Mythos des „guten Geschmacks". Fragmente einer Analyse des aktuellen Kleidungsdiskurses in zwei russischen Städten. In: *Zeitschrift für Slavistik* 2, 144–159.

LUMER, C. 1990. *Praktische Argumentationstheorie*. Braunschweig.

PAGANO, A. 1994. Negatives in written text. In: Coulthard, M. (ed.). *Written Text Analysis*. London 1994, 250–265.

БАСТРЫКИН, А.И., ШИРЯЕВ, Э.Б. 1988. *Мода, кумиры и собственное "Я"*. Ленинград.

БОЙМ, С. 2002. *Общие места. Мифология повседневной жизни*. Москва.

ГЕЛЛЕР, Л. 2000. Социалистический реализм как культурная парадигма. In: *Соцреалистический канон*. Под ред. Х. Гюнтера и Е. Добренко. Академический проект.

ГУРОВА, О. 2008. *Советское нижнее белье: между идеологией и повседневностью*. Москва.

ДЕГОТЬ, Е. 2000. От товара к товарищу. К эстетике нерыночного товара. In: Деготь, Е., Демиденко, Ю. (eds.). *Память тела. Нижнее белье советсокой эпохи. Каталог выставки*. Москва 2000, 8–19.

ДОБРЕНКО, Е. 2007. *Политэкономия соцреализма*. Москва.

ЖУКОВ, Н.Н. 1954. Воспитание вкуса. Заметки жудожника. In: *Новый Мир* 10, 159–176.

ЗАЙЦЕВ, В. 1982. *Этот многоликий мир моды*. Москва.

ЗАХАРОВА, Л. 2007. Советская мода 1950-60-х годов. In: *Теория Моды. Одежда. Тело. Культура* 3, 55–80.

КАЗАРИНОВА, В.И. 1985. *Красота, вкус, экономика*. Москва.

КРУГЛОВА, Т. 2005. *Советская художественность или Нескромное обаяние соцреализма*. Екатеринбург.

КРЫШТАНОВСКАЯ, О.В. 2002. *Бизнес-элита и олигархи: итоги десятилетия*, http://www.pseudology.org/Reklama/kryshtanovskaya%5B1%5D.pdf (06.04.2014).

МАМАРДАШВИЛИ, М. 1992. *Как я понимаю философию*. Москва.

ПЕТРОВ, Л.В. 1974. *Мода как общественное явление*. Ленинград.

ПОЛИТИЧЕСКАЯ ЭКОНОМИЯ: Учебник. 1955, 2-е изд. Москва.

РИНДИСБАХЕР, Х. 2011. Мода и идеология: от Ленина до Горбачева. Отзыв на книгу Bartlett D. FashionEast. The Spectre that Haunted Socialism. MIT Press. In: *Теория Моды. Одежда. Тело. Культура* 22. http://www.nlobooks.ru/node/2354 (05.04.2014)

РОДЧЕНКО А. 1996. Опыты для будущего. Дневники. Статьи. Письма. Записки. Москва.

РУСАНОВА, О.В. 1961. *Раздумья о красоте и вкусе*. Москва.

ЩИПАКИНА, А. 2009. *Мода в СССР. Советский Кузнецкий, 14*. Москва.

«САМОПАЛ ПОД ФИРМУ»: Подпольное производство одежды в СССР в 1960-1980-е годы

АННА ИВАНОВА, МОСКВА

В начале 1970-х годов швейный учебно-производственный комбинат в городе Казах Азербайджанской ССР вместо не пользующихся популярностью жакетов, которые он должен был производить по плану, стал тайком изготовлять модные тогда джемперы и водолазки. Эта продукция, как писала газета «*Правда*» в разоблачительной статье под названием «*Трест, который лопнул*», вызвала на рынке «настоящий бум и переполох» и нелегально продавалась в ларьках в 32 городах СССР (ШАТУНОВСКИЙ 1978: 6). Помимо производства популярных товаров комбинат также мог похвастаться высоким уровнем дисциплины: начальники «с утра до вечера ходили по цехам, следили за сохранностью станков, за чистотой и порядком, пересчитывали на складе готовую продукцию, [...] были непримиримы к лодырям и бракоделам» (ШАТУНОВСКИЙ 1978: 6). Однако через несколько лет, когда деятельностью комбината заинтересовались правоохранительные органы, организаторы эффективного «бизнеса» оказались на скамье подсудимых и получили до 15 лет лишения свободы за хищение социалистической собственности (ПОСЛЕ КРИТИКИ 1979: 3). Журналист газеты «*Правда*» в конце своей статьи восклицал:

> «Хочется узнать мнение деятелей легкой промышленности. Как они объяснят, почему этим малограмотным, абсолютно не сведущим в технике и технологии дельцам на полукустарном по существу предприятии удавалось выпускать продукцию, могущую конкурировать с изделиями нашей промышленности. Без ясных ответов на эти вопросы, [...] нельзя дать твердых гарантий, что подобный жульнический трест, лопнувший в Казахе, не возродится где-нибудь в другом месте. Нельзя будет дать таких гарантий до тех самых пор, пока идея заменить неходовой товар ходовым и извлечь из этого максимальную пользу будет приходить сначала в голову жуликам, а потом уже осенять умы некоторых наших честных, но увы безынициативных и неповоротливых работников» (Шатуновский 1978: 6).

Кто же были эти «жулики», конкурировавшие с советской промышленностью? Как они решали, что именно производить? Каковы были причины возникновения подпольного производства одежды, и насколько оно было отрефлектировано в официальном дискурсе?

В данной статье подпольное массовое производство одежды в СССР в период 1960-1980-х гг., существовавшее как альтернатива официальному фабричному производству, будет интересовать меня как пример функционирования частного предпринимательства в обществе с плановой экономикой[1]. Я выделяю два типа нелегальных предпринимателей. Первый – это люди, которые работали в официальном швейном цеху и параллельно организовывали там незаконное производство (как в вышеприведенном примере комбината города Казах). При этом я рассматриваю не тех, кто просто шил из сэкономленного сырья большее количество плановой продукции, чем

---

[1] Подпольное производство в СССР упоминается в следующих исследованиях: (SIMIS 1982: 103, MCCAULEY 2008: 333, SAMPSON 1988: 148–150)

это значилось в документах, и продавал излишек «налево». Меня интересуют предприниматели, которые в своей теневой деятельности учитывали спрос, подходили к своему «бизнесу» творчески и нелегально производили более востребованные товары, чем те, которые они должны были производить легально. Второй тип – это люди, никак не связанные со швейными фабриками, а организовавшие свое производство на дому. Среди этой группы меня будут, прежде всего, интересовать не те частные портные, которые шили штучные вещи на заказ конкретным людям, а те, которые также ориентировались на рынок и создавали вещи, пользовавшиеся спросом, для дальнейшей продажи в относительно массовом количестве (это могло быть и несколько вещей в месяц).

Материалы устной истории, архивные документы и даже открытые советские источники (пресса и кинофильмы) показывают, что подпольные предприятия по изготовлению одежды постоянно возникали на всей территории СССР. Ниже я попытаюсь описать этот феномен и его роль в обществе, а также ответить на следующие вопросы: на какие образцы одежды ориентировалось подпольное производство, откуда предприниматели брали сырье, как распространялась такая продукция и, наконец, каково было отношение к этому виду деятельности в официальной риторике. Вопрос об отношении к подпольному производству и продукции среди потребителей представляет собой тему для отдельного исследования и затрагивается в статье лишь поверхностно.

Проблема моды в СССР и частные производители

В конце 1950-х – начале 1960-х гг. государство начало уделять больше внимания материальным потребностям граждан. Началось массовое строительство жилья, развивалось производство легковых автомобилей и бытовой техники. Также стояла цель удовлетворить спрос населения на одежду. Для ее достижения открывались швейные фабрики, производились новые синтетические ткани, создавались художественные учреждения, призванные развивать советскую моду. Однако вопрос о том, каким параметрам должна соответствовать советская одежда, оставался открытым. Джурджа Бартлетт в своей книге об истории социалистической моды говорит о том, что в 1930-е годы на смену утопическому модному нарративу, предполагавшему создание функциональной моды, соответствующей новому человеку и новому обществу, приходит тип социалистической моды. Этот тип реабилитировал традиционные представления о моде, однако брал за основу консервативные каноны и не предполагал учета модных тенденций (Бартлетт 2011: 15). В конце 1950-х – начале 1960-х в социалистическую моду «вдохнули новую жизнь», советские модельеры обменивались опытом с западными, в СССР были устроены показы Кристиана Диора, увеличился импорт западной одежды. И, тем не менее, в концептуальной основе советской моды по-прежнему лежали идеи скромности, приличия, «хорошего вкуса», подразумевавшие отказ от модной динамики (Захарова 2007: 6162).

К тому же удовлетворить реальный спрос социалистической моде все равно не удавалось. Разработки советских модельеров практически не доходили до конечных потребителей: при их централизованной реализации в больших масштабах на швейных фабриках было практически невозможно воспроизвести изначальные задумки. Из-за дефицита нужных тканей и незаинтересованности работников одежда отечественного производителя неизбежно ассоциировалась у потребителей с плохим качеством (Захарова 2007: 61-62, Вайнштейн 2007: 121–122).

При этом сами потребители по мере того, как экономика восстанавливалась после войны, все активнее интересовались модой. Городское население росло, все больше людей стремились не просто обеспечить себя одеждой, но и выглядеть элегантно. С конца 1950-х годов в СССР все активнее проникала западная мода. Отчасти это происходило благодаря растущему туризму в СССР из-за рубежа и прокату западных кинофильмов[2], отчасти – благодаря официальному импорту иностранной одежды. Именно в 1960-е годы, согласно Бартлетт, в качестве реакции потребителей на консервативность социалистической моды возникает еще один нарратив советской моды – «повседневный». (Бартлетт 2011: 26) Утопический и социалистический модные нарративы, хотя и были как концепты идеологически противоположны, были задуманы сверху, соответствовали неким идеальным представлениям и получали свое воплощение только в штучных, репрезентативных примерах, но не в массовом производстве. В отличие от них повседневная мода представляла собой адаптацию модных западных тенденций самими потребителями на массовом уровне.

В условиях, когда советская швейная продукция не отвечала спросу (отчасти из-за стоящей за ней идеологии, а отчасти из-за качества конечной продукции), а количество официального импорта одежды было недостаточным, советские потребители были вынуждены искать альтернативные каналы приобретения модной одежды. С одной стороны, импортную одежду привозили из-за границы как иностранцы, так и советские граждане, побывавшие за рубежом. Она могла распространяться через знакомых, комиссионные магазины и фарцовщиков. С другой стороны, люди шили сами, ориентируясь на одежду из иностранных журналов и западных кинофильмов, или обращались к частным портным[3]. В условиях повышенного спроса на вещи, привезенные из-за границы, или сшитые «под западные», а также из-за неповоротливости советской швейной промышленности и запрещенности официального частного предпринимательства актуальным становилось подпольное производство модной одежды в СССР.

Кустари и цеховики: кампания по борьбе с пережитками начала 1960-х гг.

Проблема подпольного производства существовала в СССР с момента запрета частного предпринимательства. Как показала на примере кустарей и артелей Джули Хесслер, законодательство в отношении «частников» в период с 1920-х до 1950-х годов несколько раз менялось, однако вне зависимости от него частное производство никогда не исчезало и приобрело особенно важную роль в снабжении населения во время войны (Hessler 1998). Исследования структуры потребления населения середины 1950-х годов, которые проводились Центральным статистическим управлением СССР, показывают, что около 80% семей на территории РСФСР хоть раз обращались к покупкам вне магазинов (РГАЭ 1562-26-921: 153). При этом, если смотреть на потребительскую корзину граждан в целом, то около 20% всех непродовольственных товаров покупалось в 1950-е годы у частных лиц. Конечно, на черном рынке продавалась не только продукция, произведенная «частниками»: ЦСУ сообщали, что среди товаров, продающихся с рук, были и новые фабричные товары, продаваемые спекулянтами, и товары, бывшие в употреблении, но также и продукция, произведенная частными лицами (РГАЭ 1562-26-

---

[2] Министр культуры СССР Н.А.Михайлов писал в 1956 г. в ЦК КПСС: «В результате расширения культурных связей Советского Союза с зарубежными странами, число приобретаемых для проката в СССР иностранных кинофильмов за последнее время значительно увеличилось». (Записка министра культуры СССР Н.А.Михайлова с согласием секретарей ЦК КПСС о разрешении министерству самостоятельно решать вопрос о приобретении кинофильмов капиталистических стран) (Водопьянова 2001:499)

[3] Государственные ателье, призванные восполнить низкое качество швейной продукции и дефицит импорта, также не справлялись со своей задачей: в постановлении ЦК КПСС и Совета Министров СССР от 10 августа 1962 года «О дальнейшем улучшении бытового обслуживания населения» отмечалось, что из-за «неудовлетворительной организации обслуживания населения в существующей сети ателье, павильонов и мастерских вынуждает людей обращаться к услугам частных лиц. (Лебина 2003: 214)

382: 83-84). Из непродовольственных товаров с рук, прежде всего, покупалась именно одежда (РГАЭ 1562-26-382: 89).

Придя к власти, Хрущев с новой силой развернул борьбу против «частнособственнических пережитков»: в апреле 1956 года было принято постановление ЦК КПСС «*О реорганизации промысловой кооперации*». Если до этого ремесленники могли объединяться в артели, получать сырье и оборудование наравне с государственными фабриками и даже торговать своей продукцией (при условии уплаты крупных налогов), то теперь создание промысловых коопераций было запрещено, а существующие преобразованы в государственные швейные предприятия (Костыр-ченко 2012: 356). В условиях, когда все швейники стали вынуждены работать только в рамках установленного фабрике сверху плана, участились случаи использования госу-дарственного производства для частной деятельности: работники предприятий исполь-зовали излишки сырья для собственного производства. Еще в 1955-м году произ-водство «левой» продукции получило отражение в советском кинофильме «*Дело Румянцева*», в центре сюжета которого лежит проблема транспортировки «левого» товара с фабрики (Хейфиц 1955). В начале 1960-х годов было устроено несколько показательных процессов против подпольных производителей, действовавших в рамках госфабрик, многие из них были приговорены к высшей мере наказания (Эвельсон 1986). В закрытом письме ЦК КПСС 1962 года говорилось о необходимости борьбы с теми «темными дельцами», которые используют для частного производства государственные производственные мощности, а для сокрытия этого вступают в сговор с должностными лицами, чем наносят материальный ущерб государству и «разлагают кадры» (Хлевнюк 2009: 201). В том же письме приводились примеры только что раскрытых дел в Московской и Курской областях, Украинской, Узбекской и Киргизской СССР, где «расхитители народного добра» «получали за взятки дефи-цитное сырье», «производили из него скрытую от учета продукцию, которую затем расхищали». (Хлевнюк 2009: 202). Однако специальное слово для обозначения подпольных производителей, пользующихся производственными мощностями для изготовления товара «налево» – «цеховики» – возникает лишь в начале 1980-х годов: Жиль Фаварель-Гарриг отмечает его появление в официальных отчетах о борьбе с хищениями социалистической собственности лишь в 1981 году (Favarel-Garrigues 2011: 61), в середине 1980-х оно уже активно употребляется в открытых источниках (Буцева 1997: 605).

Ассортимент подпольных производителей: самопал и фирмА

Подпольное производство модной одежды, как уже было сказано выше, могло быть организовано двумя способами. Первый – использование существующих швейных цехов или же государственного ателье для «левого» пошива. Второй – устройство производства на дому, в одиночку или с наймом дополнительных работников. Однако вне зависимости от организации производства главным для «частников» была ориентация на модные образцы. Источником моды была западная одежда, считавшаяся в обществе культовой[4].

Американский антрополог Алексей Юрчак в своем исследовании позднесоветской повседневной культуры отмечает важность для последнего советского поколения понятия "воображаемого Запада". Иностранная музыка, одежда и атрибуты образа жизни культивировались в позднем СССР, потому что представляли собой для советских граждан символ чего-то недостижимого. Одновременно они приобретали на советской почве новые коннотации, часто сильно расходясь с западными оригиналами. Одним из

---

[4] О культе западных товаров в соцстранах см. (Bar-Haïm 1987)

элементов "воображаемого Запада" Юрчак считает феномен культа импортной одежды. Он отмечает, что важными были не бренды, а сам факт иностранного происхождения вещи. (YURCHAK 2013: 196-197)

В зависимости от масштаба и техники работы подпольного производства я выделяю два подхода подпольных производителей к производству одежды: одни производители шили вещи, по стилю похожие на западные, но не имитирующие конкретные фирмы, другие же стремились произвести одежду, которую можно было выдать за пошитую за рубежом, то есть, подделывали импортную продукцию. Ключевым в этих подделках было нашивание на одежду иностранных лейблов. В условиях, когда импортные вещи становились в обществе культовыми, стоили дорого, но были в дефиците, подпольные производители начинали сами шить «импорт». Юрчак в своем рассуждении о культе иностранной одежды отмечает, что лейбл был важен не как обозначение какой-то марки, а лишь как подтверждение принадлежности вещи к «воображаемому Западу». (YURCHAK 2013: 197)

Конечно, произвести вещь, неотличимую от импортной, было сложнее: требовались качественные ткани, современное оборудование, наличие западных этикеток и более скрупулезная работа. Один из подпольных производителей, шивший «фирменные» джинсы в 1970-х гг. в Ленинграде, вспоминает, что спрос был огромный, и потребители были заинтересованы не в разнообразии моделей, а именно в точном следовании западному образцу:

> «Люди хотели только Levis, Montana – на что приходила мода, весь народ ходил в одном и том же. Не то что «у тебя такие джинсы, а я хочу другие», наоборот: «у всех такие и мне такие тоже надо». Доходило до идиотизма: там должны были быть все вот эти пришиты этикеточки [...] Потом: настоящие джинсы они делаются на специальных машинах, которые делают цепной стежок – если посмотреть внутрь джинсов, то можно увидеть, что там строчка идет такая петельками – так вот эти петельки приходилось проделывать вручную» (ИНТЕРВЬЮ С КТ)[5].

Шить одежду, не претендующую на звание импортной, а просто более модную, чем та, которая обычно предлагалась в советских магазинах, было проще. Называлась такая продукция «самопалом» и стоила в несколько раз меньше той, что шилась «под фирмУ» («фирмОй» называлась импортная одежда). Зато ее можно было производить большими масштабами, тогда как «подделки» производились в количестве нескольких штук в месяц. Иногда цеховики, имевшие масштабное производство, пытались тоже пришивать на свою продукцию иностранные ярлыки, однако такие нетщательные подделки быстро разоблачались знающими покупателями.[6] Наличие подпольно произведенной в СССР одежды заставляло потребителей хорошо разбираться в импортной продукции, умение отличать настоящую «фирмУ» от подделки цеховиков было важным навыком. Вот как об этом вспоминает современник:

> «Вспомните вообще процесс покупки у фарцовщика: если ты идёшь покупать фирмовые штаны впервые, то берёшь с собой «опытного» друга, который проверит лейбак, деним (ёлочка у рэнглер!, диагональ у ливайс), строчку, косичку на

[5] Отчасти подобные подделки были похожи на современный контрафакт (подделку «люксовых» брендов (см. ГОРАЛИК 2009)), однако сегодня люди покупают подделку с рук по более низкой цене в условиях, когда у них нет денег на покупку оригинала в фирменном магазине. В СССР же подделка покупалась из-за отсутствия доступа к оригиналу и по той же цене, что и оригинал.

[6] См. фото 2: „Пуговица от джинсов, произведенная цеховиками в Одессе в конце 1970-х гг.“

> изнанке, клёпки, зиппер и наконец в особо скрупулёзных случаях, трутся ли, линяют ли джинсы правильно. Если друга взять не удавалось, то уж инструкцию на что смотреть при покупке «фирмы» учили наизусть» (О СОВЕТСКОЙ ФАРЦОВКЕ 2011).

Для производителей, и просто имитирующих стиль, и напрямую подделывающих импортную одежду, существовало два основных источника моделей: сама западная одежда и иностранные журналы мод. Иностранные каталоги одежды достать в СССР было не так просто. В государственных ателье портные должны были шить, ориентируясь на советские журналы, в редких случаях они могли получить журналы соцстран (ЗАХАРОВА 2007: 67-68). Доступ к западным журналам мод имели только дома моделей в Москве и Ленинграде (АЗАРХИ 2009: 15). Подпольные производители вспоминают, что моряки загранплавания и другие выезжавшие за рубеж советские граждане привозили из-за границы на продажу не только саму одежду, но и такие каталоги, как, например, «*Otto*» и «*Neckermann*». Вырезанные оттуда картинки могли передаваться из рук в руки и долго использоваться в качестве образцов (ИНТЕРВЬЮ С КТ). Другой возможный путь получения образцов – распарывание западной вещи для использования ее в качестве лекала. В книге журналиста Михаила Козырева, посвященной подпольному производству товаров в СССР, в частности одежды, приводятся воспоминания жены подпольного производителя одежды:

> «[…] Нужны были «актуальные» модели. И Рабинович их покупал. У тех самых грузинских знакомых, которые завозили их через Батуми и Сухуми. За один [спортивный] костюм Сергей Рабинович платил около 200 рублей. Потом брал портняжный нож и аккуратно, строчку за строчкой, распарывал все швы. С «разобранной» вещи снималась выкройка, и модель запускалась в производство. Увидев в первый раз, как муж собственными руками разрезает вещь, обошедшуюся в баснословные полторы месячных зарплаты советского инженера, Светлана была в шоке» (КОЗЫРЕВ 2012: 131-132).

По мере развития «повседневной» моды (БАРТЛЕТТ 2011: 26) спросом (прежде всего, среди молодежи) начинала пользоваться не модная одежда в целом, а конкретные ее элементы. В 1977-м году в статье, посвященной проблеме подпольного производства, газета «*Комсомольская правда*», цитируя одного из таких производителей, писала, что наибольшим спросом из нелегально произведенной продукции среди населения пользуются «джинсы, джинсовые костюмы, «батники» (то есть приталенные рубахи) и майки» (ЩЕКОЧИХИН 1977: 4). Действительно, начиная с конца 1960-х годов, не производившиеся советской промышленностью джинсы стали пользоваться в СССР особенным спросом. Они начали приобретать популярность еще после фестиваля молодежи и студентов 1957-го года (КОЗЛОВ 1998: 104, 114), а их привлекательность для советских граждан в 1970-е – 1980-е годы получила отражение даже в подцензурных источниках. На одной из карикатур в журнале «*Крокодил*» за 1978-й год с иронией изображен молодой человек, заявляющий своей матери «Или джинсы «Супер-райфл» или объявляю голодовку», на другой – библейский змей в качестве искушения предлагает Еве не яблоко, а именно джинсы (ГОРОХОВ 1978: 4; УБОРЕВИЧ-БОРОВСКИЙ 1978: 4). Большим спросом пользовались и футболки с иностранными надписями. Поскольку советская промышленность имела только стандартные шаблоны расцветок, а прежде всего это были геометрические рисунки (традиция, идущая еще из утопической моды 1920-х годов (ЛЕБИНА 2008: 30), то любые «принты» на обычных футболках воспринимались как символ модной молодежной одежды. Степень распространения моды на майки, а также их подпольное производство в СССР получили отражение в советском фильме 1984-го года «*Прохиндиада или бег на месте*». Один из героев говорит:

> «Ну, вы же видели эти майки с иностранными надписями – так сказать, последнее увлечение нашей молодежи? [...] Оказывается, это наше же производство – конечно, кустарное, так сказать, подпольный бизнес, но ведь целая фабрика! И делали на этом миллионы!» (Трегубович 1984)

Один из подпольных производителей из Пятигорска вспоминает, что в начале 1980-х годов большим спросом пользовались изготовленные им майки с названиями иностранных музыкальных групп (Интервью с АД).

Историк моды Ольга Вайнштейн отмечает тот момент, когда профессиональные частные портнихи в 1960-е годы начали шить «под фирму», как точку важного культурного сдвига:

> «Эта новая ситуация означала радикальную перемену в ориентации портних как культурных производителей. Если портнихи старой школы продолжали дореволюционные традиции ремесла и демонстрировали модели аристократического поведения, то молодое поколение мастериц предпочитало идти в ногу со временем и любой ценой ответить на вызов современной западной моды. Первое время портнихи старательно шили вещи в западном духе и выдавали их за «фирменные»: порой на таком изделии можно было видеть ярлык с заветными словами made in. [...] Неумелые имитации заслужили презрительное именование «самопал», а искусные воспринимались как настоящая фирменная одежда. На этом историческом витке портниха оказалась невидимой по [...] социоэкономическим причинам – гламур иностранных брендов оказался сильнее преимуществ ручной работы (Вайнштейн 2007: 123–124).

Элементы рынка: снабжение и сбыт подпольной продукции

Для производителей одежды, действовавших подпольно, всегда существовала проблема получения сырья и продажи произведенной продукции. При «цеховом» производстве производители имели доступ к казенному оборудованию и сырью: чаще всего «левая» продукция шилась из излишков ткани или из ткани, списанной по причине брака. Однако, когда поставлявшиеся на фабрику ткани не подходили для подпольного производства, цеховики искали другие источники снабжения. Так, например, бывший глава киевского отдела ОБХСС вспоминал, что главный инженер киевской галантерейной фабрики Михаил Шер в 1960-е годы договорился через друзей на Дарницком шелковом комбинате, выпускавшем нейлоновую нить для производства парашютов, о поставках ценного материала на фабрику и стал подпольно производить из него пользовавшиеся большим спросом нейлоновые рубашки (Головин 2011).

Индивидуальному же предпринимателю всегда приходилось самому изыскивать и швейные машины, и сырье. Михаил Козырев в своей книге приводит пример московского цеховика, формально работавшего в НИИ, однако имевшего дома шесть швейных машин, на которых посменно работали восемь швей (Козырев 2012: 129-134). Московский подпольный предприниматель Александр Паникин в своих воспоминаниях пишет о том, как он смог решить проблему покупки ватина для изготовления дефицитных в СССР детских пинеток:

> «Ватин я закупал [...] прямо на фабрике, поскольку этого материала нам требовались тысячи метров. [...] Фабрикам было запрещено продавать населению товары

> за наличные деньги. Реализация шла только через безналичные расчеты с торговыми организациями. Поскольку мы не были юридическим лицом с расчетным счетом, банковские каналы оплаты были для нас недоступны. А наличные деньги на фабрике никто не принял бы. [...] И вот новаторский ход — оплату партии ватина отправил на банковский счет фабрики обычным почтовым переводом! Таким способом мы вошли в безналичное обращение» (ПАНИКИН 1997: 174).

Иногда подпольные производители одежды получали ткани с производств, не имевших отношения к швейной промышленности. Так, сын ленинградского подпольного предпринимателя в своих воспоминаниях рассказывает, что его отец, работал на заводе оптических приборов и, имея доступ к замше, в которую оборачивали линзы, сумел наладить из ее остатков пошив модных тогда пиджаков, курток и юбок сначала через частных портных, а затем на базе государственного ателье (НИЛОВ 2006: 72-76). Однако для небольшого производства на дому материалы чаще не добывались на предприятиях, а покупались в магазинах или привозились из-за границы. Ленинградский подпольный производитель вспоминает: «Как выглядела тогда жизнь с этим связанная? Каждый день поход по магазинам – не выкинули ли новые ткани» (ИНТЕРВЬЮ С КТ). Используя материалы, купленные в обычных магазинах, цеховикам удавалось производить пользовавшуюся большим спросом одежду, которой советская легкая промышленность не выпускала вовсе. Тот же производитель вспоминает, как в начале 1980-х он стал производить «фирменные» пуховые пальто из подручных материалов:

> «Ты покупаешь какое-то количество детских пуховых одеял (взрослых одеял просто не было в продаже) – в них процент содержания пуха был очень высокий, перьев почти не было, – и из одного одеяла получалось полтора-два пуховика. Покупаешь болонью плюс нужна была пропитка – чтобы пух не лез. Болонья, правда, не очень котировалась потому что цвета были не очень, плюс она шуршащая такая была в отличие от того, что делали на Западе. Потом в продаже появился индийский тик –это был просто подарок: он совершенно свободно лежал - никому особо был не нужен – но не пропускает пух и цвета хорошие! Нашиваешь этикетку и продаешь за 200 рублей – оно же как настоящее» (ИНТЕРВЬЮ С КТ).

Помимо тканей, продававшихся в магазинах, подпольные производители использовали и импортную ткань. Моряки и другие ездившие за рубеж советские граждане привозили ткани из-за границы и либо продавали ее напрямую, либо сдавали в комиссионные магазины. Один из московских цеховиков вспоминает, что источником тканей могли также быть иностранцы, прежде всего аспиранты и студенты из соцлагеря, привозившие по два-три рулона ткани на продажу (ИНТЕРВЬЮ С ИХ). Немногие регулярно выезжавшие за рубеж советские граждане быстро поняли, что сотрудничать с цеховиками выгоднее, чем привозить готовую одежду: «Мой знакомый в 80-е имел возможность часто выезжать за границу, был хоккеистом в команде высшей лиги. Так вот он из-за рубежа вез не джинсы, а ткань и фурнитуру. Затем все это за хорошие деньги сдавал знакомому цеховику» (ЖВАЧКОВЫЙ ДИСКУРС 2012).

Пытаясь удовлетворить спрос населения на модную одежду и тем самым побороть подпольное производство, советская промышленность в начале 1980-х стала производить собственные джинсы. Эта продукция не пользовалась большим спросом, однако стала еще одним источником материала для подпольного пошива. Цеховики использовали советские джинсы для изготовления более качественной продукции:

«Был период, когда появились в продаже советские джинсы, они закупили какое-то количество нормального денима, но шили безобразно, сшито было как советские рабочие штаны. Вот их мы тоже покупали и перешивали, там надо было практически все переделывать, их использовали скорее просто как ткань» (Интервью с КТ).

При пошиве вещей «под фирмУ» ключевыми были не только ткани и модели, но и фурнитура и упоминавшиеся выше лейблы. Фурнитура – то есть пуговицы, заклепки и молнии – иногда тоже привозилась из-за границы (Ганулич 2007: 88). Наряду с этим ею подпольных производителей могли снабжать и другие предприниматели: на предприятиях, где были штамповочные прессы, подпольно изготовлялась фурнитура – сначала разово под заказ, а затем уже массово целыми комплектами. Лейблы западных фирм поначалу тоже изготовлялись на полиграфических предприятиях под заказ, а затем стали создаваться целые подпольные «фирмы» по печати иностранных этикеток (Нилов 2006: 102). Иллюстрацией того, что суть деятельности цеховиков часто заключалась не столько в пошиве, сколько в точной подделке западной модели, может служить рассказ одного из цеховиков о том, как для изготовления «настоящих джинсов» использовались джинсы индийского производства, продававшиеся в советских магазинах:

«Когда выбрасывали индийские джинсы, их в течение двух часов раскупали, то есть надо было вовремя попасть, отстоять сумасшедшую очередь, или иметь знакомых в магазине, или потом перекупить дороже у специальных людей. Зато потом можно было просто чуть-чуть отпороть карман, нашить букву М – это значит «Монтана», нашить лейблы – работы на час-два, а после этого это уже можно было продавать их как джинсы Монтана за 180 рублей» (Интервью с КТ).

«Фирменный» вид повышал цену товара в несколько раз. Поскольку импортные вещи почти невозможно было найти в магазине и трудно было купить с рук, покупка продукции цеховиков становилась еще одним каналом доступа к статусной одежде. Как сформулировал в интервью один из бывших цеховиков: «Если это фирменная вещь – с фирменной этикеткой, то неважно сшита она за границей или здесь, у нее должна быть соответствующая цена, потому что это фирменная вещь, то есть на нее уже молиться можно» (Интервью с ИХ).

Однако, как было сказано выше, в условиях дефицита спросом пользовались и «нефирменные» вещи, ключевым в них был западный вид, даже при плохом качестве. Бывший одесский цеховик Григорий Арбер вспоминал в интервью, что можно было изготовлять «самопальные» джинсы из подручных материалов:

«Берётся самая обыкновенная хлопчатобумажная ткань, так называемая «Орбита». Выкрашивается синькой, а потом пропитывается раствором клея ПВА. Эти штаны невозможно было надеть, они были тверды как картон. Но с лихвой соответствовали распространённому в то время народному поверью, будто настоящие джинсы должны «стоять колом»» (Арбер: как это делалось на Малой Арнаутской 2006).

Такая продукция не выдавалась за фирменную, стоила дешевле, однако тоже пользовалась спросом, т.к. отсылала к западным моделям.

Существовало несколько каналов распространения подпольно произведенной продукции. Для сбыта продукции, производившейся массово и не претендующей на звание «настоящего импорта», в первую очередь, использовались рынки или «толкучки». Еще в 1950-е годы в отчете ЦСУ сообщалось:

> «Специальные рынки для продажи подержанных вещей, кустарных изделий и новых непродовольственных товаров, оказавшихся неподходящими по фасону, размеру и т.д. имеются почти во всех крупных городах. На этих рынках в нарушение действующих правил в значительных размерах производится и спекулятивная торговля новыми непродовольственными товарами и кустарными изделиями» (РГАЭ 1562-26-382: 93).

Несмотря на многочисленные запреты, подобные рынки постоянно возникали вновь. Многие вспоминают, например, существовавшую в Москве толкучку около железнодорожной платформы «Беговая» (Ганулич 2007: 88). На рынках товары продавались с рук или из грузовиков и происхождение вещи узнать было невозможно. Тем не менее, подобные толкучки пользовались большим спросом. Один из информантов вспоминает:

> «В начале 1980-х мы были в Запорожье. Специально по совету местных знакомых пошли на толкучку – они рекомендовали ее как место где можно купить модные и импортные вещи. Нам, неизбалованным советским людям, то, что там продавалось, действительно, казалось супер-красивым, ярким и модным» (Интервью с В.Е.).

Еще одной возможностью распространения нелегально произведенной продукции была обычная розничная сеть. По договоренности с директором магазина подпольная продукция могла сбываться наравне с легально произведенными товарами. В кинофильме «*Последняя индульгенция*» показано, как кроссовки, произведенные рижским цеховиком, продавались с лотка в обычном универмаге по поддельным накладным. Информант вспоминает, что его мать, работавшая в государственном ателье и шившая «налево» модные халаты, сбывала их потом, дав взятку товароведу, в небольшом магазине при местном рынке, пришив на них «левые» ценники со штампом магазина (Интервью с С.Щ.).

Для тех вещей, которые шились в малых количествах и являлись подделкой западной продукции, боле эффективной и менее рискованной была продажа через комиссионные магазины (Нилов 2006: 76). Они брали комиссию в размере около 10%, однако в этом случае подпольным производителям при небольших масштабах производства не нужны были даже дополнительные договоренности. В газете «*Комсомольская правда*» 1977-го года так описывался сбыт подпольной продукции со слов одного из «дельцов»: «Чаще всего продаем у комиссионных магазинов. Изготовил сто маек [...] Стоишь спокойно, подходят всякие люди, тихо спрашивают: «Что есть?» Отвечаешь» (Щекочихин 1977: 4). Эффективной также была продажа левой продукции через фарцовщиков (Романов, Ярская-Смирнова 2007: 155, Вайнштейн 2007: 123). Поскольку через них чаще всего продавались вещи, привезенные из-за границы, этот способ распространения как бы подтверждал «настоящесть» левой вещи. Также под видом иностранных вещей можно было сбывать продукцию цеховиков через магазины «*Березка*» – сеть магазинов ограниченного доступа, где продавались в основном импортные товары за валюту, специальные чеки и сертификаты, выдаваемые в обмен на валюту избранным категориям советских граждан - по предварительно договоренности с сотрудниками этих магазинов (Козырев 2012: 129–134).

Для тех, кто производил одежду небольшими партиями «под фирмУ», существовали и необычные способы продажи вещей. «Статусная» одежда, будучи в дефиците, рекламировала сама себя: «Например, кто-то, кто купил сшитые мной джинсы, работает в НИИ каком-нибудь, приходит на работу в джинсах – ему, конечно, говорят «где ты такое достал?» Он говорит: «Я могу помочь вам тоже достать» и у меня появляются новые покупатели» (Интервью с КТ). Модные вещи становились и универсальным средством оплаты:

> «[У меня был знакомый цеховик]. У него всегда в машине валялось какое-то количество этих готовых изделий. И он говорил «я часто прихожу куда-то в кафе, в ресторан или в автосервис и мне не нужны деньги – я расплачиваюсь своей продукцией» (Интервью с ИХ).

Осуждение и оправдание: отношение к подпольным производителям в публичном дискурсе

Поскольку частное предпринимательство считалось чуждым социалистическому образу жизни, то отношение к нему в официальном дискурсе было негативным. Преследование подпольных предпринимателей было как идеологическим, так и уголовным. Для привлечения их к ответственности использовались обычно две главы уголовного кодекса: «*Преступления против социалистической собственности*», включавшая в себя хищение, растрату, причинение имущественного ущерба и недобросовестное отношение к охране государственного имущества (Уголовный кодекс РСФСР: 62–69), а также «*Хозяйственные преступления*», куда входили частнопредпринимательская деятельность, спекуляция, а также «выпуск недоброкачественной, нестандартной или некомплектной продукции» (Уголовный кодекс РСФСР: 87–91). Однако даже в условиях хрущевских законов, ужесточивших юридическое положение предпринимателей, оставалось небольшое пространство для легального существования индивидуальных производителей (не имевших подчиненных). Некоторые цеховики пытались действовать в рамках закона. Александр Паникин в своих воспоминаниях пишет, что старался законно доставать все материалы, покупая их у фабрик по официальным бумагам, а для производства и продажи своей продукции оформил «патент на индивидуальную трудовую деятельность». Узнать о возможности оформления подобного патента было сложно, сам Паникин пишет, что информация об этом утаивалась, к тому же многие боялись получать патенты, не желая привлекать к своей деятельности внимание правоохранительных органов. Также Паникин хотел заплатить со всего своего дохода полагающийся налог, однако, по его воспоминаниям, чиновник предложил ему занизить реальную сумму, боясь для себя последствий. Несмотря на все легальное оформления своего бизнеса, Паникин тем не менее был позднее арестован: по его словам, у правоохранительных органов не было доказательств незаконности его деятельности, однако человека, занимающегося частным производством и имеющего крупный доход, нельзя было оставить на свободе (Паникин 1997: 168, 176–178).

Действительно, помимо существующих статей уголовного кодекса, в официальной риторике педалировалось представление о том, что любая частнопредпринимательская деятельность по определению считается хищением социалистической собственности – поскольку все, что произведено в СССР, является народным достоянием. Н.Ф. Чистяков, бывший сотрудник КГБ СССР, в своих воспоминаниях, написанных в 1979-м году, рассказывает, как в начале 1960-х участвовал в разоблачении группы цеховиков. Будучи сотрудниками лечебно-трудовых мастерских психоневрологического диспансера в Москве, они наладили там производство модных шерстяных изделий. На заводах они приобретали необходимое оборудование, доставали сырье, а больные в рамках трудотерапии, официально предусмотренной диспансером, шили одежду. Затем «дельцы» договаривались с другими предприятиями, чтобы те красили и отделывали выработанный ими товар. Сбывалась продукция по договоренности в торговых палатках. Формально обвинить предпринимателей можно было лишь в том, что они платили взятки, чтобы добывать сырье. Однако Чистяков на протяжении всего своего рассказа настаивает на том, что «дельцы» занимались хищением социалистической собственности. Не поясняя, в чем конкретно состояло хищение, он концентрирует внимание читателя на том, какие крупные суммы денег были найдены у преступников, какой шикарный образ жизни они вели, и даже обвиняет их в том, что они не читали книг, не ходили в театр и кино:

> «Радужный мираж легкой наживы соблазнял. Забыв долг, утратив совесть, поправ мораль и закон, эти люди встали на путь тягчайших преступлений, разворовывая то, что мы называем священным и неприкосновенным, экономической основой нашего социалистического общества. [...] Организатора подпольного трикотажного цеха Ройфмана, так же как и Шакермана, совершенно ничто не интересовало, кроме денег и ценностей. Газет он не читал, книг тоже, в театр и кино не ходил по нескольку лет». (Чистяков 1979: 228)

Первичным в поведении цеховиков для Чистякова становится именно их чуждая система ценностей, а не конкретные преступления.

В кинофильме «*Черный бизнес*», снятом в 1965-м году по мотивам того же расследования, авторам, по всей видимости, тоже показалось, что в дословном изложении криминальность деятельности цеховиков будет для зрителей неочевидна. К реальной истории была добавлена новая линия: работники диспансера, желая обратить свои накопления в твердую валюту, договорились с иностранцами, едущими в СССР, чтобы те привезли им из-за границы золотые монеты. Однако выяснилось, что сами иностранцы являются шпионами и полученные в обмен на золото рубли используют для вербовки работников советских оборонных предприятий. Таким образом, авторы фильма давали понять, что подпольное производство модной одежды – путь к измене родине (Журавлев 1965).

Несмотря на осуждение и провозглашение необходимости борьбы с подобными преступлениями, уголовных дел именно в отношении цеховиков заводилось не так много. Жиль Фаварель-Гарриг называет подпольный бизнес самой сложной формой экономической преступности и указывает на тот факт, что подобные преступления почти не упоминаются в отчетах МВД 1970-х годов (Фаварель-Гарриг 2005: 83).

Однако помимо осуждения цеховиков с уголовной и идеологической точек зрения, чем дальше, тем больше в официальной риторике начинали звучать соображения о рациональной основе существования подпольного производства в СССР. В детек-тивном фильме 1966 года «*Два билета на дневной сеанс*» разоблачается подпольное производство на швейной фабрике в Риге. Характерно, что в фильме не говорится, какой именно товар подпольно шьют на фабрике, однако упоминаются «фирменные» этикетки:

> «Вы подумайте! – да у них здесь целый подпольный цех, работали с размахом: и представьте, на производстве у нас эта публика звезд с неба не хватала, ничем не выделялась, а тут поди ж ты, вот что значит материальная заинтересованность. – А вы посмотрите какие фабричные марки! самые заграничные – и ловко сделано! – блеск: Париж, Лондон, Стокгольм - учитывают покупателя, мерзавцы. Ведь на такой ярлык в комиссионке как мотыльки летят. – Ну что тут говорить... Нет, все-таки надо прямо сказать: пережитки – это само собой, но нету еще у нас этой гибкости, умения учитывать спрос – вот это и порождает – ведь это что ж – золотая жила, для делового человека – это все» (Раппопорт 1966: 1:22:28-1:23:27).

Из этого пассажа видно, что авторы фильма не только дают понять, что работники фабрики стараются, только если чувствуют материальную заинтересованность, но и что «левая» продукция пользуется спросом, именно потому что легальная отечественная продукция не может удовлетворить запросов покупателей.

Еще отчетливее сознание того факта, что отечественная промышленность неэффективна в производстве модных, пользующихся спросом вещей, проявляется в риторике 1970-х годов. В упомянутой выше статье из «*Комсомольской правды*» автор сетует: сами майки, на которые цеховики ставили модные западные «принты», были официально произведены на советских фабриках, а значит, достаточно было сделать немного для того, чтобы самим удовлетворить спрос молодежи. Здесь речь идет уже о том, что покупатель отчасти прав, предпочитая подпольно произведенную вещь фабричной.

> «Мне обидно стало за тех, кто отдал бешеные деньги только за то, чтобы полюбоваться мнимоиностраным клеймом на абсолютно нашенских майках. Но еще больше обидно за тех, кто эти майки произвел. Что у них, краски что ли не было? И уверен я, что люди оказавшие бесплатную услугу [подпольному предпринимателю] Мише хотя бы тем, что произвели эти майки, и телевизор смотрят, и радио слушают, и газеты читают, и молодых людей на улицах встречают. Следовательно, должны знать, что сейчас модно, а что нет. […] Я предвижу возражения, что другой, не Миша, и то что есть на прилавках наденет. Правильно. Другой наденет. И третий наденет. И четвертый. А пятый пойдет на «толкучку» доставать себе то, чего нет на прилавках или бывает редко. Шестой же поймет, что можно жить тем, что снабжать пятого модными шмотками» (Щекочихин 1977: 4).

Заключение

Советский экономический проект подразумевал создание глобальной плановой системы, которая бы запускала в производство точное количество нужной продукции, учитывая потребности людей и действуя максимально рационально. На деле система давала сбои, создавая дефициты в одном месте и перепроизводства – в другом, качество в условиях отсутствия личной заинтересованности тоже страдало. Однако в области производства и потребления модной одежды плановый подход был обречен изначально. Сама задумка просчитывания всех нужд, идея их объективности и неизменности была неприменима к личному вкусу и модным тенденциям. К тому же в условиях взаимодействия, пусть и поверхностного, советского общества с Западом, предлагавшим пример альтернативного взгляда на моду, советский подход не выдерживал конкуренции. Все это создавало почву для множества неформальных практик, в частности подпольного пошива псевдо-импортной одежды. На примере деятельности цеховиков видно, какую огромную роль играла западная продукция в советской повседневности. Самым большим спросом среди подпольно произведенной одежды пользовалась именно та, которая полностью имитировала иностранную. Находя образцы, налаживая поставки необходимых комплектующих, организуя сбыт «цеховой» продукции, предприниматели действовали согласно рыночным механизмам, деформированным из-за нелегальности их существования. Подпольные производители модной одежды в СССР «исправляли» плановую экономику за счет ее же неэффективно потраченных ресурсов: задействовали списанную ткань, перешивали плохо сделанные джинсы, увеличивали зарплату незаинтересованных работников. Находясь вне рамок правового поля, они создавали собственное рыночное пространство внутри советской системы, заслуживая сдержанное уважение даже в официальной риторике.

Summary

The article tells about the underground mass manufacturing of clothes in 1960-1980s in the USSR based on memoirs, oral history, Soviet media and films. The illegal Soviet entrepreneurs organized their production inside state factories or at home with their goal being to benefit by the demand for fashionable clothes that the state-run industry failed to satisfy. The main models for illegal production of clothes were imported items, which were extremely popular among Soviet urban citizens, especially the youth. The article shows how elements of the market worked in the planned economy, how underground producers compensated for the shortcomings of the state production and how the phenomenon of illegal clothes manufacturing was seen in the public discourse.

Библиография

BAR-HAÏM, G. 1987. The Meaning of Western Commerical Artifacts for Eastern European Youth. In: *Journal of Contemporary Ethnography* 16 (2), 205–226.

FAVAREL-GARRIGUES, G. 2011. *Policing Economic Crime in Russia. From Soviet Planned Economy to Privatization.* London.

HESSLER, J. 1998. A postwar Perestroika? Toward a History of Private Enterprise in the USSR. In: *Slavic Review* 57 (3), 516–542.

MCCAULEY, M. 2008. *The Rise and Fall of the Soviet Union.* New York

SAMPSON, S. 1988. "May You Live Only by Your Salary!": The Unplanned Economy in Eastern Europe. In: *Social Justice* 15 (3-4), 148–150.

SIMIS, K.M. 1982. *USSR, Secrets Of A Corrupt Society: The Secret World of Soviet Capitalism.* New York.

YURCHAK, A. 2013. *Everything Was Forever, Until It Was No More: The Last Soviet Generation.* Princeton.

АЗАРХИ, С.В. 2009. Один дом на Невском. In: *Теория моды* 14, 9–34.

АРБЕР. 2006. Как это делалось на Малой Арнаутской. In: *Фокус.* 14 октября 2006, http://focus.ua/society/644/ (28.03.2014)

БАРТЛЕТТ, Д. 2011. *FashionEast. Призрак, бродивший по Восточной Европе.* Москва.

БУЦЕВА, Т. et. al. 1997. *Новые слова и значения: Словарь-справочник по материалам прессы и литературы 1980-х гг.* СПб.

ВАЙНШТЕЙН, О. Б. 2007. Моё любимое платье: портниха как культурный герой в Советской России. In: *Теория моды.* 3, 101-126.

ВОДОПЬЯНОВА, З.К. 2001. *Аппарат ЦК КПСС и культура. 1953-1957.* Москва.

ГАНУЛИЧ, А. 2007. *Denim, или Все о джинсах.* Москва.

ГОЛОВИН, В. 2011. Цеховики. In: *Forbes Украина* 10, http://forbes.ua/magazine/forbes/1332812-cehoviki (21.08.2014)

ГОРАЛИК, Л. 2009. Тень роскоши: будущее люксовых подделок. In: *Теория моды* 12, 57–72.

ГОРОХОВ, Е. 1978. Или джинсы «Супер-райфл» или объявляю голодовку. In: *Крокодил* 23, 4.

ЖВАЧКОВЫЙ ДИСКУРС. 2012 In: *Сообщество «Back in the USSR»,* http://maxpark.com/community/129/content/932043 (28.03.2014).

ЧЕРНЫЙ БИЗНЕС. 1965 R: Василий Журавлев. СССР: Мосфильм.

ЗАХАРОВА, Л. 2007. Советская мода 1950–60-х годов: политика, экономика, повседневность. In: *Теория моды* 3, 55–80.

ИНТЕРВЬЮ С А.Д. 2013. Личный архив автора. 11 октября. Москва

ИНТЕРВЬЮ С В.Е. 2013. Личный архив автора. 30 сентября. Москва.

ИНТЕРВЬЮ С И.Х. 2013. Личный архив автора. 17 сентября. Москва

ИНТЕРВЬЮ С К.Т. 2013. Личный архив автора. 10 октября. Санкт-Петербург.

ИНТЕРВЬЮ С С.Щ. 2013. Личный архив автора. 1 октября. Москва.

КОЗЛОВ, А.С. 1998. *«Козел на саксе» - и так всю жизнь...* Москва.

КОЗЫРЕВ, М. 2012. *Подпольные миллионеры: вся правда о частном бизнесе.* Москва.

КОСТЫРЧЕНКО, Г.В. 2012. *Тайная политика Хрущева. Власть, интеллигенция, еврейский вопрос.* Москва.

ЛЕБИНА, Н. 2003. *Обыватель и реформы: картины повседневной жизни горожан в годы НЭПа и хрущевского десятилетия.* СПб.

ЛЕБИНА, Н. 2008. Синтетика: любимая ткань непостроенного коммунизма. In: *Теория моды* 10, 23-40.

НИЛОВ, А. 2006. *Цеховики. Рождение теневой экономики: записки подпольного миллионера.* СПб.

О СОВЕТСКОЙ ФАРЦОВКЕ 2011. In: *Живой журнал oadam*, http://oadam.livejournal.com/105110.html (28.03.2014)

ПАНИКИН, А. 1997. Записки русского фабриканта. In: *Новый Мир* 11, 152–181.

ПОСЛЕ КРИТИКИ 1979. In: *Правда.* 13 января, 3.

ДВА БИЛЕТА НА ДНЕВНОЙ СЕАНС. 1966 R: Герберт Раппапорт. СССР: Ленфильм.

РОМАНОВ, П. В., ЯРСКАЯ-СМИРНОВА, Е. 2007. Трузера и крабы для советского потребителя: будни подпольного капитализма фарцовщиков. In: *Профессии. doc. Социаль-ные трансформации профессионализма: взгляды снаружи, взгляды изнутри.* Сост. Е. Ярская-Смирнова, П.В. Романов. Москва 2007, 152-169.

РОССИЙСКИЙ ГОСУДАРСТВЕННЫЙ АРХИВ ЭКОНОМИКИ (РГАЭ) Ф.1562. Оп. 26. Д. 382; 921.

ПРОХИНДИАДА, ИЛИ БЕГ НА МЕСТЕ. 1984 R: Виктор Трегубович. СССР: Ленфильм.

УБОРЕВИЧ-БОРОВСКИЙ В. 1978. Джинсы. In: *Крокодил* 30, 4.

УГОЛОВНЫЙ КОДЕКС РСФСР. 1983. Москва

ФАВАРЕЛЬ-ГАРРИГ, Ж. 2005. Советская милиция и ее борьба с ростом экономических преступлений в эпоху «застоя». In: *Неприкосновенный запас* 42 (4), 80–85.

ДЕЛО РУМЯНЦЕВА. 1955 R: Иосиф Хейфиц. СССР: Ленфильм.

ХЛЕВНЮК, О. et.al. 2009. *Региональная политика Н. С. Хрущева. ЦК КПСС и местные партийные комитеты. 1953–1964.* Москва.

ЧИСТЯКОВ, Н. Ф. 1979. *По закону и совести.* Москва.

ШАТУНОВСКИЙ, П. 1978. Трест, который лопнул. In: *Правда.* 24 декабря, 6.

ЩЕКОЧИХИН, Ю. 1977. Подделка: диалог о ценах и ценностях. In: *Комсомольская правда.* 10 августа, 4.

ЭВЕЛЬСОН, Е. С. 1986. *Судебные процессы по экономическим делам в СССР (шестидесятые годы).* Лондон.

FROM RAGS TO RICHES?
Black Sea Ports and Consumerism in the Soviet Union, 1970s and 1980s

IRINA MUKHINA, WORCESTER

The fact that Soviet people craved western goods has been well documented, yet the meaning of this consumption, and especially its role in articulating resistance to the regime, is a matter of much debate (GUROVA 2008, EMEL'IANTSEVA 2011). David Crowley and Susan Reid write that "the will to consume represented a potential threat to communist authority" and "consumption choices could, and did, articulate resistance" (CROWLEY 2000: 14), while Katherine Verdery argues that for Soviet people, "to acquire objects became a way of constituting your selfhood against a regime you despised" (VERDERY as cited in HUMPHREY 1995: 56). Yet acquiring those objects was not an easy task to begin with. For many Soviet people, the consumption of western goods and western pop-culture was firmly linked to and made possible only by tapping into the black market, or *fartsovka*. People who were associated with the black market, *fartsovshchiki*, resold items that they acquired from western visitors for astronomical prices. People who worked in the service sector, especially in hotels, and tour guides were regularly drawn into the business. In this informal economy that circulated western goods to Soviet consumers, its main players offered a wide range of goods from clothing and items of personal hygiene to music recordings and even forbidden literature (VASIL'EV 2007).

While large urban cities had multiple channels for acquiring foreign goods (by dealing with *fartsovshchiki*, or through diplomatic ties or blat),[1] smaller, more peripheral locations represented the full range of diversity of consumer nightmares and consumer utopias that existed across the Soviet Union.[2] In Novorossiysk, a case study for this project, its residents indeed craved for western goods and appreciated them, and they had a relatively easy access to them in this small Soviet consumer utopia.[3] Partially for this reason, the residents' understanding of western fashions and styles and the choices that they made in acquiring them were distinct from their counterparts in capital cities. Moreover, the circulation of western goods with its precise acquisition and distribution channels in small port towns on the Black Sea coast resembled *fartsovka* only in

---

[1] For major studies of urban centers, see, for example, Svetlana Boym "*Common Places: Mythologies of Everyday Life in Russia*", Thomas Cushman "*Notes from Underground: Rock Music Counterculture in Russi*", Hilary Pilkington "*Russia's Youth and Its Culture: A Nation's Constructors and Constructed*", Alexei Yurchak "*Everything was Forever, Until It was No More: The Last Soviet Generation*".

[2] The terminology of consumer utopias is derived from Kate Brown's study of Soviet "gated communities" (closed cities with residents working for the top-secret military industries). Brown argues that "these communities were so attractive – such consumer utopias, in fact – that residents gave up important rights and freedoms in order to live in them" (BROWN 2012: 50). There was no shortage or deficit of anything in these places, and they were a substantial rather than a marginal phenomenon in the narrative of Soviet consumption (see BROWN 2012). In contrast, Ekaterina Emeliantseva, writing about a different closed city of Severodvinsk, concluded that regarding "consumer goods such as clothing or furniture, the situation was not much better [in Severodvinsk] than everywhere else." (see EMEL'IANTSEVA 2011)

[3] The project relies heavily on interviews (oral history) and utilizes local archives and newspapers as well.

marginal ways, if at all. In the 1970s and 1980s, residents of small port towns had a ready access to authentic foreign goods that circulated in large quantity and were readily available, even if not cheap, to most residents of these towns.

As such, port cities, especially those beyond giants like Odessa, were crucial for their role as cultural emitters of the late Soviet period and in stimulating a popular obsession with foreign goods on the periphery. While larger cities experienced tight control, smaller but no less important ports of Novorossiysk, Batumi and others created loopholes through which material objects passed in surprisingly substantial numbers. Sailors brought enough foreign clothing to meet the needs of those who could afford it, and the majority of port town dwellers flashed Wrangler jeans in the 1970s, at the time when even for Muscovites the consumption of foreign goods was limited to those with a privileged status or connections.[4] People employed by port authorities and those who purchased foreign goods exemplified the lifestyle and outlooks that many Soviet citizens beyond the boundaries of these port towns could only dream of achieving.

This access to foreign goods had important consequences for residents' attitudes to the wider world. Alexei Yurchak writes, for example, that for most Soviet people the world beyond Soviet borders, or *zagranitsa,* signified "an imaginary place that was simultaneously knowable and unattainable, tangible and abstract, mundane and exotics" to the point where "its real existence became dubious" (YURCHAK 2005: 159). Yet even if this complex perception remained true to some port cities residents and even considering that only a clear minority actually travelled overseas, it was impossible for the image of the wider world to maintain its dubious and almost illusive nature. The scope and scale of contacts was too great for the aura of mystique to survive. Not only goods but knowledge, experiences, memories and new needs crossed the border with sailors who came back home after months of international explorations. Of course, limitations of ordinary people were still significant and many who wanted to go abroad could not realize their aspirations. Yet the immediate proximity of that *zagranitsa* experience emphasize the more knowable, tangible and mundane over the abstract and dubious.

Thus, for port-town dwellers, *zagranitsa* was not so much an "Imaginary West" but a "Practical West", a specific means by which one could attain his or her goal of greater financial stability, better consumption opportunities, and a broader engagement of the world than was possible locally. Yet paradoxically, every aspiration and goal remained deeply rooted in local milieu and social realities of each and every participant. Because of this real-life connection to the West, by early 1980s people started to have relatively little concern for the intrinsic meanings of the goods. As a matter of fact, the analysis of interviews of sellers and buyers in Novorossiysk demonstrated no direct correlation between consumption of "made in" clothing and interest in western pop culture. To some extent, the consumption was less "cultured" and more material, and this is also what made it more mundane. For port-town residents at large, the craving for particular western attire was not necessarily an act of admiration of western values; instead, it was a manifestation of their social status (whether real or self-proclaimed) and a sense of fashion that was deeply embedded into realities of their daily lives. Much like their western counterparts, port-town dwellers wanted better, more beautiful, and more reliable products that met their sense of fashion, style, and taste.[5] As such, both the suppliers and consumers of small port-cities had marked differences

---

[4] The Ministry of the Merchant Marine (*Morflot*) as well as the Shipbuilding Ministry of the Soviet Union employed thousands of workers; some sailed abroad and many more did not, but a job in *Morflot* made foreign goods more readily available for all.

[5] See, for example, a discussion of consumer revolution by Natalya Chernyshova, in "Consumer Revolution? Society and Economy in the Soviet 1970s", also Vladimir Shlapentokh "*Public and Private Life of The Soviet People: Changing Values in Post-Stalin Russia*".

from their counterparts elsewhere in the country, and it is crucial to highlight some of those differences and explain the mechanism through which the goods circulated.

The rise of popular obsession with consuming western goods and pop-culture in the USSR is oftentimes linked to the movement of *stilyagi*. The members of this youth movement of the 1950s and 1960s went out of their way to buy western clothing and listen to rock-n-roll. They formed a youth subculture of the Soviet Union, and they were willing to pay any price for attributes of western culture. Sometimes that price was literal; a single piece of clothing could cost more than an average monthly wage at the time (about 120 roubles after the 1961 redenomination). More often than not, the price was also of one's wellbeing. *Militsiia* 'the Soviet police' routinely arrested *stilyagi*, destroyed their clothing, shaved their heads and stigmatized these young men and women for life. But while the movement was undeniably indicative of these youths' desire to oppose the system and rebel, the overall spread and impact of the movement tends to be exaggerated. Some recent productions, no matter how grotesque, might give an impression that the movement was predominant in the youth culture of the day. Yet despite the attention that they attracted from the state and Soviet people and continue to draw from scholars and history aficionados, *stilyagi* were a small movement which did not see any massive sprouts in various more "peripheral" regions of the Soviet Union.

On the other hand, large port cities, especially Odessa, have always had a far greater access to foreign goods that was the case for other locations in the Soviet Union. Already since the 1920s, residents of Odessa commonly exchanged vodka, caviar, Armenian cognac and various Soviet-produced goods for western clothing. Much of that clothing came off the back of foreign sailors, but it became so commonplace that even a slightest association of western clothing with envy or status was laughable. Residents did not see anything shameful either in such transaction or in wearing used clothing, and western goods were deeply appreciated both for their styles and their affordability. It was possible to exchange Soviet cotton men's underwear (that was affordable even by Soviet standards) for a pair of nicely-tailored western pants. Though the term *fartsovka* was not used and some of the principles of exchange were different from the transactions that took place in the 1970s and 1980s, nonetheless the basic principles of acquiring western goods was familiar and routine for residents of Odessa, and the goods were widely available (VASIL'EV 2007: 13–17).

Likewise, by late 1970s and into 1980s the volume of western goods that was available to most port town residents was far greater than what one could find elsewhere. Yet what made the real difference in consumption in port towns was not so much the ready availability of those goods but the channels through which they reached the consumers. To begin with, most goods crossed the border with various workers on the Soviet cargo fleet, and the sailors were the main suppliers in this circle of consumption. Unlike *fartsovshchiki*, the sailors who went abroad belonged to a well-respected, honourable, if not to say romantic, occupation, and the goods that they brought were likewise seen as honourably earned by hard labour rather than as spoils of cheating by mean speculators. Sailors and their distributors created networks that had allowed even the pickiest buyers to avoid the key moral dilemma of the Soviet consumers. Many Soviet people wanted to wear authentic western goods, but typically they "disliked the types of people who supplied them through black market channels [...] and [felt] ashamed by having to deal with them" (YURCHAK 2005: 200). This was not the case for port town dwellers, who respected and even admired the people who supplied the goods for their consumption.

Several factors made sailors stand out from the rest of the group involved in *fartsovka*. To begin with, most (though not all) sailors received extensive training in mechanical and nautical sciences and were indeed highly qualified professionals. The middle and upper echelons attended *morekhodka*, a specialized marine college with rigorous entrance requirements. It was never enough to have *blat*[6] to gain acceptance into one of those colleges; though informal networks and privileged social standing of the family helped, it was so mostly in the form of specialized instruction and access to private tutors. The educational process combined highly advanced math and science prep with almost a navy-like iron discipline. All graduates were expected to demonstrate a high level of professionalism and appropriate personal conduct that was comparable to military training. In addition, intensive program in languages (usually English) was similar to what one could find only in specialized philological universities. Though the degree and type of training varied according to one's occupation and position on the ship, nonetheless everyone had skills and specialized knowledge. These people were not simply "no one", the speculators; they were professionals who invested years into their training, and this fact was commonly known and understood by all. Their work conditions were also distinct and often seen (and justly so) as physically and emotionally challenging. A barge that was scheduled to go abroad was almost invariably away for six months at a time. Cramped living conditions and the fact that privacy was practically non-existent created emotional hardships, while it also produced a wide range of health risks. Travel to distant regions came with its share of challenges as well, and many sailors came down with cholera, malaria, and yellow fever (*Sovertskii moriak* 1960: 14). The rate of illness and even death was so high that aside from a few organizations (like hospitals), the captain of the ship had a rare individual legal right to pronounce a person dead. Even wives who stayed behind were treated with respect and envy for their material conforms but also pity and understanding as if they were single mothers. These women were bound by their duty to their husbands yet had to carry the burden of everyday life single-handedly without the support of their spouses.

Time ashore was not much easier either. Sailors received several months off to compensate for being away from home, yet such a respite was a mixed blessing. Most did not know what to do with their free time; they were not well versed in or attuned to everyday life ashore. Sailors faced similar problems when they retired. Their specialized training had no application to regular civilian life. Some found employment on small *galoshi* (the word in its literal sense means rustic rubber boots but represented boats for local transportation). Perceived as uninspiring and boring, such work at least provided enough stimulus to stay away from the bottle. Others fared even worse. These were well known challenges of the profession, and it made the rewards of the profession even more acceptable. Thus, even though sailors were more than well paid by Soviet standards (a typical monthly wage was 600 roubles or higher) and they made even more profits in bringing foreign goods for resale, their position might have generated envy but not resentment or accusations of being dirty speculators and slackers.

The suppliers of this system relied on a distribution system was also more acceptable to port town dwellers than might have been the case of *fartsovka* distribution channels. The preferred channels of distribution were almost always informal. Even though there were *komissionki*, or consignment shops, most sailors preferred to use them sparingly. Not *komissionki* but *babushki* were the most important distributors in this economy. A story of one woman (now deceased) is indicative of this process.[7] Unlike her friends with no connections to the business, she intention-

---

[6] Ledeneva defined "*blat*" as an economy of favors, or getting something "by acquaintance". For further definitions, see LEDENEVA.

[7] Several informal interviews were conducted with Baba Mania and her friends and relatives. The interviews spanned over the course of nearly fifteen years. The first interview with Baba Mania took place in August 1997 and we continued over several meetings (she died in July 1998). The relatives, including her sister (to be mentioned later), carried on with our informal conversations until the passing of Baba Mania's sister in 2007 and stepsister in

ally cultivated her image of *babushka* (she was 65+ when she did the most business), and eventually Baba Mania, as most called her, became a powerhouse in this trade. Baba Mania received sailors in her two-room apartment, which she shared with her sister and brother-in-law. The system was similar to some of the elite clubs of the present day. A sailor's background was closely scrutinized for reliability and financial security (there was an interest in building a regular clientele base rather than taking in someone who only sold an item or two occasionally). Then "an insider" had to recommend that person, and after that the sailor received the address of "the contact", i.e. Baba Mania, and an acceptable time to bring goods. Baba Mania was cheerful and welcoming and seemed to befriend everyone. She always had a bottle of vodka on her kitchen table and a smile to accompany it. But she was the final judge of what was taken in and how much one could charge for their goods. Baba Mania mostly took in high-end clothing, while the rest was either discarded as unsellable (to be distributed to friends as gifts) or was passed onto an extended network of lower-key sellers who took in what was too problematic to sell and of no interest to Baba Mania. *Tekhasy* 'jeans', Italian shoes, leather boots, and dress shirts were her favourite items because they were in highest demand and yielded highest profits. Kids' clothing ranked relatively low on her list of priorities; it was too expensive and not long-lasting enough for most consumers (an average t-shirt cost 15-25 roubles, and since kids grow, it could last only a couple of seasons at most). Baba Mania was careful not to overcharge and marked up the goods by no more than ten percent. Nonetheless, Baba Mania's profit margin came to 500-600 roubles monthly, nearly ten times her official retirement benefit and a substantial amount by all means.

Her distribution channels were analogous to her system of acquiring goods in the first place. Potential buyers from among the acquaintances were invited to see the goods in the apartment, and the most reliable and regular customers could even place orders for specific goods. But for things that did not sell to *svoi* 'insiders', Baba Mania had to go to the open-air markets and seek buyers there. In order to avoid the charges of speculation (a criminal offense in the Soviet Union), she never took more than one item with her, and even if caught selling that item, she always managed to plead innocence. Needless to say, most *militsionery* 'Soviet policemen' knew her well and relied on her services, though there were always loners who were incorruptible and who wanted to uphold the system and socialist values at all cost. Overall, as several respondents reported, *babushki* were much more reliable as distribution channels for sailors than consignment shops, and most goods that did not circulate among family and friends passed through their hands. "Newcomers" and "youngsters" went to shops with their goods, but there was always a desire to find a "contact" like Baba Mania. In this particular town, as Baba Mania remembered, there were about a dozen women like herself, and then a wild range of petty sellers (or speculators, the term she used with a degrading tone) who did not have regular clientele and did not last long in the business. The business came with its share of risks ("though only the greedy ones got prison terms," commented Baba Mania); nonetheless, the benefits were substantial as well. Aside from direct financial considerations, these women acquired so many "contacts" among various groups of people that they could even make transactions that involved property or high-deficit socialist commodities which ranged from vacation passes to cars.[8]

A widow herself (like all other "important" women), Baba Mania had her sister's and her brother-in-law's opinions to consider, not the least because they shared the apartment. Her sister

---

2012. Interviews also included former sailors of all ranks who went abroad in 1972–1982. The collection of interviews for this group is on-going.

[8] This system was reminiscent of "*blat*" as presented in Alena Ledeneva "*Russia's Economy of Favor: Blat, Networking and Informal Exchange*".

was a hard-core Communist who never criticized party decisions and supported the system to her last breath. She even insisted that the scarcity of some goods and the imperfect distribution system was one of the best achievements of the system that taught people to depart from *veshchism* 'obsession with material goods' and embrace eternal values of kindness, mutual support, and intellectualism. Ironically, these views did not prevent her from buying foreign clothing that her sister had access to, and the explanation was often rather trivial. She either liked the design of strawberries on a particular shirt, or the colour was "cute", or something similar. Consistently, this woman and many other respondents emphasized that they wanted quality clothing that was both durable and appealing. This woman shunned Soviet undergarments for herself and preferred to see her grandchildren wear colourful dresses and trousers in colours that did not fade after a few washes. But she never once saw her purchases as being in any way contradictory to her internalized values of Soviet communism.

In one way or another, all of the respondents shared this sense of accepting western goods and Soviet values. One woman was plain shocked to hear that to some, consumption apparently represented rebellion. As a young woman in her later 20s in the 1970s, she would only wear Italian and German outfits, with occasional "sprinkles" of American clothing. The items that she had – boots, coats, and pants – were expensive and not numerous, yet they made up the bulk of her wardrobe. When asked about her choices, she wondered: "Did I wear this clothing because it had something to say against the Soviet system? That's nonsense. I was a true patriot of my motherland. I loved the Soviet Union." The residents enjoyed wearing western clothing and drinking Pepsi (the first Pepsi factory opened in a port town of Novorossiysk in 1974) but they seemed to be oblivious to and ignorant of any subculture or the message of resistance per se. The interviews demonstrated that when the respondents bought western goods, they did not necessarily refuse "the broader context of socialism, its realities, possibilities, and values" (YURCHAK 2005: 204).

The explanation for this seemingly dichotomous fascination with western clothing and the support for the Soviet system might be illusive and speculative but nonetheless important to seek. The erosion of the norms and ideals of social equality and the availability of material possessions that represented the social status on the one hand and the unique political and social culture of the so-called periphery on the other hand might help explain how ordinary citizens understood and managed to combine the attributes of the two worlds in their daily lives. To begin with, the political culture of the small port towns was more conservative, system-oriented, and homogenous that what the case for major cities was. When in 1987 one of my respondents raised the question at the *Komsomol* meeting on what should be done about *perestroika*, the response of the First Secretary was that "it [was] not prudent to look to Moscow for any of this. They, the Muscovites, can afford to toy around with such things, but this nonsense is never going to come to places like ours." The same general feeling applied to youth subculture and even western pop-culture. Thus, hippy bands could be spotted in Moscow, Leningrad, L'vov and other major cities throughout the 1970s. By the second half of the same decade, the diverse groups of *fanaty* 'football hooligans', *metallisty* 'heavy-metal lovers', punks, *rokery* 'motocycle gangs', and *firmy* 'groups that controlled access to theatre box offices' were proliferating there at an amazing speed.[9] But there is no evidence to suggest that such groups were commonplace in smaller port towns or that they were

[9] See, for example, Iurii Shchekochikhin "*Allo, my vas slyshim*", William Jay Risch "Soviet 'Flower Children'. Hippies and the Youth Counter-culture in 1970s L'viv".

visibly present. To the contrary, as one of the respondents concluded, "why would well-educated people like us have anything to do with these freaks?"[10]

Not only the culture but even the slang of the subculture, including in relation to the black market, did not appear and did not circulate widely among the sailors and their customers. One study reported that Moscow and Leningrad had a well-defined group of *mazhory*, or people who specialized in getting foreign clothing for their customers. They brought clothing from one destination only and thus were known as pseudo-Americans, pseudo-Italians, and so on (FEL'DSHTEIN 1988). Yet none of the respondents have ever even heard the term. Retrospectively, during the interviews they insisted that there was no "vulgar" slang or a language of its own that emerged in relation to resale of foreign goods that sailors brought with them from abroad. Regional specialization was also problematic since most ships travelled to multiple destinations and offered sailors an opportunity to purchase goods in various locations on a single trip (with an exception of those who stayed within the boundaries of the Black Sea and sailed to Bulgaria or Turkey only). Even listening to the Soviet pop diva Alla Pugacheva had a generational divide to it. If the young adults saw her as risqué, flirtatious and seductive and wanted to listen to her songs, for these same reasons the older generation (vaguely defined) found her too provocative and repulsive to enjoy. The "golden youths" of Moscow could have listened to Bing Crosby and Louis Armstrong and worn T-shirts with Stars and Stripes and "US Army" logos on them, but no equally open signs of resistance were evident in small towns (BALL 2003: 183–185).

Moreover, private selling in open-air markets was commonplace in border regions of the Soviet Union and especially in the southern parts. Indeed, "open-air markets have existed as an integral part of the retail sector in most states in Eastern and Central Europe during socialist period. They formed a part of the second economy and an essential part of the state redistributive system in most countries, not only in the 'liberal states' of central Europe such as Poland and Hungary, but also in the Soviet Union" (HOHNEN 2003: 3).[11] Yet whereas such markets had limited presence in the capital and urban giants, they were the main providers of basic staples of life in other parts of the Soviet Union. This was so much so that most families in Novorossiysk, Kabardinka, Gelendzhik, Batumi and similar coastal towns reported that they barely ever went to state stores for basics like food and clothing in the 1970s and 1980s (except for sugar and soap). If not the open-air markets, than at least *komissionki* could yield the desired item, not the socialist distribution system. The widespread existence of these markets in the southern parts of the Soviet Union diluted notions of privateers and speculators compared to the rest of the country, and made private buying more acceptable, or at least more routine and mundane as a general practice.

Last but not least, a particular fascination with foreign goods was directly linked to people's sense of what represented their success and position in the society. This, of course, was in no ways unique to port towns. In a state of self-proclaimed equality for all, there was little room to expressing one's social status. Social classes did not cease to exist, unlike what the Soviet people were assured, and the gap between the have and have-nots reached down to all layers of the society by the 1970s and 1980s. The party elites always enjoyed special access to goods and facilities that distinguished them from the rest of the population. But for the population at large, which was becoming increasingly stratified, there were few avenues to express their social position and dis-

---

[10] This is not to say that the general population elsewhere endorsed such groups. In fact, negative stereotypes were abundant. See Risch, op. cit., for a discussion of popular perception of such subculture groups as hippies. Yet the visible lack of such subculture was also atypical.

[11] Also see: Louise I. Shelley, "The Second Economy in the Soviet Union; V. Shlapentokh, "*Public and Private Life of the Soviet People: Changing Values in Post-Stalin Russia*".

tinguish themselves from the peers. Housing was distributed by the state and property was not privately owned, and thus the housing situation could not be improved or changed even with greater-than-average financial resources. In short, property ownership could not function as a sign of one's social status. Cars, refrigerators, TV sets and other valuables were "sold" according to a distribution system and they were not purchased at will. And thus the only true outlet for visibly asserting one's social position was clothing, which was priced on a black market out of all proportion to incomes precisely because it represented more than a way to cover one's body. Aesthetic and practical considerations played a role (western clothing by all means looked more appealing than Soviet-produced counterparts), but one's sense of personal worth and status that was vested into clothing was crucially important as well.

A Soviet proverb exemplified this obsession with fashions when it proclaimed that "you judge a person first by his clothing and later by his/her intelligence." Though in its deeper meaning the proverb was meant to downplay the importance of looks (which only mattered in making that first impression) and elevate the importance of intelligence (which with time revealed the true worth of a person), many misjudged it to mean that looks and first impressions were more important than any other attribute of human life. This was especially true of younger people of the 1970s many of whom thought that "clothing [gave] young people status, prestige, and self-confidence" (FISHER 1993: 11). If clothing and consumerism were markers of personal and collective identity, then those markers were deeply social and ingrained into the fabric of everyday life.[12] Most consumers of western brands and clothing wanted to be like the people around them or better off in order to be embedded into their social milieu, not to oppose it. The clothing, that proverbial first impression, was and continues to be valued as status symbols.

Needless to say, retrospective accounts, like all memoirs and interviews, tend to be idealized, romanticized, and tainted by at least a hint of nostalgia for those good old days. The new challenges of life in post-Soviet Russia displaced many people; for those who learned to navigate the system so masterfully, "the end of communism meant more loss than gain when suddenly the rules of the game, in which they had been so proficient, radically changed. [...] the new game was much more impersonal, global, and corporate, while networks of family and friends were no longer paramount to the functioning of the system" (BREN 2012: 142) (as a side note, Baba Mania was reduced to poverty by this 'new game'). Nonetheless, these realities do not take away from a more general observation about consumption in the Soviet Union of the 1970s and 1980s. Historian John Bushnell wrote that "throughout the 1960s and 1970s Soviet society developed spontaneously and dynamically, with a booming second economy, [...] and an increasingly complex and heterogeneous urban population" (BUSHNELL 1990: 276). Though the original context of the statement refers to the rise and flourishing of youth subculture, the same would equally apply to the consumption patterns of the ever-growing number of port town residents. The volume of foreign goods that passed through port towns was so substantial that it made them part of the everyday culture. While to some residents these foreign goods in fact represented rebellion and freedom, to many more the "made-in" goods acquired added value only in the context of and in relation to socialist reality. The consumption was global and local at once, and it was becoming increasingly complex and consumer-oriented.

[12] For the discussion of consumption under socialism as part of one's individual or collective identity, see Susan E. Reid, David Crowley "*Style and Socialism: Modernity and Material Culture in Post-War Eastern Europe*".

Summary

Based on extensive oral history fieldwork and research in various port administration archives, this study investigates the role of port cities in the Soviet Union as magnets of change and cultured spaces shaped by cosmopolitanism and consumption. It demonstrates that Soviet consumers of the 1970s were far from unfortunate victims of massive shortages. Even if expensive, western clothing and styles were available to most residents of capital cities and port towns, thus shaping their tastes, their sense of style, and their personal aspirations. Specifically, ports of Novorossiysk, Batumi and others created perfect loopholes through which material objects passed in surprisingly substantial numbers. Sailors brought enough foreign clothing to meet the needs of those port town residents who could afford it. People employed by port authorities and those who bought foreign goods exemplified the lifestyle and outlooks that many beyond the boundaries of these port towns aspired to achieve. The volume of foreign goods that passed through port towns was so substantial that it made these items almost mundane. Moreover, the consumption was deeply rooted in the realities of local social milieu; the goods rarely acquired any additional meaning that could have demonstrated the opposition to the regime.

Bibliography

BALL, A. 2003. *Imagining America: influence and images in twentieth-century Russia.* New York.

BARSUKOVA, S., RADAEV, V. 2012. Informal Economy in Russia: A Brief Overview. In: *Economic Sociology* vol. 13, no. 2, 4–13.

BOYM, S. 1994. *Common Places: Mythologies of Everyday Life in Russia.* Cambridge.

BREN, P., NEUBERGER, M. (ed.). 2012. *Communism Unwrapped: Consumption in Cold War Eastern Europe.* Oxford University Press, 2012.

BROWN, K. 2012. Utopia Gone Terribly Right: Plutonium's "Gated Communities" in the Soviet Union and United States. In: Bren, P., Nauburger, M. (ed.). *Communism Unwrapped: Consumption in Cold War Eastern Europe.* Oxford 2012, 49–67.

BUSHNELL, J. 2009. An Introduction to the Soviet Sistema: The Advent of Counterculture and Subculture. In: *Slavic Review* vol. 49, no. 2, 272–277.

CHERNYSHOVA, N. 2010. Consumer Revolution? Society and Economy in the Soviet 1970s. Presented at the *ASEEES Annual Convention,* Los Angeles, CA.

CROWLEY, D., REID, S. (ed.). 2000. *Style and Socialism: Modernity and Material Culture in Post-War Eastern Europe.* Berg Publishers, Oxford.

CUSHMAN, T. 1995. *Notes from Underground: Rock Music Counterculture in Russia.* New York.

EMEL'IANTSEVA, E. 2011. "The Privilege of Seclusion: Consumption Strategies in the Closed City of Severodvinsk. In: *AB Imperio* 2, 238–259.

FEL'DSHTEIN, D. et al (ed.). 1988. *Psikhologicheskie problemy izucheniia neformal'nykh molodezhnykh ob'edinenii. Sbornik nauchnykh trudov.* Moskva.

FISHER, L. 1993. *Survival in Russia: Chaos and Hope in Everyday Life.* Boulder.

GUROVA, O. 2008. *Soviet Underwear: Between Ideology and Everyday Life/ Sovetskoe nizhnee bel'e: mezhdu ideologiei i povsednevnost'iu.* Moskva.

HOHNEN, P. 2003. *A Market out of Place? Remaking Economic, Social, and Symbolic Boundaries in Post-Communist Lithuania.* Oxford.

HUMPHREY, C. 1995. Creating a culture of disillusionment: consumption in Moscow, a chronicle of changing times. In: Miller, D. (ed.). *Worlds Apart. Modernity through the Prism of the Local.* London, New York 1995, 43–68.

LEDENEVA, A. 1998. *Russia's Economy of Favor: Blat, Networking and Informal Exchange.* Cambridge.

PILKINGTON, H. 1994. *Russia's Youth and Its Culture: A Nation's Constructors and Constructed.* London.

RISCH, W. 2005. Soviet 'Flower Children'. Hippies and the Youth Counter-culture in 1970s L'viv. In: *Journal of Contemporary History* vol. 40, no. 3, 565–584.

SHEKOCHKIN, Y. 1987. *Allo, my vas slyshim.* Moskva.

SHELLEY, L. 1990. The Second Economy in the Soviet Union. In: Los, M. (ed.). *The Second Economy in Marxist States.* London 1990, 11–25.

SHLAPENTOKH, V. 1989. *Public and Private Life of the Soviet People: Changing Values in Post-Stalin Russia.* New York.

SOVETSKII MORIAK 14. 1960. Moskva.

VASIL'EV, D. 2007. *Fartsovshchiki: Kak delalis' sostoianiia.* Sankt-Petersburg.

YURCHAK, A. 2005. *Everything was Forever, Until It was No More: The Last Soviet Generation.* Princeton.

SOMETHING NEW IN THE EASTERN MARKET
Polish Perceptions of the Developing Soviet Consumerism, 1961-1972

MILA OIVA, TURKU

In the export to the Soviet Union, we are encountering the typical buyers´ market. Therefore, it is extremely important that we take into account the quality of our export products, in order to keep up with the competition.
(A paraphrase from a report of the Polish Ministry for Foreign Trade, 1968)

At the beginning of the 1960s, Polish exporters of ready-to-wear clothes started to market their products in the Soviet Union.[1] By the end of the decade, the Soviet market had become a highly competed one. To be able to succeed in the tightening competition, the Polish exporters were forced to start analysing how to satisfy the Soviet consumer – a new actor in the field of trade activities. The aim of this article is to explain why our general understanding, according to which shortages of the planned economies marginalized consumers into insignificant actors, contradicts partly the above explained development, visible in my primary sources (KORNAI 1992: 244–248, 271, BEREND 2009: 21, HARDY 2009: 20–30). The article will tackle the contradiction by examining how Polish exporters of ready-to-wear clothes perceived the consumers´ role in the developing Soviet consumer culture, and how Polish foreign trade sales activities responded to the increasing importance of the consumers in the Soviet Union, from the early 1960s to the early 1970s. I aim to reach a more nuanced approach to the shifting role and the meaning of the consumers in the Soviet Union through the following research questions: what was the most important Soviet target group for the Polish marketers, and how did the changing Polish export activities reflect the shifting importance of the different groups? Looking at the role of the Soviet consumers from the perspective of the Polish foreign traders illuminates the more competitive part of the Soviet market – the import market – and gives the perspective of a trader from outside of the Soviet consumer culture.

The main sources of this research consist of the internal correspondence and reports of the Polish *Association of Clothing Industries (ZPO)*[2] and foreign trade companies.[3] These documents allow analysing how the Polish clothing exporters depicted the Soviet market: whose opinion – that of the Soviet wholesale purchasers, the clothing professionals or the consumers – was the most significant from the point of view of the traders? In the early 1960s the major target groups of the Polish clothing exporters were the wholesale purchasers and the clothing professionals, but towards the end of the decade the consumers started to gain more attention. The wholesale purchasers were representatives of the Soviet foreign trade organization *Raznoeksport* and the supply organizations of the Soviet republics. They were in charge of

---

[1] This article is a revised version of an article published in Finnish in *Idäntutkimus* 2, 2014. I wish to thank all the anonymous reviewers and Dr. Suvi Kansikas for their valuable comments.

[2] The Association of Clothing Industries, *Zjednoczenie Przemysłu Odzieżowego (ZPO)*, was responsible for coordinating the clothing production of the state owned factories, and starting from the early 1960s also for organizing export together with the foreign trade companies.

[3] The main exporters of ready-to-wear were foreign trade company CETEBE (1949–1962) and Confexim (1963–1971). In addition to these companies Coopexim exported clothes produced by the cooperatives´ and Prodimex clothes of the few private clothing producers. (APŁ collections 354, 355, 402 and AAN collection 351, JASIŃSKI 2011: 279-280, POLISH FOREIGN TRADE ENTERPRISES 1964).

choosing the concrete clothing models to be imported, and the price negotiations with the Polish foreign traders. The Soviet clothing professionals were a diverse group, whose common nominator had a job related to the clothing production and fashion. The designers, representatives of the retail stores and the clothing factories, art professionals and for example journalists and photographers of the magazines represented the different sections of the diversified clothing sector. They could act as arbiters in the committees, which determined what kinds of clothing models were to be considered as desirable and to be produced in the Soviet Union (ZAHAROVA 2011: 103–112, GRONOW & ZHURAVLEV 2010: 27–28). Consumers formed the third group, which was composed of the Soviet citizens, in all their diversity.

Consumer cultures are often studied as one country's internal development. By studying the development of the Soviet consumer culture from the point of view of the Polish clothing exporters, the object of the study becomes placed into a wider context of mutual communication and cultural differences between the socialist states, as well as the global trends. From the Polish perspective, the Soviet consumer culture was different from the domestic one, and it often seemed to be less developed. In general, in comparison with the Soviet Union, Poland has often been described as ideologically more tolerant, and Poles as having closer connections to Western Europe and even the United States, than Soviet citizens. The Polish foreign traders travelled extensively, and they were well aware of the trading practices in different economic systems and countries. Due to the task of the Polish foreign traders to sell their products profitably, their interest focused on how things were carried out in practice, instead of how things would have been ideologically appropriate. In the internal documentation of the Polish foreign trade sector orders were reasoned by the economic consequences, while the socialist rhetoric was conspicuous by its absence. For example, when talking about the Soviet trade, friendly cooperation between the socialist countries was not mentioned. On the other hand, topics, such as the political dominance of the Soviet Union in Poland, the emotional baggage of the Soviet-Polish history, or the reservations of the Poles against the Soviet Union, hovering beneath the official perceptions even during the socialist period in Poland, were not referred to either (cf. EISLER 2009: 263–267, SUDZIŃSKI 2009: 74).

Due to a more visible competition in foreign trade, the foreign traders had to take consumers into consideration more than in the domestic trade. The Polish clothing exporters competed on the Soviet market with the other socialist countries, especially with the German Democratic Republic (GDR), Hungary and Bulgaria, and they observed carefully the changes on that market in order to be competitive. The foreign trade between the CMEA[4] member countries was based on long term agreements, which were bound into each country's five-year plans. These agreements, however, were non-specific to the extent that they left room for negotiating in the lower levels of the economic hierarchy that was in charge of realizing the agreements. Because the CMEA barter trade was based on balanced trade quotas, the Soviet allies felt pressure to export high priced goods to the Soviet Union, in order to import cheap energy from there (STONE 1996: XI, 3–7). This caused competition between the CMEA member countries on the Soviet market. Consequently, although the domestic trade was to a large extent a sellers' market, in foreign trade competition between the producing countries prevailed (OIVA, 2014).

Preceding research has often considered mass consuming as a phenomenon characteristic solely of the Western market economy, which was developed as a consequence of the industrialization and development of the capitalist production model (SASSATELLI 2007: 13–14). Recently the consumer cultures of the socialist countries have been researched increasingly,

[4] The Council for Mutual Economic Assistance (CMEA) was an economic union of the socialist countries which functioned in 1949-1991. The founding members of the CMEA were the Soviet Union, Poland, Bulgaria, Czechoslovakia, Hungary and Romania. Albania, GDR, Mongolia and Cuba joined the union later (JASIŃSKI 2011: 175, KANSIKAS 2014: 37–38).

and the question whether consumer cultures existed at all in socialist states is no longer topical. However, still relevant questions are for example what the socialist consumer cultures were like and how they functioned. It is necessary to look at the role of the consumers in forming the consumer cultures alongside the political leaders, in order the reach a wider understanding of the phenomenon. According to Susan E. Reid and David Crowley, the current research provides two kinds of explanations for the development of consumer cultures in the socialist countries. The first version describes increased consumption as a luxury reserved for selected elite, as a reward for being loyal for the leadership. Secondly, by allowing and enabling mass consumption, the leaders legitimized their authority and maintained stability in the socialist camp (CROWLEY & REID 2010: 12–13). Both explanations give the leaders a dominant position in forming a consumer culture, and the role of the consumers is marginal. The aim of this article is to shed light to the consumers' role, and the change of lifestyles in the development of the consumer culture in the Soviet Union. This approach is in line with the increasing body of literature that underlines the important role of the consumers in forming trade and the consumer cultures in the socialist countries (cf. NEUBURGER 2012: 99–100).

The political dependency of Poland on the Soviet Union influenced Polish economic functions and trade. After World War II the Soviet Union became the most important trading partner for Poland. From the mid-1950s, the Polish economic planners started to redirect the emphasis of the Polish export production from raw materials towards increasing export of industrially produced, ready-made commodities. By the 1970s, Poland had become the second biggest importer of industrially produced consumer goods to the Soviet Union, right after the GDR (JASIŃSKI 2011: 175, 267, SUDZIŃSKI 2009: 57, 61). This development was a consequence of changes in trading practices, alongside the redirection of the production. For example, the Polish ready-to-wear exporters launched their marketing activities in the Soviet Union in the early 1960s, and over the decade Poland increased its share in the Soviet clothing import from a minor player to a significant producer. The Soviet Union was the most important client of the Polish clothing industry, since over 80% of the exports were directed to the Soviet Union (cf. GUS 1959: 55, GUS 1966: 120). The major factor behind the success of Polish export of ready-to-wear to the Soviet Union was the understanding that the importance of consumers had increased since the late 1950s, and taking this into account in the trading activities. See picture 3.

Although the export to the Soviet Union was significant to the Polish clothing production, the share of the Polish-origin items of the total amount of clothes circulating in the Soviet market was minuscule. The clothing production of the Soviet Union was vast, but the access to the good-quality and fashionable ready-to-wear clothes was more difficult for the average consumers there, than in many other socialist countries. Home-sewing or modifying of clothes at home, and using services of tailors, were the most frequently used means for acquiring desired clothing in the Soviet Union. The imported clothes were in high demand, and in order to be able to purchase them, an average Soviet consumer needed to take extra efforts (GRONOW 2012: 127, BARTLETT 2010: 160, GUROVA 2009: 49-51, IVANOVA 2012: 78-80, 155-156, ZAKHAROVA 2013, 418–423).

Professionals as Representatives of Consumers

At the beginning of the 1960s, the main target groups for Polish exporters were the Soviet trade and fashion professionals. Organizational changes in foreign trade structures in both countries in the late 1950s created more dynamic contacts between the Soviet and Polish trade organizations. In 1961, the Polish ready-to-wear exporters launched the new sales practices by organizing a sales exhibition, accompanied with a fashion show tour, in the Soviet Union. Earlier, from the late 1940s to the late 1950s, the Polish ready-to-wear clothes had been exported to the Soviet Union in small amounts, and under the supervision of the Polish Ministry for Foreign Trade. During that time, no sales exhibitions of the Polish clothes had been organized in the Soviet Union, and the Association of Clothing Industries (ZPO), or its predecessor, did not take part in the practical arrangements of the trade deals. In the late 1950s, the Polish economic administration was partly de-centralized and the Soviet import regulations of goods from socialist countries were changed (FOREWORD TO THE COLLECTION OF THE SOVIET MINISTRY FOR FOREIGN TRADE, JASIŃSKI 2011: 227). Following those reforms, the initiatives on how to arrange the Polish-Soviet trade could take place at the lower levels of the economic hierarchy. The ZPO and the Polish foreign trade companies were authorized to decide on more matters than earlier. Simultaneously trade became more dynamic, as the ZPO had a bigger interest to develop clothing export than the Ministry for Foreign Trade, which was responsible for the whole foreign trade.

As a consequence of the reforms, the ZPO and the foreign trade company CETEBE developed in 1961 new ways of selling clothes to the Soviet Union. The ZPO coordinated the design of the first Polish export collection, consisting of approximately 800 pieces of clothing, directed solely to the Soviet market in order to be able to pull the plan through. The ZPO set aside good quality fabrics and each clothing factory made designs based on the available fabrics. The ZPO and the clothing factories were pressured to design models that the Soviet purchasers would find attractive: the clothing models to be actually sold and the prices paid for them, were determined only in the negotiations between the Soviet wholesale purchasers and CETEBE in Moscow. The agreement finally reached in Moscow covered the majority of Polish clothing export sales for year 1962 (MEETING MINUTES NO. 1/III/61).

The Production Department of the ZPO paid specific attention to the appearance and design of the export collection designated to the Soviet consumers, with the focus on colours and fashionability. In order to make the Polish collection as diverse as possible, it also took into consideration the varying climate conditions of the Soviet Union and different cultural preferences of people living in different regions. It stressed particularly that although the collection was composed of products made by different producers, it had to be exhibited so that it would give an impression of a uniform Polish collection (MEETING MINUTES NO. 3/VI/61, LETTERS OF ZPO, APRIL 1961). The Polish clothing designers were ordered to design colourful designs for the Soviet market (GROUP INTERVIEW OF POLISH FASHION DESIGNERS). Polish exporters thus viewed the preferences of the Soviet consumers to be different from the domestic ones. Presenting a colourful and varied collection in Moscow had to please the eyes of the Soviet trade representatives coming from different regions of the country. The Polish collection had to differ in a positive sense from the Soviet collections, which were generally perceived as dull and monotonous (GRONOW & ZHURAVLEV 2010: 28).

The Soviet wholesale purchasers were in a decisive position in relation to the Polish export attempts. Because the total export amount was in principle agreed beforehand at the bilateral high level annual negotiations (KORNAI 2000: 350–353), the prices paid for individual clothing models dictated how many pieces of clothing the Polish clothing industry had to produce in order to reach the agreed overall sum. Production of the clothes was challenging because of the shortage of fabrics and other raw materials. Therefore the Polish clothing factories and exporters aimed at gaining the highest price as possible for their products. Although the Soviet retail purchasers had to follow the directions of their superiors and the price rates, they could also determine for which items they could pay more and for which less in the price negotiations.

In addition to the sales exhibition organized in Moscow in 1961, the Polish exporters organized fashion shows in Leningrad, Riga and Kiev. These cities were clearly important from the point of view of the clothing sale, because already in 1959 Hungary, the competitor country for Poland, had organized fashion shows in these cities. Fashion shows were not an unknown phenomenon in the Soviet Union. They were, alongside with the catalogues and magazines, an important means of disseminating the information on the newest models of the domestic Fashion Houses *doma modelej*. Especially in the 1950s and the 1960s fashion shows were popular entertainment. However, the fashion shows presenting foreign ready-to-wear clothing were still relatively rare in the early 1960s. The foreign ready-to-wear producers had been organizing fashion shows in the Soviet Union occasionally only since 1956 (GRONOW & ZHURAVLEV 2012: 119–120, 136, REPORT OF THE SOVIET CHAMBER OF COMMERCE 1963).

In order to disseminate the information on the Polish ready-to-wear clothes and to gain positive attention to them, the Polish clothing exporters directed their fashion shows to Soviet clothing professionals. The fact that Riga, the city with a relatively small population but acting as a trend setter in the Soviet fashion, was included in the fashion show tour demonstrates the importance of the clothing professionals for the Polish exporters. The committees formed by the clothing professionals determined the directions of the Soviet clothing production, and simultaneously the clothing professionals were an influential, albeit heterogeneous, discussant on fashion issues in the Soviet press. Still at the beginning of the 1960s, the clothing professionals considered that the task of the clothing production and the trade professionals was to educate the citizens to consume "correctly", and to choose products with a good taste. This was a continuum of the socialist consuming ideals born in the 1930s Soviet Union, *kul'turnost'*, which was closely related to the ideals of civilization and sophistication (ZAKHAROVA 2011: 105–108, HESSLER 2004: 198–209, KRAVETS & SANDIKCI 2013: 465–466).

The Soviet clothing professionals depicted the consumers as a uniform group, all members of which were offered similar clothes, inspired by the European classical and discreet fashion. The only factors that could, according to the clothing professionals, cause a need for variation in clothing, were geographical. The city and countryside dwellers were acknowledged to need coats of different lengths for practical reasons, and the altering climate conditions of the country, and traditions of different nationalities, could influence to a certain extent what kinds of clothes the consumers needed. Still, in the turn of the 1950s-1960s, the stylistic differentiation from the customary dressing code, such as the *stiliaga* style, was interpreted as a sign of antisocial perceptions and behaviour (ZAKHAROVA 2011: 105–108, GRONOW & ZHURAVLEV 2012: 129, 134). Therefore, the ready-to-wear sector of the Soviet Union did not take into consideration different consumer groups, such as youth or followers of certain styles.

It was important for the Polish exporters to influence certain members of the nomenclature elite, who also could be treated as the clothing professionals, and their opinions were also influential when deciding what to purchase from foreign sellers. Already in the 1930s, the members of the elite, such as influential nomenclature wives, had been dictating what was considered to be stylish and the practice had continued also after the war. Starting from the late 1950s, an important feature of the cultural capital of the expanding Soviet middle-class was to know what was fashionable in the West (BARTLETT 2010: 72, 82-84, 242). A Soviet Russian import company of knitwear *Trikotazh* used to ask diplomat students to come along to the sales exhibitions to tell what was fashionable in their circles, and what should be bought from the offered foreign collection at the beginning of the 1960s (PRIANIKOV 2007).

In addition that only selected people could decide upon the acceptable clothing, the Soviet consumers had also an unequal access to consumer goods, which varied greatly in the different areas of the Soviet Union. In major cities the offer was richer and more varied than in smaller cities, and industrial centres were better supplied than non-industrial areas (IVANOVA 2012: 78, TIKHOMIROVA 2004, HESSLER 2004: 5, 12). Also unofficial channels and trading routes influenced the variety of the available goods: in small harbour cities, where the customs control of the sailors was less strict, it was easier to purchase fashionable foreign clothing than in bigger harbour cities (see MUKHINA in this volume, ZAKHAROVA 2013, 426, KOIVUNEN 2013: 269). In major cities contacts with the tourists were also a source of consumer items (KUUSI 2013). The consuming opportunities of an individual were not determined solely by his or her wealth, but the personal networks and capability to use them were crucial. This practice was called *blat* in the Soviet Union and it was widely used (LEDENEVA 1998: 1–7).

Because of the hierarchical differences between the different regions of the Soviet Union, it was significant for the Polish exporters in which cities they presented their newest collection. The fashion shows of the Polish – and actually all the foreign clothing exporters – were concentrated in the 1950s and the early 1960s in the cities in the western part of the Soviet Union. Leningrad and Kiev were large European cities, and although Riga´s population was smaller, it was an important fashion city, alongside with Tallinn and Minsk. The Fashion Houses of the Baltic republics had a strong, though unofficial, status as disseminators of fashion trends and bellwethers of future fashion in the Soviet Union. For example, the new fashion of women's trousers as elegant street wear became prevalent in Tallinn a couple of years earlier than in the other European cities of the Soviet Union, and in the Central Asian republics spreading the fashion took even longer (CHERNYSHOVA 2013: 143, GRONOW & ZHURAVLEV 2012: 128–130).

The Soviet clothing professionals and fashion-conscious citizens of different regions had different statuses and possibilities to determine what kinds of clothes were considered as acceptable and trendy in the Soviet Union. In the eyes of the foreign clothing sellers, the European cities of the Soviet Union were the centre of dictating the trends and the other regions were to follow their lead. When comparing the urbanized and wealthy regions of the Soviet Union to the cities where the majority of the foreign fashion shows were organized, the strong Western attraction of the Soviet fashion culture becomes evident. In 1959, alongside with Russian, Estonian and Latvian republics, the most urbanized republics of the Soviet Union were Armenia and Azerbaijan (NARODNOE HOZJAJSTVO SSSR ZA 70 LET 1987, 378) and for example Baku was an important city. Further, the citizens of Turkmenistan, Kazakhstan and Russia had in average the biggest incomes in the Soviet Union in 1960 (POCKNEY 1991: 59). In spite of this, all the fashion shows organized by foreign clothing exporters in 1956–1962 were concentrated in major cities in the European part of the Soviet Union (REPORT OF THE SOVIET CHAMBER OF COMMERCE OF FOREIGN EXHIBITIONS IN THE SOVIET UNION IN 1946–1963). This demonstrates how the certain kind of cultural capital and connections to the Western world had more weight than the distribution of the urban lifestyle and average incomes in the region, when it was decided who had the power to determine good taste, and the direction of the fashion trends in the Soviet Union.

The Polish ready-to-wear exporters were well aware of the culturally determined importance of the cities in the European part of the Soviet Union in shaping the fashion trends and opinions on them. The Polish clothing exporters considered organizing fashion shows for the Soviet clothing professionals and consumers as a prerequisite for reaching successful trade agreements. Other kinds of fashion shows were not considered as influencing the sales and expanding the success of export. For example, the annual Fashion Congresses of the socialist states' were not mentioned in the documentation of the Polish exporters. In the Fashion Congresses the national collections competed, but only few models ended up to real mass production (BARTLETT 2010: 114–118, 158).

The importance of the opinion of the Soviet clothing professionals for the successful Soviet export was depicted also in the composition of the Polish export collection directed to the Soviet market. Because the Soviet clothing professionals did not consider offering youth fashion to the Soviet consumers as important, the Polish exporters did not include them to their collection in offer (LETTER OF THE PRODUCTION DEPARTMENT OF THE ZPO TO THE LABORATORY OF CLOTH INDUSTRIES). In Poland in the late 1950s the idea of a separate youth culture had been already spreading, and the Polish clothing industry had launched production of youth clothing. The Polish clothing industry was forced to take into consideration the wishes of the consumers more attentively: many Polish consumers purchased and preferred clothing imported from the West through unofficial channels, called *ciuchy*, and the officials wanted to direct consuming towards the domestic production. *Warszawskie Zakłady Przemysłu Odzieżowego* launched production of the first youth collection in 1960, and the production of Polish jeans,[5] branded *Rekord*, was launched in 1961 (PELKA 2007: 14, 52–53). Although the production of youth clothing was topical in Poland, the Polish clothing exporters did not regard it important to include them to the export collection directed to the Soviet Union. The Polish exporters thought that colourful, elegant and versatile in cuts collection would raise the interest of the Soviet customers and wholesale purchasers, but offering too modern or Western-style fashion was not considered as an asset in the Soviet market. The Polish exporters understood that as the Soviet trade and fashion professionals dictated what was imported to the country, they should be offered the kinds of clothing they considered as ideologically suitable for the Soviet consumers.

The new sales procedures and organizing fashion shows for the clothing professionals in the early 1960s paid dividends, and the amount of the exported ready-to-wear and the sums paid for them started to increase. By the end of the 1960s, Poland had reached a serious position among the importers to the Soviet market. Only the GDR exported more ready-to-wear clothes to the Soviet Union than Poland (cf. REPORT OF A COMMERCIAL DELEGATION CONCERNING TRADE NEGOTIATIONS IN THE SOVIET UNION). Until the mid-1960s clothing export was increasing without demanding further efforts from the Polish exporters, until the demands of the customer began to change in the late 1960s.

The Emergence of the Consumers

The changing demands of the Soviet consumers became visible in the foreign trade requirements in the late 1960s. In summer 1967, a Polish export delegation reported in detail the requirements of the Soviet purchasers to the ZPO. A Polish collection of 1,033 clothing models presented in Moscow had received approving evaluation, but the purchasers had given also negative remarks concerning certain models and had been reluctant to purchase some items. In addition, the Soviet purchasers had brought out new demands that had been raised by the consumers. One of the newly emerged demands caused by social changes was the increasing demand of bigger sizes. In the late 1960s, the increasing living conditions became gradually visible in the growing demand of larger clothing for the better nourished population. For the first time in 1967 the Polish clothing exporters included to the export collection clothing models for men covering sizes 56-58. However, agreement on the prices was not reached in the negotiations, and the Soviet Union did not purchase the offered models. In the bigger size clothes the problem was often that their production required more source materials, but the same sums were paid for them, as for the smaller sizes (cf. ZAKHAROVA 2013, 413). In addition to the growing physical dimensions, also the leisure and dressing habits had changed during the decade. Alongside the bigger clothes, also the demand of cheap and stylish sportswear had increased in the Soviet Union. The sportswear was not included in the Polish export collection in 1967, but the exporters delegation reported that they should be included in the future collections (cf. REPORT OF A COMMERCIAL DELEGATION CONCERNING TRADE NEGOTIATIONS IN THE SOVIET UNION).

---

[5] Jeans were valued and difficult to access consumer goods in the socialist countries. The attitudes towards consumers' demand were different in Poland in comparison to the Soviet clothing industry, because jeans production was launched in Poland over ten years earlier, in 1961, than in the Soviet Union (in 1975) (PELKA 2007: 53, BARTLETT 2010: 269). In Poland the domestically produced jeans were generally not considered as attractive as the Western imports. For example, in the late 1970s the consumers were ready to pay for the imported jeans 15 times more than for the domestic jeans. Jeans of Polish origin were not called jeans in Polish, but according to the name of the producer, such as *odry*, *elpo*, *komesy*, *justy* and *rekordy*. Domestically produced denim fabric was called either *teksas* or *tekspol* (GMYZ 2007).

The wishes and tastes of the Soviet consumers could no longer be ignored, even regarding the more dubious products, such as jeans. When in the early 1960s the Polish exporters did not even offer jeans in the export collection to the Soviet Union, by the late 1960s jeans appeared in the list of the exported clothing. Until the mid-1980s, jeans were considered officially as a symbol of the American imperialism in the Soviet Union (GRONOW & ZHURAVLEV 2010: 28). However, in practice, the Soviet importers purchased the Polish jeans. The Polish clothing industry benefited when the Soviet Union could not purchase Western jeans in big amounts due to economic and ideological reasons. The Polish clothing industry managed to adapt their jeans production so that they could sell jeans for the price-conscious Soviet wholesale purchasers in low, but profitable prices (cf. REPORT OF A COMMERCIAL DELEGATION CONCERNING TRADE NEGOTIATIONS IN THE SOVIET UNION).

The increasing awareness on the consumers' needs and demands in foreign trade was connected to the growing diversification of the Soviet retail trade sector during the 1960s. The position of the consumers improved especially in the biggest cities, and the consumers' opportunities to purchase import goods developed. Until the mid-1950s, a restricted circle of the political elite had had better access to the consumer goods than the rest of the population (HESSLER 2004: 62–69). After the late 1950s a growing number of Soviet citizens could purchase foreign goods. The attitudes towards consumption became relaxed at the same time, and the goods that were considered exclusive, became increasingly visible in the streets. It was more possible than earlier to distinguish oneself from the others by consumer goods. Different ways of dressing were not considered anymore as a social threat. The other side of the coin was that the inequality of the consumers became more visible than earlier, when the consuming opportunities of the urban population and people working in exclusive professions or with good connections, increased more than of others. The retail trade of the shortage goods in foreign currency[6] in special shops, usually called *Berezkas*, that had been launched in the late 1950s in the Soviet Union, spread both geographically and in volume along the 1960s. Foreign currency trade made the expensive Western goods accessible for increasing amount of better-off consumers (IVANOVA 2012: 5, 29, TIKHOMIROVA 2004). If earlier the majority of the consumers had more or less shared the hardships of accessing good-quality goods, now a fraction of the society had better accessibility than the others.

In addition, in the mid-1960s, the Soviet retail sector established special shops, that sold products from other socialist countries. The shops were named after foreign cities, such as *Belgrad*, *Praga*, *Budapest*, *Sofia* and *Leipzig* (BARTLETT 2010: 269, DOCUMENTS OF THE STATE DEPARTMENT STORE GUM). The retail shops specialized in the Polish goods, such as *Pol′skaja Moda*, 'Polish Fashion', and *Vanda*, 'Vanda', were established by the year 1979 (REPORT OF RAZNOEKSPORT CONCERNING IMPORT GOODS IN 1979). Unlike most of the West European imports, consumers could purchase imported socialist states′ ready-to-wear also in normal shops. Although the imports from the socialist states were less valued in comparison to the Western brand clothes, they were anyway regarded as of higher quality than the Soviet production. The Soviet consumers connected different qualities with different products of socialist countries. For example, East German clothes were regarded as practical and of high quality, while Polish clothes were considered to be distinctive. Many Soviet consumers, who did not have access to the hard currency shops, aimed to purchase clothing produced in other socialist countries (IVANOVA 2012: 158, TIKHOMIROVA 2004).

---

[6] The hard currency shop *Torgsin* had functioned in the Soviet Union already in the 1930s. Since the late 1950s the most well-known Soviet hard currency shop was *Berezka*, which was supervised by the Ministry for Foreign Trade. The shop chain functioned in several Soviet republics and under local names. Hard currency shops were established also in the other socialist countries. In Poland, established in the early 1970s, they were called *Pewex*, in Czechoslovakia *Tuzex*, and in Bulgaria *Corecom* (IVANOVA 2012: 5, CROWLEY & REID 2010: 19, JASIŃSKI 2011: 269).

The Soviet-produced ready-to-wear was less appreciated among Soviet consumers. They were perhaps the most dissatisfied with the clothing industry and trade of the whole domestic consumer goods production. Despite the improvement attempts, Soviet shops could not offer fashionable and high quality domestically produced ready-to-wear. The increasing expectations of Soviet consumers became evident even in the clothing sections of the flagship department stores, such as the Moscow State Department Store GUM. In the 1960s, the amount of visitors of the fashion exhibition hall of GUM decreased dramatically. It was said that this was caused by a radically increased competition between the fashion organizations at the Soviet market and that GUM had lost its monopolistic position in Moscow. Soviet consumers had become increasingly aware of the prevailing trends and more critical, and they compared the models offered by GUM to the models offered by other domestic and foreign producers. The availability of attractive ready-to-wear for the solvent urban consumers was increased yet more by establishment of boutiques selling exclusive domestic production for higher prices, alongside with the average clothing shops and department stores (GRONOW & ZHURAVLEV 2012: 127,136, GRONOW & ZHURAVLEV 2010: 28, 33).

The gradually increasing importance of consumers and consuming in the Soviet economy and everyday life, caused the diversification of the Soviet retail trade and the growing attention to the consumers in the import sector in the 1960s. Simultaneously the Polish exporters depicted this change as a tightening competition. The products, shops selling the products and consumers were divided more visibly than earlier into different categories of value in the Soviet market. Polish exporters competed in the 'second best' category alongside the other socialist countries. This category was accessible for a wider range of consumers than the Western imports were, but simultaneously the prices could not be too high. Soviet retail shops reported to the central trading organizations and through them to the wholesale purchasers, which products were sold quickly, and which remained in the shelves of the shops. Consumer surveys were conducted continuously from the 1950s through the 1970s (REPORTS OF THE ADMINISTRATION OF TRADE ON INDUSTRIALLY MADE GOODS IN 1954, 1955, 1966 AND 1971). Although a product remaining unsold was not as big problem for the shop keeper in the planned economy as it is in the market economy, having desired items in sale was benefit for the shop employers also in the socialist system. Alone the access to these clothes gave more power for the shop assistants both in the official and unofficial economic activities. In order to increase the demand for Polish clothes, the Polish clothing industry needed to confirm not only the wholesale purchasers, but also a vast amount of Soviet consumers.

Response to the Increasing Requirements

The appearance of the consumers' needs to the Soviet foreign trade purchasers' demands in the late 1960s forced the Polish clothing exporters to renew their portfolio and develop their marketing strategies. The attempts to respond to the Soviet consumers' demands were visible in the Polish export practices already in 1969. In that year the Polish Ministry for Foreign Trade organized in the premises of the Soviet Exhibition of Achievements of the National Economy (VDNKh) in Moscow an exhibition entitled *Peoples' Republic of Poland 25 years.* The exhibition was a great endeavour of the whole Polish foreign trade sector, the major aim of which was to strengthen the position of the Polish made machines, equipment and industrially produced consumer goods in the Soviet market. The objective of the exhibition was to lose the reputation of Poland as solely an exporter of raw materials, coal and fabrics, and to emphasize the image of Poland as a technically developed producer country (REPORT ON PLANNING THE 'PEOPLE'S REPUBLIC POLAND 25 YEARS').

Although the exhibition was to present the whole variety of Polish industrial production, from heavy industry to the production of consumer goods, the ready-to-wear clothing had a special role in the exhibition. By presenting widely and in an attracting manner clothing models, which had been gaining reputation in the socialist world, the Polish Ministry for Foreign Trade aimed to create a modern image of the whole country. The clothes were exhibited under four themes: work and everyday life, school and college, sport and leisure, as well as play. In order to emphasize the modernity of the Polish production, new products were included in the exhibition, for instance youth clothing was presented in the exhibition. Demands of the young consumers could not be ignored anymore, therefore youth clothing was included in the export collection designed for the Soviet market in 1970. In addition sport clothing, which absence was noted in 1967, was widely presented in the exhibition. (REPORT ON PLANNING THE 'PEOPLE'S REPUBLIC POLAND 25 YEARS', FOREIGN TRADE COMPANY COOPEXIM'S REPORT ON A JOURNEY TO MOSCOW).

The tastes of Soviet consumers changed in a similar manner as the tastes also elsewhere in the modern world: youth fashion with jeans became widely distributed and the sportswear occupied the room of classical suits in the late 1960s. What was considered as a decent way of dressing, behaviour or gestures, relaxed in the Soviet Union during the 1960s. Similarly like in the West, a change towards individual and less formal behaviour and clothing was visible. In the Soviet Union, however, this development was slower and more moderate than in the West. It was also distinctive to the Soviet consumer culture that goods were not thrown away lightly and they were reused thoroughly, because their accessibility was at that time difficult (GRONOW 2012: 131, BULGAKOVA 2008, GUROVA 2009: 48–49).

The display of the products in the *Peoples' Republic of Poland 25 years* exhibition was directed above all to the consumers. This denotes that the consumers' desires were not taken into consideration only in the offered selection, but consumers were considered also as a decisive group influencing the sales. For instance, fashion shows presenting 300 outfits were organized in a daily basis at the exhibition. Alongside with the shows, the exhibition visitors were offered different service points, such as a fashion tips point, a tailor, a while-you-wait repair of shoes, a make-up studio, a hairdresser and a laundry (REPORT ON PLANNING THE 'PEOPLE'S REPUBLIC POLAND 25 YEARS'). It is thus evident that the exhibition was targeted above all to the consumers, and not so much for wholesale purchasers or clothing professionals. By giving fashion tips to the visitors, the exhibition served the consumers in a new way promoting Polish ready-to-wear.

In the late 1960s taking into consideration Soviet consumers was not only important for the Polish ready-to-wear exporters, but their importance had also grown in the whole Polish foreign trade sector. The growth of the Polish national economy had been slowing down during the 1960s, and the economic planners attempted to stimulate economic growth by investing in export production (JASIŃSKI 2011: 243–244). The importance of the industrially produced consumer goods had increased in the Polish foreign trade. Their share in Polish export had increased from the 9% share in 1957 to 16% in 1970, simultaneously with the increase in the total export (LANDAU & TOMASZEVSKI 1985: 275). The share of the ready-to-wear clothes and other textile products at the time was approximately half of the total volume of export of industrially produced consumer goods (GUS 1966: 18–19). The growing importance of consumer goods was illustrated by a shift in exhibition portfolios between the late 1950s and the late 1960s: a Polish exhibition organized in Moscow in 1959 had not presented ready-to-wear clothes at all (REPORT OF THE SOVIET CHAMBER OF COMMERCE 1963, ANNUAL REPORT OF THE POLISH CHAMBER OF FOREIGN TRADE 1959). Ten years later, in the exhibition organized in 1969, the ready-to-wear clothes and consumer goods had an important role in creating a positive and modern image of the development of Poland. This demonstrates that the Polish clothing industry had succeeded in increasing its role in the internal hierarchy of the Polish economy.

Analysing the internal reports, it is easy to note the increasing importance of Soviet consumers and the tightening competition on the Soviet market besides the developing exhibition activities. The reports stated that the growing average incomes of the Soviet consumers led to the increasing demand of higher quality goods on the Soviet market. One of the reports warned that the Polish exporters could no longer think that they could continue exporting poor quality products to the Soviet Union. Arrogant attitude towards consumers was considered to harm the reputation of all the Polish export products, and above all, the future export prospects (REPORT ON POLISH-SOVIET TRADE OF THE POLISH MINISTRY FOR FOREIGN TRADE 1968, CLASSIFIED REPORT OF THE OFFICE OF THE COMMERCIAL ADVISER AT THE EMBASSY OF POLAND IN MOSCOW 1972).

Polish ready-to-wear exporters sought balance between the increasing demands of the Soviet consumers, the export quotas of the Polish Ministry for Foreign Trade and the production problems of the planned economy. The report of the Ministry for Foreign Trade demonstrates that some Polish foreign trade professionals considered that it was possible to export lower quality goods to the Soviet Union. The management of the Ministry for Foreign Trade regarded this attitude misleading and endangering Poland's competitiveness and reputation. However, the Polish clothing industry could not always provide the best possible quality to the Soviet market. The shortage of raw materials, the Soviet wholesale purchasers' strict price control, and the massive production quantities were factors that often lowered the quality of the end products (GROUP INTERVIEW OF POLISH FASHION DESIGNERS). In order to overcome the contradicting expectations, Polish exporters could use their professional knowledge of the unequal Soviet market: they could send the products of lower quality to the more remote locations of the Soviet Union without serious threat of receiving customers' complaints. Similarly, exporters could deliver the major Soviet cities only with the high quality goods, because consumers in the major centres would immediately complain about a lower quality (INTERVIEW OF A POLISH EXPORTER). In general, however, the clothing produced in Poland for the Soviet market was of better quality than the clothes produced for domestic sales. The ready-to-wear produced for export, but not sold for some reason, were greatly desired by the Polish consumers (PELKA 2007: 60, 149–151).

Consumers and the Social Change

Soviet consumers made their voices heard for Polish clothing exporters during the 1960s. This development took place because Soviet wholesale purchasers needed increasingly to take into consideration escalating consumers' demands. Simultaneously the role of clothing professionals in dictating what was desirable in the Soviet clothing culture seems to have decreased.

As the material conditions of the citizens of the socialist states improved and the awareness of the living standards outside the socialist world increased, their expectations and demands concerning their living conditions expanded (CROWLEY & REID 2010: 7). Although the consumers' expectations increased in all the socialist countries gradually after the mid-1950s, taking into consideration the Soviet consumers' needs and expectations became a necessity in ready-to-wear retail and wholesale trade only along the 1960s. This was also the conclusion reached by Crowley and Reid regarding that the East Central European countries: they became consumer cultures approximately ten years earlier than the Soviet Union (CROWLEY & REID 2010: 11). Because the Polish clothing industry had to take into consideration the desires of the consumers already since the late 1950s, they were better prepared than their Soviet colleagues to make changes in their production, and take into consideration the diversifying needs of the Soviet consumers. At the same time the priority position of foreign trade helped the Polish export in comparison to the Soviet domestic production. The more bureaucratic and fragmented Soviet clothing industry turned more slowly to meet the newly emerging expectations.

It is extremely interesting that the importance of consumers appeared in the 1960s. During the reign of Nikita Khrushchev (1953–1964) the living conditions of the population were taken into account more than earlier and consuming became more tolerated. However, the reforms launched in the Khrushchev period became more visible in the trade sector during the succeeding era of Leonid Brezhnev (1964–1982), although the Brezhnev period has been often called as a period of stagnation. Also Chernyshova comes to the same conclusion, as she writes that the changes made during the Khrushchev period were merely rhetoric, while during the Brezhnev period the consumers became visible for real (CHERNYSHOVA 2013: 2).

Summary

In this article I show how Soviet consumers became noteworthy for Polish exporters by the late 1960s. What was the reason for this change, then? I argue that it is one-sided to explain this development solely by the changing moods of the leaders and their willingness to allow consumerism to develop in order to gain legitimacy. The Polish foreign trade reports are a source that allows us to see that the Soviet consumers began to participate in determining the directions of the development of the Soviet consumer culture. Although certain administrative and legal changes acted as prerequisites, the changing force came from the consumers. The reasons for the increasing role of the consumers can be found in the global developments causing social changes during that time. Although in the planning economies the role of the state in regulating consuming was bigger than in the market economies (FEHÉRVÁRY 2009: 428), the general European factors influencing consuming habits were not unknown in the socialist countries either.

Bibliography

Archival sources

ANNUAL REPORT OF THE POLISH CHAMBER OF FOREIGN TRADE FOR YEAR 1959, Archiwum Krajowy Izby Gospodarczej (KIG), Sprawozdania.

CLASSIFIED REPORT OF THE OFFICE OF COMMERCIAL ADVISOR AT THE EMBASSY OF POLAND IN MOSCOW ON SOVIET ECONOMY IN 1972, Archiwum Akt Nowych (AAN) 2/351/30/11.

DOCUMENTS OF THE STATE DEPARTMENT STORE GUM DATED IN 1964, Tsentral'nyi Arkhiv Goroda Moskvy (TsAGM) f 474 o 1 d 238 and d 239.

FOREIGN TRADE COMPANY COOPEXIM´S REPORT ON A JOURNEY TO MOSCOW, dated 23rd of December 1970; Archiwum Akt Nowych (AAN) 2/351/64/14.

FOREWORD TO THE COLLECTION OF THE SOVIET MINISTRY FOR FOREIGN TRADE 1951-1960, Rossijskij Gosudarstvennyi Arkhiv Ėkonomiki (RGAE) F 413.

MEETING MINUTES NO. 1/III/61 OF READY-TO-WEAR CLOTHES GROUP OF THE COUNCIL OF EXPORT OF ZPO, dated 14.3.1961, Archiwum Państwowe w Łódzi (APŁ) 39/874/0/1925.

MEETING MINUTES NO. 3/VI/61 OF MEETING OF THE READY-TO-WEAR CLOTHES GROUP OF THE COUNCIL OF EXPORT OF ZPO, dated June 6, 1961, Archiwum Państwowe w Łódzi (APŁ) 39/874/0/1925.

LETTER OF THE PRODUCTION DEPARTMENT OF THE ZPO TO THE LABORATORY OF CLOTH INDUSTRIES ON PREPARATIONS OF THE EXPORT COLLECTION, dated May 4, 1961, Archiwum Państwowe w Łódzi (APŁ) 39/874/0/1936.

LETTERS OF THE DIRECTOR OF THE PRODUCTION DEPARTMENT OF ZPO TO THE CLOTHING FACTORIES IN APRIL 1961, APŁ 39/874/0/1936.

REPORT OF A COMMERCIAL DELEGATION CONCERNING TRADE NEGOTIATIONS IN THE SOVIET UNION, dated June 7, 1967; Archiwum Państwowe w Łódzi (APŁ) 39/874/0/1946.

REPORTS OF THE ADMINISTRATION OF TRADE ON INDUSTRIALLY MADE GOODS IN 1954, 1955, 1966 AND 1971; Tsentral'nyi Arkhiv Goroda Moskvy (TsAGM), f 297 o 1 d 123; d 148; d 617 and d 873.

REPORT OF THE FOREIGN EXHIBITIONS´ DEPARTMENT OF THE SOVIET CHAMBER OF COMMERCE ON FOREIGN EXHIBITIONS IN THE SOVIET UNION IN 1946-1963, dated in 1963; Rossijskij Gosudarstvennyi Arhiv Ekonomiki (RGAE) F 635 o 1 d 566, part 1.

REPORT ON POLISH-SOVIET TRADE OF THE DEPARTMENT OF COMMODITY EXCHANGE OF THE POLISH MINISTRY FOR FOREIGN TRADE IN 1968, part II, Archiwum Akt Nowych (AAN) 2/351/63/13.

REPORT OF RAZNOEKSPORT CONCERNING IMPORT GOODS IN 1979, Rossijskij Gosudarsvennyi Arkhiv Ėkonomiki (RGAE), f 413 o 32 d 407.

REPORT ON PLANNING THE "PEOPLES´ REPUBLIC OF POLAND 25 YEARS" -EXHIBITIon to be held in Moscow in June 1969, date September 7, 1968, Archiwum Akt Nowych (AAN) 2/351/3/38.

Interviews

GROUP INTERVIEW OF POLISH FASHION DESIGNERS (BORN 1943, 1947, 1947, 1949 AND 1949), Łódź, Poland, June 30, 2011.

INTERVIEW OF A POLISH EXPORTER (BORN 1950), Łódź, Poland, December 3, 2011.

Literature

BARTLETT, D. 2010. *FashionEast: The Spectre That Haunted Socialism.* Cambridge.

BERENDT, I.T. 2009. *From the Soviet Bloc to the European Union. The Economic and Social Transformation of Central and Eastern Europe since 1973.* USA.

BULGAKOVA, O. 2008. *The Factory of Gestures. Body Language in Film.* (DVD). Stanford.

CHERNYSHOVA, N. 2013. *Soviet Consumer Culture in the Brezhnev Era.* Great Britain.

CROWLEY, D., REID, S. E. 2010. Introduction: Pleasures in Socialism? In: D. Crowley, D., Reid, S.E. (ed.). *Pleasures in Socialism: Leisure and Luxury in the Eastern Bloc.* Illinois 2012, 3–50.

EISLER, J. 2009. Bratni naród? Stosunek społeczeństwa polskiego do obywateli ZSRR. In: *W objęciach wielkiego brata. Sowieci w Polsce 1944–1993.* Pod redakcją Konrada Rokickiego & Sławomira Stępnia. Warszawa 2009, 263–273.

FEHÉRVÁRY, K. 2009. Goods and States: The Political Logic of State-Socialist Material Culture. In: *Comparative Studies in Society and History* 51 (2), 426–459.

GŁÓWNY URZĄD STATYSTYCZNY POLSKIEJ RZECZYPOSPOLITEJ LUDOWEJ (GUS). 1959. *Statystyka Handlu Zagranicznego. Przywóz i wywóz towarów według krajów 1958.* Warszawa.

GŁÓWNY URZĄD STATYSTYCZNY POLSKIEJ RZECZYPOSPOLITEJ LUDOWEJ (GUS). 1966. *Rocznik Statystyczny Handlu Zagranicznego 1965.* Warszawa.

GMYZ, C. 2007. Pożądanie w kolorze blue. In: *Tygodnik Wprost*, 30 (1283).

GRONOW, J. 2012. Soviet modernity: the case of Soviet fashion. In: Alapuro, R., Mustajoki, A., Pesonen, P. (ed.). *Understanding Russianness.* London 2012, 125–136.

GRONOW, J., ZHURAVLEV, S 2012. A Window to the West and Door to the East. The Tallinn Fashion House as a Part of the Soviet Fashion Design System. In: *Mood ja külm sõda - Fashion and the Cold War.* Estonia 2012, 108–137.

GRONOW, J., ZHURAVLEV, S. 2010. Soviet Investment in Flamboyance. Fashion Design at GUM, the State Department Store at Moscow. In: *Baltic Worlds* III 2, 26–33.

GUROVA, O. 2009. The Life Span of Things in Soviet Society. Notes on the Sociology of Underwear. In: *Russian Studies in History* 48:1, 46–57.

HARDY, J. 2009. *Poland´s New Capitalism.* London.

HESSLER, J. 2004. *A Social History of Soviet Trade: Trade Policy, Retail Practices, and Consumption, 1917-1953.* Princeton.

IVANOVA, A. 2012. *Gosudarstvennaia torgovlia na inostrannyiu valiutu v ierarkhii i kul'ture potrebleniia sovestkogo obshchestva, 1958-1991 gg.* Moskva.

JASIŃSKI, L.J. 2011. *Bliżej centrum czy na peryferiach? Polskie kontakty gospodarcze z zagranicą w XX wieku.* Warszawa.

KANSIKAS, S. 2014. *Socialist Countries Face the European Community. Soviet Bloc Controversies over East-West Trade.* Frankfurt am Main.

KOIVUNEN, P. 2013. *Performing Peace and Friendship. The World Youth Festival as a Tool of Soviet Cultural Diplomacy, 1947–1957.* Tampere.

KORNAI, J. 1992/2000. *The Socialist System. The Political Economy of Communism.* Oxford.

KRAVETS, O., SANDIKCI, Ö. 2013. Marketing for Socialism: Soviet Cosmetics in the 1930s. In: *Business History Review* 87 03, 461–487.

KUUSI, H. 2013. Accidental Traders – Finnish Tourists in the Soviet Union in the 1950s-1970s. In: Heinonen, V., Peltonen, M. (ed.). *Finnish Consumption. An Emerging Consumer Society between East and West.* Helsinki 2013, 206–227.

LANDAU, Z., TOMASZEWSKI, J. 1985. *The Polish Economy in the Twentieth Century.* Kent.

LEDENEVA, A. 1998. *Russia´s Economy of Favours. Blat, Networking and Informal Exchange.* UK.

MUKHINA, I. 2013. From Rags to Riches. Port Cities and Consumerism in the Soviet 1970s and 1980s. In: *Fashion, Consumption and Everyday Culture in the Soviet Union between 1945 and 1985*, Conference at the University of Salzburg.

N.N. 1987. *Narodnoe khoziaistvo SSSR za 70 let*. Moskva.

NEUBURGER, M. 2012. The Taste of Smoke. Bulgartabak and the Manufacturing of Cigarettes and Satisfaction. In: Bren, P., Neuburger, M. (ed.). *Communism Unwrapped. Consumption in Cold War Eastern Europe*. Oxford 2012, 91–115.

OIVA, M. 2014. Selling Fashion to the Soviets. Competitive Practices in Polish Clothes Export in the Early 1960s. In: Ilich M., K. Miklóssy, K. *Competition in Socialist Society*. Great Britain 2014, 71–88.

PELKA, A. 2007. *Teksas-land: moda młodzieżowa w PRL*. Warszawa.

POCKNEY, B.P. 1991. *Soviet Statistics since 1950*. Great Britain

PRIANIKOV, P. 2007. Udavila nemtsev za kopeiku. Kak vneshniaia torgovlia cdelala doch' trotskista khoroshei znakomoi korolevy Elizavety II. In: *Russkaia zhizn'* 17 (8).

SASSATELLI, R. 2007. *Consumer Culture: History, Theory and Politics*. London.

STONE, R.W. 1996. *Satellites and Commissars: Strategy and Conflict in the Politics of Soviet-Bloc Trade*. Princeton.

SUDINSKI, R. 2009. Etapy i kierunki oraz metody i formy ekonomicznego uzależnienia Polski od ZSRR w latach 1944-1989 na tle pozostałych krajów bloku komunistycznego. In: *W Objęciach Wielkiego Brata. Sowieci W Polsce 1944-1993*. Pod redakcją Konrada Rokickiego & Sławomira Stępnia. Warszawa 2009, 57–94.

TIKHOMIROVA, A. 2004. V 280 kilometrach ot Moskvy: osobennosti mody i praktik potrebleniia odezhdy v sovetskoi provintsii (Iaroslavl', 1960–1980-e gody). In: *Neprikosnovennyi zapas* 5 (37).

ZAKHAROVA, L. 2011 *S'habiller à la soviétique: La mode et le Dégel en URSS*. Paris.

Graphics

Export of Polish clothing and underwear to the Soviet Union (thousand złoty), 1958–1981. Source: GUS foreign trade statistics (see picture 3)

Abbildung 1:
Photograph from the Soviet magazine *Sovetskaia zhenshchina* in 1946, No 2

Abbildung 2:
Пуговица от джинсов, произведенная цеховиками в Одессе в конце 1970-х гг.

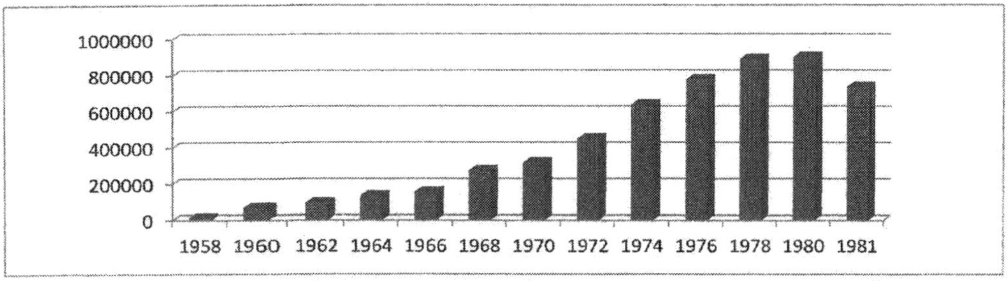

Abbildung 3:
Export of Polish clothing and underwear to the Soviet Union (thousand złoty), 1958–1981.
Source: GUS foreign trade statistics

Abbildung 4:
Zhertva Mody 'Victim of fashion' (Kassil', 1968)

Abbildung 5:
Moda 'Fashion' *(Bashkortostan Kyzy,* 1970)

Abbildung 6:
Семейные фотографии Трубицыных

Abbildung 7:
DVD-Intro zum Musikfilm „*Stiljagi*“ (Regie: Valerij Todorovskij, 2008)

Abbildung 8:
Die Konsomol-Versammlung (aus dem Musikfilm „*Stiljagi*“; Regie: Valerij Todorovskij, 2008; 1:29:11)

Abbildung 9:
Nach der Perestrojka (aus dem Musikfilm „*Stiljagi*“; Regie: Valerij Todorovskij, 2008; 2:04:53)

Abbildung 10:
Aleksandr Baženov: Podražateli (o. J.)

Aleksandr Baženov (1904–1983) war Maler und Karikaturist und bereits ab 1926 Mitarbeiter bei Krokodil. Der Text auf der Karte lautet: «Мы спорить с Дарвиным не будем / В его ученье нет изъяна / Он прав: / В далёком прошлом люди / Произошли от обезъяны. // Все было бы так, как шло от века, / Но рок-н-ролл сместил все планы, / И в этом танце / Человека / Не отличишь от обезьяны.»

Abbildung 11:
Egor Gorochov : Illustration zu *„Garri“*

Egor Gorochov (1924–2006), Karikaturist, ab 1948 künstlerischer Redakteur bei *Krokodil*.

Abbildung 12:
Kukryniksy: Poganki (1960)

Kukryniksy ist das Akronym für Michail Vasil'evič Kuprijanov (1903–1991), Porfirij Nikitič Krylov (1902–1990) und Nikolaj Aleksandrovič Sokolov (1903–2000). Die drei waren mehrfach ausgezeichnete Maler und Karikaturisten (und nicht zu verwechseln mit der russischen Rock-Gruppe, die seit 1997 unter diesem Namen auftritt). Der Text auf der Bildkarte stammt von dem bekannten Feuilletonisten und Satiriker Ėmil' Krotkij (Pseud. Ėmmanuil Jakovlevič German, 1892–1963) und lautet: «Иностранцы!! Иностранки!! / Нет, от пяток до бровей / Это – местные поганки, / Доморощенный ‹Бродве›!».

MAKING YOURSELF BEAUTIFUL?
Appearance, Body and "Girl's Dignity" in the Life of Young Women in the 1950s-1960s

YULIA GRADSKOVA, STOCKHOLM

"Men look at women. Women watch themselves being looked at... She has to survey everything she is and everything she does because how she appears to others, and ultimately how she appears to men, is of crucial importance for what is normally thought of as a success in her life,"– wrote John Berger in his book dedicated to visual culture (BERGER 1972: 46-47). The fashion scholar Malcolm Barnard also claimed that historically in many cases women were reduced to their appearance while creation and maintenance of a style or an appearance became something like a defining feature of femininity (BARNARD 1996: 115).
How relevant all of it was for the Soviet young women of the 1950s-1960s? What was the relationship between femininity norms, nice look and fashionable clothes? How different were the norms for beauty and what did they mean for young women?

Previous researches on Soviet fashion and beauty have shown that in the 1950-1960s the Soviet discourse on look, beauty and fashion was rather contradictory. On the one hand, it was proved that the Soviet women were suffering from the shortages of nice, feminine and fashionable clothes (see VAINSTEIN 1996, LEBINA & CHISTIKOV 2005). On the other hand, the research on Soviet dress makers, clothing industry and advice publications showed that "fashion" not only did not disappear from the Soviet everyday life, but that the Soviet government attempted to organize production of fashionable clothes and expected Soviet people, in particular women, to dress with the taste (ZHURAVLEV &GRONOW 2005, KELLY 2001, GRADSKOVA 2007 a, GRADSKOVA 2012). Indeed, Catriona Kelly in her study of advice literature wrote about consumerism becoming important part of the Soviet ideology of universal plenty that led to a certain conflict with "retaining the moral elevation and material disinterest" (KELLY 2001: 314-315). However, the contradictions of Soviet interpretations of beauty and their connections to femininity appear to be even more striking when we start analysing individual memories on everyday beauty practices. In particular, if we take into account existent differences among women depending of their place of living, age, education, ethnicity, or religious traditions of their families.

The article is based on the analysis of advice publications and women's magazines as well as on the interviews with women born mainly between 1932 and 1947; the interviews were collected in Moscow and in Ufa (the capital of Bashkortostan).[1] I analyse the recommendations on beauty and everyday beauty practices of younger women, those who were seen in 1950-1960s as constructors of the future communist society. In order to study the Soviet beauty practices I use a feminist approach of thinking through body (see DAVIS 1997: 1-23) and an intersectional approach. Indeed, according to Kemberlé Crenshaw, the different axes like class, gender and ethnicity should be approached as interacting in order to understand complex hierarchies and discrimination systems (CRENSHAW 1989: 40). Thus, in this article I will focus on how advice publications present women as a group different from men with respect to social norms and expectations around their appearance. At the same time I will also explore how women discussed their experiences of getting beautiful and/or fashionable look.

---

[1] The interviews were collected as a part of my PhD research in 2003-2005. Some ideas discussed in this article first appeared in my dissertation "Soviet People with Female Bodies. Performing Beauty and Maternity in Soviet Russia in the mid-1930s-1960s" Stockholm University, 2007.

Also I will take into account differences among women in the cross-section of their belonging to a particular professional or ethnic group, being younger or older and as living in a particular region.

Good look, morality and femininity in Soviet advice literature

An important part of the Soviet "standard" vocabulary of beauty was dealing with *vkus* 'taste'. To possess "good taste" presupposed that people were dressed well. A "good taste" was seen as the result of education: everyone interested in looking nice should know "the laws of harmony", make "a correct choice" of fabric or "fashion" and choose matching garments. At the same time, "bad taste" was frequently associated with deviant value systems rather than to bad aesthetic education. The deviant value system included not only *meshchanstvo* 'philistinism' – too much interest in expensive and decorative clothes and hairstyles – but also norms connected to age-specific behaviour and control over sexuality.

Due to certain opening of the country after Stalin's death and appearance of certain (even very limited) availability of choice of garments and accessories compared with the post-war years, some aesthetic advice for young people started to be seen as an especially important part of education of the young people. The advice on clothes and look constituted a significant part of this campaign, however, in most of the publications the nice look was discussed in the contexts of personal behaviour and self-improvement. The terms "beautiful" and "not beautiful" were used mainly as normalizing categories in an attempt to manipulate the consumption, behaviour and sexuality of young people through aesthetic arguments. The "bad taste", for example, started to be more and more associated with foreign style clothes; it was also assumed that there are connections between thinking about a remarkable look and lack of attention to moral behaviour and lack of interest in education[2] (see picture 4: *Zhertva mody* 'Victim of fashion') were drawn. At the same time, in spite of recognizing importance of new styles, the Soviet advice publications continued prizing "naturality" of look as the most valuable one.

For example, in the 1960s the leading Soviet women's magazine *Rabotnitsa* started publishing a special section for young women *Podruzhka* 'Female friend' as well as a lot of advice on look and clothing connected to spending of the leisure time. Along with presenting new garments, including shorts and trousers for young women, publications did not forget to remind about colour combinations ("it is good if shorts and a sun cap are of the same colour", *Moda* 1966) and that having too big brooch exposes a "bad taste" rather than beauty (MARGOLINA 1964, POSLEDITE 1966). At the same time almost all the publications stressed that it was the young body per se that was the most beautiful.

The publications by the Soviet writer Lev Kassil' (elected member of the Soviet Academy of Pedagogical Sciences in 1965) are very characteristic for the contradictory views on new styles and new consumption practices. Justifying the importance of fashion, Kassil' showed himself at the same time as being very preoccupied by aesthetic style that, according to him consisted in respect to the "natural" body: "And the most important issue is that every woman should first of all choose the style and tone of the dress matching her appearance and corresponding to her natural features" (KASSIL' 1958: 27).

"The natural features" here had to remind the woman-reader that her look is an important part in the gendered communication and that too much "extra" accessories would rather damage her look not only from the view point of the Soviet ideology of social equality and modesty, but also from the view point of the observation of the gender norms. Indeed, it is *de-*

[2] It is interesting to note that in the court decision on Pussy Riot performance 50 years later it was possible to read the accusation of their behavior that is aimed for "changing moral, norms of appropriateness, relationship to family, sexual relationships" see N.N. 2012.

vichie dostoinstvo 'girl's dignity' that is not less important than style (KASSIL' 1968: 11). Kassil' also stressed that woman should be attractive and the aim of changing styles to avoid certain tiredness of the spectator (KASSIL' 1968: 71).

Still, most of the publications on beauty not only reminded on attractiveness of the natural body, but also advised how to make it more attractive through the use of special techniques or garments. The contradictions of the new aesthetic discourse for youth could be followed, for example, by considering the book by the Estonian author Iina Asamaa *"How to Behave"* first published in Estonian (1965) and later translated into Russian. Due to the fact that the book's first audience was not the Russians who grew up in Soviet families, but the Estonian youth where a lot of pre-war cultural traditions were still preserved from the independence time, the author managed to merge the Soviet advice with the legacy of the Western middle class culture. Along with traditional insistence on modesty of appearance and behaviour and respect for naturalness, the book brought many new aspects to the problems of taste and choice. Firstly, it not only approved of the use of makeup, stating, "proper use of make up in these days shows a person's level of education and culture," (ASAMAA, 1971: 221) but gave explicit explanations on the eye-brow pencil and lipstick application (ASAMAA 1971: 202, 219). Secondly, it approved a particular style of clothes for youth, including bright colours and trousers for women. Thirdly, the book gave a lot of psychological advice about using clothes and communication (for example, on need to avoid steering on somebody's outfits) (ASAMAA 1971: 16).

On the other hand, the book included some pieces of advice that were rather gender-specific and allowed some norms of behaviour that seemed to be in discrepancy with the ideology of Soviet style, where man and woman were supposed to be "equal" in social communication of different kind. For example, the book uses "Dame" when it is discussed who is supposed to be first in shaking hands and saying "Hello" and advises that if a man is meeting a couple on the street it is a man, not a woman, who should be greeted first (ASAMAA 1971: 58). Furthermore, norms of taste and good manners, according to the book, were very age-specific: if sitting with crossed legs per se was declared not to be inappropriate for a woman anymore, it still was considered to be so for a young woman – a girl[3] (ASAMAA 1971: 31).

The gender-specific norms of behaviour are also visible in other Soviet publications for youth. For example, the book written by Aleksandr Dorokhov in the same period of time and addressed to young people warned:

> "Some of [girls] think that they should not be different from the most libertine boys. They walk with the wide steps and swing their arms while walking, they speak by a specially rough voice and use a lot of the rude words that they know that boys are using while alone, they are giggling loudly and generally behave very provocatively, almost spitting with their leaps.
>
> If they would be able to understand how does it harm them depriving from the charms of femininity! The girls should show the example to boys and get their attention not by using rudeness, but by showing softness, modesty and self-control. These are qualities that make a girl to be beautiful." (DOROKHOV 1969: 60)

This passage points out several gender differences in look and behaviour (like rudeness/softness, free movements/restrain). Indeed, the book creates the image of the woman and, in particular the young woman, as a subject of bigger social surveillance than in the case of the young man.

After this short analysis of the discourses of taste and beauty for youth on the base of the Soviet publications, I intend to analyse how issues of beauty were presented in stories of women that were young in 1950-1960s.

---

[3] *Devushka* 'girl' is a word that has clear connotations of virginity in Russian.

Beauty and different femininities

The Soviet publications insisted on taste and aesthetics being central for the discussion of beauty and femininity. Indeed, the idea of the good taste was presented as if based on a kind of expert knowledge on aesthetics that clearly divided women's appearance into corresponding to certain norms or not. However, the collected stories show that women's ideas about what was beautiful differed a lot depending on women's place of living, profession, education as well as ethnic and religious traditions. I will show that these different views on "beauty" expressed in the interview process created simultaneously different statuses and femininities.

Many of my older informants, especially those who worked in cities as accountants, engineers and doctors stressed the difference between the look they should have at the work place (in this case aimed mainly professional occupations in public places) and the "Sunday best" – the nice dress for visiting friends and going to parties. My informant from Ufa, F, who started to work as teacher at a rather young age stressed, for example: "The teacher always had to be taut. She should have serious dark dresses." The "Sunday best" in its turn had to be produced from the most expensive cloth and to be of much more varied colours. Even if this tradition was more characteristic for the 1930s-1940s, the collected interviews show that up to the beginning of the 1960s these traditions continued to be observed by many city women.

On the other hand, the interview material shows that in the 1950s and, in particular in the 1960s, the number, diversity and importance of the establishments aimed for producing beautiful look in the cities grew immensely. Large department stores displayed at least two or three styles of dresses, coats and shoes, there were specialized shops for perfume and accessories, beauty salons, hairdressers and fabric shops. In all of these places women interacted as consumers. It was very different from the first post-war decennia when, according to many of my older informants, *tolchok* the 'black market' and home production of clothes were the most important for the "good look". Several of my informants, who were young in the late 1950s-1960s, mentioned some remarkable purchases they made – high quality shoes, a nice dress or perfume. At the same time, along with an open system of shops and services, a hierarchical structure of special or exclusive services was developed and diversified. Thus, V, who worked in a secret military company in Moscow from the early 1960s, stated that at that time the beauty services within the company were very good. There were not only shops and hairdressers, but at the hairdresser's it was possible to get some cosmetic services for free. In its turn, possibilities of free use of beauty services indicated special privileges and higher social status.

Together with differences connected to the work place, profession and education, the regional differences in the use of beauty facilities were considerable as well. While my Moscow informants remember the late 1950s and 1960s as a period when ready-to-wear clothes including coats, dresses, hats and baby-clothes were widely available, an informant like U, coming from a provincial town in the Urals, would recall shops as having a very limited choice of everything that meant that the services of private dressmakers and/or shopping trips remained vital to the local population. Thus, U's mother, a waitress in a restaurant, had her private dressmaker who also made dresses from scratch for U. Another informant, T, who was from an industrial city in northern Kazakhstan, in the mid-1960s was a student in Moscow and complained about shortages of clothes and told about her experience of buying fashionable garments privately in the student dormitory. However, she stressed that she looked extraordinarily fashionable at her home town in Kazakhstan with the shoes and clothes she had bought in Moscow state trade facilities.

Such differences in accessibility of stuff and institutions of beauty led to the production of a kind of beauty stratification, where complex combination of place of work and living as well as profession resulted in different looks. At the same time, the "appearance" influenced young women's statuses and choices. T, for example, remembered that when she was a young single mother and had a rather tough economic situation, her female friend made her to buy a new coat arguing that she should find a husband and that nobody would marry her in such a coat she has now.

In spite of the fact that starting from the 1920s the ideas of "good taste" and "good look" were presented as universal and guided by modern aesthetic principles, they usually promoted the Western (European style) dress as aesthetic, while the traditional ethnic look in case of ethnic minority women was declared mainly to be "backward".[4] Although the attitude to the "national dress" started to change already in the late 1940s under the influence of the universal fashion interests in folklore,[5] the "national elements" in dress were still set mainly for a kind of theatrical representations of minorities as a part of the Soviet community (see PILKINGTON & YEMELIANOVA 2003; about use of national traditions and language in Tatarstan as folklore see also FALLER 2011). While the loud campaigns against non-hygienic and damaging health ethnic dress were left in the 1930s (NUKHRAT 1930: 44), still for many young women living in ethnic regions and autonomous Soviet republics the problem of look was connected to the problem of ethnic identity. Indeed, my Bashkir and Tatar informants discussed uneasy relationships towards "modern" city dress (in this case usually addressed as "Russian") in difference to local traditions. Thus, one of the informants, mother of six children proudly said that from time to time she travelled to the nearby city with other women from the village and came back with the clothes for her daughters. She was proud that they could allow themselves to wear city style clothes and by this was "fashionable". On the other hand, several informants from Ufa expressed their concerns with the new "modern" fashion, in particular, with the situations when very young women wore a lot of makeup and short dresses – it was seen as a challenge to the local traditions as well as to ethnic interpretations of differences between the married woman and the "young girl". F said, for example, that young Bashkir women usually did not wear too much makeup, while it were "the Russian girls" who wore "tight clothes" and, had "too long skirts with big pockets, or too narrow skirts like a pencil". Another informant from Ufa, A, also noted that it was a big difference between how Russian and Bashkir girls were dressed: the last looked more modest than the first.[6] On the base of the collected stories it is possible to see that different looks not only indicated ethnic and religious identities, but also contributed to the production of different modes of femininity in the cross-section of gender and ethnic standards.

Still, the stories of most young informants (born in the late 1930s-1940s) show that fashionable clothes became more important and the homogenization of look happened to a big extend due to fashion pages in magazines and to films, including some foreign films that were accessible for youth. The Bashkir language magazine for women *Bashkortostan Kyzy*, launched in 1968, also presented the same year a collection of the mini-dresses similarly to the central publications of fashion models (like in *Rabotnitsa*) the same year. Most of the presented clothes had at the same time a Bashkir style ornament (see picture 5 *Moda* 'Fashion'*)*. Furthermore, two of my informants who grew up in two different small cities (one of them was Russian living in North Kazakhstan and the other was Tatar living in small city in the Urals) told about their attempt to follow Brigitte Bardot's style in the film about Babette by wearing self-made dresses, made according to their impressions from the film (GRADSKOVA 2012).

[4] More about Bolshevik culturalisation of dress and resistance to it see GRADSKOVA 2008.

[5] See, for example, fashion pages from the women's magazine in Tatar language *Azat Hatyn* and the article "Following the people's style" in *Zhurnal mod.*

[6] On modesty see more in GRADSKOVA 2009.

How to get a beautiful look?

Unlike the beauty given by nature, becoming beautiful was connected with some investments in the form of money, time or human resources. Different societies can be studied and classified on the basis of the main principles of how their economies of beauty function. The traditional society is characterized by time-consuming beauty techniques (for example, long evenings of sewing dowry clothing) and natural resources (home-made clothing and shoes). The beauty economy of industrial societies is mainly based on monetary resources. If more money is invested, high-quality textiles and more sophisticated fashion are accessible.

My interviews indicate that the role of money in Soviet beauty practices during the whole studied period was important. As in a market economy the accessibility of beauty artefacts was very dependent on the income. A, who was a student in Ufa in the early 1950s, said that jewellery was rather inaccessible for young people – they hardly could buy earrings or other decorations. The beauty accessories were sold "in special shops" and, probably for "rich people". "Rich", thus, was presented in the story as a marker of differences, although A. herself in an earlier part of the interview stated that young women in Ufa in the period of her youth were rather "similar" and "modest" in their looks.

The interviews suggest, however, that in spite of the importance of mostly money based, public as well as semi-legal beauty infrastructure (like buying clothes from foreigners in the student dormitory as F did), in the 1950s-1960s beautiful look continued predominantly to be produced at home. The home-produced beauty required a lot of skills, time and imagination. Most of the women I interviewed learned to sew already in their childhood (by older female relatives or at school) and considered it "normal" to sew, knit and make hair-dresses at home, but in most of the cases they were proud of their results. Exceptions were rare and informants expressed how difficult it could be when one lacked such kind of knowledge. Thus, S from Moscow considered her abilities to sew as a very important resource for becoming beautiful – she not only sewed nice dresses for herself, but also made a nice dress for her older sister who put it on when she went to university. Sewing techniques, according to my informants, became especially important later, during the periods of pregnancy when the body shape was changing and the more standardized clothes that could be bought in the shops did not fit any more. The most important use of sewing and knitting techniques was, however, not applied to make new clothing from scratch but rather to embellish or improve existing garments. Usually, old dresses were used again and were refashioned several times.

Hairdressing was another important qualification that had to be learned in order to reach a nice everyday look, not to speak about a more special one. While the perm, according to my older informants, was done at the hairdresser's only 2-3 times a year during the 1940s-early 1950s, my younger informants went to hairdressers once a month for a setting. Also everyday maintenance usually required the use of specific products and equipment for revitalising the curls.

School, students' dormitory and workplace, according to the interviews, played an important role in the development of qualification for beauty. For example, G from Ufa told me that copying embroidery patterns from one another was very popular in the student dormitory where she lived. Several other informants told about learning sewing patterns and sewing techniques at the work place from the co-workers, while in several stories the beauty models were presented as a subject for discussions and collective experimenting. According to F from Ufa, for example, the "most fashion interested girls in the students' dormitory" did curls by heating up iron sticks.

Concluding the part on self-made beauty in the memories of women who were young in the 1950s-1960s, it is important to stress, that the need of learning and using these techniques was presented as obvious for women, but not for men. According to my informants, the men in their surrounding (except for *stilyagi* in the story of P from Ufa and M from Moscow)[7] used more frequently clothes made outside of the home.

Young bodies, attractiveness and surveillance

As we could read in the advice publications, the young women were expected to be moral, hardworking and not sexually frivolous, they had to look as "girls" and be different from "women". At the same time young women had to care about looking nicely and behaving "differently" from young men. The collected stories often contain parts that show difficulties and contradictions in addressing these demands and expectations while remembering different periods of own life. Indeed, even those of my informants who were involved in experimenting with looks in their youth (first of all during their student years), in other parts of the interview insisted on the importance of morality and appropriateness as defining factors for life and happiness of a woman. P from Ufa, for example, told a lot about her student years and experimenting with changing her hair colours. Still, discussing her work as a school teacher in the early 1970s she stressed that she had individual conversations with girls who behaved too frivolously. For example, she also told girls who came to school with makeup or extravagant hairstyle: "You're going to be a mother. Somebody will love you. So you should get rid of these habits." A Moscow informant, M, who in her young years was proud to have a private (illegal) dress-maker and telling about herself as "a girl of fashion" and a representative of "that generation of the 1960s" later presented herself as a supporter of the Soviet modesty norm. Also she pictured her interest for clothes in her "young years" as an unfortunate affliction of young people:

> "But all of us were youngsters in the 60s. You understand? We were singing Okudzhava songs. We went to that famous Grushin festival. And it was the true 60s generation! It was a very interesting youth. But I have to tell you, that we also had these stilyagas... And our boys, they were trying even to make these trousers, you know, like stove pipes. It was great. The girls were doing this hair style [shows on her head]... We had all of this and it all passed. This is the time of youth. We had to recover from it as from illness, and now I am recovered." (M)

Nevertheless, having a special style clothes or just an ordinary modest look, the young woman, according to my informants, was expected to demonstrate her difference to men. According to P from Ufa, for example, "a woman did not have to be particularly beautiful, but feminine, soft and kind instead." At the same time, woman's body was presented as particularly vulnerable to ageing and had to be protected and cared about. Answers to my questions about the use of makeup pointed to this temporal dimension. For example, G from Ufa said:

> "I didn't use curlers, lipstick or makeup. I started to use lipstick after I became 30 years old. [Pause] We were told that if a woman were to use makeup at an early age she would lose the natural colour of the skin. [With added emphasis] Indeed, it's true. Those who didn't use makeup preserved their beauty better." (G)

According to this informant, makeup is good only when it serves for the imitation of youthfulness that has already faded, an opinion shared by several other informants from different cities.

The women's stories indicate that natural, healthy skin and hair was a sign of good looks and signalled sexual attraction and healthy offspring. Indeed, the interviews show that hairstyle and makeup also conveyed information about proper or deviant female sexuality. Ac-

[7] About stilyagi-men remaking their clothes see, for example, KIMERLING 2007: 82.

cording to some of my informants, the use of makeup was especially risky for the appearance of young girls since obvious traces of makeup in her face immediately associated her with the appearance of a sexually experienced woman.

> "We were girls and we looked like girls... One time my friend and I... She was from Odessa. We went to Odessa. We were students at that time and went to the seaside. She told me: 'You should dye your eyebrows.' I have a very pale face, so I dyed my eyebrows; I have a picture [of me] that I've kept until now. You know, it gives such an impression! Can you imagine an attractive young girl that suddenly was converted to a kind of a woman of the street! I cried and cried, but they said that I had 6 months guarantee [of the preservation of the colour of the eyebrows]. I was doing sun bathing back then [The informant hoped that the sun bathing would fade the dye quicker]. But when I came home, my mother said: 'Oh God! What did you do to yourself!'" (M)

Unlike women who were expected to be at least feminine if not outstanding beauties, men could easily be considered attractive for other qualities. Hence, in speaking about the importance of beauty for men and women my informants highlighted some differences: "Besides his good looks he also had something very special" (P about her husband), "I never liked good-looking men, but I liked intelligent men". (C)

Concluding, it is possible to say that the question posed at the beginning of this article could be answered positively. How did young women look and dress, what models did they choose, how did they use cosmetics was very important for their femininity and would be recognized as correct and "normal". While the advice for youth on clothes, aesthetics and behaviour in the 1950s-1960s became more diverse and permissive than in the previous period, it is still easy to follow the "special" relationships to the clothes and looks the "girls" were expected to have.

During these years the beauty practices were institutionalized through the bigger availability and services provided by stores, hair and cosmetic salons, as well as through the stronger influence of beauty ideas that were infiltrating into Soviet cities through films and fashion models from the other side of the Iron Curtain. At the same time, the ideals of "natural beauty" and modesty continued to be promoted by the advice literature while woman continued to be declared "equal to man". It contributed to controversial expectations from and demands for the young women who with their bodies had to demonstrate both attractiveness and restrain.

The stories of my informants show that the fashionable look required a lot of efforts, time and creativity, particularly, taking into account the situation of shortages of goods and clothes. At the same time the stories prove that young women not only were doing a lot of efforts for making themselves to "look nice", but had sometimes different ideals with respect to beauty, not least, depending on their educational and ethnic background. Thus, differences in the look contributed to different statuses and were connected to "invisible" Soviet hierarchies (for example, between "woman from the centre" and "provincial woman" or between "our women" (belonging to the body of the particular nation) and "other women". Different looks could also influence individual success and marked individual biographical trajectories. Nevertheless, it was an expression and preservation of the "femininity" (in its different interpretations), that was in the focus of the stories of practically all my informants.

Summary

This article is dedicated to the study of beauty practices in the 1950s-1960s and their importance for the Soviet femininity construction. In the focus of the article is the analysis of the expectations on how young women (girls) should look and behave as well as the exploration of the diversity of beauty practices in connection to femininities in the cross-section of social, ethnic and geographical differences between women. The woman's body is approached as an important means for a "beautiful look" as well as an object for the social surveillance. The article is based on the analysis of advice publications and women's magazines as well as on the interviews with women born in the 1930s-1940s in the USSR.

Bibliography

ASAMAA, I. 1971. *Kak sebia vesti.* Tallinn (first published in Tallinn in Estonian in 1965).

BARNARD, M. 1996. *Fashion as Communication.* London and New York.

JOHN, B. 1972. *Ways of Seeing.* London

CRENSHAW, K. 1989. Demarginalizing the intersection of race and sex: A black Feminist Critic of Anti-discrimination Doctrine. Feminist theory and Anti-Racist Politics. In: *University of Chicago Legal Forum,* Chicago 1989, 139-167.

DAVIS, K. 1997. *Embodied Practices. Feminist Perspectives on the Body.* London.

DOROKHOV, A. 1969. *Eto stoit zapomnit',* Moskva.

FALLER, H. 2011. *Nation, language, Islam: Tatarstan's sovereignty movement.* Budapest.

GRADSKOVA, Y. 2007. *Soviet people with female bodies: performing beauty and maternity in Soviet Russia in the mid 1930-1960s.* Stockholm University Doctoral Dissertation.

GRADSKOVA, Y. 2007a. "We were very upset if we didn't look fashionable": Women's Beauty Practices in Post-war Russia. In: Rebecca Kay (ed.). *Gender, Equality and Difference during and after State Socialism.* Palgrave, 21-40.

GRADSKOVA, Y. 2008. From 'Backwardness' to 'Modern Culture'? 'Beauty' and 'Femininity' during the Soviet Cultural Modernization from the 1930s to the 1960s. In: Olofsson, K. (ed.). *From Orientalism to Postcoloniality,* Huddinge 2008. http://www.diva-portal.org/sh/

GRADSKOVA, Y. 2012. Femininity and Beauty Practices in Soviet Russia in the 1950-1960s. In: McNeil, P., Wallenberg, L. (eds.). *Nordic Fashion Studies.* Stockholm 2012, 3-18.

GRADSKOVA, Y. 2009. How Can Women's Stories about Beauty and Maternity Help Us to Study Soviet Social History of the 1930-1960s? In: Obertreis, J., Stephan, A. (ed.). *Oral history and (Post-)Socialist Societies.* Essen 2009, 187-201.

KASSIL', L. 1958. Devushka so vkusom. In: *Rabotnitsa* 4 1958, 27.

KASSIL', L. 1968. *Delo vkusa.* Moskva.

KELLY, C. 2001. *Refining Russia. Advice Literature, Polite Culture and Gender from Catherine to Yeltsin.* Oxford.

KIMERLING, A. 2007. Platforma protiv kalosh, ili Stiliagi na ulitsakh sovetskogo goroda. In: *Teoriia mody. Odezhda. Telo. Kultura.* 2007:3, 82-99.

LEBINA, N., CHISTIKOV, A. 2003. *Obyvatel' i reformy: kartiny povsednevnoi zhizni gorozhan v gody NEPa i khrushchevskogo desiatiletiia.* St.Petersburg.

MARGOLINA, L. 1964. Broshki na ves. In: *Rabotnitsa* 4, 29.

N.N. 1966. Moda turistam. In: *Rabotnitsa* 5, 22.

NUKHRAT, A.1930. *Bytovaia rabota potrebitelskoi kooperatsii v natsionalnykh raionakh.* Moskva.

N.N. 2012. *Khuligany v khrame zadirali nogi immitiruia tantsy.* http://www.newsru.com/arch/russia/22aug2012/pr_verdict_txt.html (04.08.2014),

PILKINGTON, H., YEMELIANOVA, G. 2003. *Islam in Post-soviet Russia. Public and Private Faces.* London, New York.

N.N. 1966. Posledite za soboi, pozhaluista. In: *Rabotnitsa* 6, 30.

VAINSTEIN, O.1996. Female Fashion, Soviet style. The bodies of Ideology. In: Goshilo H., Holmgren, B. (ed.). *Russia, Women, Culture.* Indiana University Press. 1996, 64-94.

VISHLENKOVA E., MALYSHEVA S., SAL'NIKOVA A. 2005. *Kazanskoe zhitie* (and Ervard Turnerelli. *Kazan' i ee zhiteli).* Kazan'.

ZHURAVLEV, S., GRONOW, J. 2005. Krasota pod kontrolem gosudarstva: osobennosti i etapy stanovle-nia sovetskoi mody. In: *The Soviet and Post-Soviet Review* 32, 1-92.

List of the informants

U. – born in 1947 in a small city in Ural, interviewed in Moscow.
T. – born in 1946 in a small city in Northern Kazakhstan, interviewed in Moscow.
S. – born in 1945 in Far East, spent her childhood mainly in Moscow, interviewed in Moscow
P.– born in 1939 in a village in Bashkortostan, interviewed in Ufa.
V. – born in 1939 in Moscow, interviewed in Moscow.
F. – born in 1937 in a city in Ural, interviewed in Ufa.
G. – born in 1935 in Bashkortostan, interviewed in Ufa.
O. – born in 1935 in a village in Bashkortostan.
M. – born in 1933 in Minsk, spent her young years in Moscow
E. – born in 1932 in a village in Bashkortostan, interviewed in Ufa.
A. – born in 1932 in a village in Bashkortostan, interviewed in Ufa.
H. – born in 1927 in a village in Bashkortostan, interviewed in Ufa.
C. – born in 1922 in a village near Riazan', interviewed in Moscow.

Pictures

Zhertva mody 'Victim of fashion' from Kassil' 1968, 96.
Moda 'Fashion' from *Bashkortostan Kyzy* 1970 1, 24.

ЧТО НУЖНО ДЛЯ СЧАСТЬЯ? ЭСТЕТИЧЕСКАЯ ИНСЦЕНИРОВКА ЖЕНСКИХ БУДНЕЙ В СОВЕТСКИХ ЖУРНАЛАХ И КНИГАХ ПО ДОМОВОДСТВУ 1950-Х – 1960-Х ГОДОВ

ЕЛЕНА ХУБЕР, ЗАЛЬЦБУРГ

Фаза развития женской идентичности, которая создавалась и преобразовывалась за счет слияния политических концепций, традиционных ценностей и норм, а также реальных фактов, представляет нам в 1950-ых-1960-ых годах независимую, успешную, образованную и воспетую идеологией женщину, которая успевает делать карьеру и одновременно устраивает свою личную жизнь. Но одновременно в визуальной репрезентации женщины советскими средствами массовой информации, в содержании многочисленных дискурсов о ее положении в обществе и семье, и, наконец, в отношении ее реальной жизни постоянно проявляются противоречия. С одной стороны ее роль как мать, жена и работающая женщина четко определена, достижение равноправия женщины, поставленное целью советским государством и ее свобода (во всех ее понятиях) находятся в постоянном процессе улучшения. Многочисленные законы и политические программы, критика в средствах массовой информации о несправедливом обращении с женщиной на работе и дома, и наконец теоретические дискуссии и предложения улучшения уровня ее жизни социологами и демографами говорит о том, что государство уверенно владеет обстановкой в этом вопросе. С другой стороны, анализируя женские журналы и книги по домоводству, мы можем заметить попытку конструирования женской идентичности, которая не только явно про-тиворечила критике несправедливого отношения с женщиной, но и отчасти усугубляла ее положение.

Учитывая общественные, экономические и политические изменения в стране, а также идеологические нормы и проектировки периода оттепели, нужно поставить вопрос о том, насколько принципы советской гендерной политики с ее общественными идеологическими дискурсами с одной стороны и неофициальные, существующие внутри семьи и ее окружения ценности, с другой стороны формировали женский индивидуум, и, наоборот, как она сама реагировала на все эти влияния. Конечно, благодаря актуальному уровню исследований в этой области такие понятия как двойная и тройная нагрузка, равноправие в процессе разрушения (MARGOLINA 1994: 54) или кризис мужественности уже не новые. Наоборот, становится интереснее понять, как женщины сами видели свою роль в обществе и семье. Эксперимент эмансипации не удался или она была ловко заменена своенравием[1] (понятием «*Eigen-Sinn*») и комплексной презентацией самой себя? Наконец здесь поставлен вопрос о том, как формировались взаимоотношения между женщиной, государством и семьей на индивидуальном и структурном уровне?

Отправная точка этого исследования лежит в объединении гендерных исследований и исследований в области одежды. В официальном дискурсе 1950-ых – 1960-ых годов обсуждение концепции советского вкуса было поставлено на передний план, а женская идентичность была конструирована с учетом понятий моды, эстетики и красоты. Как следствие одежду, если рассматривать ее исключительно как предмет потребления, следует понимать как медиум или способ конструированиия полов. Па основании женских

[1] Перевод иностранных слов, выражений, цитат, имеющихся в данной статье, сделан мной – Е.Х.

журналов и журналов моды, а также книг по домоводству в этой статье будет предпринята попытка, проанализировать визуальную репрезентацию женщины в ее (рабочем) быту, что даст нам возможность понять не только реальную ситуацию тех лет, но и идеологические и культурные ценности и правила советского общества. Для этого выборочно будет рассмотрен ряд журналов *Работница* и *Советская женщина*, а также публикации середины 1950-ых – 1960-ых годов, которые рассматривают понятия моды, эстетики и норм поведения. На основании их анализа будет исследован вопрос о том, насколько принципы конструирования полов и их различий можно рассматривать под влиянием этих понятий. Основным предметом обсуждения проблемы здесь является то, насколько и действительно ли официальные дискурсы стабилизировали традиции женской роли в обществе и семье и наоборот, как эти уже заданные концепты идентичности поддерживались или ликвидировались самой женщиной. Другими словами, фокусируя свое внимание на эти дискурсы, мы получаем точный анализ общественных норм и ценностей того времени. В конечном счете, предписанные в них жизненные установки можно рассматривать не только как факт воздействия »Wirkung« на социокультурное развитие общества, но и как его результат »Auswirkung« (Heimerdinger 2006: 57).

Центральными аспектами изображения советского женского быта являлись в первую очередь женственность и красота. При этом понятие красоты рассматривалось через призму разнообразных областей частной и общественной жизни. Конечно, в основном это были вопросы внешнего вида, поведения и конкретно одежды, они объединяли в себе требования простоты, скромности и чувства меры. Далее в женском сознании сформировывался тот факт, что к не менее важным качествам привлекательной и, в общем, идеальной женщины относились одновременно материнство, склонность к созданию семьи и успех в работе. Только наличие этих компонентов делало ее примером для других и обеспечивало стабильное социальное положение.

Эстетизация работающей женщины и понятие женственности

Рассматривая многочисленные публикации середины 1950-х по 1965-е годы на тему эстетики и красоты, можно заметить, что руководящую роль в дискуссии о том, какие качества объединяет в себя культурный уровень советского индивидуума и общества в целом, на первый план ставится его внутренняя красота. В общем, социальный импульс, подталкивающий общество на обсуждение вопросов вкуса и эстетического сознания, обосновывается фактом повышения уровня жизни, а также материальных и культурных потребностей населения, а вместе с тем и необходимостью, правильно, а главное самостоятельно использовать полученные знания в этой области. Конечно, на основании уже имеющихся исследований в этой области усиленное внимание вопросам вкуса и красоты можно аргументировать дружественными связями с Западом, чья повседневная культура или отдельные ее стороны могли подорвать основу социалистического образа жизни. Этот аргумент поддерживается тем фактом, что в основном дискуссии на тему вкуса и вообще манеры поведения базировались на том, чтобы показать и объяснить смысл социалистической культуры за счет выявления провалов или в целом категоричного отрицания именно западной культуры.

Одновременно здесь забывается тот факт, что период оттепели фактически был периодом советской истории, где существовали экономический подъем и внутриполитическое ослабление контроля государства над личностью, а вследствие этого требовалось создание новой жизненной модели, отвечающей этим новым явлениям в советском обществе. Начало новой культурной парадигмы в 1950-ых – 1960-ых годах очерчивалось, прежде всего, легитимацией частной жизни и как следствие созданием «мещанского уютного» стиля жизни, а также стремлением окружить себя эстетически красивыми предметами быта:

«С каждым годом меняется облик всей страны, растут новые села, районы и новые города, и стиль современности является нам в простоте, изяществе, лаконичности. [...] Меняется не только внешний вид городов, становится другой и делается краше вся жизнь в них. [...] Много добротных, красивых и разнообразных товаров создает наша легкая промышленность. Сейчас стало гораздо легче выбрать вещь по своему вкусу.» (Дубровская 1961: 1)

Многочисленные публикации начинаются с подобным обращением к советскому читателю, а для каждого простого человека такие понятия как эстетика, стиль и элегантность являлись уже чем-то обычным, так как найти их можно было не только в узком кругу научных работ, но и во многих вполне доступных в продаже журналах и книгах. Эстетическим идеалам не зря была уделена настолько серьезная роль, независимо от социальных и политических трансформаций она оставалась единст-венным кри-терием стабильности и определяла создание и сохранение новых традиций в быту:

«Эстетический идеал служит критерием, на основе которого человек оценивает действительность, в нем воплощены общественные интересы людей, их представления о лучшем. Эстетический идеал переплетается с другими общественными идеалами: социальными, политическими, нравственными. Каждый человек оценивает различные явления с позиций существующего эстетического идеала, но в зависимости от своих индивидуальных особенностей.» (Шубин 1987: 40)

Создание собственного индивидуального пространства, которое было возможно с приобретением собственной квартиры, вызвало в действие новый процесс переосмысления области семьи и супружества. Внезапная культурная либерализация частной жиз-ненной сферы и возможность концентрирования интересов и забот индивидуума на уз-ком кругу его семьи и друзей предполагало создание новых эстетических идеалов и ценностей. В особенности это касалось актуализации семейных ценностей и перераспределения ролей в отношении мужчины и женщины. При этом государство не оставалось в его единственной роли контрольного органа, а ловко регулировало вопросы социальной политики и семьи, направление и тематику официальных дискурсов с помощью идеологических организационных устройств, и в результате формировало представления о женственности и мужественности в общест-венном сознании. Само общество, а в этом примере семья и ближайшее социальное окружение индивидуума, перенимают при этом на себя форму горизонтального контроля (Захарова 2009: 244. Здраво-мыслова 2004: 315) и ответственность за то, что эти принципы будут правильно и самостоятельно приведены в исполнение каждым.

Здесь тип регулировки семейных взаимоотношений и в отдельности женского вопроса напоминает русское дореволюционное общество:

“Die Herrschaft des Mannes über die Frau in Russland beruhte auf der patriarchalen Tradition der erweiterten Familie. [...] Das Gewaltmonopol über die Frau und die Autorität lagen bei dem Ältesten in der Familie. [...] Verlor die Familie ihren männlichen Teil, ging die Gewalt an die Frauenseite über. Insofern war eine aktive Teilnahme von Frauen, besonders Witwen, an gemeinschaftlichen Entscheidungen keine Seltenheit.”[2] (Margolina 1994: 54)

---

[2] «Господство мужчины над женщиной основывалось на патриархальных традициях семьи в широком смысле. [...] Монополия власти над женщиной и авторитет находились в руках старейшего. [...] Если же

Перефразируя понятие *власти* через понятие своеволия или своенравия женских актеров *»Eigen-Sinn«*, в поле зрения попадает вопрос об их (со)организации и определении женской роли и идентичности как продукта социокультурных и поли-тических процессов в общественной и личной жизненной сфере. Так как социальные проблемы и конкретно освещение личного пространства в конце 1950-х годов стали предметом многочисленных дискуссий в средствах массовой информации, то в резуль-тате создается специфическая форма женского конструирования и репрезентации самой женственности, которые символично формируются и представляются через внешний вид женщины и в первую очередь через ее одежду.

Рассматривая многочисленные изображения женщин в журналах или специальной теоретической и практической литературе, в глаза бросается достаточно ограниченный выбор типажей. Как и в 1930-е годы здесь можно выделить два типа женщин – это женщина в рабочем процессе и (замужняя) женщина с ребенком. Культурные формы женского образа действий находятся в непрерывном процессе трансформации, в котором создаются новые модели женского конструирования и в тоже время видоизменяются или рушатся вообще старые «сталинские» модели. Остается только умение заменить форму эстетики и эстетизации на хитрую иллюзию, через которую переносятся и стабилизируются новые идеалы. Как и в 1930-е годы, когда фотография была использована не только для идеологических (конструирование полов), но и экономических (потребление) или культурных целей, *журнал* в качестве медиума/ коммуникативного средства перенимает на себя функцию посредника и умело при-водит в процесс эстетизацию женственности.

Центральная роль одежды в смысле конструирования полов и их дифференциации объясняется следующим высказыванием: “Eines der ersten Dinge, die beim Geschlechterverhältnis auffallen, ist nicht, wie Freud annahm, das unterschiedliche Geschlecht, sondern seine Markierung: die unterschiedliche Kleidung und die damit verbundenen unterschiedlichen Tätigkeiten in Räumen und Zeiten.”[3] (KATSCHNIG-FASCH 1987: 130, здесь GAUGELE 2002: 9) Это означает, что в конструировании одежды социокультурные представления о женственности и мужественности выявляются через выкройку, цвет, форму и материал. (см. GAUGELE 2002: 9). Четкая дифференциация в женской и мужской одежде определяется через отклонение или наоборот присвоение определенных символов одежды. Кроме того, идентичность групп и иерархическая лестница во взаимо-отношении обоих полов символично выражается через жесты, осанку, одежду и другие факторы, имеющие к этому отношение (KOTTHOFF 1994: 171, здесь GAUGELE 2002: 10).

Доминантным образом в изображении женщин в советских журналах из двух представленных можно назвать образ работающей женщины, причем под рабочим процессом здесь не подразумевается работа в публичной сфере, т.е. на предприятии, в бюро или на политическом собрании, но и в частности в ее личном пространстве. Это относится и к репрезентации ее красоты и женственности, так как в отличие от начала 1930-х годов в период оттепели эти оба типажа женской телесности были тесно связаны. Мы не видим четкого различия между женственностью работающей женщины и той, изображение которой было четко ориентировано на красоту, как, например, артистический тип, который был популярен в начале 1930-х годов. Интересно, что женщины, которые

семья теряла свою мужскую часть, власть переходила на женскую сторону. В этом отношении активное участие женщин, а в особенности вдов, в общественных вопросах было не редкостью.»

[3] «Одно из первых обстоятельств, которые бросаются в глаза касаемо взаимоотношений полов, это не их различие, как предполагал Фрейд, а различная одежда и связанные вместе с ней различные виды действий во времени и пространстве.»

репрезентировали конкретно внешнюю красоту (актуальные модные тенденции, прически или бижутерию) независимо от того, в позитивном ли (в репортажах или статьях о моде и стиле) или негативном смысле (критика моды и стиля), часто изображены именно в рисунке, а не в фотографии. Это, скорее всего, связано с попыткой реконструировать красоту и женственность искусственно и тем самым идеально, что делает ее так называемым объектом вожделения. Искусственные идеалы красоты сами по себе будут реализованы читательницами, но эта цель достигается путем сознательного эстетического влияния или обмана реальной жен-щины неестественным, созданным идеологически сформированным образом. Эстети-ческое изображение работающей, успешной женщины становится предметом подра-жания для реально существующей, но и не только для нее самой, а и для ее супруга, который видит ее в этой роли, как что-то само собой разумеющееся.

Возможно, что только одежда для занятий в публичной сфере деятельности является той оболочкой, которая меньше всего подчеркивает дифференциацию полов, чем это делает одежда для работы в частном пространстве. Через первую обладательнице приписывается маскулинизированный образ и тем самым навязывается специфическая социальная роль, которая предоставляет ей некое признание в мужской сфере деятельности. Здесь большую роль играет видимость эстетического, так как с одной стороны авторы многочисленных публикаций заставляют нас в контексте визуального и текстуального изображения женщины поверить в существование равноправия[4], в то же время между этими изображениями и реальностью существует разнобой, который опрокидывает этот образ.

Чтобы заменить мужчину на его рабочем месте, женщине нужно принять ряд мужских черт:

> “Will eine Frau beruflich erfolgreich sein, muß sie männliche Einstellungen übernehmen. Für ihren Körper hat das zur Folge, daß sie vermehrt männliche Hormone ausschüttet. Das bedeutet eine verringerte Produktion von Sexualduftstoffen. Und gerade diese östrogenabhängigen Duftstoffe sind es, die den Mann anmachen.”[5] (KAPLAN 1989, здесь LOSCHEK 1991: 212)

Одежда становится инструментом конструирования дифференциации полов:

> “In allen vorindustriellen Gesellschaften spiegelt das jeweilige Insgesamt von männlichen oder weiblichen Tätigkeiten sich in einem Satz geschlechtsspezifischer Werkzeuge wider […] Wenn man ein Werkzeug ergreift und benutzt, setzt man sich zu dem zugehörigen Geschlecht in Beziehung. Daraus ergibt sich, daß der Umgang der beiden Geschlechter primär ein sozialer ist.”[6] (ILLICH 1983: 59, здесь GAUGELE 2002: 75)

---

[4] см. например: БУЖКЕВИЧ, М. 1956. Делегат съезда. In: *Советская женщина* 2, 7–8; Из дневника ткачихи Любы Парфеновой. 1967. In: *Работница* 10, 8–10; ФЕДОРОВА, Л. 1968. Как вам работается… In: *Советская женщина* 12, 20–21; КАРПОВА, Е. 1971. Это и есть равноправие. In: *Советская женщина* 8, 6–7; МИХАЙЛОВ, В. 1965. День Музы Федоровны. In: *Советская женщина* 2, 30–31.

[5] «Если женщина хочет быть успешной, то она должна перенять на себя мужские особенности. Для ее организма это означает, что она должна выделять мужские гормоны. Это означает сниженную выработку сексуальных ароматизаторов. Но именно эти зависимые от эстрогенов ароматизаторы делают женщину привлекательной для мужчины.»

[6] «Во всех преиндустриальных обществах конкретная совокупность мужских и женских сфер деятельности отображается в одном комплекте специфических инструментов, относящихся к тому или иному полу […] Взяв в руки и используя какой-то из этих определенных инструментов, индивидуум тем

На основании этого высказывания становится понятно, что женщине просто необходимо облачать себя в подчеркнуто мужскую одежду, чтобы иметь признание прежде всего мужского пола. В особенности это касается ее, если она хочет занимать или действительно занимает некую высокую позицию. Через общественный дискурс и собственный индивидуальный опыт (небрежное отношение к семье и как следствие плохо воспитанные дети, разочарованный супруг и даже развод), а также за неимением поддержки со стороны семьи, которая даже винит женщину в ее неудачах, ей непрерывно указывается на то, что у нее есть первостепенные обязанности в жизни. Вступая в профессиональную жизнь, она вторгается в мужскую сферу, что в общест-венном дискурсе представляется как совмещение первостепенной и второстепенной роли женщины. Отдача времени в пользу карьеры и политической деятельности при-знаются обществом до тех пор, пока она наряду с этим успевает исполнять свою роль как мать и жена.

Одежда при этом перенимает функцию столпа, на котором держатся основы культурного конструирования и дифференциации полов. На примере рабочей одежды, а в особенности брюк, можно увидеть точные специфические признаки того или иного пола. Мы видим как в публичной, так и частной сфере деятельности едва ли не принужденную женственность, которая обнаруживается путем навязывания ей ношения юбок и платьев. В первую очередь брюки рассматриваются как мужская часть туалета и поэтому либо совсем отвергаются, а если и принимаются, то в редких случаях (в профессиональной деятельность их советуют одевать для особо тяжелой или грязной работы).

Далее фактическое признание женщины в мужской профессиональной сфере осуществляется за счет ее отречения от типично женских признаков в одежде и в ее общем внешнем виде. Это возможно, например, через категоричный отказ от любого украшательства, так как оно считается типичным для женщины:

> «Желание дополнительно украсить рабочую одежду, свойственное иногда женщинам, не достигает своей цели, так как противоречит деловой обстановке. Не стоит, например, заменять ситцевую косынку, сделанную в одном цвете с воротничком халата, более дорогой, шелковой, которая вовсе ни к чему не подходит. Тем более не следует носить на производстве серьги, бусы, колье. Они предназначены для нарядной одежды.» (Ефремова 1969: 10)

Снисходительно или почти иронично сочувственно описываются женщины, которые в рабочем процессе хотят быть привлекательными и в мужской одежде чувствуют себя неуютно:

> «Лиза не просто переодевалась в комбинезон, но […] устраивала себе прямо-таки гардеробную. Она приходила в лодочках-гвоздиках и чулках эластик, накрахмаленная юбочка, […] и на отвороте блузки неизменно сияла эмалевая брошка-квадрат […].
> Вечером, переодевшись, Лиза стремилась выйти не со всеми, а выскользнуть раньше, чтобы никто не видел ее в потоке строительных рабочих. […] – Я иду – и ни один человек не скажет, что я на стройке работаю, – с гордостью заявляла Лиза.» (Левина 1961: 93)

самым определяет свое отношение к тому или иному полу. Из этого следует, что связь с полом характеризуется в первую очередь через социальные факторы.»

Несмотря на строгость рабочей одежды женщины часто не воспринимались серьезно или в лучшем случае над ними брали «отцовство» коллеги мужского пола:

> « – Раз – два – взяли! Кто не взял, тому легче! – крикнул демобилизованный моряк и по-хорошему подмигнул девушке-студентке, которая, должно быть, потому, что была в лыжных брюках и кедах, не пожелала остаться с женщинами, а толкала машину рядом со своим товарищем, плечом к плечу.» (Левина 1960: 95)

Менее привлекательным был тот факт, что рабочая одежда женщинам на предприятии выдавалась либо неподходящего размера, либо плохого качества, что можно рассматривать как насмешку или хотя бы как отсутствующую готовность интегрировать женщину в рабочий процесс.[7]

Женщинам четко давали понять, какую ответственность они принимают на себя, участвуя в рабочем процессе, а передача этого неофициального смысла читательницам производилась визуальным путем, через осознанно выбранную осанку и жесты. На фотографиях мы часто видим женщину конкретно в рабочем процессе, она находится в почти скованной позе, концентрирует свой взгляд на коллегах или деловых бумагах, редко улыбается или смотрит в камеру. Почти без эмоции и без каких-либо определенных жестов она тем самым выражает свою компетенцию и весомость. Отсутствие эмоций здесь все же не отрицает самого чувства счастья, но оно видимо лишь в ее индивидуальном пространстве, в свободное время, а если и проникает в рабочий процесс, то в виде легкой улыбки или жеста внутреннего сияния или удовлетворения.

Эстетическая инсценировка работающей домохозяйки и матери

Одежда для работы в домашней обстановке воплощает в себя символ создания индивидуального пространства. В связи с политическими и экономическими изменениями тема домашнего уюта становится ведущей в общественном дискурсе и символизирует мещанский стиль жизни, а вместе с тем и стремление к эстетически кра-сивому окружению, которое характеризирует весь период оттепели. Именно в 1950-ые -1960-ые годы дискуссиям о домашней одежде и общем внешнем виде индивидуума в домашней обстановке (в присутствии партнера или без него) было уделено много внимания. Эстетизация домашнего быта и его обитателей, а также приватизация семьи в общем смысле требовали переосмысления женской роли.

Вопрос о разделении домашних обязанностей отображается в многочисленных дискурсах. С одной стороны критики осуждали проблемы в неравномерном перераспределении домашних дел и тем самым отсутствие равноправия в семье:

> «Советские социологи и демографы доказывали наличие бытового неравенства мужчин и женщин, преодоление которого является задачей коммунистического строительства. Исследования бюджетов времени выявили, что женщины-работницы уделяют домашнему хозяйству в 2–2,5 раза больше времени, чем мужчины и соответственно располагают меньшим временем для роста квалификации и развития потенциала личности. Женские занятия составляют основу домашнего хозяйства и поглощают столько внерабочего времени, что образуют своего рода вторую смену женщин-работниц.» (Здравомыслова 2004: 317)

---

[7] См. например: N.N. 1962. Халат «вообще». In: *Работница* 7, 9; Черепахова, Э. 1965. Эхо домостроя. In: *Работница* 3, 14 – 15; Давыдов, И. 1966. «Девушкам вход воспрещен». In: *Работница* 2, 18 – 19; Франковский, А. 1965. А не про наш ли завод? In: *Работница* 8, 29; N.N. 1966. „Не для женщин“. In: *Работница* 7, 10; Массова, Б., et.al. 1958. Работницам – удобную спецодежду. In: *Работница* 10, 22 – 23.

Но действительная проблематика этого вопроса виделась в том, что женщина слишком много времени уделяла работе. Ее настоящей предписанной государством и обществом ролью оставалась роль матери и жены. При этом традиционные патриар-хальные нормы подвергались критике, а единственным решением проблемы виделись малоуспешные попытки расширить область бытовых услуг и ускорить процесс механизации домашнего хозяйства.

В результате государство вообще официально отходит от поиска решения семейных проблем и принимает на себя роль критического наблюдателя. Аргументируется это решение тем, что вопрос правильного распределения семейных обязанностей между супругами должен решаться ими самими, так как сам факт их исполнения относится к одним из основ семейных отношений. К тому же конкретно женщине указывается на то, что профессиональная деятельность так и иначе не является гарантом ее равноправия (как пример публикуются статьи об угнетении женщин на Западе, которые обязаны работать, чтобы элементарно выжить). Эстетизация работающей женщины в домашней обстановке через ее визуальную и текстуальную репрезентацию в сущности только подчеркивает настоящую позицию государства в этом вопросе.

Одежда становиться средством различия между мужчиной и женщиной и укрепляет роль женщины на различных уровнях. Роль домашней одежды как средство конструирования полов объединяет в себе ее практическое назначение, социальную функцию и изготовление. Она воплощает в себе то, что можно понимать как эстетическое представление о правильной и неправильной женской идентичности, и как манера себя вести отличает мужчину от женщины в общественном понятии:

> “Bekleidung (wie Sprache) befriedigt nicht nur die praktischen Bedürfnisse und den persönlichen Geschmack ihrer Träger, sondern dient dazu, die Umwelt zu bezeichnen und die Normen der Umwelt zu befriedigen […] jeder paßt sich in seiner Sprache und seiner Bekleidung seinem Milieu an.”[8] (Bogatyrev 1971: 85, здесь Gaugele 2002: 27)

В то время как работающая в общественном пространстве женщина в своей репрезентации в первую очередь в одежде и во всем внешнем поведении перенимает на себя мужские черты, то от женщины, работающей дома, требуется воплощение идеалов женственности и красоты. Контраст между типично женским и мужским внешним видом заметно усиливается и тем самым через одежду усиливается иерархия между мужским и женским полом. Чтобы покрыть весь спектр деятельности женщины в личном пространстве набором необходимой домашней одежды, ей предлагается особая категория одежды, так называемое домашнее платье (менее брюки). Этим делается акцент на женственности и слабости (слабый пол). Гардероб для дома эстетизируется, а работа по дому сама по себе преуменьшается или приукрашивается.

> «Закончив домашние хлопоты, снимите его (передник, Е.Х.) и останьтесь в платье, в котором проведет весь вечер, если никуда не идете и не ждете гостей.
> Но даже если кто-нибудь и зайдет случайно, вам не придется стесняться своего вида: на вас чистое, отглаженное, приятное домашнее платье.

---

[8] «Одежда (как и язык) удовлетворяет не только практические потребности и личный вкус ее носителя, но и служит для того, чтобы описывать окружающий мир и удовлетворять его нормы и правила […] каждый приспосабливается сам в своем языке и одежде к своему окружению.»

> Гардероб для дома может быть очень невелик, но в нем непременно должны быть: тапочки или легкие туфли и одно-два платья или сарафан с блузками. [...]
> Кроме платьев, нужен легкий халатик, который надевают только утром, вставая с постели, да перед сном.
> Обязательно надо иметь два-три передника. Лучше, если они предназначены для разных работ: для уборки и стирки, для стряпни и один парадный. [...]
> Хорошо, если фигура позволяет вам носить брюки. Их можно надевать дома в холодные зимние дни, а также для прогулок и поездок за город. [...]
> Для домашнего физического труда удобен хлопчатобумажный полукомбинезон.» (Дубровская 1961: 4)

Подобные советы для домашнего гардероба можно найти во многих других книгах по домоводству или журналах. Создание не отвечающей реальности приукрашенной действительности (трата времени и физический труд нигде не упоминаются) происходит при помощи ауры элегантности и возвышенности (даже если они достигаются простотой и скромностью в одежде), которая возникает вокруг одежды и служит инструментом для обмана читательницы. Граница между рабочей одеждой и одеждой для отдыха частично смыта, чтобы лишить первую функции именно рабочей или спецодежды, и тем самым не дать женщине чувствовать себя обособленной от общества: «Приятно, вернувшись с работы, переодеться в свежую, удобную и красивую одежду. Молодым, стройным женщинам идут платья с приталенным лифом и расширенной книзу юбкой – это и модно да и удобно для домашних дел.» (Семенова 1963: 31). Дополнительно можно рассматривать халаты длиной до колен, брюки или расширенные юбки как признанные обществом символы женской эмансипации и тем самым расширение женской мобильности и свободы. То, что с утверждением одежды для работы дома визуализируется демонстрация постоянного занятия делом и подразумевается ее фактическая занятость, как вид социального давления на женщину, не ставиться под вопрос.

Прежде всего, обращаясь к женщине, авторы повышают в ее глазах имидж домашнего халата (причем не только в Советском Союзе), который по их словам можно носить буквально всегда и везде как модное дневное платье, тем самым рас-ширяя границы частной сферы и не чувствуя себя служанкой в домашней обстановке. Каталог «*Quelle*» 1969-го года описывает халат под лозунгом “aktuelle Mode für den wichtigsten Beruf der Welt”[9] (Quelle F/S 1969: 86, здесь Gaugele 2002: 231). В Советском Союзе халат вообще имел особое положение, даже во времена дефицита его можно было купить без особых проблем. На страницах журналов мод халаты каждый сезон твердо держали места, а в многочисленных публикациях на тему моды и стиля описанию того, как изготовить или украсить халат декоративными элементами, всегда уделялось должное внимание.

Вообще изготовление одежды для дома, а здесь конкретно халата служило критерием для оценки женской компетенции, а сами предметы одежды – демонстра-цией постоянного занятия делом. Кроме того, самостоятельно сшитая или хотя бы хорошо заштопанная одежда являлась признаком работы хорошей домохозяйки и жены, хотя официально все виды рукоделия рассматривались как хобби. Текстильная ручная работа была определена как определенно женская работа еще в дорево-люционной России. При этом умение шить, как средство конструирования полов, заменило профессионализм этого мастерства на обычную домашнюю работу и в результате окончательно установило роль женщины в семье.[10] Эта традиция продол-жила свое существование в

---

[9] «актуальная мода для самой важной профессии мира»

[10] О специфике гендерных аспектов шитья см. Руан 2009: 35–70.

Советском Союзе, и вследствие этого умение шить и сам процесс шитья стали чем-то само собой разумеющимся. Каждая женщина должна была понимать смысл построения выкройки, делать ее или хотя бы уметь переносить ее с образцов в журналах и книгах, а также не только уметь шить, но и переделать какую-то вещь для разных целей (подогнать по форме, придать новый вид). Естественность этой практики развивалась в первую очередь во времена дефицита швейных изделий, материала или швейных принадлежностей (см. Гурова 2009: 46-57). Далее способность шить отметала факт отсутствия культурного развития в вопросах моды и стиля. Это аргументировалось тем, что этой проблемы просто не может существовать ввиду наличия многочисленных статей, а также доступности не только их, но и книг по домоводству, а в особенности широкого распространения выкроек советских модельер-ов, которые можно было найти в любом женском журнале (см. Захарова 2006: 186-201). Учитывая разнообразный выбор курсов кройки и шитья, скромный бюджет и дефицит уже не воспринимались как препятствие на пути к качественной и стильной одежде не только для женщины, но для всей ее семьи.

> „Каждая женщина – горожанка, колхозница – должна [...] непременно уметь шить!
> Научиться шить, хотя бы для своих детей и для себя, - очень важно. Курсов кройки и шитья в городах много. В Москве они существуют при самых различных организациях, даже при домоуправлениях. Возможность научиться шить имеет буквально каждая москвичка. Такие кружки можно организовать везде.
> Во многих сельских районах сейчас открывают ателье и при них сразу же создают курсы кройки и шитья. В колхозы выезжают художники-модельеры и помогают разобраться в том, что кому подходит, советуют, что и как шить. [...]
> Когда умеешь шить, легче определить, что тебе идет, что не идет, найти свой стиль. Зная свой стиль, уже не трудно одеться к лицу, а главное, как мы уже говорили, в процессе производства, работы развивается эстетический вкус.
> Покупать дешевую материю и заказывать из нее платье в дорогом ателье нет смысла. [...] Умея шить, вы свободны в выборе, купите дешевое или дорогое – то, что вам по душе.» (Русанова 1962: 119)

Умение шить, как профессиональная деятельность, потеряла свою ценность, она стала неоплачиваемой деятельностью и способом времяпрепровождения. Те женщины, которые все же зарабатывали шитьем на жизнь, сталкивались с различными проблемами: они считались низкоквалифицированным персоналом и соответственно этому оплачивались. Кроме того, они должны были работать невидимыми для государства и тем самым идти на риск выполнения запрещенной частной или подпольной деятельности (см. Вайнштейн 2007: 110).

В закрытом женском коллективе учиться шить или давать кому-то шить на заказ предмет одежды является специфическим гендерным опытом самомоделирования. Занятие шитьем в школе или конкретно здесь курс кройки и шитья взрослой для взрослой женщины можно рассматривать как подготовку или утверждение ее роли как жена и мать. Феминизирование или оженствление текстильной индустрии (в этой области были заняты в основном женщины), которое было популярным не только в Советской России, но и в Европе, “begann mit einer geschlechtsspezifischen Selektion im textilen Industrieunterricht, parallel zum sinkenden Lohnniveau in den Textilbetrieben.”[11] (Ladj-

[11] «[...] началось со специфической гендерной селекцией на текстильно-промышленных занятиях параллельно к спаду уровня зарплаты в текстильных предприятиях.»

TEICHMANN 1983: 80, здесь GAUGELE 2002: 133). Это привело к тому, что в общественном сознании не оставалось сомнения в том, что домашняя рабочая сфера в общей сложности является женской сферой, так «женская работа», была переимено-вана в «домашнюю работу (или домашнее хозяйство)» (см. LADJ-TEICHMANN 1983: 80, здесь GAUGELE 2002: 133).

Последняя и важная роль домашней одежды рассматривается под аспектом поддерживания семейных отношений. Одежда, как и общая эстетическая манера поведения, регулируют противопоставление вожделения и отвращения к партнеру и тем самым способствуют балансу в супружеских отношениях. Ольга Вайнштейн при-дает халату с его украшательством, цветочками и ленточками, а также с подходящими к нему тапочками с помпончиками некую специфическую функцию, которая утверждает образ идеальной домохозяйки, а также символизирует собой мещанский стиль и личную жизнь (ВАЙНШТЕЙН 2010). Так халат принимает на себя одновременно эстетическую (с перспективы идеологии) и эротическую (интимность семейной сферы и супружество) функцию. Государство, отойдя от решения личных семейных вопросов, взяло на себя роль семейного терапевта и наблюдателя и в этой роли обращалось в первую очередь к женщинам, когда речь шла о решении семейных проблем. Плюсом для женщины, по мнению общества и специалистов в этом вопросе, было то, что она своей внутренней (добросердечностью, терпением и заботливостью) и внешней красотой могла проявить, прежде всего, свою компетентность и превосходство и в результате хотя бы неофициально считаться главой семьи. Одновременно требование к «текстильному» образу женщины и вообще ее общему внешнему виду подчеркивает как раз таки противоположность этого аргумента. Она рассматривается как «украшение своего мужа» и всего семейного пространства. “Das weibliche Äußere […] repräsentiert nicht nur das »schöne Eigentum«, sondern auch das Abgespaltene und Unterdrückte des männlichen Wesens.”[12] (KATSCHNIG-FASCH 1987: 131; здесь GAUGELE 2002: 206). Это мнение поддерживается рядом публикаций, которые указывают на то, что грязная домашняя одежда и вообще неряшливый внешний вид женщины могут разрушить любые любовные отношения. При этом подчеркивается, что неготовность женщины одеваться стильно и красиво дома, как она это делает в общественности, приводит к тому, что она теряет уважение в глазах партнера и остальных членов семьи, а наоборот ее привлекательный внешний вид заставляет и мужа работать над супружескими отношениями.

> “So gesehen ist das Hausfrauenleitbild, das über Kittel und Mode die Angleichung von Beruf und Haushalt suggeriert genauso ein gesellschaftlicher Kompensationsversuch bei der Reduktion der Frauen auf die Hausarbeit und auf die ökonomische Abhängigkeit vom Mann wie das Postulat der permanenten aktiven Körperpflege: »Und der heimkehrende Gatte findet in seiner wohlgepflegten Frau gerade das Ideal, das er sonst bei anderen Frauen zu finden glaubt.«”[13] (GAUGELE 2002: 227).

В заключение, опираясь на тезис Сони Марголиной, мы можем определить понятие советского матриархата под аспектом сознательного подчинения женщины мужчине. Она использует свою женственность как универсальное средство, которое помогает ей

[12] «Женская внешность […] репрезентирует не только «красивую собственность», но и осколок и подчиненное мужскому существу.»

[13] «Можно сказать, что образец домохозяйки, который внушается через халат и моду, а также приравнивание домашней работы к карьере, является общественной попыткой компенсации ограничения роли женщины на уровень домашнего хозяйства и ее экономическую зависимость от мужа, так же как и постулат о постоянном уходе за собой: «И муж, приходящий домой, видит в своей жене тот идеал, который он не нашел бы ни в одной другой женщине.»

как в личной жизни, так и в целом в обществе достичь определенных целей (см. MARGOLINA 1993: 66). Одновременно у нее нет альтернативы, "[…] Familiensinn, Mütterlichkeit oder besondere Fähigkeiten bei der Beziehungsgestaltung bei den Frauen als naturgemäß erwartet bzw. verlangt."[14] (SCHOR-TSCHUDNOWSKAJA 2001: 87). Эти ожидания трансферируются в первую очередь через одежду и принимаются на горизонтальном уровне контроля (общество) под аспектом хорошего вкуса. Государство и общество существуют с идеологической точки зрения в созвучности друг с другом. Для женщины же это означает работу над преодолением многих противоречий и как следствие невыполнения этой работы фрустрацию и приспособление к такой сложной ситуации. "Die sowjetische Frau ist das Ergebnis einer kulturellen Neurose, die im Zusammenstoß zwischen der durch die Modernisierung erzwungenen Modernität und den traditionellen oder romantischen Vorstellungen über die Rolle der Frau in der Familie und in der Gesellschaft entstanden ist."[15] (MARGOLINA 1993: 66). За счет искажения реальности, которая вырисовывается через постоянное разногласие и согласование идеологических и общественных норм, женщина не может найти возможность для удовлетворения своих потребностей. Этот факт особенно виден в ее одежде, которая служит символом обмена между женщиной и внешним миром, а также как "ritualisierte Form des Geschlechtsverhaltens"[16] (KOTTHOF 1994: 172, здесь GAUGELE 2002: 251).

Summary

The paper shows, how the concept of a new taste was placed in the foreground in the official discourse of 1950s to 1960s and how female identity was built by such terms as aesthetics and beauty. Therefore, especially clothing as a consumption good will be taken as an example and by reference to fashion and women magazines, as well as advice booklets, closely analyzed. The presentation will go particularly into the individual practices of clothing manufacture by women. Item of clothing as a good of primary need helps to understand the impacts on the whole process from the manufacture to the consumers and unveil interrelationship between state and society in detail.

Библиография

BOGATYREV, P. 1971. The Functions of Folk Costume in Moravian Slovakia. In: Sebeok, T. (ed.). *Approaches to Semiotics* 5. The Hague, Paris.

ВАЙНШТЕЙН О. 2007. Мое любимое платье. Портниха как культурный герой в Советской России. In: *Теория моды* 3, 101–126.

ВАЙНШТЕЙН, О. 2010. «В соответствии с фигурой»: полное тело в советской моде. http://www.polit.ru/research/2010/05/25/vainshtein.html# (13.09.2013).

GAUGELE, E. 2002. *Schurz und Schürze. Kleidung als Medium der Geschlechterkonstruktion*. Wien.

GUROVA, O. 2009. The Life Span of Things in Soviet Society. Notes on the Sociology of Underwear. In: *Russian Studies in History* 48, 1, 46–57.

ДУБРОВСКАЯ, Г., et.al. 1961. Вы у себя дома. In: *Приложение к Журналу мод* 2, 1–4.

ЕФРЕМОВА, Л. 1969. *Одежда для работы и дома*. Москва.

ЗАХАРОВА, Л. 2006. «Наиболее распространенной является форма прямого пальто с однобортной застежкой»: о советской моде эпохи «оттепели». In: *Неприкосновенный запас* 1, 45, 186–201.

ЗАХАРОВА, Л. 2009. Мода или режим социального нивелирования. In: Кондратьева, Т., Соколов А. (ed.). *Режимные люди в СССР*. Москва 2009, 243–256.

---

[14] «[…] склонность к семейной жизни, материнство и другие навыки для создания личных отношений от женщины ожидаются или даже требуются.»

[15] «Советская женщина – это результат культурного невроза, который возник в результате столкновения принудительных новшеств и традиционных или романтических представлений о роли женщин в семье и обществе.»

[16] «ритуализированная форма поведения того или иного пола

Здравомыслова. Е., et.al. 2004. Государственное конструирование гендера в советском обществе. In: *Журнал исследований социальной политики* 1, 3-4, 299–321.

Heimerdinger, T. 2006. Alltagsanleitungen? Ratgeberliteratur als Quelle für die volkskundliche Forschung. In: *Rheinisch-westfälische Zeitschrift für Volkskunde* 51, 57–71.

Illich, I. 1983. *Genus. Zu einer historischen Kritik der Gleichheit.* Reinbek.

Kaplan, L. 1989. Ein Mann bleibt ein Mann. In: *Petra* 2, без указания стр.

Katschnig-Fasch, E. 1987. Projektionen und Inszenierungen. Überlegungen zu einer geschlechtsspezifischen Interpretation der Kleidung. In: Beitl, K., Bockhorn, O. (ed.). *Kleidung-Mode-Tracht. Referate der österreichischen Vokskundetagung 1986 in Lienz (Osttirol).* Wien 1987, 127–146.

Kotthoff, H. 1994. Geschlecht als Interaktionsritual? In: Goffmann, E. *Interaktion und Geschlecht*, Frankfurt am Main 1994, 159–194.

Ladj-Teichmann, D. 1983. *Erziehung zur Weiblichkeit durch Textilarbeiten.* Weinheim.

Левина А. 1960. Сам и сейчас. In: *Юность* 8, 95.

Левина, А. 1961. Для людей. In: *Юность* 8, 93.

Loschek, I. 1991. *Mode. Verführung und Notwendigkeit. Struktur und Strategie der Aussehensveränderungen.* München.

Margolina, S. 1993. Herrschaft der Frau. Das sowjetische Matriarchat und das Ende des Totalitarismus. In: Jansen, M., Walch, R. (ed.). *Frauen in Ostereuropa: erweiterte Dokumentation der Tagung "Frauen in Osteuropa" vom 9. - 11. Okt. 1992.* Wiesbaden 1993, 51–67.

Margolina, S. 1994. *Rußland. Die nicht zivile Gesellschaft.* Reinbeck bei Hamburg.

Ruane, Ch. 2009. *The Empire's New Clothes: A History of the Russian Fashion Industry, 1700-1917.* New Haven, London.

Русанова, О. 1962. *Раздумья о красоте и вкусе.* Москва.

Семенова, Е. 1963. Как одеваться на работе и дома. In: *Работница* 8, 31.

Schor-Tschudnowskaja, A. 2001. Das Ideal der Frau. Eine qualitative Analyse sowjetischer "Benimmbücher". In: Ritter, M. (ed.). *Zivilgesellschaft und Gender-Politik in Russland.* Frankfurt am Main 2001, 67–93.

Versandhauskatalog Quelle F/S 1969.

Шубин, Г. 1987. *Мода и эстетическая культура.* Москва.

НОВАЯ ОДЕЖДА, НОВАЯ ЖИЗНЬ: Мода в определении советской идентичности в период позднего социализма (конец 1970-х -начало 1980-х гг.)*

НАТАЛЬЯ СТАРОСТИНА, ЯНГ ХЭРРИС

Одной из самых больших проблем, с которыми советский человек сталкивался в годы позднего социализма, был дефицит товаров народного потребления. (HANSON 2003; NOVE 1992.) В магазинах, продававших одежду, обувь и товары для дома, советский покупатель имел весьма ограниченный выбор: советская легкая промышленность, очевидно, не поспевала за требованиями моды. Старомодная, плохо сидящая одежда унылых расцветок отнюдь не соответствовала стремлению советских людей одеваться модно. На фоне хронического дефицита красивой модной одежды советское государство создавало альтернативные возможности одеваться модно и красиво. Растущая популярность всевозможных курсов кройки и шитья, где проходило обучение моделированию модной одежды и вышивке, и которые большинство клубов и домов культуры предлагали за символическую плату, стали панацеей против отсутствия модной одежды на прилавках магазинов. В поздние 1970-ые – 1980-ые годы следование моде стало важной характеристикой советской идентичности. Всевозможные книги и буклеты приводили цитаты из пьесы А.П.Чехова «*Дядя Ваня*»: «в человеке всё должно быть прекрасно: и лицо, и одежда, и душа, и мысли...», а также из романа А.С.Пушкина «*Евгений Онегин*»: «быть можно дельным человеком и думать о красе ногтей.» Если в 1950-ые годы слепое следование моде считалось признаком поверхностности, ограниченности и бездуховности, то в 1970-ые и 1980-ые годы неумение красиво одеваться становится смешным. В нескольких советских фильмах тема моды как важного механизма создания новой идентичности отражает смену идеологической парадигмы в отношении к ней: мода окончательно стала атрибутом советской идентичности, а в массовой культуре она уже является частью советского образа жизни.

Не быть мымрой! Мода в фильме Служебный роман

В одном из популярнейших советских фильмов «*Служебный роман*» (1977) следование законам моды и приобретение модной одежды сыграли значительную роль в преображении главной героини Людмилы Прокофьевны Калугиной (ТЯЖЕЛЬНИКОВА 2003: 101; MACFADYEN 2003). Действие фильма происходит осенью 1976 года в Москве.[1] Людмила является начальницей одного из статистических управлений Москвы и

---

* Я бы хотела поблагодарить Татьяну Васильевну Трубицыну за предоставленные первоисточники, которые я использовала в этой статье.

[1] Фильм поставлен по пьесе «*Сослуживцы*», написанной Эльдаром Рязановым (род. в 1927 г.) и Эмилем Брагинским (1921-1998) в 1971-ом году.

руководит десятками сотрудников. Ее подчиненные боятся и не любят ее, так как, с одной стороны, Людмила ревностно относится к своим обязанностям и ожидает такого же рвения от своих сотрудников, а с другой стороны, они высмеивают ее неспособность привлекательно одеваться и наслаждаться жизнью. Людмиле всего лишь 36 лет, но выглядит она старше своего возраста, за глаза Калугину даже называют „мымра“ (СЛУЖЕБНЫЙ РОМАН 1977, 1-ая серия, 02:30 – 02:33.) В начале фильма мы видим ее в старомодном плохо сшитом костюме грязно-бурого цвета и голубой рубашке; на лице некрасивые очки в роговой оправе. У нее плохая стрижка и полное отсутствие какой-либо укладки на голове. Ее обувь неэлегантна: на ногах у нее некрасивые туфли, которые визуально полнят и укорачивают ее ноги. Ее невзрачный и неухоженный вид резко контрастирует со значительными карьерными успехами, которых она достигла. Людмилу Прокофьевну ценит начальство, она регулярно участвует в заседаниях в министерстве. К тому же Калугина хорошо разбирается в современной поэзии, не без удовольствия листает журналы, изданные на Западе, и не прочь заняться генеральной уборкой у себя в квартире. Но, несмотря на это, Калугина глубоко одинокий человек, она не только не имеет друзей среди коллег на работе, свою личную жизнь ей наладить тоже не удалось. В прошлом у нее был неудачный роман, который закончился тем, что ее друг женился на ее подруге.

В подчинении Калугиной находится большой коллектив. В нем трудится много женщин. В утренние часы многие из них вытаскивают косметички и начинают накладывать макияж. В коллективе работает Анатолий Ефремович Новосельцев: ему сорок лет, он разведен и воспитывает в одиночку двух сыновей. В некотором смысле он олицетворяет жизнь советского служащего. Анатолий живет от зарплаты до зарплаты и старомодно одет, он носит костюм, брюки которого слишком коротки, а пиджак плохо сидит. Новосельцеву чужды карьерные амбиции Калугиной, и он отнюдь не горит на работе, как его коллега Калугина. В начале фильма она даже распекает Новосельцева за ошибки в его статистическом отчете, на основании которого Министерство советской промышленности будет планировать производство товаров народного потребления. Калугина упрекает его в том, что именно из-за таких нерадивых работников в советских магазинах не хватает необходимых товаров. Мы видим и Ольгу Петровну Рыжову, подругу Новосельцева со студенческих времен; она, как и Анатолий Ефремович больше заботится о своей семье, нежели о работе.

События стремительно разворачиваются, когда в коллективе появляется Юрий Григорьевич Самохвалов, с которым Новосельцев и Рыжова учились в одном институте. Самохвалов прекрасно одет, обходителен и представляет собой само мужское очарование. Юрий Григорьевич настоящий карьерист. Он приходит в коллектив как заместитель Калугиной, и, желая иметь Новосельцева на своей стороне, предлагает ей именно его кандидатуру на место начальника отдела легкой промышленности. Людмила Прокофьевна отвергает кандидатуру Новосельцева, аргументируя это множеством ошибок, которые он допустил в своем отчете. Тогда Самохвалов предлагает Новосельцеву «приударить» за Калугиной, чтобы новая должность досталась ему. Эта перспектива приводит Новосельцева в смятение: он признается, что боится свою начальницу «как волка» (СЛУЖЕБНЫЙ РОМАН 1977, 1-ая серия, 25:35 - 25:39). Самохвалов приглашает своих новых коллег в гости. Именно там Новосельцев и должен очаровать Калугину. Получается это у него плохо. В разговоре он прыгает с одной темы на другую и пытается обсудить то сбор грибов, то поэзию. Людмила Прокофьевна не проявляет никакого интереса к неловким попыткам Анатолия поухаживать за ней. Несмотря на свою робость и неожиданно для самого себя и своих коллег он вдруг взрывается и обвиняет свою начальницу в том, что она черствый и сухой человек, а также плохой руководитель. На следующий день Людмила Прокофьевна вызывает Новосельцева к себе в кабинет. Новосельцев ожидает увольнения, поэтому он старается спасти ситуацию, бормоча почти смешные извинения. Людмила Прокофьевна начинает плакать, неожиданно для себя она делится с подчиненным, что совершенно одинока и ненавидит праздники, потому что ей не с кем их справлять. Калугина жалуется на то, что ей только 36 лет, а свое одиночество приходится заполнять работой. Новосельцев потрясен этой неожиданной исповедью, он удивлен, что Калугиной, которую зовут старухой, всего лишь 36 лет. Анатолий Новосельцев советует ей приобрести модную одежду и намекает, что она некрасиво одевается.

У Калугиной нет подруг (она “ликвидировала всех подруг”) и она избегает любого общения (СЛУЖЕБНЫЙ РОМАН 1977, 2-ая серия, 40:30 - 40:35). В фильме подчеркивается связь между ее полным невежеством в вопросах моды, старомодным, плохо пошитым костюмом, в котором она каждый день неизменно появляется на работу и ее неловкостью в социальном плане. В интерпретации Рязанова плохо сидящая одежда и невнимание к внешнему виду не являются признаками одухотворенности, высокого духовного напряжения и полного самоотречения. Наоборот, старомодная одежда делает человека смешным, нелепым и затрудняет его общение с людьми. После разговора с Новосельцевым Людмила Прокофьевна решает обратиться за помощью к своей секретарше Верочке. Калугина не очень хорошо разбирается в людях, и поэтому просит рассказать ей об ее подчиненном Новосельцеве. Верочка же обладает самыми подробными сведениями обо всех сотрудниках статистического управления и понимает динамику отношений в этом коллективе гораздо лучше своей начальницы.

Верочка является полной противоположностью Калугиной. Она всегда одета по последней моде, «оклад у нее секретарский, а туалеты сплошь заграничные» (СЛУЖЕБНЫЙ РОМАН 1977, 1-ая серия, 07:15 - 07:20). На протяжении всего фильма Верочка появляется в модных нарядах – красиво расшитых блузках, сарафанах, брюках клеш, женственных сарафанах, элегантных жакетах – и все это она дополняет модными аксессуарами. В начале фильма Людмила Калугина показывает свое презрительное отношение к попыткам своих подчиненных выглядеть модно и красиво. Она с возмущением говорит об объявлении в женском туалете, в котором говорится о продаже женских колготок. А когда Верочка спрашивает совета своей начальницы о том, нужно ли ей купить кожаные сапоги на высокой платформе, Калугина отмечает их как *очень вызывающие*, после чего Верочка немедленно принимает решение о покупке (СЛУЖЕБНЫЙ РОМАН 1977, 1-ая серия, 23:40 – 24:05). Но Верочка вовсе не глупа и не поверхностна, у нее есть свои четкие представления о чести и к тому же она обладает чувством сострадания и справедливости. Когда Людмила решает изменить свою жизнь, она для начала просит Верочку рассказать ей о моде и модных тенденциях. На протяжении этого комического диалога Людмиле становится понятно, как плохо она одевается и как жалко она выглядит в глазах своих подчиненных. Секретарша объясняет Калугиной, что ее лицо требует внимания косметолога. Невежество Калугиной в отношении моды проявляется, например, в том, что она не знает, что такое клубный пиджак, она не знакома с салонами красоты и ко всему этому обладает неженственной походкой. Но Людмила Прокофьевна быстро усваивает уроки моды и полностью меняет свой гардероб. Она приглашает Новосельцева к себе в гости. На ней длинное вечернее платье и она сделала красивую прическу. Новосельцев влюбляется в Людмилу Прокофьевну. На следующий день Калугина появляется на работе в новом модном платье, с модной прической и макияжем. Ее преображение становится настоящей сенсацией среди подчиненных.

Самохвалов в свою очередь, которого докучают знаки внимания Рыжовой, а у него в студенческие годы был с ней роман, но он сейчас женат и к тому же не находит свою бывшую пассию привлекательной, решает передать любовные письма Рыжовой активистке месткома Шурочке. Шурочка отличается назойливостью, беспардонностью, любопытством и бестактностью. Она давно забросила свои прямые обязанности бухгалтера и полностью растворилась в общественной работе. Последняя представлена в фильме таким навязчивым и нелепым занятием, как покупка тяжелой статуэтки бронзовой лошади с крыльями для одного из сотрудников бюро по случаю его юбилея. Шурочка одета плохо и не следит за собой. В некотором смысле она олицетворяет активистку-общественницу, как будто оставшуюся в прошлом. Шурочка не имеет никакого уважения к частной жизни, напротив, она считает, что личная жизнь сотрудников должна быть дос-тоянием коллектива. Узнав о том, что Самохвалов передал письма Рыжовой Шурочке, Анатолий Ефремович дает ему пощечину, тем самым продемонстрировав свои представления о мужской чести. В отместку тот пытается разорвать отношения между Калугиной и Новосельцевым, но это у него не получается. Фильм имеет счастливый финал: Людмила Прокофьевна и Алексей Ефремович поженились, и у них родился мальчик.

Одной из важных тем в фильме является красивая модная одежда. Когда Людмила Прокофьевна решает внести изменения в свою жизнь, она начинает в первую очередь с внешнего вида. Эта трансформация ознаменовывает и значительные изменения в характере Людмилы: она становится раскрепощенной, перестает быть трудоголиком, превращается в более мудрую начальницу и даже выходит замуж, обретая свое личное счастье. Фильм показал советскому зрителю, как важно следовать моде, быть ухоженным и привлекательно одеваться. Вместе с тем фильм подчеркнул тот факт, что человек должен быть красив и внутренне. Самохвалов, который носит красивые костюмы, уверен в себе и импозантен, тем не менее оказывается подлецом. «*Служебный роман*» стал одним из самых популярных советских фильмов: около 58 миллионов зрителей увидели его в кинотеатрах СССР, а телевизионный показ фильма собрал еще большую аудиторию. По результатам опроса журнала «*Советский Экран*» этот фильм стал лучшим фильмом 1978-го года – а Алиса Фрейндлих и Андрей Мягков, которые исполнили роли Калугиной и Новосельцева – лучшими актерами года. Невозможно недооценить важность картины для формирования особого языка и особого советского менталитета. До сих пор россияне помнят фразы из «*Служебного романа*»: фильм разлетелся на цитаты и стал одним из самых важных культурных событий в советской истории 1970-ых годов. Кроме того, он конструировал понимание моды как важной составляющей советской идентичности. В соответствии с моралью этой картины, мода помогает человеку стать интереснее и счастливее, а чтобы начать новую жизнь, нужно всего лишь обратить пристальное внимание на свою манеру одеваться.

Вместе с тем «*Служебный роман*» не ставил себе задачу объяснить советскому зрителю, где именно можно было приобрести красивую одежду. У Людмилы Проко-фьевны – высокая должность и есть собственная служебная машина Волга с шофером. В картине не представлен такой факт, что, как всякий руководитель, она может покупать одежду в специальных распределителях, которые были в распоряжении советской элиты. Понятно, что Людмила Прокофьевна при ее самоотверженной отдаче на работе едва ли в такой короткий срок могла освоить искусство кройки и шитья и создать сама свои новые наряды. В «*Служебном романе*» есть один интересный кадр: секретарша Верочка берет пряжу и начинает вязать (Служебный роман 1977, 2-ая серия, 17:08 – 17:11). Для советского зрителя этот эпизод является знаковым: женщина, которая умеет вязать, смо-жет красиво одеваться при любых обстоятельствах.

Мода, душа, любовь или Создай себя заново

Многие позднесоветские фильмы тесно связывали женственность, привлекательность, очарование со способностью женщины модно одеваться. В первой половине 1980-ых годов в Советском Союзе были выпущены два фильма, которые завоевали всеобщую любовь зрителей, - «*Влюблен по собственному желанию*» (1982) и «*Самая обаятельная и привлекательная*» (1985). Оба фильма исследуют тему женского одиночества и предлагают рецепты для его преодоления. В фильме «*Влюблен по собственному желанию*» главный герой, бывший спортсмен Игорь Брагин, работает на заводе, спивается и глубоко неудовлетворен своей жизнью. Его спортивная карьера, по его мнению, не задалась. Несмотря на многочасовые тренировки, он все же оказывался вторым на пьедестале, ему не удавалось занять место победителя. В конце концов, Брагин решает бросить спорт и работать на заводе. Случай сводит его с Верой Силковой, которая живет вместе с мамой и младшим братом. Вера работает обычным библиотекарем, но, несмотря на монотонность ее работы, к ее исполнению она подходит исключительно ответственно. Девушка много читает, и хотя она обладает душевной глубиной и духовностью, внешне Вера непривлекательна и, возможно, поэтому одинока. Вера носит бесформенные кофты и длинные темные юбки, которые визуально полнят ее. Познакомившись с Игорем, она решает помочь ему обрести счастье и новый смысл в жизни. Для достижения этой цели она предлагает, используя модные техники аутотренинга, влюбиться друг в друга. В откровенном разговоре Игорь дает понять Вере, что она плохо одевается, неинтересно и непривлекательно выглядит, и что ей следует сбросить лишний вес.

Эти слова задевают Веру, однако, она действительно решает кардинально изменить свой внешний вид. Она начинает заниматься спортом и, стремясь одеваться модно, покупает с рук у спекулянтки кофточку, на которую тратит весь свой аванс, то есть почти половину своей зарплаты. Однако спекулянтка оказывается мошенницей. Под видом красивой кофточки Вере подсунули половую тряпку. Тот факт, что девушка вообще обращается к такому рискованному виду приобретения одежды, указывает на ее дефицит в советских магазинах. Более того, в картине есть показательный пример уровня обслуживания советской торговли: Вера просит продавщицу посоветовать, какая одежда ей будет к лицу. Та, желая поскорее отвязаться от нее, небрежно бросает, что весь товар в зале, и тем самым игнорирует ее просьбу.

Есть в фильме и пронзительные сцены. Вера советует Игорю найти хобби, на что он решает помогать родственникам в поиске могил солдат Великой Отечественной войны. Так, Вера находит братскую могилу и сообщает вдове солдата о местонахождении этого памятника. Сцена, в которой вдова с детьми приезжает на могилу своего мужа, является одной из самых сильных в фильме... Игорь видит красоту Вериной души. Эксперимент – влюбиться по собственному желанию – удался, и, в конце концов, Игорь действительно влюбляется в Веру. Девушка в свою очередь совершенно преображается в фильме. И что немаловажно, стала одеваться со вкусом. Картина «*Влюблен по собственному желанию*» по опросам читателей журнала «*Советский экран*» стала лучшим фильмом 1982-го года, около 30-ти миллионов зрителей увидели этот фильм. Как и «*Служебный роман*», фильм разлетелся на цитаты и предоставил готовые рецепты советским гражданам, а в особенности гражданкам, как стать счастливыми.

Фильм «*Самая обаятельная и привлекательная*» стал еще одним хитом советского кинематографа, в нем также затрагивается тема модной одежды и указывается на значительную роль моды в преобразовании идентичности. В этом фильме, созданном в 1985-ом году, главные роли были сыграны Ириной Муравьевой и Александром Абдуловым. В картине зритель переживает превращение Надежды Клюевой, инженера-конструктора, из невзрачной женщины в «женщину-шарм», женщину с изюминкой. Фильм начинается с интересной ситуации: главная героиня, патрулирующая городской район в роли дружинницы, наблюдает кражу в магазине. Надежда, не задумываясь, бросается в погоню за ворами; завязывается драка и, хотя она получает безобразный синяк под гла-зом, ее задача выполнена, и преступники задержаны. Клюева возвращается домой и на пути неожиданно встречает свою студенческую подругу Сусанну. Та работает психологом и параллельно пишет диссертацию о преодолении одиночества в пределах мегаполисах. Она решает помочь Надежде в налаживании ее личной жизни, а подходящей кандидатурой должен выступать избалованный красавчик Володя Смирнов. Он работает в одном отделе с Надеждой и является полной ее противоположностью, так как презрительно относится и к общественной работе и, собственно, к ней самой. План Сусанны отчасти удается, на Клюеву обращают внимание даже двое ее коллег: женатый Михаил Дятлов, который не прочь завести любовницу, и холостой Леша Пряхин. Но Пряхин родился в деревне и, по мнению Сусанны, является слишком неинтересной целью для эксперимента. Но именно Володю Наде покорить не удается. Кроме того, она понимает, что муж Сусанны, которого подруга покорила с помощью ее психологических приемов, отнюдь не верен своей жене. У фильма довольно неожиданный финал: Надя понимает, что ее коллега Гена, невзрачный молодой человек из другого отдела, с которым она разделяет увлечение настольным теннисом, и есть тот самый мужчина, с которым она может быть сама собой.

Несмотря на разочарование в методах аутотренинга, Надя действительно преображается в фильме и становится обаятельной женщиной. Новая одежда помогает ей в создании нового образа. И здесь героине приходится прибегать в нелегальному методу получения модной одежды: подруга приводит Надежду в квартиру фарцовщика. Предложенные им наряды, в том числе комбинезон якобы от Кардена и свитер стоят баснословно дорого. Чтобы их приобрести, Наде приходится занять у подруги деньги. Довольно иронично показана и ее неискушенность в вопросах моды и правил подпольного приобретения одежды. Фарцовщик насмешливо задает вопрос: «Она что, с Урала?», тем самым подчеркивая ее провинциальность и неумение оценить предложенный им дефицитный товар (САМАЯ ОБАЯТЕЛЬНАЯ И ПРИВЛЕКАТЕЛЬНАЯ 1985, 27:30 - 27:35). Надя появляется на работе в новом свитере, который ей к очень лицу. Но она так и не решается надеть дорогой комбинезон от Кардена. Сцена дает понять, что фарцовщики – это не вполне подходящий и к тому же рискованный источник приобретения красивой и модной одежды. Одежда, предлагаемая фарцовщиками, может выглядеть странно и безвкусно, а поэтому она неподходящая для создания образа настоящего советского человека. Фильм быстро завоевал популярность среди населения. Его просмотрели около 45-ти миллионов человек.

Таким образом, эти три хита советского кинематографа, которые увидели миллионы зрителей, заострили внимание публики на хорошей модной одежде как важном компоненте облика современника и современницы. Вместо того, чтобы превозносить скромность и высмеивать женщин, которые следуют моде, эти фильмы представили моду как положительное явление, как средство для изменения своей жизни в лучшую сторону. Фильмы продемонстрировали преобразующее влияние моды на женскую личность: модная одежда открывает новые перспективы перед человеком и показывает возможности, необходимые для изменения своей судьбы. Женщина, которая модно одевается, имеет большие шансы обрести личное счастье, преодолеть застенчивость, стать более уверенной в себе и найти новых друзей. С другой стороны, целью фильмов, которые я рассматриваю в данной работе, не является ответ на вопрос, как же именно эти три героини смогли существенно изменить свой гардероб? Зрителю понятен только тот факт, что покупка одежды у спекулянтов и фарцовщиков чревата неприятностями.

Три девицы под окном пряли поздно вечерком, или Новые модели организации досуга советских женщин

Многие советские женщины превосходно умели шить и вязать, и эти талантливые рукодельницы и мастерицы создавали современную модную одежду для себя и своих близких. Советское кино подчеркивало, что улучшение советского быта может начаться с такой простой вещи как швейная машинка. В частности, в художественном фильме «*Девушка со швейной машинкой*», созданном на киностудии Грузия-фильм режиссерами Михаилом Чиаурели и Георгием Шенгелая в 1980-м году, рассказывается история энергичной девушки Маквалы, которая закончила техникум кройки и шитья имени Кирова. В самом начале фильме Маквала возвращается в свое родное село и обещает председателю колхоза, что в течение полугода оденет всех односельчан в модную одежду. На афише фильма написано «Даешь «высокую моду» в высокогорные районы!» (https://ru.wikipedia.org/wiki/Девушка_со_швейной_машинкой). Маквала приходит на прием к председателю и убеждает его построить салон мод. Председатель с насмешкой относится к ее идее, он указывает ей на тот факт, что в селе есть гораздо более насущные задачи: сбор урожая, строительство библиотеки и бани и многие другие. Но, несмотря на первоначальные трудности, энтузиазм и настойчивость девушки помогают ей в создании салона и ателье. Так, речь председателя открывает показ мод в новом салоне: «сейчас уважаемая наша портниха продемонстрирует, какую одежду рекомендуется носить нашему колхознику, чтобы каждый и рабочий и выходной день стал для него праздником» (ДЕВУШКА СО ШВЕЙНОЙ МАШИНКОЙ 1988, 25:50 - 26:00). Надо сказать, что некоторые фасоны, которые создала Маквала, не могут не удивить своей непрактичностью, в частности имеется в виду мужской белый костюм с жилетом для выходного дня или белый жакет для женщины средних лет. Без сомнения, белый цвет – цвет маркий и непрактичный, и он бы быстро потерял свой привлекательный вид из-за частых стирок или требовал химической чистки.

Конструирование советской идентичности, в которой следование моде занимает не последнее место, отражало большие возможности для приобретения навыков кройки и шитья, которые в период позднего социализма были предоставлены советским женщинам. В 1970-ые и 1980-ые годы они могли подписаться на журналы «*Крестьянка»* и «*Работница»*, которые публиковали выкройки для самостоятельного пошива одежды и детальные инструкции по кройке, шитью, вязанию и вышиванию. Многие дома культуры и клубы за минимальную плату предлагали курсы кройки и шитья или вязания. В советских школах в течение шести лет, с четвертого по десятый класс, обязательным предметом был курс по домоводству, в котором девочки учились кроить, шить, вязать. Благодаря этим курсам они умели самостоятельно шить юбки, блузки, платья, предметы нижнего белья и многое другое. Такая государственная политика смягчала последствия затяжного кризиса отечественной легкой промышленности, которая многие годы финансировалась по остаточному принципу, к тому же она помогала советским гражданам найти способы по преодолению дефицита и смягчала очевидную неповоротливость плановой экономики, не успевающей за быстро меняющейся модой. Развитие рукодельных талантов посредством школьного обучения и всевозможных курсов помогало советским женщинам создавать модную одежду. Эта политика сыграла важную роль в формировании положительного отношения к моде, которая более не рассматривалась как антисоветский атрибут, а наоборот, стала частью советского образа жизни.

Я выросла в Советском Союзе, и в моем доме до сих пор хранится немалое количество выкроек и журналов, которые помогали советским женщинам красиво одеваться. Моя мать, Татьяна Васильевна Трубицына, несмотря на свое высшее образование, профессию инженера-технолога по производству станков и напряженный рабочий график, научилась прекрасно шить, вязать крючком, спицами и на вязальной машине, создавать изделия из кожи, освоила макраме и многие другие техники рукоделия. Ее изумительное мастерство, организованность и трудолюбие не перестают поражать меня и по сей день. Благодаря тому, что в выходные дни моя мама и бабушка Елена Анисимовна Платонова посвящали многие часы кройке, шитью и вязанию, наша семья – мама, мой отец, я, моя сестра и бабушка - всегда были прекрасно одеты в нарядную и модную одежду. Для этой статьи я попросила свою маму поделиться несколькими изданиями из ее коллекции, содержащими советы по шитью и рукоделию. С обложки третьего выпуска за 1985-ый год журнала «*Шейте сами*», изданного в Ленинграде и являющимся приложением к журналу «*Мода*», на нас смотрит красивая молодая женщина в модном клетчатом пальто, кроме того, на ней рубашка с галстуком. (ШЕЙТЕ САМИ 1985: обложка) Журнал создан под эгидой Минлегпрома РСФСР и выпущен тиражом в 150 000 экземпляров, стоимость выпуска один рубль и 20 копеек. (ШЕЙТЕ САМИ 1985: 1) Выпуск начинается небольшой статьей искусствоведа Л.А.Биллевич:

> «Главными требованиями, предъявляемыми сегодня к современной одежде, попрежнему остаются требования практичности, удобства. Как и в предыдущие годы, основное внимание в модной одежде уделяется форме и очертанию плечевого пояса. Ведь именно он придает моделям современный вид. В изделиях всех ассортиментных групп разными средствами достигается расширенная, прямая или плавно-округлая линия плеч. Самыми модными являются рукава покроя кимоно, реглан, рубашечного типа непременно с заниженными проймами. Несмотря на относительную стабильность моды, каждый сезон приносит что-нибудь новое, свое. Сегодня изменения в моде касаются в основном деталей.» (БИЛЛЕВИЧ 1985: внутренняя страница обложки.)

Слова «мода» или «модный» упоминаются одиннадцать раз. Автор завершая статью, указывает на то, что «современная мода очень разнообразна» и что есть те, которые с удовольствием принимает все модные начинания и те, которые очень избирательны в этом вопросе. Интересно, что варианта *не следовать моде* в статье не рассматривается вообще. В журнале представлены выкройки разнообразных платьев, юбок, блузок и жакетов, повседневная одежда и нарядные платья на разные размеры. В журнале также есть и выкройки одежды для мужчин, женские и мужские куртки, платье-пальто и «остро модное платье для каждого дня». Имеется несколько моделей и выкроек и для полных женщин. Рекомендуемые материалы на данный сезон – это шерстяные, шелковые и трикотажные ткани.

В добавление к журналам, которые выходили на регулярной основе, советские покупательницы также могли купить и небольшие памфлеты-раскладушки «*Вяжите сами*», «*Вяжите спицами*» и другие (Вяжите сами 1986; Вяжите спицами 1988). Журналы для женщин «*Крестьянка*» и «*Работница*» издавались тысячными тиражами. Они содержали бесплатные приложения, по которым читательницы могли научиться вязать на спицах, шить одежду себе и своим родным.

Каково было отношение Советского государства к моде? В 1970-ые годы мода стала важным элементом советской идентичности, как показывает искусствовед Ирэн Андреева в своих мемуарах. Работая в Виалегпроме (Всесоюзном институте ассортимента лёгкой промышленности и культуры одежды), Андреева исследовала западные модели, переиначивала их на советский лад и старалась угадать моду сразу на два года: «Мне было предписано анализировать зарубежную моду, соотносить ее новинки с возможностями отечественной промышленности и выжимать из полученного гибрида рекомендации для советской моды на два года вперед» (Андреева 2009: 146). В своих рекомендациях она должна была считаться с нуждами советской промышленности. Так, на протяжении многих лет советская промышленность категорически отвергала идею производства колготок вместо чулков, так как такое новшество требовало использования в три раза больше материала и тем самым затрудняло выполнение плана в срок (Андреева 2009: 154). Ирэн Андреева вспоминает, что она прекрасно одевалась в Москве, потому что, во-первых, у нее было много знакомых первоклассных портних, а во-вторых, у нее было несколько знакомых продавщиц, которые оставляли ей красивую одежду, и, в-третьих, она периодически заглядывала в сельские магазины, в которых можно было найти прекрасные импортные товары (Андреева 2009: 142, 143, 145, 147). Ирэн вспоминает, что порой ей приходилось сталкиваться и с гримасами моды. Так, например, штапельное вискозное полотно темных расцветок или трикотажные панталоны из хлопка, как элемент нижнего белья, считались самыми неженственными и безобразными материалами, которые можно было найти в советской торговле, В странах же Средней Азии эти вещи имели большой успех: женщины шили из этого материала платья, а на штанишки нашивали разноцветную тесьму, «кусочки традиционной цветастой шелковой ткани и вышитый кант с кисточками» что позволяло им одеваться в традиционную одежду (Андреева 2009: 161).

Ирэн также вспоминает, что в 1970-ые годы правительство стало гораздо благосклоннее относиться к моде. Так, ее приглашают дать лекции о моде в различных государственных и партийных организациях: «В это время меня все чаще и чаще стали приглашать читать лекции о моде руководителям промышленности и даже пропаганды разных уровней, вплоть до Высшей партийной школы (Андреева 2009: 150). Она считает, что в 1970-ые годы вкус стал одним из основополагающих элементов моды. Этот мнение подтверждают многочисленные публикации в прессе. В частности, в статье «*Гримасы моды*», опубликованной в бесплатном приложении к журналу «*Крестьянка*» в 1975-ом году, художник-модельер А.Семынина пишет о безвкусной одежде, которую носит современная молодежь:

> «Если говорить об одежде, то она должна сливаться с человеком, а не кричать о себе самостоятельно, скрывать недостатки фигуры и подчеркивать ее достоинства. Как подобрать такую одежду, могут подсказать взрослые, понимающие в этом толк люди, родители.» (Семынина 1975: без стр.)

В приложениях к журналу «*Крестьянка*» можно было найти и советы, которые могут позабавить современную российскую женщину. Выкройки бюстгальтеров 1-2 и 5-6 размеров можно найти в бесплатном приложении №7 к журналу «*Крестьянка*» за 1979 год (Савицкая 1979: 7). Выкройки для матерчатых сумок, в том числе подробное объяснение, как такую сумку можно украсить вышивкой с олимпийской символикой Москва-1980, находятся в этом же бесплатном приложении. А вот и рекомендация для создания ручек к сумке:

> «Сумки из ткани очень удобны. Женщина может сшить ее сама из пестрой или одноцветной ткани, украсить вышивкой, тесьмой, сплести шнур для ручек... Сумка будет еще наряднее и неповторимей, если к ней приделать ручки в виде двух пластинок, вырезанных из фанеры, плексигласа или другого плотного материала. Мы даем четыре чертежа (рис. 2) для таких ручек. Для сумки надо выпилить 2 ручки. Ручки из фанеры протрите наждачной бумагой и, если они очень светлые, покрасьте их густоразведенной марганцовкой – дерево потемнеет. Не забудьте сделать дырочки по нижнему краю ручек. К сумке ручки прикрепляют суровыми нитками или сутажом с помощью толстой иглы.» (Сумки из ткани 1979: 7)

Есть выкройки и модели для детей и мужчин: бесплатное приложение к журналу «*Крестьянка*» № 2 за 1979-ый год посвящено мужской одежде. В разделе «*Сшейте мужчинам*» представлены выкройки и руководство по шитью мужской рубашки приталенной формы с закругленными разрезами на боках, а также куртки с капюшоном с подкладкой (Овсянникова 1979: без стр.). В этом же приложении находятся и рекомендации по вышивке салфеток фиалками (Еременко 1979: без стр.). Увы, я не нашла статей, которые были бы названы «*Сшейте женщинам*» и призывали советских мужчин шить куртки и пальто для женщин. Довольно забавно то, что в приложении, где содержатся сложные и трудоемкие в исполнении модели мужской куртки и рубашки есть и руководство по игре в шахматы.

Сложно представить, что у советской женщины хватило бы времени на то, чтобы совмещать работу и одновременно быть матерью, женой, хозяйкой, мастерицей и при этом интересоваться игрой в шахматы.

Заключение

В своей статье я показала, что в конце 1970-ых и в начале 1980-ых годов мода становится весомым элементом советской ментальности. Фильмы, которые я проанализировала, указывают на значительную роль красивой модной одежды в изменении идентичности советской женщины. Картины учат женщин не только совершенствовать свой внутренний мир, но и обратить внимание на внешний вид. Здесь я бы хотела подчеркнуть несколько важных моментов. Во-первых, в конце 1970-ых – начале 1980-ых годов мода реабилитирована: одеваться модно становится важно и необходимо. Немодно и некрасиво одетая женщина становится предметом насмешек. Во-вторых, государство помогает советским женщинам овладеть искусством шитья, вязания, вышивания, а также выпускает большое количество журналов, которые помогают женщинам одеть себя и свою семью модно и со вкусом. Тем не менее, не совсем понятно, где советские женщины могли найти материалы, необходимые для создания красивой модной одежды. В-третьих, советская мода – это образовательный и цивилизационный проект, в котором профессионалы моды, искусствоведы и художники-модельеры учат женщин одеваться со вкусом и по фигуре. В этом отношении мода становится важным компонентом в создании культурного советского человека и в повышении культурности советского населения.[2] Мода становится необходимым признаком культурности, как это акцентирует фильм *«Девушка со швейной машинкой»*. При этом задача советских модельеров намного сложнее, чем цель дизайнеров в западных странах, так как советские специалисты должны были предугадать модные тенденции на два года вперед, чтобы подготовить промышленность к созданию новых моделей, как об этом рассказывают мемуары Андреевой. В-четвертых, популяризация моды становится важным государственным проектом, в котором желание женщин нравиться окружающим, а также их индивидуальный вкус помогают преодолеть недостатки планирования и работы легкой промышленности.

Такое распределение гендерных ролей означало наличие тройной нагрузки для женщин, которые одновременно работают, занимаются домашним хозяйством, воспитывают детей, а на выходных еще и обшивают свою семью, вяжут из прибалтийского мохера свитера, делают сумки и салфетки и украшают красивыми вышивками ткани скучных расцветок. Для многих женщин рукоделие стало настоящим хобби. Однако это также означало, что в свободное от работы время, следуя моделям и выкройкам из журналов, женщина создавала модную одежду для всей своей семьи. Журналы конструировали поведение советских женщин, рекомендуя им беспрестанно заботиться об уюте своего жилья и о своем внешнем виде.

Summary

Many late Soviet films tie femininity and charm with a woman's ability to follow fashion's trends Sluzebnyj roman '*Office Affair*' (1977, El'dar Riazanov), Vljublen po sobstvennomu zelaniiu '*Fallen in Love by Own Choice*' (1982, Sergey Mikhaelian), and Samaia obajatel'naia i privlekatel'naia '*The most charming and attractive*' (1985, Gerald Bezhanov). Films portray women's experience as much enriched by their capacity to follow the fashion trends and praise women's ability to sew, to knit, and to make modern clothes for themselves. Films represent a woman who follows fashion and take care of her body and visual appearance as the one who is more likely to fall in love and to marry. These messages in Soviet cinema coincided with a large number of opportunities for Soviet women to develop excellent skills of a seamstress. In the 1970s and 1980s, Soviet women could subscribe to illustrated magazines Krest"ianka '*A Peasant Woman*'and Rabotnitsa '*A Working Woman*' which provided patterns for sewing and knitting clothes. Many dressmaking and knitting courses were offered for a small pay. This fashion politics helped to alleviate the outcomes of the ongoing sharp crisis of the Soviet light industry that resulted in the economics of deficit and chronic shortages. These efforts to make women capable of producing modern-looking clothes for themselves and for their families played a crucial role in exonerating fashion from the attributes of presumably anti-Soviet lifestyle. My article emphasizes the deep effects of individual production of fashionable clothing on the identity of a Soviet woman.

Библиография

АНДРЕЕВА, И. 2009: *Частная жизнь при социализме: отчет советского обывателя*. Москва,

БИЛЛЕВИЧ, Л.А. 1985. Главными требованиями. In: *Шейте сами* 3 (31), внутренняя сторона обложки.

ДЕВУШКА СО ШВЕЙНОЙ МАШИНКОЙ. https://ru.wikipedia.org/wiki/Девушка_со_швейной_машинкой. (09.20.14)

ЕРЕМЕНКО, Т. 1979. Фиалки для салфетки. In: Бесплатное приложение к журналу *Крестьянка* 2, без указания страниц.

ИГРАЙТЕ В ШАХМАТЫ. УРОК № 9. 1979 In: Бесплатное приложение к журналу *Крестьянка* 2, без указания страниц.

---

[2] О важности культуры и культурности в создании советского человека написано немало статей, в том числе статья Вадима Волкова (VOLKOV 1999: 210-230).

HANSON, P. 2003. *The Rise and Fall of the Soviet Economy: An Economic History of the USSR from 1945*. London, New York.
MACFADYEN, D. 2003: *The Sad Comedy of El'dar Riazanov: An Introduction to Russia's Most Popular Filmmaker*. Montreal, McGill.
НАДГОРНАЯ, И. 1975. Для домашнего уюта 6, In: Бесплатное приложение к журналу *Крестьянка* 6, без указания страниц.
NOVE, A. 1992. *An Economic History of the USSR, 1917-1991*. London, New York.
ОВСЯННИКОВА, Т. 1975. Детям к лету. In: Бесплатное приложение к журналу *Крестьянка* 6, без указания страниц.
ОВСЯННИКОВА, Т. 1979. Сшейте мужчинам. In: Бесплатное приложение к журналу *Крестьянка* 2, без указания страниц.
САВИЦКАЯ, Т. 1979. Сшейте сами. In: Бесплатное приложение к журналу *Крестьянка* 7, без указания страниц.
СЕМЫНИНА, А. 1975. Гримасы моды. In: Бесплатное приложение к журналу *Крестьянка* 6, без указания страниц.
СУМКИ ИЗ ТКАНИ. 1979. In: Бесплатное приложение к журналу *Крестьянка* 7, без указания страниц.
ТЯЖЕЛЬНИКОВА, В.С. 2003. «С жульем, допустим, надо бороться!» Неформальная экономическая активность в 1960-е годы (по фильмам Э. Рязанова). In: *Отечественная история* 6, 101 – 108.
ШЕЙТЕ САМИ. Модели одежды 1985. In:. Приложение к журналу *Мода* 3 (31). Издание Минлегпром РСФСР.
VOLKOV, V. 1999. The Concept of Kul'turnost': Notes on the Stalinist Civilizing Process. In: Fitzpatrick S. (ed.) *Stalinism: New Directions*. London, Paris, 210-230.
ВЯЖИТЕ САМИ 1988. Киев.
ВЯЖИТЕ СПИЦАМИ 1986. Киев

Фильмография

ВЛЮБЛЕН ПО СОБСТВЕННОМУ ЖЕЛАНИЮ. 1982 Р: Сергей Микаэлян. СССР: Ленфильм.
ДЕВУШКА СО ШВЕЙНОЙ МАШИНКОЙ. 1980 Р: Михаил Чиаурели, Георгий Шенгелая. СССР: Грузия-фильм.
САМАЯ ОБАЯТЕЛЬНАЯ И ПРИВЛЕКАТЕЛЬНАЯ. 1985 Р: Геральд Бежанов. СССР: Мосфильм.
СЛУЖЕБНЫЙ РОМАН. 1977 Р: Эльдар Рязанов. СССР: Мосфильм.

Фотография

Сделанные в 1970-ые - начале 1980-ых годов фотографии показывают мою семью, семью Трубицыных – моих родителей Татьяну Васильевну и Анатолия Алексеевича; мою сестру Елену Анатольевну и мою бабушку Елену Анисимовну Платонову. За исключением военной формы моего отца, школьной формы моей сестры, костюма Деда Мороза и одежды моего отца на фотографии, сделанной на юге, все без исключения платья сшиты моей матерью, Татьяной Васильевной, с помощью моей бабушки. Даже костюм и головной убор Красной Шапочки на мне – произведение рук моей мамы и бабушки (см. фото 6).

DER NYLONKRIEG IM SOWJETISCHEN LITERARISCHEN DISKURS DER 1960ER JAHRE

JULIA HARGAßNER, SALZBURG

Говорят, что будет сердце из нейлона.
Говорят, что двести лет стучать ему…
Может это, по науке, и резонно,
А по-нашему, ребята ни к чему.
Igor' Šaferan

Der lyrische Text dieses seit Ende der 1960er Jahre bekannten Liedes reflektiert die implizite Eigen-Fremd-Opposition, die der Stoff Nylon an sich hat. Nylon steht im Zentrum der beiden Erzählungen, die in diesem Beitrag analysiert werden, Samuil Šatrovs „*Nejlonovaja šubka*" (1962) und Sergej Dovlatovs „*Krepovye finskie noski*" (1986). Diese Texte spielen ungefähr zur gleichen Zeit, in den 1960er Jahren, auf die als historischen Kontext in den Analysen Bezug genommen wird. Trotz der deutlichen Unterschiede zwischen den Auffassungen des Nylon-Themas der beiden Autoren, sind die folgenden Thesen in diesen literarischen Werken nachweisbar. Nylon spielt eine bedeutende Rolle für die kompositorische Struktur dieser Texte, mittels seiner werden Oppositionen innerhalb der sowjetischen Gesellschaft aufgedeckt und die Mängel der sozialistischen Planwirtschaft nachgewiesen. Im Fokus dieser Untersuchung steht die Frage nach der Wechselwirkung des Nylon-Themas in der erzählten und der realen Welt: Wie sind die mit Nylon verbundenen historischen Realien in den sowjetischen literarischen Diskurs eingeflossen? Inwieweit spiegeln die Texte die außerliterarische Realität wider?[1] Inwiefern tragen die Texte, insbesondere jener von Dovlatov, dazu bei, dass Nylon in der sowjetischen Wirklichkeit negativ konnotiert wird? Im Zentrum steht der längere Text von Šatrov, im letzten Teil werden die Thesen mit dem Text von Dovlatov abgeglichen.

Ein historischer Exkurs soll die gesellschaftliche Bedeutung der Nylonwaren verdeutlichen, um die Vorgeschichte der Ereignisse darzustellen, die in den Erzählungen behandelt werden: Die amerikanische Firma DuPont eröffnete mit der Entwicklung des Nylons Mitte der 1930er Jahre eine neue Epoche in der Konsumwarenproduktion. Angefangen mit den von Frauen heiß begehrten Nylonstrümpfen erweiterte DuPont die Produktpalette und produzierte weitere Kleidungsstücke aus diesem Material. Während amerikanische Konsumenten die Vorteile der Faser schon Jahrzehnte genießen konnten, blieb dieser Stoff sowjetischen Konsumenten vorenthalten. Erst nach dem Zweiten Weltkrieg kamen die ersten Nylonerzeugnisse in die Sowjetunion und wurden zum Objekt der Begierde. Der Stoff aus den feindlichen USA war nicht leicht zu bekommen und betonte das Statussymbol seines Besitzers.

Eine ausführliche Analyse der Situation in der Sowjetunion hinsichtlich synthetischer Stoffe zwischen 1950 und 1960 bietet die russische Historikerin Natalija Lebina in ihrem Artikel „*Pljus chimizacija vsej strany*" (LEBINA 2002) an. Zu Beginn der 1950er Jahre war die Produktion moderner Stoffe in der Sowjetunion in Verzug. Ein halbes Jahr nach Chruščevs Machtantritt 1955 initiierte er eine Diskussion über die Einführung des technischen Fortschritts in die sowjetische Wirtschaft, wobei der Kunstfaserproduktion absolute Priorität zu-

[1] Die Frage nach der Verbindung zwischen Literatur und Realität steht seit langem im Fokus literaturhistorischer und literaturtheoretischer Diskussionen. In diesem konkreten Analysefall beziehe ich mich auf die Lotmansche Auffassung: „Die Kunst erkennt das Leben, indem sie es nachbildet" (LOTMAN 1972: 22). Die zu analysierenden fiktionalen Erzählungen stellen ertragreiche Beispiele der künstlerischen Auseinandersetzung mit einem aktuellen Thema der Gegenwart, wie Nylon es in den 1960er Jahren war, dar und führen auch zu Erkenntnissen über die enge Verbindung zwischen Kunst und Realität.

gesprochen wurde. Im Mai 1958 fand ein Plenum des ZK der KPdSU statt, an dem eine Erweiterung von Lenins berühmtem Motto vorgeschlagen wurde, es sollte heißen: „Kommunismus – das ist Sowjetmacht plus Elektrifizierung des ganzen Landes und Chemisierung der Volkswirtschaft" (NARYŠKIN 1986: 238). Das Programm umfasste ein breites Spektrum von Maßnahmen zur Propagierung chemischen Wissens im sowjetischen Volk mit dem Ziel, synthetische Stoffe bekannt und beliebt zu machen. Nikita Chruščev, selbst ein starker Synthetik-Befürworter, trug mit Stolz eine kaukasische Pelzmütze aus Kunstfaser. Ende der 1950er Jahre begann die Produktion synthetischer Socken, Anfang der 1960er Jahre konnte man Nacht- und Unterwäschesets aus Nylon und Kapron in Geschäften erwerben. Es folgte eine Ausdehnung der Produktion auf Kleider, Anzüge und Mäntel aus Synthetik. Im Laufe dieser Kampagne erfolgte ein konsequenter Austausch der Stoffe im Handel: Anstatt Baumwolle, Seide, Leinen und Wolle wurden synthetische Stoffe produziert und zum Verkauf angeboten. Das Juni-Plenum des ZK der KPdSU beauftragte im Jahr 1960 die sowjetische Textilindustrie, die jährliche Produktion von synthetischen Stoffen in Frankreich, Großbritannien und der BRD zu übertreffen (NARYŠKIN 1986: 541). Jedoch war dieser Plan nicht leicht zu erfüllen. So konnte man die Produktion von Nylonhemden für Männer erst Anfang der 1970er Jahre starten. Die stark beworbenen sowjetischen Kunstpelze erwiesen sich im Vergleich mit ausländischen als schwer, farblich eintönig, meist schwarz, und mit einem spezifischen Geruch. Diese Faktoren verstärkten die Vorliebe sowjetischer Bürger für Importwaren und führten zum Aufblühen des Schwarzmarktes.

Um den sowjetischen Konsum Mitte des letzten Jahrhunderts zu beschreiben, bedarf es einer zeitlichen Systematisierung. Eine Zweiphasen-Charakterisierung der Konsumpolitik sozialistischer Länder schlägt Stephan Merl vor (MERL 1997: 206ff). Demnach tritt nach dem Tod Stalins die zweite Phase ein, die Stephan Merl als „Systemlegitimation aus der Konsumorientierung" bezeichnet. Kennzeichnend dafür ist die Opposition zwischen systemstabilisierenden und systemsprengenden Effekten des Konsums, die letztendlich zum Zerfall der sozialistischen Wirtschaft führten. Laut Ol'ga Gurova gliedert sich die sowjetische Konsumpolitik in vier Phasen,[2] die jeweils die sowjetische Ideologie reflektieren. Die 1960er Jahre, um die es in diesem Artikel geht, lassen sich in die dritte Phase einordnen, die unter dem Einfluss der westlichen Konsumkultur verläuft. Diese Phase (GUROVA 2005: 16-20) beginnt nach dem Tod Stalins im Jahr 1953 und dauert bis in die 1970er Jahre, in denen sie von der vierten Phase der *razveščestvlenija* ‚Entdinglichung' abgelöst wird. In den 1950er und 1960er Jahren gewinnt Konsum im sowjetischen ideologischen Diskurs an Bedeutung. Diese Änderung der ideologiebeladenen Konsumpolitik erfolgt vor dem historischen Hintergrund des Tauwetters, das durch viele Kulturkontakte mit dem Westen und insbesondere den USA gekennzeichnet ist. Der Begriff „sowjetischer Geschmack" legte das dominierende Konzept der 1960er Jahre in der Sowjetunion fest. Diesen sowjetischen Geschmack bestimmten die Attribute *prosto* ‚einfach' und *celesoobrazno* ‚zweckmäßig'. Der offizielle Diskurs gründete den sowjetischen Geschmack auf die Opposition zum ausländischen bzw. amerikanischen Geschmack im Kontext des ideologischen Wettbewerbs. Unterschiedliche Konsumkonzepte untermauerten das Spannungsverhältnis sozialistischer und kapitalistischer Wirtschaftssysteme im Kalten Krieg (RÜTHERS 2010: 35ff).

In diesem Zusammenhang ist der Vorschlag des amerikanischen Soziologen David Riesman aufschlussreich. Im März 1953 fand in Boston an der Amerikanischen Kunst- und Wissenschaftsakademie eine Konferenz über Totalitarismus statt. Die mitwirkenden Wissenschaftler versuchten theoretische und praktische Wege zu finden, um den Totalitarismus in der Welt zu bekämpfen. Unter die gegenwärtigen totalitären Systeme subsumierte man die

[2] Die Soziologin Ol'ga Gurova gibt in ihrem Buch „*Vešči v sovetskoj kulture*" (2005) eine detaillierte Beschreibung der vier Perioden sowjetischer Konsumgeschichte, die unter unterschiedlichen ideologischen Akzenten verliefen.

sozialistischen Länder unter der Führung der Sowjetunion. Zu diesem Zeitpunkt war der Eiserne Vorhang in Churchills berühmter Fullton-Rede schon gefallen und der Kalte Krieg hatte begonnen. In der Diskussion der Bostoner Konferenz schlug David Riesman vor, die stärkste Waffe der amerikanischen Gesellschaft, ihre Konsumwaren, im Krieg gegen Russland einzusetzen:

> „Why don't we produce consumer goods to the utmost of our capacity, and then flood the Russian population, by aerial bombardment, with all kind of stuff: jeeps in Odessa, nylons on Moscow, and so forth [...]. The whole point of our system is its productivity; let's show the world that it really can produce. These really *are* 'our rules'." (FRIEDRICH 1954: 378).

Dieser Vorschlag von Riesman wurde unter dem Titel „Nylon war" bekannt. Die originelle Idee, die Sowjetunion nach den Regeln der amerikanischen Konsumgesellschaft spielen zu lassen, scheint auch funktioniert zu haben. Der künstlerische Diskurs der Sowjetunion von den 1950er bis in die 1970er Jahre reflektiert das Eindringen des amerikanischen Produkts Nylon in die Sowjetunion. Die Auswirkungen sind sensationell: Nylon deckt Problemstellen der sowjetischen Gesellschaft auf, Nylon unterminiert die sozialistischen Prinzipien der Planwirtschaft und fördert die negativen Seiten des sowjetischen Alltags zutage.

Ein plakatives Beispiel der künstlerischen Auseinandersetzung mit dem Thema Nylon stellt die satirische Erzählung von Samuil Michajlovič Šatrov *„Nejlonovaja šubka"* dar. Dieser 1962 erschienene Text[3] handelt von einem im Ausland gekauften Nylonpelzmantel, der über zahlreiche Besitzer schließlich als Tierunterlage in einer Schweinezucht landet. Der Autor, der über mehrere Jahrzehnte für das satirische Magazin *„Krokodil"* tätig war, skizziert den langen Weg des Nylonpelzmantels und zeigt dabei die Anziehungskraft des importierten Kleidungsstücks auf, die es auf „die negativen Elemente" der sozialistischen Gesellschaft ausübt. Die Aufgabe eines echten Satirikers besteht laut zeitgenössischer Kritik darin, die sozialen Phänomene zu brandmarken, die in einem bestimmten historischen Moment die größte Herausforderung für das Volk, die Partei und den Staat darstellen (ERŠOV 1966: 9). Sie warf Šatrov vor, dass die handelnden Personen der Erzählung nur oberflächlich gezeichnet und nicht tiefgründig dargestellt seien (ERŠOV 1966: 258). Dennoch ist *„Nejlonovaja šubka"* eine gelungene Entlarvung bedeutender sozialer und wirtschaftlicher Probleme der damaligen UdSSR. Diese auf Oppositionen aufgebaute Erzählung enthält starke sozialistische Propagandazüge, die in dem turbulenten Sujet zum Teil etwas konstruiert wirken. Der künstliche Stoff Nylon treibt die Sujetentwicklung voran und legt verschiedene Oppositionen offen.

Der Nylonpelzmantel dient als Lackmustest in der Erzählung. Die handelnden Personen kann man in Bezug auf Nylon in zwei Gruppen teilen: in gute sowjetische Bürger und solche, die durch ihre negativen Eigenschaften auffallen. Alle, die den Mantel haben wollen und/oder damit Geld verdienen, gehören zu der letzten Gruppe. Es sind Mitarbeiter des Kommissionswarengeschäfts, die ihren eigenen Profit schlagen, Ehemänner, die ihr Geld nicht ehrlich verdienen, Ehefrauen, die keine anderen Interessen als Kleidung haben, Schmarotzer und Spekulanten. Ihre Weltanschauung wird wie folgt festgehalten: „Шкаф с тряпками – вот твое мировоззрение. За такой шкаф ты продашь меня, семью, любовь! За два шкафа я куплю у тебя солнечную систему, нашу Галактику, Млечный Путь!" (ŠATROV 1962: 52). Materielle Güter bestimmen ihr Leben und führen somit zum Konflikt mit der sozialistischen Ideologie.

---

[3] 1974 kommt die Musikkomödie *„Nejlon 100%"* in die sowjetischen Kinos, die auf dem *Buch „Nejlonovaja šubka"* basiert.

Die erste Gruppe wird dem gegenüber von ehrlichen sowjetischen Bürgern gebildet, für die Konsumwaren nicht der einzige Sinn des Lebens sind.[4] Die Ehepaare Motoviliny und Korž sehen den Nylonpelzmantel nicht als Objekt der Begierde, sondern wollen ihn seiner direkten Bestimmung nach als Kleidungsstück und nicht als Statussymbol nutzen.

Kennzeichnend ist der Umgang mit dem Mantel für die Figur Inga Fedorovna. Als sie noch den Status der Ehefrau des Rechtsanwalts Sugonjaev genießt, ist sie bereit, sich zu erniedrigen und auf den Knien um den Mantel zu bitten (ŠATROV 1962: 88). Nach dem Tod ihres Mannes muss sie selbst für sich sorgen, und am Ende der Erzählung zeigt sie kein Interesse an dem Kleidungsstück mehr. Ihr Leben bekommt eine andere Erfüllung, da Inga Fedorovna erfährt, dass nicht Kleidung,[5] sondern Arbeit zur seelischen Befriedigung führt. Diese Erkenntnis spiegelt die sozialistische Vorstellung vom Leben, in der nicht der Konsum, sondern die Arbeit den zentralen Anker des menschlichen Lebens darstellt (MERKEL 1999: 17; GOLDSCHWEER 2013: 6). Die Erzählung *„Nejlonovaja šubka“* trägt somit zur Erziehung des idealen sowjetischen Menschen bzw. seines Geschmacks bei, deren sozialistische Grundidee die geistige Dominanz über das Materielle bildet.

Veščizm,[6] ‚ein erhöhtes Interesse an materiellen zum Nachteil geistiger Dinge‘ (EFREMOVA 2005: 274), bedingt die Verhaltensweisen beider Gruppen. Dieser Mitte der 1970er Jahre entstandene Begriff stellt eine Auswirkung des entwickelten Sozialismus in der UdSSR dar (LEBINA 2006: 85). Die Vertreter der ersten Gruppe verabscheuen die Priorität des Materiellen im Leben, sie übernehmen damit die sowjetische Normeinstellung zu Konsumwaren (GUROVA 2005, 25ff),[7] die Mitglieder der zweiten weichen von der Normeinstellung zu Konsumwaren ab. Die Gedanken des erfolgreichen Schweinezüchters Koržs betonen die wiederkehrende Opposition von eigen und fremd und weisen darauf hin, dass eine solche Verhaltensweise auf keinen Fall sowjetisch ist: sie ist entweder fremden Gedanken oder vorsowjetischen Zeiten zuzuschreiben: „То ли их чужим ветром занесло, то ли они поросль от старого, трухлявого корня“ (ŠATROV 1962: 89). Die Metapher *чужой ветер* ‚fremder Wind’ für Fremdeinfluss impliziert eine bestehende Opposition, die die positiven Eigenschaften dem Eigenen zuordnet und das Negative als fremd ansieht. Die Opposition bestätigt die von Monika Rüthers erwähnte Wertehierarchie sowjetischer Moral: „Arbeit und Produktion sind hoch angesehen, Handel und Konsum dagegen niedrig“; abgesehen davon war „sowjetische Konsumkritik Kapitalismuskritik“ (RÜTHERS 2010: 54). Auf dem 25. Parteikongress 1976 warnte Leonid Brežnev vor „Rezidiven kleinbürgerlicher Psychologie“ (NARYŠKIN 1986: 162), die für die kapitalistische Gesellschaft typisch seien. Die Erzählung nimmt die letzte vierte Phase der sowjetischen Konsumgeschichte vorweg, die unter dem Motto *razveščestvlenije* ‚Entdinglichung‘in die 1970er Jahre fällt (GUROVA 2005: 20). Die von *veščizm* besessenen Figuren der Erzählung *„Nejlonovaja šubka“* sind den sozialistischen Prinzipien fremd und werden mithilfe des Verfahrens der Satire zur Schau gestellt und verurteilt.

Auf eine unkonventionelle Wendung im sowjetischen *veščizm*-Diskurs verweist Natalija Lebina: Der Kampf gegen den veščizm sollte sowjetische Bürger von der Suche nach Alltagsgegenständen ablenken (LEBINA 2006: 85). Stephan Merl erwähnt in seiner Konsumanalyse der osteuropäischen Staaten eine „innere Immigration“ in den Konsum (MERL 1997: 206),

---

[4] „Вещи не составляли единственного смысла ее жизни.“ (ŠATROV 1962: 11)

[5] „Инга Федоровна была увлечена новой, своеобразной работой. Быть может, впервые в жизни она с удивлением узнала, что не только вещи могут приносить радость.“ (ŠATROV 1962: 263)

[6] „Повышенный интерес к вещам, к обладанию ими в ущерб духовным интересам.“ (EFREMOVA 2005: 274)

[7] Die sowjetische Normeinstellung zu Konsumwaren äußert sich in folgenden Punkten: 1. Der sowjetische Mensch ist von Konsumwaren unabhängig. 2. Eine Anhäufung von Konsumwaren soll nicht zum Ziel werden. 3. Konsumwaren sollten nach einem vernünftigen Bedarf erworben werden. 4. Der sowjetische Mensch soll einen anderen nicht nach materiellen Dingen beurteilen. 5. Sowohl die Menge, als auch die Form von Konsumwaren soll für den sowjetischen Menschen unbedeutend sein.

die durch einen mangelhaften Konsum verursacht und schließlich für das Scheitern des kommunistischen Regimes in Osteuropa verantwortlich war. Im literarischen Text Šatrovs parallelisiert Nylon die Realien des sowjetischen Gesellschafts- und Konsummodells. Die Erzählung zeigt, dass der Wunsch nach schöner und modischer Kleidung mit dem Sozialismus nicht ausgelöscht werden kann. Darüber hinaus wird die Unfähigkeit des Systems angesprochen, die Bedürfnisse aller Bürger nach Kleidung zu befriedigen.

Am Anfang der Erzählung wird diskutiert, welchen Wert der Nylonpelzmantel im Gegensatz zu Echtpelz haben kann. Diese Opposition von echt vs. unecht spiegelt die reale Situation der Kunstfaser in der Sowjetunion wider. Die Epitheta, die den Nylonmantel in der Erzählung begleiten, sprechen für sich selbst: „Шубка легка, как пушинка, и горяча, словно доменная печь. Она согреет вашей даме не только душу, но и сердце“ (ŠATROV 1962: 9), „бесценная вещь“ (ŠATROV 1962: 19), „сказочная шубка – королева зарубежного ширпотреба“ (ŠATROV 1962: 33), „серебристое чудо“ (ŠATROV 1962: 74), „тряпка, достойная царицы Тамары“ (ŠATROV 1962: 141), „нейлоновое диво“ (ŠATROV 1962: 282). Diesen lobenden Eigenschaften stehen die realitätsbezogenen Charakteristika gegenüber, die der Kommissionswarenverkäufer aufzählt, um den Preis zu senken:

> „Передо мной не каракуль, не песец и даже, извините, не задрипанный кролик. Передо мной всего-навсего нейлон. Разве это мех? [...] Если мех делают из нефти, из древесных опилок, из дыма, это уже не мех, а черт знает что!“ (ŠATROV 1962: 13 -15).

Mitte der 1960er Jahre waren Pelzmäntel auf den Straßen sowjetischer Städte selten zu sehen. Echter Pelz war für einfache Bürger unerschwinglich (LEBINA 2002: 85). Die Möglichkeit, Kunststoffpelzmäntel zu kaufen, wurde mit Freude angenommen. Die traditionelle russische Vorliebe für den Echtpelz musste aus wirtschaftlichen Gründen den Platz für synthetischen Pelz räumen.

Aufschlussreich in diesem Zusammenhang ist der Preiswandel, den der Nylonpelzmantel erfährt. Anfangs um zweitausend Rubel erhältlich, erreicht der Preis den Höhepunkt von fünfeinhalbtausend Rubel. Die Schlussfolgerung liegt nahe – der Nylonpelzmantel ist wertvoll. Jedoch bringt es die Opposition eigen vs. fremd aus dem Gleichgewicht. Die letzte Episode der Erzählung balanciert diese wieder aus. Korž löscht das Feuer in seiner Schweinezucht mit dem Nylonpelzmantel, und setzt damit den Mantel nicht als Ziel, sondern als Mittel ein, mit dem man sozialistisches Eigentum retten kann. Die letzte Verwendung des ausländischen Pelzmantels festigt die Abwertung des fremden Kleidungsstücks, in dem es als Tierunterlage benutzt wird.

Eine weitere zentrale Opposition der Erzählung ist das Stadt-Land-Verhältnis innerhalb der sowjetischen Gesellschaft. Nylon unterstreicht diese Spannung. Am stärksten tritt sie in dem Kommissionswarengeschäft zutage, als der prominente Schweinezüchter Korž ein Geschenk für seine Frau sucht. Die Verkäufer überschütten Korž mit klischeehaften Vorbehalten gegenüber Dorfbewohnern und versuchen, ihm von dem Kauf abzuraten: „Таких элегантных вещей деревня не носит! [...] А вот короткие плюшевые жакеты там в большой моде“ (ŠATROV 1962: 75 -76). Matil'da Semenovna gibt dem Schweinezüchter den guten Rat, auf den Markt zu gehen und einen Haargarnmantel um dreihundert Rubel zu kaufen. Als Reaktion darauf kauft der verärgerte Kolchosechef den Mantel um einen überteuren Preis von fünftausend Rubel. Dies führt zur Eskalation, die im Fazit der erstaunten Verkäuferin gipfelt: „Сначала дорогие колхознички дерут с нас три шкуры за молоко, а потом набивают свои сундуки нейлоном!“ (ŠATROV 1962: 78). Der unerwartete Ausklang dieser Auseinandersetzung wird als „гримасы товарооборота“ (ŠATROV 1962: 82) bezeichnet. Eine sogenannte „Grimasse des Warenumsatzes“ äußert sich im Transfer einer heiß begehrten ausländischen Ware aus der Stadt, wo sie dementsprechend geschätzt werden kann, in die tiefe Provinz, in ein Dorf. Dies entspricht allerdings nicht der sowjetischen Versorgungshierarchie, die Monika Rüthers als ein spezifisches Merkmal der sowjetischen Konsumgeschichte beschreibt. Demzufolge wurden sowjetische Städte ihrer Rangordnung entsprechend beliefert, beginnend mit den Hauptstädten bis zu den kleinen Provinzstädten. Die Dorfbewohner waren die letzten in der Reihe und konnten Konsumwaren oft überhaupt nicht bekommen (RÜTHERS 2010: 41–42). Die überraschende Wendung in der Erzählung zielt also auf die Aufwertung des Dorfes ab und steht im Dienste der sozialistischen Propaganda.

In diesem Zusammenhang lohnt es sich, die Geldfrage in den Blick zu nehmen. Bis zu diesem Zeitpunkt konnten sich den Nylonpelzmantel nur die Bestverdiener leisten, von denen die meisten durch unehrliche oder gesetzeswidrige Handlungen zu Geld kommen. Der Mantelkauf eines erfolgreichen Kolchosechefs manifestiert die Gleichstellung von Dorf- und Stadtbewohnern, angesichts der Tatsache, dass Kolchosemitglieder erst unter Chruščev einen regulären Lohn erhielten (RÜTHERS 2010: 42). In der Erzählung wird erwähnt, dass eine Haushaltshilfe in der Stadt dreihundert Rubel monatlich bekommt, während Melkerinnen in einer Kolchose nicht weniger als eineinhalbtausend Rubel verdienen (ŠATROV 1962: 68). Kolchosemitglieder sind damit in die Liste der Bestverdiener aufgestiegen, was die propagandistischen Ansätze der Erzählung offenbart. Das positive Image des sowjetischen Dorfes bzw. der sowjetischen Kolchose bleibt auf der guten Seite der Opposition eigen vs. fremd. Die tatsächliche Eignung des Nylonpelzmantels für die Bedingungen im Dorf wird in der Aussage von Koržs Ehefrau vage angedeutet: „Очень уж она в глаза бьет. Как-то неудобно. Право слово, неудобно...“ (ŠATROV 1962: 280). Das prächtige Kleidungsstück passt weder optisch noch praktisch in das Kolchoseleben und entspricht keinesfalls den Lebensumständen sowjetischer Kolchosen und sowjetischer Ideologie als solcher. Das ins Auge stechende Kleidungsstück steht in Widerspruch zu dem für den sowjetischen Geschmack charakteristischen Begriff *skromno* ‚bescheiden‘; es lässt sich nicht in die Synonymreihe *ser'eznyj, nadežnyj, čestnyj, partijnyj* ‚ernst, zuverlässig, ehrlich, parteiangehörig‘ (VAJNSTEJN 2010) einordnen.

Der Nylonpelzmantel entlarvt fremde Elemente der sowjetischen Gesellschaft, da er auf sie eine Anziehungskraft ausübt. Im Vorwort findet man eine detaillierte Auflistung der *negativen Typen*:[8] Spekulanten, Faulenzer, Randalierer und anderer Schmarotzer. Spekulanten im russischen Sinne des Wortes[9] sind in dieser Erzählung breit vertreten. Es gibt zwei unterschiedliche Typen: die einen, die in einem Betrieb ihre illegalen Machenschaften durchführen, und die anderen, die sich freiberuflich, außerhalb eines sozialistischen Betriebs bereichern. Ein brillantes Beispiel der innerbetrieblichen sowjetischen Spekulation stellen die Direktoren des Kommissionswarengeschäftes Venja und Matil'da Semenovna dar. Es ist der Zyklus von Kauf und Verkauf zur eigenen Bereicherung, der dieser Erzählung zugrunde liegt: „Наименее ходовые товары продавали в установленном порядке. Веня и Матильда Семеновна сбывали модные вещи, минуя продавцов. Разница между комиссионной и продажной ценой оседала в их бездонных карманах.“ (ŠATROV 1962: 19). Der mehrmalige An- und Verkauf des Mantels bringt ihnen einen Reingewinn von viertausend Rubel.

Ein Beispiel externer Spekulanten gibt die Figur Gogoberašvili ab, der jedoch am Ende als Opfer dasteht. Am Kauf und Verkauf des Nylonpelzmantels verliert er fünfhundert Rubel. Dank Gogoberašvilis Vorgeschichte wird ein Muster des illegalen Handels in der Sowjetunion offen gelegt. Die Machenschaften jenseits des Gesetzes und der Planwirtschaft decken den wahren Grund dieser wirtschaftlichen Umstände in der Sowjetunion auf. Gogoberašvili of-

---

[8] „Повесть «Нейлоновая шубка» построена как повесть-обозрение, которая показывает галерею отрицательных типов: спекулянтов, обосновавшихся в комиссионном магазине, лодыря и дебошира, устроившегося пресвитером общины евангелистов, и других стяжателей и тунеядцев.“ (ŠATROV 1962: Vorwort)

[9] Спекулировать ‚Aufkauf und Verkauf von Besitzwerten, Lebensmitteln, Massenbedarfsartikeln u.ä. aus Profitsucht, gew. durch ungesetzmäßige Preistreiberei; (missbilligend) aus etw./jdm. Vorteil ziehen‘ (GOTTLIEB 1998: 127)

fenbart, dass er auf die Marktsituation prompt reagiert. Die Warenpalette, die er rasch an Käufer liefert, reicht von Zitrusfrüchten, Trikotage aus Wolle, Lorbeerblatt, Nähmaschinen bis zu Mimosen (ŠATROV 1962: 129). Alle diese Waren sind in der Sowjetunion unter dem seit den 1930er Jahren etablierten Begriff *Defizit* (GUROVA 2005: 14) bekannt: Es gibt eine starke Nachfrage, aber keine Möglichkeit, sie zu kaufen. Daraus folgt, dass sowjetische Spekulation auf dem „fruchtbaren Boden" des *Defizits* gewachsen ist. Spekulanten, die zum eigenen Profit Defizitwaren an sowjetische Bürger lieferten, riskierten jedes Mal verhaftet und verurteilt zu werden. So warnt ein junger Mann Gogoberašvili vor einer Razzia gegen Spekulanten auf den Moskauer Märkten (ŠATROV 1962: 150). Solche Razzien sind von Nikita Chruščev persönlich ins Leben gerufen worden, denn er glaubte an die Hilfe der breiten Öffentlichkeit im Kampf gegen fremde Erscheinungen in der sozialistischen Gesellschaft wie Spekulation, Bestechlichkeit und Schmarotzertum (BOGDANOV 2012). Im Zuge der propagandistischen Aufklärung der Erzählung *„Nejlonovaja šubka"* weist der bekehrte Gauner Evsej Mironovič Gogoberašvili darauf hin, dass die Sowjetmacht Spekulation in der Zukunft unbedingt beseitigen wird: „Придет время, и большевики займутся мимозами. [...] В борьбу за мимозу включаются партком, местком и комсомол. [...]. Они умеют работать. Поверьте мне. У них золотые руки и золотые головы!" (ŠATROV 1962: 162).

Die rosigen Perspektiven, Spekulation zu bekämpfen, wurden erst mit der von Gorbačev initiierten Perestrojka wahr, als Einzelerwerbstätigkeit[10] offiziell erlaubt wurde. Der literarische Diskurs der *„Nejlonovaja šubka"* rechnet jedoch schon in den 1960er Jahren mit den beiden Spekulantentypen ab. Ausgerechnet Gogoberašvili nennt Venja „Гниль ты спекулянтская!" (ŠATROV 1962: 167), dank dem Nylonpelzmantel wird auch Gogoberašvilis Niederlage offensichtlich. Im Laufe der Zeit muss Venja fliehen und sein Äußeres mit chirurgischer Hilfe ändern, damit er der verdienten Anklage entgeht. Als eine der Ursachen tritt der Nylonpelzmantel zutage. Venja behauptet, er sei von Gott erschaffen worden, um sein Gehalt monatlich zu erhöhen.[11]

Mithilfe des Nylonpelzmantels wird sogar die Kirche einer Prüfung unterworfen. Eine Fortsetzung der Liste der negativen Typen stellt die evangelische Gemeinde dar, an deren Spitze sich ausschließlich suspekte Gestalten befinden. Die spannungsreiche Beziehung des sowjetischen Staates zur Religion ist allgemein bekannt. So ist es kein Zufall, dass Venja als negativ abgestempelte Figur in seiner letzten Aussage Gott erwähnt. Das Aufdecken der verlogenen Führung der evangelischen Gemeinde in dieser Erzählung bestärkt die propagierte Negation jeglichen religiösen Glaubens. Der Werdegang des Bruders Serafim bzw. San'ka Buchvostov lehnt sich an Biographien vieler Heiliger an: erst im Gefängnis wird er auf den richtigen Weg mithilfe eines geistlichen Lehrers geleitet. Jedoch anstelle des Glaubens haben für ihn Bequemlichkeit und materielle Güter Priorität. Die Bibel langweilt San'ka und bringt ihn zur Verzweiflung.[12] Den Predigtstoff entnimmt er antireligiösen Broschüren, denn sie sind „einfach und interessant zu lesen" (Šatrov 1962: 121). Während Bruder Serafim dem Glauben kritisch gegenübersteht, erweist sich die Prophetin Taisija als eine überzeugte Gottesanbeterin. Sie wirbt neue Mitglieder für die Sekte und verfolgt dabei ihre eigenen Interessen. Taisija sucht Hilfe bei Himmelsvertretern, um ihre eigenen Kleider zu retten.[13] Eingebettet in leidenschaftliche Gebete um ihr Seelenheil träumt sie vom Nylonpelzmantel und schmiedet Pläne über eine zweite Taufe Inga Fedorovnas mit der Absicht, sie in einen Trancezustand zu ver-

[10] Am 19. November 1986 wurde in der UdSSR das Gesetz über Einzelerwerbstätigkeit verabschiedet.

[11] „Вы знаете, Матильдочка, почему появилась на свет эта шубка? Бог создал ее, чтобы ежемесячно увеличивать нашу реальную зарплату." (ŠATROV 1962: 168)

[12] „Санька пытался читать Библию, но не мог. Одолевал сон, сомнения и богохульные мысли." (ŠATROV 1962: 121)

[13] „Инга Федоровна тоже пыталась сделать своим союзником какого-нибудь представителя неба, чтобы спасти свои вещи." (ŠATROV 1962: 127)

setzten und zur Spende des Nylonpelzmantels zu bringen. Als Inga Fedorovna Bruder Serafim um einen Rat bittet und erzählt, dass Taisija ihr empfiehlt, auf materielle Güter zu verzichten und den Mantel an die Sekte zu übergeben, zeigt sich der Nylonpelzmantel erneut als Lackmustest für die Oppositionsreihe eigen vs. fremd, echt vs. unecht, gut vs. schlecht. San'ka, der sich immer mehr von der Religion abwendet, verkündet in der Rolle des Presbyters Serafim: „Господь бог не носит нейлона. [...] Носите сами!" (ŠATROV 1962: 122). Somit werden die Übergabe des Nylonpelzmantels und der Betrug im Namen Gottes verhindert. Gauner San'ka muss sein religiöses Abenteuer abbrechen und wird zu einem ordinären LKW-Fahrer. Schlüssig ist San'kas Vergleich der Sektenmitglieder mit Spekulanten in einer Warteschlange vor einem Geschäft.[14] Aus Sicht der sozialistischen Norm erweisen sich die beiden Gruppen als negative Elemente der Gesellschaft. Mithilfe des Nylonpelzmantels gelingt es San'ka, sich auf der positiven Seite der Opposition einzureihen und die Gläubigen und Spekulanten auf der anderen Seite zu verorten. Diese semantische Differenzierung anhand des vestimentären Handelns der Sektenoberhäupter verurteilt Prophetin Taisija als Person, die ausschließlich von materiellen Dingen geleitet ist.

Das Thema Nylon im literarischen Diskurs findet seine Fortsetzung in Sergej Dovlatovs Sammelband *„Čemodan"*. Die selbstkritisch-ironischen Erinnerungen des Autors an sein Leben in der UdSSR sind mit Kleidungsstücken verbunden, die sich in seinem Reisekoffer befinden. Das Kapitel *„Krepovye finskie noski"* widmet sich dem finnischen Nylonerzeugnis. Die Nylonsocken aus dem Dovlatov-Text, Ende der 1960er Jahre erschienen, bestätigen die These, dass Nylon die dunklen Seiten der sowjetischen Gesellschaft und Wirtschaft aufdeckt. Dem jungen Studenten Dovlatov wird ein illegales Geschäft angeboten, durch das er ans große Geld kommen kann. Man kauft finnische Nylonsocken, nach denen eine große Nachfrage besteht, für sechzig Kopeken und verkauft sie am Schwarzmarkt für sechs Rubel. Das Schema der Bereicherung ist einfach und verspricht einen Reingewinn für jeden Beteiligten von fünfhundertsiebenundsechzig Rubel. Die ausländische Ware kommt aus Finnland und gelangt durch *Farcovščiki*[15] zum Käufer. *Farcovka* ist eine Weiterentwicklung sowjetischer Spekulation, spezialisiert ausschließlich auf den Verkauf ausländischer Konsumgüter. Jedoch wird der illegale Handel in dieser Erzählung mit einer wirkungsvollen Maßnahme des sowjetischen Staates unterbunden. *Farcovščik* Fred bezeichnet es als eine Katastrophe: „Все магазины завалены креповыми носками. Причем советскими креповыми носками. Восемьдесят копеек – пара. Качество не хуже, чем у финских. Такое жэ синтетическое дерьмо..." (DOVLATOV 2002: 302). Über Nacht wurden die Geschäfte in Leningrad mit sowjetischen Nylonsocken beliefert. So bleiben zweihundertvierzig Paar finnischer Nylonsocken für mehrere Jahrzehnte in Dovlatovs Besitz.

Nylon zeigt in dieser Erzählung eine Reaktion des sowjetischen Staates auf die starke Nachfrage nach ausländischen Waren in der Sowjetunion. Fred bezeichnet sie als eine Gemeinheit der sozialistischen Wirtschaft,[16] die allerdings im Rahmen des Nylonkriegs als ein vorübergehender Sieg der Sowjetunion betrachtet werden kann. Dennoch führte in der Realität dieser Schritt der sowjetischen Planwirtschaft nicht zum endgültigen Sieg im Nylonkrieg. Der enttäuschte Fred erkennt die Ursache dafür:

> „Знаю я нашу блядскую промышленность! Сначала она двадцать лет кочумает, а потом вдруг – раз! И все магазины забиты какой-нибудь одной хреновиной. Если

[14] „Несмотря на горящие глаза, на постные лица, на поднятые к небу бороды, трясуны не походили на людей, охваченных молитвенным экстазом. Скорее их можно было принять за спекулянтов, что поутру собрались у дверей универмага в надежде первыми заскочить в здание и схватить прибыльный отрез или дефицитную кофточку." (ŠATROV 1962: 11)

[15] *Фарцовка* ‚Schwarzhandel mit ausländischen Artikeln' (FREIDERICH 1976:163)

[16] „Кто мог ждать такой подлянки от социалистической экономики?!" (DOVLATOV 2002: 302)

уж зарядили поточную линию, то всё. Будут штамповать эти креповые носки – миллион пар в секунду...“ (DOVLATOV 2002: 302).

Diese emotional beladene Erklärung reflektiert die Rigidität der Planwirtschaft und ihre Unmöglichkeit, auf die sich ständig ändernde Nachfrage zu reagieren. Zugleich wird die Parallelisierung der Realität und der Fiktion offensichtlich. In Wirklichkeit führte diese Maßnahme in der UdSSR zu einer kurzzeitigen Minderung der Schwarzmarktaktivitäten. Dennoch bedurfte es einer konstanten Nachverfolgung von Konsuminteressen der Bevölkerung und einer konsequenten Auffüllung des einheimischen Marktes mit den gewünschten Waren, um den Schwarzmarkt endgültig auszulöschen. Die Zukunftsperspektiven aus Freds fiktionaler Prophezeiung sind in der geschichtlichen Realität nachverfolgbar, in der die Unfähigkeit der sowjetischen Wirtschaft zu einer schnellen Reaktion auf Konsumentenbedürfnisse eine Tatsache war. Die Erzählung scheint aus dem Leben gegriffen zu sein und weist viele Parallelen zur sowjetischen Vergangenheit auf.[17]

Die russischen Bezeichnungen für die Nylonsocken *sintetičeskoe der'mo* und *chrenovina* bezeugen die rein negativen Eigenschaften der Ware, unabhängig vom Land der Herstellung. Aber während die finnischen Socken als Defizitware um sechs Rubel am Schwarzmarkt gekauft werden, bleiben die einheimischen in den Geschäften liegen. Zum Teil basiert dieses Phänomen auf einer mythologisierten Vorstellung sowjetischer Bürger über die Qualität ausländischer Waren, die a priori besser sei (LEBINA 2006: 173). Zum Teil liegt die Ursache dafür im Defizit: Die stärkste Nachfrage genießen diejenigen Waren, die am schwierigsten zu bekommen sind. Es besteht ein direkter Zusammenhang zwischen Konsumwarenmangel und der Bedeutung dieser Waren: je schwieriger es ist die Ware zu kaufen, desto höher ist der Wert dieser.[18]

In der Erzählung Dovlatovs sind die finnischen Nylonsocken deutlich als ein semiotisches Zeichen der Freiheit lesbar. Die Hauptfigur setzt dieses Zeichen bewusst ein, um die eigene Nonkonformität zu manifestieren und den Regimerahmen zu sprengen. Für die Hauptfigur Dovlatovs besteht eine lange Liste weiterer Waren, die er nach seinem Fiasko mit den finnischen Nylonsocken am Schwarzmarkt vertreibt. Es sind ausländische Waren: Bolonja-Mäntel, deutsche Stereoanlagen, amerikanische Zigaretten, eine japanische Fotoausrüstung. Auffällig ist, dass es Massenkonsumgüter sind, die man in der Sowjetunion tatsächlich nicht leicht kaufen konnte.

Kennzeichnend für beide literarischen Reflexionen der Nylonkleidungsstücke ist der Ursprung dieser Waren: Sie sind aus dem Ausland mitgebracht worden. Die ersten einzelnen Nylonerzeugnisse wurden – wie fast alle Neuheiten und Defizitwaren – von sowjetischer Prominenz eingeführt, das heißt von Parteifunktionären, Wissenschaftlern und Künstlern, die die Möglichkeit hatten, ins Ausland zu reisen, wie beispielsweise der Chirurg Motovilin in „*Nejlonovaja šubka*“. In diesem Zusammenhang verhält sich Nylon entsprechend der üblichen Verbreitung von Mode in der Gesellschaft, und zwar nach dem top-down-Mechanismus (SIMMEL 1911: 182). Zu einem späteren Zeitpunkt findet man andere Wege, um größere Mengen an Waren in die UdSSR zu bringen, wie die zwei finnischen Cousinen aus Dovlatovs Erzählung, deren Mütter Russinnen waren. Ein weiteres Mal wird mithilfe des Nylons die enge Verbindung der Fiktion mit den sowjetischen Alltagsrealien veranschaulicht.

So gesehen zeugen die beiden literarischen Texte von dem nicht offiziell erklärten Nylonkrieg, der ausländische Konsumwaren als Waffe gegen die mangelhafte Versorgung in der

[17] Erzählberichte finnischer Touristen über ihre Erfahrungen in der Sowjetunion von den 1950er bis in die 1970er Jahre bezeugen die Einfuhr von Nylonwaren. Nylonstrümpfe und -hemden waren die beliebtesten Kleidungsstücke, die am Schwarzmarkt in der UdSSR die stärkste Nachfrage genossen (vgl. KUUSI 2013: 218).

[18] „Der nie überwundene Konsumgütermangel wirkte sich auf die Bedeutung und Gebrauch von Dingen aus. Die Dinge waren wichtig, weil Mangel herrschte.“ (RÜTHERS 2010: 55)

Sowjetunion einsetzt. Der Nylonkrieg[19] dauerte im Rahmen des Kalten Krieges bis zum Zerfall der Sowjetunion 1991. Der Nylonkrieg in Bezug auf Nylonerzeugnisse kam Anfang der 1970er Jahre zu seinem Ende, als die sowjetische Industrie die Fließbandproduktion diverser Nylonkleidungsstücke aufnahm. Genau in dieser Zeit kam Nylon aus der Mode und die Nachfrage erlosch von selbst.

In den angeführten literarischen Beispielen erweist sich Nylon nur dann als wertvoll, wenn es sich um ausländische Waren handelt. Das ausländische Nylon bringt die sowjetische Wirtschaft aus ihrem stabilen Gleichgewicht, deckt den Nachholbedarf auf und regt die Wirtschaft zu Veränderung und Modernisierung an. Dennoch bezieht sich die starke Nachfrage nicht auf die Qualität der Nylonerzeugnisse, sondern basiert auf ihrem ausländischen Ursprung. Das Nylon aus dem Ausland sprengt die offensichtlich auf Propagandabasis aufgebaute Oppositionsreihe von eigen vs. fremd, echt vs. unecht, gut vs. schlecht, die insbesondere in Šatrovs Text zur Geltung kommt. Das ausländische Nylon zeichnet sich als Gegenstand der sowjetischen Spekulation und *farcovka* aus und symbolisiert das Fremde und das Negative. Wenn das „fremde" ausländische Nylon zu dem sowjetischen, also „eigenen" wird, bricht das künstlerische Oppositionssystem zusammen.

In der Realität zerstörte das Aufkommen des sowjetischen Nylons die vorher bestehenden Spannungen: Die Nachfrage verschwand und das sowjetische Nylon führte die starre sozialistische Planwirtschaft vor, indem die aus der Mode gekommenen Nylonkleidungsstücke, für die es nun keine Nachfrage mehr gab, massenhaft und auf Dauer produziert wurden. Die reale Konfrontation zwischen dem sowjetischen und dem ausländischen Nylon hat kurzzeitig stattgefunden und endete mit dem langen Bestehen des sowjetischen Nylons. Dennoch wurde das sowjetische Nylon weder in der Realität, noch im literarischen Diskurs positiv konnotiert. Die von Riesman vorgeschlagene kapitalistische Aktion trug auch dazu bei, dass die sozialistische Planwirtschaft Mitte der 1980er Jahre abgeschafft wurde und sowjetische Konsumenten zumindest ansatzweise eine freie Auswahl an Konsumgütern bekamen. Das ausländische Nylon im literarischen Diskurs der 1960er Jahre spielt, wie diese Analyse bestätigt, eine bedeutende Rolle im Aufdecken verschiedener wirtschaftlicher und sozialer Probleme in der Sowjetunion der 1960er Jahre.

Die literarischen Texte Šatrovs und Dovlatovs, so lässt sich zusammenfassend sagen, weisen das ganze Spektrum gegensätzlicher Einstellungen zum Nylon auf und bauen eine Sequenz von Oppositionen auf. Zunächst sind die Autoren selbst Vertreter unterschiedlicher Haltungen dem sowjetischen Staat gegenüber. Šatrov, ein treuer Regimeanhänger, schreibt im Geiste der Zeitschrift *„Krokodil"*, propagiert die sowjetische Weltanschauung und bekämpft zugleich die Mängel mit dem satirischen Wort. Dovlatov, ein namhafter Regimekritiker, hinterfragt nicht nur den sowjetischen Alltag, sondern schlichtweg alles, inklusive seiner selbst. Während Šatrov regelmäßig in der Öffentlichkeit zu Wort kommt, gelingt es Dovlatov nur gelegentlich, unter Umgehung der staatlichen Anweisungen, seine Texte zu veröffentlichen. So wurde der Sammelband *„Čemodan"* zuerst im Ausland publiziert. Kennzeichnend für die gegensätzlichen Positionen der Autoren ist auch das Schicksal der beiden Erzählungen, *„Nejlonovaja šubka"* und *„Krepovye finskie noski"*: Der Sammelband *„Čemodan"* geht in den Kanon der sowjetrussischen Literatur ein und wird in mehrere Sprachen übersetzt, das Werk Šatrovs gerät in Vergessenheit.

Trotz der unterschiedlichen Autorenhaltungen symbolisiert Nylon in beiden literarischen Texten den Westen. Während Šatrov den importierten Nylonpelzmantel als Lackmustest für alle negativen Erscheinungen in der Erzählung einsetzt, manifestieren die finnischen Nylon-

[19] „Das strategische Konzept des Nylon War sah vor, durch die Infiltration der Sowjetunion mit Konsumgütern wie den begehrten Nylonstrümpfen Erwartungsdruck aufzubauen. Die Sowjetregierung sollte durch ihre Bevölkerung gezwungen werden, in die Konsumgüterindustrie zu investieren statt in Raumfahrt und Rüstung." (RÜTHERS 2010: 44)

socken in der Erzählung Dovlatovs eine Möglichkeit der freien Wahl und sind somit eine Erscheinungsform der Freiheit. Die Höhepunkte der beiden Erzählungen veranschaulichen es am besten. In der Erzählung Šatrovs wird der Nylonpelzmantel als Tierunterlage im Stall verwendet, wodurch seine Wertlosigkeit unterstrichen wird. In der Erzählung Dovlatovs nimmt die Hauptfigur die Nylonsocken in die Emigration mit, als Erinnerung an die eigene Ungehorsamkeit in der UdSSR, an die Jugend und Freiheit.

Summary

In March 1953 at a conference on Totalitarianism in Boston, David Riesman, an American sociologist, suggested a way for winning the Cold War. The idea was simple: the US had to bombard the Soviet Union with American consumer goods in order to initiate unrest in the socialist system. Although the war was not declared officially, it went down in history as the Nylon War. This paper aims to reveal the effects of this war in the Soviet literary discourse of the 1960s. The paper analyses two literary texts, "*The Nylon Fur Coat*" by Samuil Shatrov (1962) and Sergey Dovlatov's story "*Finnish Crepe Socks*" (1986), to reveal nylon's intrusion into the Soviet Union in the 1960s. The influence of the western nylon on the Soviet consumers reflects the Soviet mythologized view of imported clothing, which was better than domestic by definition. Furthermore, nylon reveals the rigidity of the planned economy and its inability to satisfy the demands of the Soviet consumers. The Western nylon takes a secure place on the negative side of the conflict between good and bad but, unexpectedly, the Soviet nylon cannot be judged positively either.

Bibliographie

BOGDANOV, S. 2012. Popytki Chruščëva aktivizirovat' bor'bu s ėkonimičeskoj prestupnost'ju v SSSR. In: *Vestnik aktivista.* 19.08.2012. http://www.vestarchive.ru/issledovaniia/1964-popytki-ns-hrysheva-aktivizirovat-borby-s-ekonomicheskoi-prestypnostu-v-sssr.html (15.07.13)

DOVLATOV, S. 2002. *Čemodan.* In: Dovlatov, S. *Sobranie sočinenij.* Band 3. Sankt-Peterburg 2002, 287–405.

ERŠOV, L. 1966. *Sovetskaja satiričeskaja prosa.* Moskva.

FRIEDERICH, W. / GEIS, S. 1976. *Russisch-Deutsches Neuwörterbuch.* München.

FRIEDRICH, C. J. (ed.) 1954. *Totalitarianism. Proceedings of a conference held at the American Academy of Arts and Sciences.* Cambridge.

GOLDSCHWEER, U. 2013. Frau und Konsum: Genderaspekte der sowjetischen Konsumkultur. In: Norhejl, R., Gorfinkel, O. et al (ed.). *Genderdiskurse und nationale Identität in Russland. Sowjetische und postsowjetische Zeit, München,/ Berlin, Washington D.C., 181–196.*

GOTTLIEB, K.H.M. 1998. *Sprachfallen im Russischen.* 5. Aufl. Moskau.

GUROVA, O. 2005. *Ljudi i vešči v sovetskoj kul'ture.* Novosibirsk. http://sitemaker.umich.edu/olga.gurova/files/nz.pdf (20.07.2013)

KUUSI, HANNA. 2013. Accidental Traders – Finnish Tourists in the Soviet Union in the 1950s-1970s. In: Heinonen, V., Peltonen, M. (ed.). *Finnish Consumption. An Emerging Consumer Society between East and West.* Helsinki, 206–229.

LEBINA, N. 2002. Plus chimizacija vsej strany. In: *Rodina 9/2002,* 82–86.

LEBINA, N. 2006. *Ėnciklopedija banal'nostej. Sovetskaja povsednevnost': kontury, simvoly, znaki.* Sankt-Peterburg.

LOTMAN, J. 1972. *Vorlesungen zu einer strukturalen Poetik.* München.

MERKEL, I. 1999. *Utopie und Bedürfnis: die Geschichte der Konsumkultur in der DDR.* Köln, Wien.

MERL, S. 1997. Staat und Konsum in der Zentralverwaltungswirtschaft. Rußland und die ostmitteleuropäischen Länder. In: Siegrist, H., Kaelble, H. et al (ed.). *Europäische Konsumgeschichte. Zur Gesellschafts- und Kulturgeschichte des Konsums (18. bis 20. Jahrhundert).* Frankfurt am Main, 205–241.

NARYŠKIN, B. 1986. *KPSS v rezolucijach i rešenijach s"ezdov, konferencij i plenumov CK. Band 9: 1956 – 1960.* Moskva.

RÜTHERS, M. 2010. Kampf der Lebensstile. American way of life und sowjetische Konsumgeschichte im Kalten Krieg. In: Hansel, M., Rohrwasser, M. (ed.). *Kalter Krieg in Österreich. Literatur – Kunst – Kultur.* Wien 2010, 35–58.

ŠATROV, S. 1962. *Nejlonovaja šubka.* Moskva.

SIMMEL, G. 1911. Die Mode. In: Bovenschen, S. (ed.). *Die Listen der Mode.* Frankfurt am Main 1986, 179–207.

VAJNŠTEJN, O. 2010. V sootvetstvii s figuroj: polnoe telo v sovetskoj mode. http://polit.ru/article/2010/05/25/vainshtein/ (25.07.2013)

HOT STYLE MEETS COLD WAR
Kleidung als Distinktionsmerkmal in dem Film „*Stiljagi*"

DAGMAR BURKHART, MANNHEIM

Der vestimentäre Code gehört zu jenen nonverbalen Zeichenrepertoires, die vor allem zur Signifikation und Kommunikation von Individualität oder Konformität in Sozialbeziehungen dienen. Sich-Kleiden bedeutet „zeichenhaftes Handeln" (BURKHART 2010: 209). Erstmals 1936 verwendete der russische Ethnologe und Semiologe Petr Bogatyrev in Zusammenhang mit traditioneller Kleidung den Zeichenbegriff und definierte Tracht als besonderes semiotisches System, in dem verschiedene Funktionen, etwa die Markierung eines Festtags, einer Trauerzeit oder einer Altersstufe, zum Ausdruck gelangen (BOGATYREV 1971: 6, 340, 532). Modische Kleidung indes ist primär ein Lifestyle-Phänomen, und nicht Ausdrucksform von kollektivem Denken oder Moralität. Wer auf individuellen Stil Wert lege, sei „weder besser noch schlechter" [als die Übrigen]. „Einfach nur anders", erklärt daher der in Anlehnung an westliche Rock'n'Roll-Mode gestylte Protagonist des russischen Musical-Films „*Stiljagi*" Mėls der Komsomol-Sekretärin Katja, die ihn zu den asketischen Idealen des Kommunistischen Jugendverbands zurückholen möchte und jegliche Stil-Diversifikation ablehnt.

Der Film kam am 25. Dezember 2008 in die Kinos. Er behandelt die Auseinandersetzungen zwischen dem Komsomol und der am Westen, vor allem an den USA orientierten urbanen Subkultur russischer Jugendlicher Mitte der 1950er Jahre, die mit ihrer hedonistisch und konsumeristisch fundierten Selbstdarstellung das sozialistische System herausforderten. Im Mittelpunkt steht der aus dem Arbeitermilieu stammende Student Mėls und seine Metamorphose zu einem „Stiljaga". Fasziniert von dem aufregend Andersartigen, das die Stiljagi verkörpern, und verführt von den Reizen Polinas (Pol'zas), die einer Moskauer Stiljagi-Gruppe angehört, beschließt er, sich neu zu erfinden. So wird aus dem grauen Komsomolzen Mėls wie im Märchen von der Verwandlung des hässlichen Entleins in einen schönen Schwan, der an auffallend bunter Kleidung, Jazz, Boogie, Rock'n'Roll und Erotik interessierte Mėl. Er lässt sich ein grün-gelb kariertes Jackett nähen, dicke Kreppsohlen unter seine Schuhe kleben und kämmt sich seine pomadisierten Haare zu einer Tolle. Mit dieser neuen, provokanten Aufmachung und seinen im Eilverfahren erlernten Boogie-Woogie-Künsten hat er die Bedingung zur Aufnahme in die Stiljagi-Gruppe erfüllt, doch Polina treibt weiterhin ihren Spott mit ihm. Nachdem er seinen Komsomol-Ausweis zurückgegeben und daraufhin seinen Studienplatz verloren hat, kauft er sich auf dem Schwarzmarkt von einem arbeits- und mittellosen Musiker ein gebrauchtes Saxophon. Er lernt es binnen kurzer Zeit – vor allem nachdem ihm der Geist von Charlie Parker erschienen ist – durch heimliches Anhören eines amerikanischen Radiosenders spielen, tritt von da an in einer Musikgruppe auf und wird endlich von Polina anerkannt und geliebt. Bald jedoch stellt die Realität ihre Liebesromanze auf eine harte Probe: Als die schwangere Polina von ihrer Mutter, einer linientreuen, dogmatischen Lehrerin, verstoßen wird, nimmt Mėls Vater das Paar großzügig in seiner kleinen Wohnung auf. Selbst nachdem Polina ein dunkelhäutiges Kind zur Welt gebracht hat, zeigen er und Mėl eine Toleranz, die schließlich sogar die rassistische Hysterie von Polinas Mutter etwas zu dämpfen vermag. Am Ende finden sich Mėl und Pol'za, die als gestresste Mutter ihr Stiljaga-Outfit zugunsten praktischer Kleidung und kurzer, ungefärbter Haare abgelegt hatte, im alten Stil als Paar inmitten einer heterogenen, bunten Menge der Nach-Perestrojka-Zeit auf dem Moskauer „Brodvej", der nun wieder seinen vorsowjetischen Namen „Tverskaja ulica" trägt.

In den USA lief diese „musical dramedy", eine Mischung aus Musical, Drama und Komödie, unter dem Titel „*Hipsters*". Der Film wurde beim Toronto International Film Festival, Nashville Film Festival und dem Cleveland International Film Festival gezeigt, wo er der Publikumsfavorit war. Er gewann den Audience Choice Award beim Anchorage International Film Festival 2009 und verschiedene andere Preise, etwa viermal den renommierten russischen *Nika*. 2008 wurde er in Russland zum besten Film des Jahres gekürt.

Um das russische Publikum nicht mit dem amerikanischen Genrebegriff *Musical* vor den Kopf zu stoßen, lief die Promotion des Streifens unter der Bezeichnung *muzykal'nyj fil'm* ‚Musikfilm'. Auch der Arbeitstitel des Films „*Bugi na kost'jach*"/„*Boogie on the Bones*" wurde zugunsten des Titels „*Stiljagi*" fallen gelassen, um eine Assoziation mit dem Horrorfilm-Genre zu vermeiden (ISAKAVA 2009: 1–2).

An Drehorten wie Minsk, Moskau und Petersburg sowie im Studio entstanden, kam „*Stiljagi*" (russisch „*Стиляги*", etwa ‚von modischem Stil Besessene, Stiljäger') Ende des Jahres 2008[1] im postsowjetischen Russland als Farbfilm mit Musik, Gesang und Tanzeinlagen in die Kinos.[2]

Die Rollen der Erwachsenen wurden mit bekannten russischen Schauspielern besetzt; für die Rollen der Stiljagi und Komsomolzen wählte Todorovskij 19 bis 20jährige Laien, die beim Casting außer der Schauspielbegabung auch eine gewisse Gesangsfähigkeit zeigten, denn alle mussten selbst singen: „Es wäre seltsam gewesen, wenn ein junger Bursche [im Film] mit der Stimme eines Pavarotti gesungen hätte (TODOROVSKIJ 2008: 3).

Der Tradition des klassischen Musicals folgend, wird die Handlung in „*Stiljagi*" stets von Musik und Tanz begleitet, und von den Figuren gesungene Songs markieren die wichtigsten Punkte der Geschichte.

Blick zurück ins Graue: zwischen Stalins Tod und der Tauwetter-Periode

Die Story des Films ist im Jahr 1955 angesiedelt, also zwei Jahre nach Stalins Tod, aber noch vor dem XX. Parteitag der KPdSU 1956, auf dem Chruščev in seiner berühmten Geheimrede Stalins Verbrechen anprangerte und damit die (allerdings nur kurz dauernde) Tauwetter-Periode einleitete. Dieses Jahr 1955 zeigt besonders deutlich die Gleichzeitigkeit des Ungleichzeitigen: Während in den USA Bill Haley & His Comets – gekleidet in großkarierte Jacketts und mit pomadisierter Haartolle – den bahnbrechenden Song „*Rock Around the Clock*" spielten, Elvis Presley, der künftige „King of Rock'n'Roll", mit seiner Rhythm-and-Blues-Musik und lasziv hüftkreisend vorgetragenen Rock-Songs wie „*Heartbreak Hotel*" und „*Hound Dog*" erste Erfolge erzielte und James Dean (in Levi's-Jeans, T-Shirt und roter Nylon-Jacke[3] als Zeichen der Auflehnung) in dem Jugendgang-Film „*Rebel Without a Cause*"

---

[1] Fünfzig Jahre nach der Uraufführung (1958) von Dmitrij D. Šostakovičs Operette „*Moskva–Čerëmuškki*", in der die Probleme Wohnungssuchender in Moskau im Musical-Stil, aber mit satirisch-kritischen Untertönen thematisiert wurden.

[2] Länge: 132 Minuten; Regie: Valerij Todorovskij; Drehbuch: Jurij Korotkov und Valerij Todorovskij; Kamera: Roman Vas'janov; Produzenten: Leonid Lebedev, Leonid Jarmol'nik, Vadim Gorjainov, Valerij Todorovskij und Television Channel Russia; Produktion: Kinokompanija Krasnaja Strela, Telekanal Rossija; Darsteller: Anton Šagin (Mėls/Mėl), Oksana Akin'šina (Polina/Pol'za), Evgenija Brik (Katja), Maksim Matveev (Fedor/Fred), Ekaterina Volkova (Bėtsi), Igor' Vojnarovskij (Bob), Konstantin Balkiriev (Dryn), Sergej Garmaš (Mėls' Vater), Irina Rozanova (Pol'zas Mutter), Oleg Jankovskij (Freds Vater), Leonid Jarmol'nik (Bobs Vater) u.a.; Art director: Vladimir Gudilin; Kostüme: Aleksandr Osipov; Choreographie: Oleg Gluškov und Leonid Timcunik. Musik: Konstantin Meladze; Originalsongs aus den 1980er und 1990er Jahre von Vjačeslav Butusov und der Gruppe „Nautilus Pompilius", Fedor Čistjakov und „Nol'", Andrej Makarevič und „Mašina Vremeni", Mike Naumenko und „Zoopark", Natal'ja Pivovarova und „Kolibri", Vladimir Šachrin und „ČajF", Valerij Sjutkin und „Bravo", Viktor Coj und „Kino", Garik Sukačev und „Brigada S".

[3] Die leuchtend rote Windjacke, kreiert von Kostümdesigner Moss Mabry, die James Dean in dem Film trägt, wurde zur Stilikone. Auch sein Mädchen, gespielt von Natalie Wood, trägt Rot: einen weiten roten Mantel. Die vom Regisseur bewusst gewählte Farbe Rot steht als Symbolfarbe für Leben, Blut, Herausforderung, Trotz und

einen Aufsässigen spielte, wurde die Alltags- und Unterhaltungskultur in der UdSSR von diametral entgegen gesetzten Faktoren bestimmt. In den russischen Kinos dominierten „wartime and post-war productions with good, educational content, promoting both patriotism and Soviet socialist values" (FÜRST 2006: 213; 2010: 224). Gemeint sind Filme wie „*Dobroe utro*" (‚Guten Morgen!'),[4] „*Pervyj ėšelon*" (‚Die erste Staffel'), „*Sčastlivaja junost'*" (‚Glückliche Jugend') oder „*Attestat zrelosti*" (‚Reifezeugnis'), alle aus dem Jahr 1955. Es herrschte eine die Bürger reglementierende offizielle Politik und Planwirtschaft, die keine Rücksicht auf individuelle Bedürfnisse der Sowjetmenschen und ihren Wunsch nach freier Wahlmöglichkeit nahm. Im Gegensatz zur Nomenklatura, die einen gehobenen Lebensstandard pflegen konnte, lebte die Masse in einer Mangelwirtschaft:

> „Ewige Schlangen, Defizit und schlechte Versorgung mit der notwendigen Ware waren Teil des Alltags geblieben. Die reale Kleidung des größten Teils der Bevölkerung war ein Abbild der totalitären Herrschaft und der sowjetischen Wirtschaft, die weder dem individuellen Geschmack und den Anforderungen des Konsumenten entsprach, noch sich darum bemühte, zwar einfache, aber qualitativ zufriedenstellende Kleidung auf den Markt zu bringen" (HUBER 2011: 253f.),

von einer ästhetisch anspruchsvollen ganz zu schweigen. Diese Defizite konnten durch Kommissionsläden, private Schneider, Selbst-Nähen und einen florierenden Schwarzmarkt nur unzureichend ausgeglichen werden. Auch der Musik-Sektor litt unter der repressiven sowjetischen Kulturpolitik und ihrem verlängerten Arm, den staatlichen Plattenfirmen. Schallplatten mit der begehrten Swing- und Rock'n'Roll-Musik wurden Mitte der 1950er Jahre von Soldaten („frontoviki"), die in Mitteleuropa stationiert waren, von Seeleuten, Diplomaten, Touristen und Schwarzmarkthändlern („farcovščiki") in Umlauf gebracht. Oder aber – ein einmaliges Phänomen der Musikgeschichte – man kopierte die in BBC, Voice of America und Radio Svoboda gehörte bzw. auf dem Schwarzmarkt erworbene oder von Freunden ausgeliehene Rock'n'Roll-Musik mit Hilfe von (zum Teil selbstgebauten) Sonographen auf ausgediente Röntgenaufnahmen, die in runde Form geschnitten und eventuell mit einem Cover versehen wurden. Da auf diesen Flexidiscs die Knochen der durchleuchteten Personen durchschimmerten, hieß die aufgenommene Musik „Muzyka na rebrach" (‚Musik auf Rippen', SEETHALER 2011, o.p.).[5]

Die Mitgliedschaft im Kommunistischen Jugendverband *Komsomol* für Vierzehn- bis Achtundzwanzigjährige wurde von den Jugendlichen mehrheitlich wahrgenommen, weil z.B. die Zulassung zum Studium davon abhing. In Routine erstarrt und meist von Erwachsenen geführt, denen der Komsomol nur als „Durchlauferhitzer" (GOEHRKE 2005: 349) für ihre Parteikarriere diente, konnte der Jugendverband viele der Heranwachsenden nicht mehr wirklich erreichen.

Sowohl bei den Komsomolzen wie auch bei den Stiljagi handelt es sich um Gruppierungen, deren spezifischer Habitus nach Pierre Bourdieu das gesamte Auftreten der jeweiligen Person, im Einzelnen also den Lebensstil, die Sprache, die Kleidung und den Geschmack, ausmacht. Die Gruppierungen agieren jeweils in einem „sozialen Feld", d.h. einem Kräftefeld, in dem die Beteiligten um Macht konkurrieren und versuchen, ihre Positionen und Repräsentationen durchzusetzen. Laut Bourdieu ist Habitus als „System verinnerlichter Muster" (BOURDIEU 1970 : 143), als erworbene Disposition, die zu einer zweiten Natur geworden ist, zwar dauerhaft, aber nicht unveränderlich. Dies hieße für die Stiljagi, dass sie nach der Sozia-

---

Kühnheit. Rot sollte dem Lebensgefühl von Heranwachsenden im Generationenkonflikt Mitte der 1950er Jahre in den USA farblichen Ausdruck verleihen und Fanal-Wirkung zeigen (vgl. YOUNG 2012: 164–169).

[4] Alle Übersetzungen aus dem Russischen stammen von mir, D.B.

[5] Daher war anfangs „*Bugi na kost'jach*" oder „*Boogie on the Bones*" (‚Boogie auf den Knochen') als Filmtitel für „*Stiljagi*" im Gespräch. Einige der heute als Sammlerstücke heiß begehrten „Röntgenschallplatten" („roentgenizdat") finden sich im Moskauer Radio-Museum. In den 1960er Jahren wurde die Röntgenschallplatten durch Tonbandaufnahmen („Magnitizdat") abgelöst.

lisation im Elternhaus (primärer Habitus), in der Schule und im Komsomol (sekundärer Habitus), später durch Imitation und Verinnerlichung „westlicher" Gestik, Körperhaltung sowie Wahl der Kleidung und des Musikstils einen weiteren Habitus erworben haben: ein Fall von Überprägung.

Valerij Todorovskijs Streifen „*Stiljagi*",[6] der all diese Themen aufgreift, will kein historischer Film oder soziologischer Dokumentarstreifen im strengen Sinn sein, sondern eher „fantasija, počti skazka" (‚eine Phantasie, beinahe ein Märchen', TODOROVSKIJ 2008: 2). Er vermittelt aber in seiner Semiotik durchaus Einblicke in das triste Alltagsleben und die ideologische Repressivität der Ära, die sich auditiv in der Kriminalisierung westlicher Musik und visuell in der erzwungenen Uniformität einer vor allem in Grau, Braun und einem dunklen Grau-Blau gekleideten Bevölkerung ausdrückt. Diese warenästhetisch gesehen unattraktive, schlecht geschnittene, funktionale Einheitskleidung wird im Film immer wieder demonstriert: etwa bei Massenszenen auf der Straße und beim Wochenendtanz im Gor'kij-Park, bei der Komsomol-Versammlung sowie in der Konfektionsabteilung eines Kaufhauses, als Mėls sich neue Kleidung kaufen möchte und angesichts des tristen Einerleis resigniert weggeht, um sich an einen illegal arbeitenden Hinterhofschneider zu wenden. Auch wenn die Kamera die Bewohner der *kommunalka* (‚Gemeinschaftswohnung'), wo Mėls' Vater mit seinen beiden Söhnen in zwei kleinen Zimmern haust, filmt, einmal aus der Vogelperspektive in Aufsicht auf die offengelegten Gemeinschafts- und Privaträume, sind alle in Grau oder Braun gekleidet.

Der Historiker Carsten Goehrke spricht von einer sowjetischen „Fassadengesellschaft", in der die Lage beschönigende Propagandaphrasen und die schnöde Wirklichkeit weit auseinanderklafften (GOEHRKE 2005: 270). Es ist die Zeit des Kalten Krieges, der in seiner schärfsten Ausprägung von 1947 bis 1972 bzw. als fortwährender Ost-West-Konflikt bis 1989 dauerte. In dieser bipolaren Welt, wo sich das kommunistische und das kapitalistische System in Konfrontation gegenüber standen, zeigte sich der Konkurrenzkampf beider Systeme nicht nur auf militärischem (Wettrüsten) und ökonomischem Gebiet (Planwirtschaft vs. Markwirtschaft), sondern auch in der Verbreitung ideologischer Propaganda. Ihre Aufgabe bestand darin, den jeweiligen Einfluss des gegnerischen Systems auf das eigene einzudämmen und zurückzudrängen. Wenn also seit Ende der 1940er Jahre die Stiljagi den afroamerikanisch geprägten Jazz, Boogie Woogie bzw. später den Rock'n'Roll und die dazu gehörende Kleidung und lässig-liberale Lebenseinstellung (oder was sie dafür hielten) aus den USA übernahmen, wurden sie von der Bevölkerungsmehrheit als Vaterlandsverräter und Systemfeinde im Sinne einer „fünften Kolonne" betrachtet und verurteilt. „Gde tvoi idealy? Ty pljunul na nich" (‚Wo sind deine Ideale? Du hast auf sie gespuckt!') und „Ty za jarkie trjapki vragu prodaešsja!" (‚Für ein paar grelle Fetzen verkaufst du dich dem Feind!'), schreit deshalb die linientreue Komsomol-Führerin Katja dem abtrünnigen Mėls ins Gesicht (1:31:29). Dieser aber, anstatt vor versammelter Komsomol-Gruppe Selbstkritik zu üben, geht durch die graue Masse der wie in einem Amphitheater sitzenden Komsomolzen nach vorne zum Rednerpult und gibt wortlos seinen Ausweis zurück. Filmästhetisch wird die Sequenz bestimmt durch den Gegensatz zwischen dem *einen* bunten Stiljaga und der unifarben blaugrauen Versammlung (Abbildung 7) sowie durch die dramatisch gesteigerte Rhetorik und Gestik der Anklägerin, deren Rede in einen Sprechgesang nach dem Song „Skovannych odnoj cep'ju, svjazannych odnoj cel'ju" (‚Geschmiedet zu *einer* Kette, verbunden durch *ein* Ziel') von Vjačeslav Butusov der Perestrojka-Kultgruppe „*Nautilus Pompilius*" übergeht, unterstrichen durch den anschwellenden Rap der Komsomolzen.

---

[6] Die Bezeichnung „stiljagi" für Anhänger des westlichen „way of life" wurde von dem Feuilletonisten Dmitrij Beljaev geprägt (*Krokodil* 10.03.1949: 10). Die Stiljagi selbst nannten sich *štatniki* (‚Fans der Vereinigten Staaten von Amerika') oder *čuvaki* und ihre Mädchen *čuvachi*.

Stil-Revolte in der Uniformitätsgesellschaft

Von der ideologischen Dauerberieselung durch politische Phrasen und Parolen abgestumpft, sah ein Teil der russischen Jugend Mitte der 1950er Jahre das Heil in der US-amerikanischen Rock'n'Roll-Kultur – eine Stil-Revolte, die in den 1970er Jahren eine Neuauflage erlebte, als „die Jugend mit Hingabe die Ausgeburten ‚westlicher Dekadenz' wie lange Haare für Männer, Jeans, Miniröcke, Twist, Beat, Rock- und Popmusik" (GOEHRKE 2005: 349) anbetete. Nach seinen Textvorlieben gefragt, verwies Valerij Todorovskij u.a. auf Viktor Slavkins Stück „*Vzroslaja doč' molodogo čeloveka*" (‚Die erwachsene Tochter eines jungen Mannes', 1979), dessen Handlung in der Brežnev-Zeit der siebziger Jahre angesiedelt ist (TODOROVSKIJ 2008: 2).

In der langweiligen, farblosen, freudlosen und nüchternen Alltagskultur des Gros der Sowjetgesellschaft wirken die *stiljagi* (‚style hunter') der 1950er Jahre mit ihrem nonkonformistischen, bunten und die geltenden Regeln herausfordernden Lifestyle wie Paradiesvögel (Abbildung 8). Die Mehrheitsgesellschaft erfreute sich aber nicht an ihrer Gegenkultur oder tolerierte sie, sondern beschimpfte sie als „Papageien", „Affen", „Faulenzer" (‚tunejadcy'), „Abschaum" (‚podonki') u.ä. Man reagierte aggressiv auf sie wie auf Deviante, Hooligans, Schmarotzer und Verräter, die bekämpft werden müssen. Es kam zu Verhaftungen wegen Schwarzhandels; Stiljagi wurden auf der Straße angepöbelt, von der Universität relegiert und aus dem kommunistischen Jugendverband ausgeschlossen; in der Presse tobte eine Propagandaschlacht gegen die durch Kleidung, Tanz, Musik und eigenen Jargon von der Mehrheitsgesellschaft Abweichenden: „Segodnja ty igraeš' džaz, a zavtra – Rodinu prodaš'!" (‚Heute spielst du Jazz, und morgen verrätst du die Heimat!'); „Džaz ne naša muzyka" (‚Jazz ist uns fremd/ist nicht unsere Musik'); „Oni pozorjat našu molodež'!" (‚Sie bringen unsere Jugend in Verruf!'); „Pod čužuju dudku!" (‚[Sie tanzen] nach einer fremden Pfeife!') und „Obez'jany sredi nas!" (‚Die Affen sind unter uns!') – so lauten die Schmähtexte zu Stiljagi-Karikaturen, die in der „*Pravda*", in der „*Komsomol'skaja Pravda*" und in der Satire-Zeitschrift „*Krokodil*", die auch im Film durch Text-Bild-Einblendungen zwischen Tanzszenen zitiert werden. Die farbigen Cartoons der auflagenstarken Zeitschrift „*Krokodil*", die meist „von bekannten Malern und Grafikern stammten, erreichten jedoch das Gegenteil. Sie verbreiteten ungewollt einen Kanon des Stiljaga-Bildes bis weit in die Provinz hinein. Das Ergebnis war ein auch dort gesteigertes Modeinteresse" (DMITRIEVA 2012: 33).

Bevorzugte Räume der Stiljagi waren „sturmfreie" Privatwohnungen („chaty"), nicht-öffentliche Clubräume und Keller, aber auch glamouröse Cocktail-Bars (etwa im Moskauer Hotel „Ukraina" oder im Leningrader „Sajgon") und im öffentlichen Raum der so genannte „Brodvej" (‚Broadway') oder einfach „Brod": in Moskau die linke Seite der Gor'kij-Straße zwischen Puškin-Platz und Ochotnyj rjad, in Leningrad der Nevskij prospekt. Dort sandten sie durch ihre Aufmachung und ihr arrogantes Auftreten visuelle Signale, die der Kommunikation mit Gleichgesinnten dienten, die „normalen" Sowjetmenschen jedoch verstörten, abschreckten oder empörten. Eine ähnliche dandyhafte Aufmachung trugen Mitte der 1950er Jahre auch die „Teddy Boys" in Großbritannien zur Schau, nur dass sie von den offiziellen Stellen und den Bürgern nicht kriminalisiert oder diskriminiert, sondern toleriert wurden. Die Stiljagi als Dissidenten zu bezeichnen, wäre allerdings falsch, denn sie wurden zwar verspottet und gejagt, aber nicht politisch verfolgt und verurteilt oder ausgebürgert wie die Dissidenten und Samizdat-Autoren der 1970er Jahre. Als Stiljagi wollten sie nicht „wie alle" sein, sondern einfach nur „anders". Sie hatten keine oppositionellen politischen Überzeugungen, sondern waren schlicht von dem „menschlichen, biologischen Bedürfnis erfüllt, auf irgendeine Weise von der grauen Menge abzustechen", betonte Todorovskij in einem Interview. Mit ihrem extrovertierten Auftreten und ihrem Kleidungsstil verletzten sie jedoch die „allgemein akzeptierten Normen und wurden so ungewollt zu ‚Feinden' des Systems" (TODOROVSKIJ 2008: 1).

In dem Film „*Stiljagi*" wird die Stil-Revolte der russischen „Hipster" in der Uniformitätsgesellschaft effektvoll durch farbliche Kontraste semiotisiert: Die „normalen" Sowjetbürger (‚žloby')[7] treten, selbst bei dem in einer Anfangssequenz gefilmten Tanz im Gor'kij-Vergnügungspark, in verschiedenen Abstufungen von quasi Nicht-Farben wie Grau und Braun auf: langweilige Kleidung zu langweiliger Musik. Dagegen zeichnen sich Kleidung, Schuhwerk und Accessoires der Rock'n'Roll-begeisterten Stiljagi durch eine ganze Palette leuchtender Farben aus – Pink, Hochrot, Gelb, Orange, Violett, Blau und Grün. Auch auffallende Muster wie Karos, Streifen und Bordüren sind Bestandteil des vestimentären Codes. Dazu gehören breitschultrige, nach unten schmal zulaufende Jacketts, bunt gemusterte Hemden, Schuhe auf hohen Kreppsohlen (‚mannaja kaša'), schmale Krawatten mit Bildmotiven, Ringelsocken und eine pomadisierte Haartolle (‚kok') bei den Jungen, enganliegende Kleider und Blusen, Petticoats, Nylonstrümpfe mit markierter Längsnaht und Strapsen, langer Zigarettenspitz, auffallende Täschchen, Halsketten und Ohrclips sowie ein grelles Make-up bei den Mädchen und möglichst großflächige Sonnenbrillen für beide Geschlechter.

Allerdings wird die Rolle der Mädchen im Film „*Stiljagi*" im Gegensatz zu ihrer in der Realität vergleichsweise sekundären Position um des Glamours willen aufgewertet. In Wirklichkeit übernahmen die männlichen Stiljagi, um sich vom heroischen Gebaren der Kriegsheimkehrer abzuheben, in ihrer Kleidung (nicht in ihrem Auftreten) feminine Züge: Farbe, Muster, Modebewusstsein, „Stil". Von den weiblichen Stiljagi heißt es in Memoiren von Zeitzeugen wie Alekej Kozlov nur, sie seien auffallend elegant gekleidet gewesen.

Allerdings erregten die Stiljagi beiderlei Geschlechts, und so wird es auch in Todorovskijs Film vermittelt, Anstoß auch auf Grund der erotischen Signale, die sie mit ihren engen Hosen, ihren Brust und Taille markierenden Blusen, zu weiten Röcken sowie ihrem körperbetonten Tanzstil aussandten. „The sexuality of stylish girls and boys", schreibt Juliane Fürst in ihrer Analyse der sowjetischen Nachkriegsjugend, „was thus an uncomfortable sight to officialdom (and, as many *stiliagi* testify, for many members of the public) – both because it reminded the authorities of their limitations and because it broke the taboos surrounding postwar gender relations" (FÜRST 2010: 224). Das provozierend freizügige, scham- und angstfreie Gebaren der Stiljagi machte die Ambivalenzen und Widersprüche der sowjetischen Sexualmoral deutlich, die zwar die reproduktiven Aspekte vorehelicher Sexualbeziehungen akzeptierte, ihre hedonistischen Seiten aber verdammte.

Zweimal kommt es in dem Film zu Überfällen der grau uniformierten, verbissenen Komsomolzen (‚družinniki') auf die grell-bunt gestylten, akrobatisch tanzenden und lachenden Stiljagi: Beim ersten Mal, ziemlich am Anfang von „*Stiljagi*" (0:05:25), gefilmt im Schuss-Gegenschuss-Verfahren, stürmen sie mit großen Scheren bewaffnet[8] eine Rock'n'Roll-Party und zerschneiden auf das Kommando ihrer Anführerin Katja hin die pomadisierten Haartollen, Kleidung, Krawatten und Nylonstrümpfe der überrumpelten Stiljagi (0:05:47). Mėls wird von Katja befohlen, die geflohene Polina zu verfolgen und zu attackieren, doch er verliebt sich in sie, obwohl sie ihn keck in einen Wassergraben stößt. Beim zweiten Überfall im Gor'kij-Park etwa in der Mitte des Films (1:15:45) übt Katja Rache an Mėls, nachdem sie ihn bei einem Treffen in ihrer Wohnung mit Hilfe eines ehedem modischen, eleganten Kleids ihrer Mutter vergeblich zu verführen (und für ihre Sache zurückzugewinnen) versucht hat: In einem durchaus als Schändung verstandenen Akt der Aggression schneidet sie eigenhändig die langen, blondierten Haare ihrer Konkurrentin Pol'za („ėtoj prostitutki!", 1:43:24) ab, wäh-

[7] Zum Subkultur-Jargon der Stiljagi vgl. KOZLOV 1998.

[8] Diese filmrhetorisch höchst affektgeladene Sequenz zitiert den bekannten russischen Ein-Blatt-Druck (Lubok) „*Cyrjulnik chočet raskol'niku borodu strič'*" (‚Der Barbier möchte einem Altgläubigen den Bart abschneiden'). Die zaristische Regierung „ließ dieses Blatt drucken, um sich über die Halsstarrigkeit der Altgläubigen lustig zu machen" (CLAUDON-ADHEMAR 1975: 19; 33) und lieferte damit gleichzeitig ein beredtes Zeugnis der eigenen Intoleranz.

rend der protestierende Mėls von Komsomolzen festgehalten wird und seiner Geliebten nicht zu Hilfe kommen kann.

Mėls, dessen Name ein Akronym aus „Marks, Ėngel's, Lenin, Stalin" darstellt, wurde bei seiner Vorstellung in der Stiljagi-Gruppe kurzerhand „entstalinisiert", indem man ihm ironisch vorschlug, das „s" am Ende wegzulassen und sich im amerikanischen Stil einfach „Mėl" zu nennen, so wie auch Fedor zu Fred und Igor' zu Bob wurden. In ihrer Brandrede vor der Komsomol-Versammlung macht ihm Katja genau dies zum Vorwurf: Verrat am „heiligen Namen" Stalins, und die Komsomolzen senken, als sie den Namen des Diktators hören, ängstlich ihre Köpfe.

Bob, tagsüber der dickliche Röntgenassistent Boris in einer Polyklinik, in der Freizeit der schrill gekleidete und sinnlich tanzende Stiljaga, tritt bereits in der Eingangssequenz des Films in Erscheinung: In weißer Berufskleidung (Kittel und weißer Kappe, die seine Tolle verdeckt) ruft er einen Patienten aus dem Wartezimmer zum Röntgen, und wird dann – Schnitt – zu Hause dabei gefilmt, wie er auf eine aussortierte Röntgenfolie Rock-Musik kopiert und danach die Folie zu einer runden Schallplatte schneidet. Er ist es auch, der Mėl nicht nur Boogie-Woogie-Tanzen im Hamburger und kanadischen Stil beibringt, sondern auch das alternative Lebensgefühl und utopie-skeptische Wertesystem seiner Stiljagi-Gruppe formuliert, indem er die Leistungs- und Fortschrittsideologie der Stalinisten konterkariert: „Zdes' ne nado bystree, vyše, sil'nee. Zdes' nužen drajv." (‚Es ist hier nicht notwendig, dass alles schneller, höher und stärker läuft. Was hier nötig ist, das ist Drive/Schwung.', 0:27:45). Die Leichtigkeit des Seins als Lebensgefühl der Stiljagi wird von Bobs Vater auf den Punkt gebracht, als er über seinen Sohn sagt: „V strane, gde nel'zja daže gromko čichnut', čtoby ne popast' pod Ugolovnyj kodeks, on prosto tancuet." (‚In einem Land, wo man nicht einmal laut niesen darf, ohne gegen das Strafrecht zu verstoßen, da tanzt er einfach.', 0:29:19).

Fred (Fedor), als Diplomatensohn nicht nur smarter Repräsentant der Jeunesse-dorée, sondern auch Anführer der bunten Stiljaga-Gruppe, klärt Mėl über die unterschiedlich zu klassifizierenden Mädchen auf und informiert ihn (auf der Basis des indischen *Kamasutra*) über die Möglichkeiten der freien Liebe in der Gruppe. In der Wohnung seiner Eltern inszeniert er Stiljaga-Partys, auf denen ekstatisch getanzt, geliebt, gekifft und mit Valuten gehandelt wird. Er entscheidet sich indes – von seinem Vater vor die Wahl gestellt – für einen Karriereposten an der Botschaft in den USA. Bedingung ist die Eheschließung mit einer Amerikanerin, und diese Hochzeit wird im Film unter Einbeziehung sämtlicher Kitschelemente aus amerikanischen Melodramen (*„Love Story"* u.ä.) parodistisch als surreale Bildsequenz der Hochzeitsgesellschaft vor der Kirche performiert, begleitet vom schrillen Klagegesang dreier Stiljaga-Mädchen mit schwarzverschmiertem Augen-Makeup.

„Stiljagi" ist nach Aussage des Regisseurs zwar nicht als reine Komödie konzipiert, doch gibt es in dem Film viele komische und Slapstick-Momente: etwa die Szene, als die nach dem Komsomolzen-Überfall auf rosa Riemchen-Highheel-Sandaletten geflüchtete und gestürzte Polina ihren Verfolger Mėls, der ihr naiv zu Hilfe eilen möchte, in einen Wassergraben stößt, oder die Sequenz, als Mėl in Freds Wohnung in Erwartung einer Erotikszene mit Polina sich auszieht und in seiner unerotisch-grauen Unterwäsche an der Bettkante sitzt, als plötzlich die Tür aufgeht und die ganze Stiljagi-Gruppe lachend hereinplatzt; oder aber die Sequenz in Katjas Wohnung, als Mėl ihr den Stiljaga-Tanzstil vormachen soll, und er in dieser fremden Umgebung und unter Katjas ungnädigen Blicken vollends äffisch wirkt; als Fred seinem Mops in der Badewanne das Fell rosa färbt und Freds Vater in seinem Schreibtisch einen pinkfarbenen Büstenhalter findet etc. (1:20:49).

> Todorovskij hat selbst erklärt: „Rasskazyvat' pro stiljag s ser'eznym vidom – nevozmožno. Oni byli chuligany: duračilis' i 24 časa v sutki iskali priključenij. Na svo-ju golovu." (‚Über die Stiljagi mit ernstem Blick zu erzählen, ist unmöglich. Sie waren

Hooligans: führten sich närrisch auf und suchten 24 Stunden lang Abenteuer. Ohne Rücksicht auf Verluste.', TODOROVSKIJ 2008: 3).

Intertextualität, interfilmische Referenzen und Zitate

Nach seinen Quellen, also Archivmaterial, Prätexten und Präfilmen, befragt, äußerte Todorovskij, er habe neben alten Zeitungsfeuilletons und Ausgaben der Zeitschrift „*Krokodil*" aus den 1950er Jahren auch auf die Memoiren einstiger Stiljagi wie Aleksej Kozlov, dem Saxophonisten (auch Mėl wird Saxophonist!), und Viktor Slavkin, dem Autor, zurückgegriffen (TODOROVSKIJ 2008: 2). In seiner audiovisuellen Rhetorik, d.h. der „auf Wirkung bedachten Art der Kommunikation" (JOOST 2008: 10), referiert der Musical-Film „*Stiljagi*" auf eine Reihe von Präfilmen, die sich in zwei Klassen einteilen lassen. Im ersten Fall dreht sich die Story um zwei feindliche Familien oder rivalisierende Gruppen; im zweiten Fall um konträre politisch-ideologische Systeme. Prototyp der ersten Klasse ist „*West Side Story*", der mit zehn Oscars ausgezeichnete US-amerikanische Tanzfilm von Robert Wise und Jerome Robbins aus dem Jahr 1961. Er basiert auf dem gleichnamigen Musical von Leonard Bernstein (1957), dem Ur-Musical schlechthin, in dem Opernelemente, Jazz und Unterhaltungsmusik kombiniert waren. Der Film beginnt mit einer Szene aus der Vogelperspektive auf New York. Die Kamera fokussiert das Upper-West-Side-Viertel zweier Banden, der weißen amerikanischen „Jets" polnischer Abstammung und der aus Puerto Rico zugewanderten „Sharks". Die durch unterschiedlichen Gruppen-Kleidungsstil markierten rivalisierenden Banden provozieren sich gegenseitig und liefern sich ein „Tanzduell", das beinahe in eine Schlägerei ausartet. Noch kommt dem die Polizei zuvor, sie kann aber nicht verhindern, dass sich die beiden um die Vorherrschaft im Viertel kämpfenden Gangs später tödlich bekriegen. Da der Film genau wie das Musical auf dem „*Romeo und Julia*"-Thema basiert, steht im Mittelpunkt der Handlung das unglückliche, aus den zwei feindlichen Gruppierungen stammende Liebespaar: hier der Amerikaner Tony, Anführer der „Jets", und dort die Puertoricanerin Maria, Näherin in einem Brautmodengeschäft und Schwester des „Sharks"-Anführers Bernardo. Nach zahlreichen Auseinandersetzungen und Zweikämpfen auf der Straße, in einem Drugstore, unter einer Autobahnbrücke und in einer Disco kommt das von Rivalität, Missverständnissen und Eifersucht gespeiste Drama zu einem tödlichen Ende: Tony wird erschossen und stirbt in Marias Armen.

Demgegenüber endet das 1978 mit John Travolta und Olivia Newton-John verfilmte Rock'n'Roll-Musical „*Grease*" (1971; Regie: Randal Kleiser), dessen Handlung genau wie die von „*West Side Story*" und „*Stiljagi*" in den 1950er Jahren angesiedelt ist, mit einem Happy End. „*Grease*" – der Titel bedeutet ‚Schmiere, Pomade', bezogen auf den Frisurstil der Jungen – behandelt eine Liebesromanze im High School Milieu einer amerikanischen Kleinstadt, wo sich die weibliche Gruppe der auffallend gestylten „Pink Ladies" und die männliche der „T-Birds", die mit den „Scorpions" rivalisieren, gegenüber stehen. Trotz Wirrungen und Intrigen findet das Liebespaar Danny und Sandy schließlich zusammen und entschwebt nach der letzten Musicalnummer in einem offenen Sportwagen (Roadster)[9] himmelwärts.

Den Ausgangspunkt der zweiten Klasse von „*Stiljagi*"-Präfilmen, in denen sich Vertreter zweier feindlicher politischer Systeme gegenüber stehen, bildet der von Hollywood-Erfahrungen des russischen Regisseurs Grigorij Aleksandrov geprägte sowjetische Film „*Cirk*" aus dem Jahr 1936. Die Story des Films handelt von der amerikanischen Zirkus-Tänzerin May Dixon, die in den USA rassistischen Angriffen ausgesetzt ist, weil sie ein Kind dunkler Hautfarbe hat. Bei einem Gastspiel in der Sowjetunion dagegen erlebt sie Toleranz und – durch die Liebe des sowjetischen Zirkusartisten Martynov – Aufnahme in die Solidargemeinschaft.

---

9 Ein „Grease"-Zitat im Film „*Stiljagi*" ist zweifellos der offene Roadster, in dem Fred zusammen mit seinem gefärbten Mops über den Moskauer „Broadway" fährt.

Bei dem gemeinsamen Marsch am Ende des Films „*Cirk*" tragen alle Teilnehmer, um die kollektive Gesinnung zu demonstrieren, einheitlich weiße Kleidung: die Frauen wadenlange Röcke, die Männer Hosen, und Rollkragenpullover. Mary Dixon, die vorher in schwarzer Perücke und „Blauer-Engel"-Aufmachung quasi entfremdet tanzen musste, hat sich von ihrem deutschen Impresario getrennt und marschiert nun fröhlich, gekleidet wie alle anderen, in der ersten Reihe der politischen Parade. Die ideologische *message* liegt bei der Schlusssequenz im gemeinsamen Singen der inoffiziellen sowjetischen Hymne „Široka strana moja rodnaja [...] Ja drugoj takoj strany ne znaju, gde tak vol'no dyšet čelovek" (‚Weit ist mein Heimatland [...] Ich kenne kein anderes Land, wo der Mensch so frei atmet', 1:26:45).

Auf den russischen Film folgten Reaktionen aus Hollywood: „*Ninotchka*" mit Greta Garbo aus dem Jahr 1939, Regie: Ernst Lubitsch. Hier findet die linientreue Kommunistin Yakushova, die zur Kontrolle ihrer drei mit dem Verkauf von Zaren-Juwelen beauftragten sowjetischen Genossen nach Paris geschickt wurde, Gefallen am kapitalistischen Lebensstil. Sie lernt den Grafen Leon kennen, der sie in das Pariser High Society Leben einführt und sie beschwört, nicht nach Russland zurückzukehren. Ein extravaganter spiralförmiger Hut fungiert als Dingsymbol für den westlichen Kapitalismus: Zunächst von der Protagonistin als dekadent verspottet, wird der Hut zum Objekt ihrer Begierde, das sie möglichst schnell zu erwerben trachtet. Auch in dem Remake „*Silk Stockings*" aus dem Jahr 1957 mit Fred Astaire und Cyd Charisse, als Tanzfilm konzipiert, verfällt die sowjetische Kommissarin Ninotchka der Warenästhetik des kapitalistischen Systems. Sie wirft ihre schwarzen wollenen Strümpfe weg, kauft sich ein weißes, ärmelloses, hoch geschlitztes Seidenkleid, dazu Seidenstrümpfe und Spitzenunterwäsche und posiert damit im Striptease-Stil vor ihrem Spiegel.

Todorovskij äußerte in einem Interview, er habe seit jeher die amerikanischen Musicals der 1930er bis 1950er Jahre, die Filme mit Fred Astaire und Gene Kelly geliebt. Ein ernsthafter und systematischer Zugang zu diesem Genre finde sich allerdings nur bei Grigorij Aleksandrov mit seinen Filmen „*Veselye rebjata*", „*Vesna*" und „*Cirk*" (TODOROVSKIJ 2008: 2). Nach dieser Aussage des Regisseurs nimmt es nicht wunder, dass es in seinem Streifen Referenzen auf beide Film-Klassen gibt: Erstens stehen sich auch in „*Stiljagi*" zwei antipodische Gruppen gegenüber, aus denen ein Liebespaar zueinander findet, wobei Kleidung ein wichtiges Distinktionsmerkmal darstellt. Zweitens bildet sich das Liebespaar durch Überschreiten einer politisch-ökonomischen Systemgrenze, nur dass im Falle des durch heutige Emanzipationsvorstellungen geprägten „*Stiljagi*"-Films der junge Mann ins „gegnerische" System überwechselt, und nicht die Frau, wie dies in den Präfilmen der Fall ist.

Ein ideologisch wichtiges „*Cirk*"-Zitat in „*Stiljagi*" ist das mit einem Schwarzen bei einer flüchtigen Begegnung in Moskau gezeugte farbige Kind der weiblichen Hauptfigur und die Intoleranz auf Seiten der feindlichen Gruppe (hier vertreten durch Pol'zas kommunistische Mutter), wodurch der „Mythos von der rassismusfreien Sowjetunion" (FRANZ 2011: 343), dekonstruiert wird. Toleranz und Akzeptanz für ihren kleinen Ivan alias Džon erfährt Polina dagegen von Seiten der Wir-Gruppe: der Stiljagi und der einfachen Bewohner der Gemeinschaftswohnung. Hautfarbe wird dabei nicht als negatives Distinktionsmerkmal aufgefasst, sondern quasi als individuelles „Kleid" im Sinne einer ersten Körperhülle angenommen. Polinas starrsinnige Mutter mit ihrem strengen, grauen Kostüm, und Mèls gutmütiger, verständnisvoller Vater mit seiner legeren Aufmachung in Unterhemd und knielangen Turnhosen, verkörpern zwei Typen des sozrealistischen Films, die in „*Stiljagi*" ironisch reinterpre-tiert werden: Polinas Mutter, die unerbittliche Politkommissarin, und Mèls Vater, den ehrlichen, schlichten russischen Menschen mit einer weiten Seele. In einer kurzen, zunächst blaugrauweißen Sequenz des Films (1:11:39) erinnert sich der Vater an seine eigene Jugend, als er singend, lachend, Harmonika spielend von der Front heimkehrte. Die schäbige, überwiegend mit Frauen (Kriegerwitwen) belegte Kommunalka und der den Einzelnen zugemessene minimale Wohnraum zeugen jedoch von enttäuschten Hoffnungen und der niederen Lebensqualität im Nachkriegs-Russland. Aus diesem Grund freut sich Mèls Vater, dass es dem Sohn besser geht als ihm selbst, und beglückwünscht ihn zu seiner famosen neuen Aufmachung als Stiljaga. Pol'zas Mutter dagegen attackiert ihre gestylte Tochter mit hasserfüllten Vorwürfen: „Wie soll ich Menschen führen, wenn ich in meinem eigenen Haus eine Spionin aufgezogen habe?" (0:15:01)

Blick voraus in Multicolor: Perestrojka und Pluralismus

Ganz in der „Anything goes"-Haltung und Darstellungsweise der Postmoderne spielt Todorovskij mit den Zeitebenen. Deshalb macht er Vorgriffe auf die Ära der „glasnost'" und „perestrojka" sowohl was den pluralistischen Stilmix in der Kleidung als auch die Musik und die Songs betrifft. Der Film, in dem wie bei jedem Musical die Performanz über die Repräsentation siegt, erreicht das zeitgenössische Publikum durch – in den Texten leicht veränderte, aber immer erkennbare – Musik bekannter russischer Gruppen der späten 1980er und der 1990er Jahre.[10] „Stiljagi" mündet mit Mèls Song *„Do svidan'ja, milyj drug"* (‚Auf Wiedersehen, lieber Freund') nach dem Lied *„Šaljaj-valjaj"* (1996) der Gruppe „ČajF" in die Gegenwart, wo endlich Alterität und Vielfarbigkeit erlaubt sind: Der Film kulminiert schließlich in der panoramaartigen Schluss-Sequenz, in der eine stetig wachsende Menge junger Leute auf der Tverskaja ulica Mèl und Pol'za, die Stiljaga-Helden der 1950er Jahre, mit Punkern, Dandies, Rastafari-Jüngern und Hippies der Perestrojka-Periode vereint (Abbildung 9). Und dies geschieht nicht wie in dem sowjetischen Film *„Cirk"* in geordneter Formation gleich Gekleideter, sondern in einer bunten Ansammlung von Menschen, die ihre Individualität nicht zuletzt in ihrer freien Wahl von Kleidung und Outfit zum Ausdruck bringen. In einem der Interviews erklärte der Regisserug:

> „Ja ne stavil zadaču rekonstruirovat' ėpochu. Tema kartiny – večnaja potrebnost' čeloveka byt' svobodnym. Byt' ne takim, kak vse. Idti protiv tečenija." (‚Ich habe mir nicht die Aufgabe gestellt, eine Epoche zu rekonstruieren. Thema des Films ist das ewige Bedürfnis des Menschen, frei zu sein. Nicht so zu sein wie Alle. Gegen den Strom zu schwimmen', TODOROVSKIJ 2008: 1).

Eine weitere grundlegende Botschaft des Films ist in einer Sequenz enthalten, welche die Begegnung von Fred und Mèl wiedergibt: Fred, der als Diplomat aus New York zu Besuch nach Moskau gekommen ist, klärt den seinem Stil treu gebliebenen Mèl darüber auf, dass es in den USA überhaupt keine in der Art der Stiljagi gekleidete Jugend gibt und dass alles mehr oder weniger ihre eigene Phantasie war (2:02:00).

„No my že – est'!" (‚Aber uns gibt es!', 2:02:38) erwidert Mèl, der sich seinen Traum vom richtigen Leben im falschen, von einem Leben in individueller Freiheit und Vielfarbigkeit, wofür Amerika stand, nicht nehmen lassen möchte und Fred vorwirft, er sehe mit seinem Hut und in seinem dunkelgrauen Outfit von weitem nun selbst aus wie einer der „žloby" (‚Normalos'). Als daraufhin Fred seinen eleganten Mantel über dem gediegenen Anzug zurückschlägt und Mèl das eingenähte Etikett zeigt, macht er eine Aussage über die Bedeutung von Qualität, die durchaus im Sinne der philosophischen Dichotomie von Schein und Sein, *phainomenon* und *noumenon*, äußere Erscheinung und inneres Wesen zu verstehen ist: „Glavnoe – ėto lejbl, to, čto na vnutrennej storone. Glavnoe – kačestvo, to, čto vnutri."

---

[10] Hier irrt Norbert Franz, der meint, der Soundtrack von *„Stiljagi"* bestehe aus nur „leicht überarbeiteten Originalen der 1950er Jahre" (FRANZ 2011: 346). Auch Baz Luhrmann, Regisseur des in die Pop-Kultur verpflanzten Films *„Romeo and Juliet"* (1996), hat in seinem Musicalfilm *„Moulin Rouge"* (2001) auf vorhandene Songs zurückgegriffen.

(‚Wichtig ist das Label, das, was sich auf der Innenseite findet. Wichtig ist die Qualität, das, was drinnen ist.', 2:01:44).

So repräsentiert Fred, der die jugendliche Stiljaga-Phase als bloße Etappe im Sinne der „rites de passage" durchlaufen und im Erwachsenenstatus überwunden hat, das Vernunft- und Realitätsprinzip, Mėl dagegen das Wunsch- und Nostalgieprinzip: „Ėtot stil' pobeždaet strach, / Ėta divnaja, zlaja, smešnaja ėpocha / Nas s toboju ne sterla v prach" (‚Dieser/unser Stil besiegt die Angst, / Diese wundervolle, schlimme, lächerliche Epoche / Hat uns beide nicht zugrunde gerichtet', 2:05:06), heißt es in Mėls Abgesang auf den „abtrünnigen" Fred.

Andererseits verweist der implizite Autor durch Freds Äußerung generalisierend auf den Charakter von Mode und Styling als einem Äußerlichen, welches dem eigentlichen Wesen, der Substanz des Menschen als einem Innerlichen, lediglich attribuiert ist.

Summary

Valery Todorovsky's film musical *Stilyagi* (2008), set in the Cold War USSR of the 1950s, tells the story of the transformation of the hero Mėls from loyal member of the Komsomol to "stilyaga" Mėl – member of the urban subculture, and his love story with Polina (Pol'za). Todorovsky's stilyagi (hipsters) are shown as the very embodiment of anti-conformism and 'revolt' into stylish bright fashion as means of distinction against grey Soviet mainstream society. The film reaches out to contemporary audiences with the music of the late 1980s and 1990s, and to present-day Russia, which eventually allows otherness and multi-colouredness: In the final panoramic sequence the film culminates in an ever-growing mass of young people strolling down Tverskaia Street, uniting Mėls and Pol'za, the stilyaga heroes of the 1950s, with punks, dandies, rastafari people and modern-styled hippies of the Perestroika period.

Bibliographie

BIENK, A. 2008. *Filmsprache. Einführung in die interaktive Filmanalyse.* Marburg.

BOGATYREV, P. 1971. *Voprosy teorii narodnogo iskusstva.* Moskva.

BOURDIEU, P. 1970. *Zur Soziologie der symbolischen Formen.* Frankfurt.

BULGAKOWA, O. 1995. Film-Phantasien im Wettbewerb. In: Adaskina, N. et al. (ed.). *Berlin – Moskau 1900–1950.* München 1995, 361–365.

BURKHART, D. 2010. Vestimentärer Code und Affekte in der russischen Literatur. In: *Welt der Slaven* LV, H. 2, 209–233.

CLAUDON-ADHEMAR, C. 1975. *Populäre Druckgraphik Europas: Russland.* München.

DMITRIEVA, M. 2010. Jazz and Dress. Stilyagi in Soviet Russia and Beyond. In: Pickhan, G., Ritter, R. (ed.). *Jazz Behind the Iron Curtain.* Frankfurt a. M. 2010, 239–255.

DMITRIEVA, M. 2012. Bikinarze und Stiljagi. Die sozialistische Jugend und ihr amerikanischer Kleidungsstil. In: *Mitropa. Jahresheft des Geisteswissenschaftlichen Zentrums Geschichte und Kultur Ostmitteleuropas*, 32–36.

EDELE, M. 2002. Strange Young Men in Stalin's Moscow: The Birth and Life of the Stiliagi, 1945–1953. In: *Jahrbücher für Geschichte Osteuropas* 50, H. 1, 37–61.

FRANZ, N. 2011. Hollywood – Moskau – Hollywood: *Cirk, Ninotchka* und andere. Oder: Ein kleines Kapitel Kinogeschichte als Beziehungsgeschichte. In: Franz, N., Kunow, R. (ed.). *Kulturelle Mobilitätsforschung: Themen – Theorien – Tendenzen.* Potsdam 2011, 311–352. http://opus.kobv.de/ubp/volltexte/2011/5743/pdf/moku01_S311_351.pdf (05.03.2014)

FÜRST, J. 2006. The Importance of Being Stylish: Youth, Culture and Identity in Late Stalinism. In: Dies. (ed.). *Late Stalinist Russia: Society Between Reconstruction and Reinvention.* New York, 209–230.

FÜRST, J. 2010. *Stalin's Last Generation. Soviet Post-War Youth and the Emergence of Mature Socialism.* Oxford.

GOEHRKE, C. 2005. *Russischer Alltag.* Bd. 3: *Sowjetische Moderne und Umbruch.* Zürich.

GÜNTHER, H. 2007. Von Hollywood zu „*Volga–Volga*": Zur Entstehung des hybriden Genres der sowjetischen Filmkomödie. In: *Zeitschrift für Slawistik* 52, 435–446.

HUBER, E. 2011. *Mode in der Sowjetunion 1917–1953.* Wien.

ISAKAVA, V. 2009. Valerii Todorovskii: Hipsters (Stiliagi, 2008). Review. In: *KinoKultura* 25. http://www.kinokultura.com/2009/25r-stiliagi.shtml (06.03.2014)

HICKETHIER, K. 1993. *Film- und Fernsehanalyse.* Stuttgart, Weimar.

JOOST, G. 2008. *Bild-Sprache. Die audio-visuelle Rhetorik des Films.* Bielefeld.

KIMERLING, A. 2007. Platforma protiv kaloš, ili Stiljagi na ulicach sovetskogo goroda. In: *Teorija mody* 3, 81–99.

KOZLOV, A. 1998. *Kozel na sakse: i tak vsju žizn'.* Moskva.

KOZLOV, A. 2009. *Proischoždenie slova „stiljaga" ili otkuda proizošlo slovo stiljaga.* http://www.koryazhma.ru/usefull/know/doc.asp?doc_id=121 (14.03.2014)

METZ, Christian 1972. *Semiotik des Films.* München.

RUDOVA, L. 2004. Stiliagi. In: Millar, J. R. (ed.). *Encyclopedia of Russian History.* Vol. 4. New York 2004, 1478–1479.

SEETHALER, K. 2011. Röntgenschallplatten – Knochen, die rocken. In: *Spiegel Online,* 11.08.11. http://einestages.spiegel.de/static/topicalbumbackground/23303/1/knochen_die_rocken.html (17.03.2014)

SLAVKIN, V. 1996. *Pamjatnik neizvestnomu stiljage.* Moskva.

TODOROVSKIJ, V. 2008. „Stiljagi". Interview mit Valerij Kičin von der *Rossijskaja gazeta.* http://www.rg.ru/2008/12/17/stilyagi.html (23.03.2014)

STILJAGI UND DIE VESTIMENTÄREN CODES DER *MOLODAJA PROZA*

CHRISTINE ENGEL, INNSBRUCK

Tauwetter und *Molodaja proza*

Im sowjetischen Kulturkampf der 1950er Jahre vertraten viele Schriftsteller Positionen des sogenannten Tauwetters und stellten sich mit ihren Werken auf die Seite der „Neuerer“. Ihr Anliegen war es, nicht nur den gesellschaftlichen und politischen Aufbruch nach dem Tod Stalins (5.3.1953) zu verstärken, sondern vor allem auch die ästhetische Starre der Literatur der späten Stalinzeit aufzubrechen. Bereits im Vorfeld des II. Schriftstellerkongresses (Dezember 1954) wurde harsche Kritik an der Konfliktlosigkeit, der Austauschbarkeit und der Mittelmäßigkeit der literarischen Produktion geübt. Mit *lakirovka dejstvitel'nosti* ‚Schönfärberei der Realität‘ prägte Vladimir Pomerancev in seinem vielbeachteten Artikel *„Ob iskrennosti v literature“* (POMERANCEV: 1953) eine treffende Chiffre für den Zustand der damaligen Literatur. Dem Gefühl des allgemeinen Aufbruchs verliehen klimatische Metaphern eines nahenden Frühlings Ausdruck, wie z. B. Nikolaj Zabolockijs Gedicht *„Ottepel'“* (1953) oder Il'ja Ėrenburgs gleichnamiger Kurzroman (Teil I 1954, Teil II 1956). Dieser breit rezipierte literarische Text lieferte in kompakter Form zugleich ein Muster, das auch von anderen Autoren und Autorinnen aufgegriffen wurde:

- Das sowjetische Leben ist kalt und frostig geworden
- Die Helden aus Politik und Wirtschaft haben sich oft als Tyrannen herausgestellt und sind indifferent gegenüber dem Allgemeinwohl
- Wichtig sind die Menschen, die aber nicht als Masse, sondern als Individuen existieren und die man auch als solche darstellen sollte
- Auch Emotionen sind realistisch und können nicht nur in rationalen Kategorien dargestellt werden – Liebe, Mitleid, Angst und Neid sind Teil unseres Lebens (ENGEL 2011: 350)

Unter den gesellschaftspolitisch engagierten Schriftstellern[1] waren auch einige junge, wie Anatolij Gladilin (*1935), Vasilij Aksënov (*1932) und Anatolij Kuznecov (*1929). Sie orientierten sich mit ihrer sogenannten *Molodaja proza* ‚Junge Prosa‘ bzw. *Jeansprosa,* wie Aleksandar Flaker dieses gesamtosteuropäische Phänomen treffend bezeichnet (FLAKER 1975), am Modell von Jerome D. Salingers Roman *„The Catcher in the Rye“* (1951): Aus der Perspektive eines Teenagers wird Fundamentalkritik an der moralischen Verkommenheit der Erwachsenenwelt und ihrer Verlogenheit geübt, bzw. genauer am Auseinanderklaffen zwischen hehren Worten und dem tatsächlichen Verhalten. Als Publikationsorgan für die Erzählungen und Kurzromane diente die neue Zeitschrift *Junost'* (gegründet 1955). Obwohl diese sich zwar primär an ein jugendliches Publikum wandte, war die intendierte Leserschaft der *Molodaja proza* dennoch die Welt der Erwachsenen. Für die damalige Zeit verfolgte diese Prosa einen recht erfrischenden Ansatz, der sich vor allem vom inzwischen verknöcherten Produktionsroman abheben sollte: Die jugendlichen Protagonisten bedienen sich einer stili-

[1] Die Verwendung der maskulinen Form trifft den Sachverhalt, denn die *Molodaja proza* war eine Angelegenheit von männlichen Schriftstellern. Die Schriftstellerinnen Nadežda Usova und Inna Goff publizierten zwar in diesem Umfeld, erreichten aber nur einen begrenzten Bekanntheitsgrad und wurden auch nicht in den Kanon dieser literarischen Richtung aufgenommen.

sierten Umgangssprache und lassen Slangausdrücke aus der Jugendsprache in ihre Rede einfließen. Außerdem ist der Schauplatz des Geschehens nicht die Fabrik, sondern die Straße oder ein Café – und wenn schon Fabriksgelände, dann nicht die Werkbank, sondern die Raucherecke; und man ist verliebt und denkt dabei nicht an das Wohl der Baustelle. Vor allem aber lehnt man den von der älteren Generation vorgezeichneten Karriereweg ab und besteht auf dem Recht eigener Erfahrungen. Um diese Haltung auch visuell zu vermitteln, pflegen die Protagonisten einen Kleidungsstil, der sie nicht nur von den üblichen grauen Anzugträgern abhebt, sondern auch – so wie ihre Musik – in einer internationalisierten Jugendkultur verankert. Ein treffendes Beispiel dafür ist der siebzehnjährige Dima, die Haupt-figur in Aksënovs *povest'* ‚Kurzroman' *„Zvëzdnyj bilet"* (1961), der von seinem älteren Bruder folgendermaßen beschrieben wird:

> „Я смотрю, как мелькают впереди его чешская рубашка с такими, знаете ли, искорками, штаны неизвестного мне происхождения, австрийские туфли и стриженная под французский ежик русская голова." (Aksënov 1990: 57)[2]

Stiljagi, čuvaki, čuvichi ...

So wenig aufregend Dimas Bekleidungsstil für heutige Ohren klingen mag, war er für die damalige Sowjetunion doch ein sehr starkes Signal. Damit begab sich die *Molodaja proza* nämlich auf ein ideologisch vermintes Terrain, wo *stiljaga* ‚Beatnik, Hipster' als ein zentraler Kampfbegriff galt. Als die Autoren der *Molodaja proza* auf den Plan traten, war der Begriff *stiljaga* bereits diskursiv verfestigt und rief in der allgemeinen und vor allem in der veröffentlichten Meinung eine ganze Reihe von negativen Konnotationen hervor – solche wie Parasit, Bildungsverweigerer, Rowdy u.a.m. Etabliert worden war der Begriff nämlich bereits zu Beginn des Kalten Krieges, als Stalin den Kampf gegen *nizkopoklonstvo pered zapadom* ‚Kriecherei vor dem Westen' und gegen den „Kosmopolitismus" ausrief.

Als soziales Phänomen betrachtet, kamen nach dem Krieg auch in der Sowjetunion jugendliche Cliquen auf, die sich nach US-amerikanischem Vorbild farbenfroh kleideten – aus ihrer Sicht also mit Stil – und Anhänger von Jazz und modernen Tänzen waren. Ihre Kleidungsmerkmale waren enge Hosen, gestreifte Socken, Schuhe mit dicken, hellen Microporsohlen; darüber ein farbiges, oft auch kariertes Jackett, an den Schultern gepolstert und um zwei Nummern zu groß; um den Hals trugen sie eine schmale, auffallende Krawatte, unter der Nase pflegten sie einen dünnen Schnurrbart und das Haar wurde zu einer hohen Tolle frisiert. Im Prinzip war dieser Habitus ein Statement männlicher Jugendlicher. Untereinander bezeichneten sie sich als *čuvaki* ‚Kumpel'. Ihre gleichgesinnten Partnerinnen, die sie *čuvichi* nannten, waren zwar auch modisch gekleidet, spielten aber eine untergeordnete Rolle. *Čuvaki* und *čuvichi* trafen sich in einer *chata*, das heißt in einer ‚sturmfreien Bude' ohne Eltern, wenn möglich überhaupt leerstehend – eine solche zu organisieren, hatte neben den Kleidungsfragen oberste Priorität.

Die Asymmetrie zwischen den Geschlechtern war nicht zuletzt auch dadurch bedingt, dass die Mädchen, wenn sie sich solchen Treffen anschlossen, gesellschaftlich sehr viel riskierten (siehe Abbildung 10). Litvinov schreibt darüber in seinen Erinnerungen, die als Gespräche mit ehemaligen „Mitstreitern" angelegt sind:

> „Сегодня, вспоминая о стиляжных временах, некоторые называют тусовку стиляг чуть ли не мужским клубом. [...] Причина понятна: если парень-стиляга сразу-же объявлялся хулиганом, то девушка – девицей легкого поведения, а то и прос-

[2] Die Seitenangaben der Zitate aus den Werken von Aksënov, Gladilin und Kuznecov beziehen sich auf den Reprint in *Ottepel'*.

титуткой, а в тогдашнем пуританском обществе репутация проститутки была гораздо хуже репутации хулигана.
Как вспоминает Алексей Козлов, «все школьницы и студентки были воспитаны в исключительно строгом духе, носили одинаковые косички и венчики, одинаковые темные платья с передниками», что явно констрастировало с внешним видом «чувих»: короткая стрижка-«венгерка», туфли на высоком каблуке, клетчатые юбки.“ (LITVINOV 2009: 67)

Hinzu kommt noch, dass die männlichen Jugendlichen mit Mode letztlich wesentlich effektvollere Signale setzen konnten als die Mädchen. Wie Vinken in ihrem Buch über Tendenzen der europäischen Mode seit der Moderne ausführt, kam die vorerst letzte Periode einer vestimentären Zurschaustellung männlicher körperlicher Vorzüge mit der Französischen Revolution an ihr Ende (vgl. VINKEN 2013: 16). Seither gibt der Anzug den Ton an, der das Korporative betont (vgl. VINKEN 2013: 49), was in der Sowjetunion besonders gerne aufgegriffen wurde. Ein Abrücken von diesem verordneten Korpsgeist, wie es die *stiljagi* tun, trifft in dieser männlich dominierten Gesellschaft daher einen zentralen Nerv.

Der Film „*Stiljagi*“ von Valerij Todorovskij (2008)[3] und auch das zunehmende akademische Interesse an alltagskulturellen Phänomenen der Sowjetzeit bot einen Anlass für neuere Publikationen zu diesem Thema (z. B. LITVINOV 2009, DMITRIEVA 2010, MOSKOVSKIJ BIT). Allerdings waren die *stiljagi* keineswegs ein so verbreitetes Massenphänomen oder gar eine politische Protestbewegung, wie der Film vermuten lässt, denn die Jugendlichen rekrutierten sich auffallend häufig aus den Kreisen von Parteifunktionären und nützten die Möglichkeiten, die ihnen die Position der Väter bot. Gerade dieser Umstand war dafür ausschlaggebend, dass sich diese Gruppe als diskursiver Turnierplatz im Kampf zwischen „Neuerern“ und „Traditionalisten“ anbot.

„*Stiljaga*“ von Dmitrij Beljaev

Es besteht weitgehende Übereinstimmung darin, dass die Initialzündung für die Kampagne gegen den Typ des *stiljaga* durch den gleichnamigen Feuilletonartikel des linientreuen Publizisten und Schriftstellers Dmitrij Beljaev (1909–1990) erfolgte (vgl. KOZLOV 2009). Dieser Artikel, der in der satirischen Zeitschrift *Krokodil* im Juli 1949 erschien, enthält bereits alle wichtigen Diskursbausteine mitsamt der von offizieller Seite erwünschten Bewertung, sodass eine nähere Betrachtung lohnend ist. Der erste Teil des Artikels ist als Gespräch zwischen einem kundigen Landwirt und dem in Agrarfragen unerfahrenen Verfasser-Ich angelegt. Die beiden unterhalten sich auf einem Getreidefeld über taube Ähren und degenerierte Blumen, die der Agronom als Unkraut ausreißt, und in denen der Verfasser eine Parallele zum *stiljaga* sieht:

„Прошлым летом со знакомым агрономом брели по ржаному полю.
И вот я заметил один, резко выделяющийся из массы ржи колос. Он был выше всех остальных и гордо покачивался над ними.
– Смотрите, – сказал я агроному, – какой мощный, красивый колос! Может быть, это какой нибудь особенный сорт?
„Агроном безжалостно сорвал колос и протянул мне:
– Пощупайте: в этом красивом колосе совсем нет зерен. Это колос тунеядец, он берет влагу и все прочее от природы, но не дает хлеба. В народе его называют пустоколоска. Есть и цветы такие в природе – выродки. Они часто красивы на вид,

[3] Vgl. zu diesem Musikdrama den Beitrag von D. BURKHART im vorliegenden Band.

но внутренне бессодержательны и не плодоносят, называются пустоцветом. Так вот и этот колос…
– Колос стиляга! – воскликнул я.
– Стиляга, – повторил я и рассказал агроному следующую историю.“
(BELJAEV 1949)

Die Geschichte, die der Verfasser dann im zweiten Teil des Artikels zum Besten gibt, spielt in einem Studentenclub. Als dort nach einem Literaturabend zum Tanz aufgefordert wird, erscheint plötzlich ein auffallend gekleideter junger Mann, der sich, wie der Berichterstatter meint, ähnlich den tauben Ähren durch Äußerlichkeiten hervortun will, und daher der Lächerlichkeit preisgegeben wird:

„Он имел изумительно нелепый вид: спина куртки ярко оранжевая, а рукава и полы зеленые; таких широченных штанов канареечно горохового цвета я не видел даже в годы знаменитого клёша; ботинки на нем представляли собой хитроумную комбинацию из черного лака и красной замши.
Юноша оперся о косяк двери и каким-то на редкость развязным движением закинул правую ногу на левую. Обнаружились носки, которые, казалось, сделаны из кусочков американского флага – так они были ярки.“ (BELJAEV 1949)

Körperverrenkungen beim Tanzen, ein legerer Umgangston mit Mädchen und Abweichungen von der damals bereits in den Status einer sakralen Unantastbarkeit erhobenen Literatursprache vervollständigen das Sündenregister des jungen Mannes. Ganz im literarischen Stil der Stalinzeit wird die Angelegenheit noch weiter im Detail erklärt, sodass der Leser schließlich auch noch die Kluft ermessen kann, wie weit sich ein *stiljaga* vom gängigen Bildungsideal, das der Innerlichkeit und dem Guten und Schönen gleichgesetzt ist, entfernt hat:

„Стилягами называют сами себя подобные типы на своем птичьем языке. Они, видите ли, выработали свой особый стиль – в одежде, в разговорах, в манерах. Главное в их «стиле» – не походить необыкновенных людей. И, как видите, в подобном стремлении они доходят до нелепостей, до абсурда. Стиляга знаком с модами всех стран и времен, но не знает, как вы могли убедиться, Грибоедова. Он детально изучил все фоксы, танго, румбы, линды, но Мичурина путает с Менделеевым и астрономию с гастрономией. Он знает наизусть все арии из «Сильвы» и «Марицы», но не знает, кто создал оперы «Иван Сусанин» и «Князь Игорь». Стиляги не живут в полном и в нашем понятии этого слова, а, как бы сказать, порхают по поверхности жизни…“ (BELJAEV 1949)

Franty, poganki, sornjaki…

Die Kampagne gegen die *stiljagi* zeichnet sich durch eine ungewöhnliche Langlebigkeit aus. So schuf z. B. Boris Timofeev, ein bekannter regimekonformer Satiriker, zehn (!) Jahre später, die Figur des Garri (siehe Abbildung 11).

In seinem Gedicht „*Garri*“, das so wie der Artikel von Beljaev in der Zeitschrift *Krokodil* publiziert wurde, zeichnet er ein im Wesentlichen unverändertes Kondensat eines *stiljaga*:

„В самом модном пиджаке, / С видом безразличным, / Франт с колечком на руке / Ходит «львом столичным»… / На прическу посмотри: / Он завит игриво, / Только пусто там, внутри, / Под волнистой гривой. / Как шнурочек, тонок ус, / Нету ярче шляпы…/ В третий раз бросает вуз / Иждивенец папы. / Был он Гришей, но сейчас

> / Носит имя Гарри... / Каждый день в обычный час / Гарри на бульваре. / Вон, собой любуясь, встал, / На девиц глазея. / Книг давно он не читал, / Не бывал в музеях. / Вот на выставку собак / Он пойдет, пожалуй: / Все увидят как-никак / Галстук небывалый! / Он всегда блеснуть не прочь / Пошлым анекдотом, / Протанцует хоть всю ночь —/ Мастер по фокстротам. / [...] Кто же этот франт? Сорняк / В нашем огороде!“ (TIMOFEEV 1959)

Wenn man schon von Langlebigkeit spricht, so soll auch noch erwähnt werden, dass eine Figur wie Garri in der russischen Literatur nicht neu ist, sondern Anleihen nimmt beim *ščëgol'* ‚Geck, Stutzer (botan. Regenpfeifer)‘, einer Negativfigur der Aufklärung, wie man sie bei Aleksandr Sumarokov, Aleksandr Griboedov oder auch in der satirisch-aufklärerischen Zeitschrift *Živopisec* von Nikolaj Novikov findet.

Timofeev beließ es nicht nur bei seinem Garri, sondern veröffentlichte ein Jahr darauf ein weiteres satirisches Gedicht mit dem Titel „*Sornjaki*“, in dem er das Unkraut und die *darmoedy* ‚Schmarotzer‘ der Gesellschaft aufzählt: Schwarzhändler von ausländischem Plunder, Bettler, die sich als Invaliden ausgeben, frömmelnde Quacksalberinnen, Ausbeuter-Vermieter von Datschen, „Goldkinder“, die auf Kosten ihrer (Funktionärs-)Eltern leben. Ihnen allen soll nun ein weiteres Mal mit dem Ausreißen begegnet werden, verschärft durch das geflügelte Wort: „Wer nicht arbeitet, soll auch nicht essen“:

> „Вырвать их из нашей грядки! / Есть у нас свои порядки – / Тверд закон для наших мест: / «Кто не трудится – не ест!..»“ (TIMOFEEV 1960: 6)

In der Reihe der gesellschaftlichen Schädlinge kommt Timofeev hier auch ausnahmsweise auf die Mädchen rund um die *stiljagi* zu sprechen – herausgeputzt, leichtsinnig und arbeitsscheu:

> „Вот девица-молодица / Разодета в пух и прах, / Папы, мамы не боится. / Каждый вечер на балах. / Финтифлюшка, белоручка, / Попрыгунья-недоучка. / Ей чужих хватает средств. / ...Не работает, а ест!“ (TIMOFEEV 1960: 6)

In der sowjetischen Presse wurde das verbale Arsenal gegen *stiljagi* zusätzlich noch mit *p'janstvo* ‚Trunksucht‘ und *chuliganstvo* ‚Rowdytum‘ verknüpft, sowie mit der Vorstellung der ‚Ansteckung‘ bzw. der aggressiven Verbreitung, was Anschlussmöglichkeiten zu anderen damals laufenden Kampagnen eröffnete (siehe Abbildung 12). Die Tageszeitung *Pravda* positionierte sich hierbei an vorderster Front und lieferte zwischen 1955 und 1963 an die vierzig Beiträge mit dem Stichwort *stiljaga.* Solche Beiträge waren nicht nur auf das Feuilleton beschränkt, sondern fanden auch in Berichte über Komsomolzen- bzw. Parteiversammlungen oder über Gerichtsverhandlungen Eingang. So z.B. wird über ein *tovariščeskij sud* ‚Kameradschaftsgericht‘ berichtet, wobei die „Delinquentin“ als jemand dargestellt wird, der unter Kuratel des Kollektivs gestellt werden muss:

> „Простили как-то также и одну молоденькую ткачиху, которая связалась с шалопаями-стилягами, стала хуже работать, пришла на вечер в клуб пьяная. Когда ближе познакомились с жизнью девушки, узнали, что она — сирота, ее удочерила одна бездетная чета, все было хорошо. Но вот умерла приемная мать, приемный отец женился, и начались нелады с молодой мачехой... Коллектив взял шефство над этой девушкой.“ (KONONENKO 1960)

Nicht zuletzt findet der Begriff *stiljaga* auch in den Erziehungsdiskurs Eingang. So werden z. B. in der *Pravda* Eltern und Parteiorganisationen dafür verantwortlich gemacht, dass die Kinder vor derart schädlichen Einflüssen bewahrt werden:

> „Партийные и комсомольские организации обязаны принять меры к тому, чтобы оградить детей от влияния разложившихся и хулиганствующих элементов, пьяниц и дебоширов, всякого рода «стиляг» и других проводников буржуазной морали. Особенно остро стоит вопрос о борьбе с хулиганством. Известно, что хулиганы охотно вербуют своих последователей и помощников среди неустойчивой части учащихся, и это им подчас удается." (KOMSOMOL I ŠKOLA 1955)

Die Protagonisten der *Molodaja proza*

In einem derart aufgeladenen Klima traten also die Autoren der *Molodaja proza* an, um mit ihren Protagonisten ein Bild von Jugendlichen als Träger der Aufbruchsstimmung und des Neuen zu entwerfen. Um sich zu positionieren, mussten sie irgendwie sowohl mit der neuen Jugendmode als auch mit dem damals üblichen traditionellen Kleidungsstil umgehen. Der als korrekt angesehene Stil sah für heranwachsende männliche Jugendliche – so wie für einen Erwachsenen – ein Jackett von unauffälliger Farbe, ein sauberes weißes Hemd (bevorzugt aus der damals neu aufgekommenen Nylonfaser) und eine unauffällige Krawatte vor, ergänzt durch geputzte Schuhe und eine gebügelte Hose. Eine plumpe Umwertung der beiden Stile wäre wenig zielführend gewesen und wäre zudem bei den Zensurinstanzen und bei den Lesern auf wenig Gegenliebe gestoßen: Man konnte weder die jugendlich-arrivierten Jackettträger einfach zu negativen Figuren stempeln, noch den Typus des *stiljaga* als Hoffnungsträger anpreisen. Ein solches Vorgehen wäre zudem auch an der Absicht der Autoren vorbeigegangen: Sie verstanden den Aufbruch des Tauwetters ja als ein Programm, das zwar den Bruch mit dem Stalinismus signalisieren sollte, keineswegs jedoch einen mit dem Kommunismus, denn die eingeschlagene Richtung sollte geradewegs zurück führen zu den Leninschen Prinzipien, zum reinen, nichtkontaminierten Urzustand des Kommunismus. Es galt also, nicht aus Schwarz ein Weiß zu machen, sondern mithilfe von geschickten Modulationen von einer Tonart in eine andere zu wechseln.

Zu alledem mussten auch noch gewisse Grundregeln des Sozialistischen Realismus beachtet werden, die ja mit Anbruch des Tauwetters keineswegs außer Kraft gesetzt worden waren. Zu diesen Anforderungen gehörte unter anderem, dass Wertungen von Gut und Böse klar erkennbar sein müssen, sodass dem Leser ein eindeutiges Orientierungssystem vermittelt wird. Um dieser komplexen Aufgabe gerecht zu werden, arbeiten die Autoren der *Molodaja proza* mit kontrastierenden jugendlichen Figuren, die sie mit verschiedenen Abstufungen von Kleidercodes und deren Bewertungen versehen. Anhand von drei Schlüsselerzählungen sollen im Folgenden mögliche Varianten solcher Modulationen veranschaulicht werden.

Anatolij Kuznecov *„Prodolženie legendy"*

Anatolij Kuznecov war mit seiner Tagebucherzählung *„Prodolženie legendy"* (1957) einer der Begründer der *Molodaja proza*. Tolja, der Ich-Erzähler, sieht die Hochschule und die Aufnahmeprüfung nicht als seinen Weg und setzt sich mit unbestimmtem Ziel in einen Zug Richtung Sibirien. Auf der Reise lernt er viele Leute kennen, nette und auch solche mit zweifelhaftem Charakter. Dadurch bekommt er einen Einblick in die Mannigfaltigkeit des Lebens, der weit über das hinausgeht, was ihm die Schule vermitteln konnte und wollte. Obwohl in der Erzählung eine gewisse Annäherung der Literatur an die Erfahrungswirklichkeit zu vermerken ist, was eine generelle Grundtendenz der Literatur des Tauwetters ist, endet die Erzählung doch in der Erfüllung der Vorgaben des Produktionsromans und des Rufes der Partei zu den

Großbaustellen des Landes: Tolja heuert in Irkutsk beim Bau des großen Wasserkraftwerks an und erkennt in der Industriearbeit das Ziel seines Lebens. Darüber hinaus will er aber als Fernhörer doch noch ein Studium absolvieren, und erfüllt durch die Vereinigung von Hand- und Kopfarbeit das Ideal der Zeit.

In Kleiderfragen riskiert der Autor, was Tolja betrifft, nicht viel: Der junge Mann sitzt mit einem Jackett bekleidet im Zug und erfährt im Laufe der Erzählung eine Nobilitierung, als er im Werk seinen Blaumann erhält und sich zu einem richtigen Arbeiter mausert:

> „Тем не менее я тоже был горд своим комбинезоном в бетоне, своими сизыми от налипшего цемента сапогами и рукавицами, которые я небрежно вытащил из-за пояса и швырнул на подоконник. Мне было приятно, что в моей походке появилось что-то неуклюжее, широкое, рабочее…“ (KUZNECOV 1990: 85)

Die negativ gezeichnete Kontrastfigur ist Vitja, sein Schulfreund, der immer mehr ins *stiljaga*-Milieu abgleitet. Er kommt aus einer Funktionärsfamilie, betrachtet die Prinzipien des Kommunismus aber äußerst utilitaristisch und rückt sein eigenes Wohlergehen in den Vordergrund. Mithilfe von Signalen, die dem Diskurs um die *stiljagi* entnommen sind, wird dem Leser deutlich gemacht, dass er Vitjas Einstellungen nicht gut heißen kann. Das zeigt z. B. sein Brief an Tolja, den er während seiner Vorbereitung auf die Aufnahmeprüfung schreibt:

> „Не представляешь ты себе, как мне тут невесело. Синусы не лезут в голову. Вокруг – *стильные ребята, девчонки в штанах* гоняют по улице на велосипедах, играют в волейбол, *танцуют по вечерам под магнитофон* – словом, развлекаются напропалую. Среди них я один, как идиот, сижу и зубрю котангенсы, вызывая насмешки.“ (KUZNECOV 1990: 35; kursiv C.E.)

Tolja, der sich seinem Freund zunehmend entfremdet, erinnert sich in einer anderen Szene zurück an die Schulzeit, als Vitja sich schon damals einiges zuschulden kommen ließ. Nicht nur, dass er sich über Pavka Korčagin, den unangefochtenen Helden des sozrealistischen Bildungsromans *„Kak zakaljalas' stal'“* (1934) von Nikolaj Ostrovskij lustig gemacht hatte, war er auch noch bisweilen in grellen Jacketts in die Schule gekommen:

> „Наконец Витька явился в школу *разодетый в ядовито-зеленый костюм, в узких брюках, туфлях с пряжками и на микропоре* и заявил, что прожить без бед, без нужды, весело – вот мудрость жизни, потому что жизнь коротка, а молодость еще короче. Комсорг сказал ему: *«Эх ты, стиляга!»* А Витька возразил и доказал, *что «стиль» – это удобно и хорошо.*“ (KUZNECOV 1990: 56; kursiv C.E.)

Vervollständigt wird Vitjas Sündenregister durch Jazz, Boogie Woogie, Rock 'n' Roll sowie durch Microporsohlen und importierten Stoff:

> „Пока я добыл магнитофон «Яуза», записываю с приемника джазы. Эх, Толя, «буги-вуги» – доисторическое дерьмо! Мы тут в одной компании затеяли попробовать «рок-н-ролл». Говорят, потрясающая вещь. В Москве появились новые туфли на каучуке – мечта! Мне шьют костюм из импортного материаль-чика. Короче: пора обретать человеческий облик.“ (KUZNECOV 1990: 167)

Mode und Kleidung sind in dieser Erzählung, wie aus den Beispielen hervorgeht, eng mit der Frage des Charakters verbunden. Was die Hauptfiguren betrifft, sind die Fronten zwar klar gezogen, aber eine gewisse Bewegung lässt sich bei Nebenfiguren beobachten. So z. B.

wird Lëša, dem Tolja im Zug begegnet, als ein im Prinzip sympathischer junger Mann charakterisiert, der jedoch immer wieder klaut. Er ist, wie es heißt, fast geckenhaft gekleidet, genauer gesagt mit einer Knautschlederjacke und mit Chromlederstiefeln (KUZNECOV 1957: 11). Da solche Kleidungsstücke aber nicht zum Dresscode der *stiljagi* gehören, heißt das, dass Lëša sich zwar allzu sehr um sein Äußeres kümmert und auch noch andere charakterliche Fehlentwicklungen aufweist, dass aber berechtigte Hoffnung besteht, mit einem guten Kollektiv aus ihm einen „richtigen Menschen" zu machen.

Der zweite Fall ist Miša, ein junger Lehrling, mit dem Tolja, der inzwischen ein allseits geschätzter Arbeiter ist, beim Kraftwerksbau ins Gespräch kommt. Miša ist trotz seiner Jugend „ideologisch gefestigt", kleidet sich aber dennoch modisch, ja trägt sogar *stiljaga*-belastete Microporsohlen. Sein Statement, dass beides vereinbar sei, verdient besondere Beachtung:

> „– Ты, Мишка, удивительный человек. Но ты стиляга.
> Мишка удивленно осмотрел свой костюм, свои новые туфли на микропоре и вдруг прорвался потоком брани:
> – Дурак! Ничтожество! Глупости только и знаешь болтать! Что же, всякий хорошо одетый человек по-твоему – стиляга? Стиляга – это социальное явление. Ты спроси у него: откуда он взял это? На чей счет он живет? Что он ищет в жизни? *Стиляга – это не микропора на ногах, это микропористая душа!*" (KUZ-NECOV 1990: 164; kursiv C.E.)

Dieser Figur kommt in der Erzählung also die entscheidende Funktion zu, beim *stiljaga*-Phänomen das Modische vom sozialen Phänomen einer sich üppig bedienenden Funktionärskaste mit ihren aus ideologischer Sicht missratenen Kindern zu trennen. So wie die Tauwetterliteratur generell, zielt auch hier die Kritik nicht auf die hohen Parteikader ab, sondern begnügt sich mit der mittleren Ebene. Eine solche implizite Kritik an den Vätern der *zolotye deti* ‚Goldkinder' ist zwar schon lange ein fixer Bestandteil des *stiljaga*-Diskurses, aber der Versuch der Abkoppelung der Kleidungsfragen ist dem Autor Kuznecov zugute zu halten.

Anatolij Gladilin „*Chronika vremen Viktora Podgurskogo*"

Viktor, der Hauptprotagonist der *povest'* „*Chronika vremen Viktora Podgurskogo*" (1956) von Anatolij Gladilin ist an und für sich ein begabter junger Mann, der jedoch die Aufnahmeprüfung an die Hochschule nicht ernst genug genommen hat. Er ist durchgefallen, hat daher keinen Studienplatz bekommen und hängt mit seinem Freund Dima tage- und wochenlang herum, während seine Freundin Nina, in die er über beide Ohren verliebt ist, sich zielstrebig dem Studium widmet. Sein Selbstwertgefühl gewinnt er erst wieder zurück, als er in einem Labor eine Arbeit aufnimmt. Die Neuerungssignale dieser *povest'*, die auf der Handlungsebene nach recht traditionellem Schema verläuft, liegen in der Art der Darbietung, d.h. in der wechselnden Erzählperspektive und dem breiten Raum, der den verliebten Emotionen des jungen Mannes geboten wird.

Der vestimentären Ausstattung kommt in dieser Erzählung eine neue, wichtige Funktion zu: Sie soll der Leserschaft einen Spiegel vor Augen halten, wie überzogen ihre Reaktion auf modisch gekleidete Jugendliche ist. Daneben erfüllt sie auch noch die Funktion, die Stimmung des Protagonisten zu begleiten: Als Viktor am Anfang der Erzählung die Nachricht von der nicht bestandenen Prüfung bekommt, ist er entsprechend geknickt. Das Herbstwetter und seine Kleidung runden das Bild des Jammers ab: Mit völlig durchnässten Schuhen, ohne Hut und mit hochgestelltem Kragen steht er im strömenden Regen, die Hände in den Taschen seines Regenmantels vergraben, den Gürtel zugeschnürt. Ganz anders war das noch im Sommer, als er zur Aufnahmeprüfung in einem neuen Anzug angetreten war. Diesen beiden Kleidungssignalen, die Viktor im gemeinhin akzeptierten Stil verankern, wird zwei Seiten später mit einem lose getragenen karierten Hemd die modische Variante hinzugefügt, was bei einer älteren Frau eine schreckhafte Reaktion auslöst:

> „Женщина вошла в подъезд и вздрогнула. В темноте стоял человек и курил. И, наверное, это был страшный человек, стоявший с определенной целью. Он не спускал глаз с освещенных окон первого этажа в доме напротив. *Женщина успела заметить, что человек был одет в ковбойку с расстегнутым воротом. Волосы его спадали на лоб. Такую прическу обычно носят хулиганы.*
> Человек – на вид ему было лет двадцать – внимательно оглядел ее. Ноги женщины сделались деревянными. Стараясь идти спокойно, она медленно прошла мимо. Поднялась на второй этаж. Нет, шагов за ней не слышно. Позвонила и быстро оглянулась. Нет, за ней никто не стоит." (GLADILIN 1989: 324; kursiv C.E.)

Wie wichtig dem Autor der Aspekt der Aufklärung seiner Leserschaft ist, kann man daran ermessen, dass er dasselbe Verfahren noch einmal anwendet, und zwar in der Szene, als Freunde zu Viktor in die *kommunalka* ‚Gemeinschaftswohnung' kommen:

> „В темную переднюю ввалились два парня.
> – Витя дома? – спросил один из них и, пройдя дальше, уверенно нашел выключатель, зажег свет.
> Бабке сначала стало не по себе. Но при свете она увидела, что ребята городские, с виду не хулиганы; а тот, что пониже, черненький, на грузина похожий, был в куртке такого пронзительно синего цвета, какой она видела только в праздник у девок на платьях. Бабка успокоилась, потому что вспомнила: «Да, вот в той комнате живет мать с сыном, сына зовут Витя», – и бойко ответила: – Да там нет никого!" (GLADILIN 1989: 325)

Gladilin positioniert seine jugendlichen Figuren also in einem vestimentären Sowohl-als-auch, um die Botschaft zu vermitteln, dass auch ganz normale Jugendliche eine *kovbojka* ‚kariertes Cowboyhemd' und eine Haartolle tragen können. Selbst wenn ihr Kleidungsstil bisweilen gewöhnungsbedürftig sei und ihr Betragen gegenüber der älteren Generation nicht immer makellos, lässt der Autor durchaus mit Ironie wissen, müsse man sich nicht gleich vor ihnen fürchten.

Vasilij Aksënov „*Zvëzdnyj bilet*"

Am elaboriertesten verfährt Vasilij Aksënov in seiner *povest'* „*Zvëzdnyj bilet*" (1961) mit Bekleidungsfragen. Für Dima, seine beiden Freunde und Galja – das Quartett, um das die Geschichte sich entwickelt – sind ihre spitzen Schuhe und die „stilvollendeten", farbenfrohen Kleidungsstücke ebenso Anlass zur Freude wie die neue Musik, zu der die Clique im Hof tanzt. Um die Harmlosigkeit dieser Vergnügungen zu vermitteln, fällt dem älteren Bruder von Dima eine wichtige Rolle zu: Viktor ist die Mediationsfigur zwischen der allgemeinen Meinung über *stiljagi* und einer entkrampfteren Sicht auf Jugendliche. Viktor selbst ist über jeden Zweifel erhaben, denn er ist der Traummann der frühen 1960er Jahre: ein junger Wissenschaftler, der an seiner Habilitation in Physik arbeitet und im Raumfahrtprogramm tätig ist; ein Mann mit Haltung, der seinen Weg geht und gegenüber seinen Vorgesetzten ein offenes Wort riskiert, selbst wenn ihm daraus Nachteile erwachsen. Die Artikulation der üblichen gesellschaftlichen Vorurteile mit den Stichwörtern *nakip'* ‚Abschaum', *vyrodki ‚Entartete'*, *sbrod* ‚Mob' ist dagegen die Aufgabe eines seiner Kollegen. Dieses Gespräch zwischen den beiden ist eine Schlüsselszene und gibt Viktor die Gelegenheit, solche Einstellungen zu kommentieren und zurechtzurücken:

„На площадке возле станции, как всегда вечером, полно молодых ребят. Они сидят на барьере и стоят кучками. […]
– Посмотри на них, – говорит Борис, – посмотри на их лица. Просто страх берет.
– Брось! — говорю я. – Нормальные московские ребята. Просто выпендриваются друг перед другом, вот и все.
– Нормальные московские ребята! – восклицает Борис. – Ты считаешь этот сброд нормальными московскими ребятами?
– Конечно! Самые обычные ребята.
– Нет, это выродки. Накипь больших городов.
– Ну тебя к черту, Борька! Димку моего ты, надеюсь, знаешь?
– Ну?
– Смею утверждать, что он самый нормальный московский малый. А он тоже часто торчит здесь, и, если бы ты его не знал, не отличил бы от всех. И в его адрес метал бы свои громы и молнии.
– А что твой Димка?
– Ну, что Димка?
– Он недалеко от них ушел. Тоже хорош твой Димка!
– Ну, знаешь, Борис!..
– А что? Скажешь, у Димки есть какие-то жизненные планы, какие-то порывы, есть что-то святое за душой? В голове у него магнитофонные ленты, девчонки и выпивка. Аттестат получил позорный …
– Довольно! – резко обрываю я, – Хватит о нем!
Черт его знает, каким он стал, этот мой друг Боря. Тоже позер! Любит, видите ли, «правду-матку в глаза резать».“ (AKSËNOV 1990: 64-65)

Trotz der im Prinzip positiven Bewertung der Clique, darf beim Leser jedoch nicht der Eindruck entstehen, dass diese Jugendlichen, die vorerst weder die Aufnahmeprüfung machen wollen, noch sich in den Arbeitsprozess eingliedern, ja die sogar für ungewisse Zeit ins Baltikum statt nach Sibirien aufbrechen, die neuen Vorbilder wären. Ihr Habitus wird daher als eine vorübergehende Jugendtorheit apostrophiert, und die weitere Entwicklung der Erzählung lässt ahnen, dass Dima sich am Ende Viktors Kleidungsstil aneignen wird – und der bindet sich, wie er betont, zum Rendezvous mit seiner Freundin eine Krawatte um. Das positive Potenzial der Clique wird wiederum dadurch unterstrichen, dass sie selbst nie als *stiljagi* bezeichnet werden, dass aber sehr wohl Nebenfiguren vorkommen, die alle schlechten Erwartungen, die mit *stiljagi* verbunden werden, erfüllen. So muss z. B. Viktor seine Freundin gegen die derben Übergriffe übler Typen verteidigen. Diese sind sofort als negative Figuren zu erkennen, da sie statt einer Krawatte nur eine Schnur umgebunden haben und zudem noch einen Schnurrbart tragen:

„Я [Виктор] повернулся к парням. У всех троих вместо галстуков висели на шее шнурки, а один был даже с усиками. Мой Димка ни за что не нацепил бы на себя шнурок. Все, что угодно, он может нацепить на себя, но не такую похабную веревочку.“ (AKSËNOV 1990: 63)

Dima selbst trägt an anderer Stelle dazu bei, um sich von solchen negativen Typen abzugrenzen; denn er macht deutlich, dass er keineswegs zu den *farcovščiki* ‚Schwarzhändlern‘ gehört, also zu denen, die Mode nicht als harmloses Vergnügen, sondern als illegale Geschäftemacherei sehen. Die Kleidungsstücke, die Dima trägt, sind nämlich alle legale Importware und stammen, wie der eingangs zitierten Charakteristik zu entnehmen ist, aus der Tschechoslowakei und aus dem neutralen Österreich. Die *farcovščiki* dagegen, so legt der Subtext nahe, verstoßen gegen das Gesetz und werden daher zu Recht verfolgt.

Mit solchen Manövern kann Aksënov einiges erreichen: Indem er die Mitglieder der Clique als Pubertierende darstellt, die nur etwas ausprobieren wollen, niemandem etwas Böses anhaben, und indem Dima letztlich gewillt ist, in die Fußstapfen seines inzwischen tödlich verunglückten Bruders zu treten, nimmt der Autor dem vergifteten Diskurs um die *stiljagi* den Wind aus den Segeln. Die Kritikaster wiederum stehen als Traditionalisten da, als zu alt fürs Neue und als Provinzler – mit einem Wort als solche, die die Zeichen der Zeit nicht erkennen. Andererseits werden Jackett, Krawatte, weißes Hemd und gebügelte Hose herausgelöst aus dem Kontext der Vätergeneration, die in der *Molodaja proza* ja gleichbedeutend ist mit Fehlentwicklungen in der Stalinzeit, und erfahren durch die sympathische Identifikationsfigur von Viktor einen Transfer in die nächste Generation.

Die Mädchenfiguren der *Molodaja proza*

Es wurde bereits erwähnt, dass *stiljagi* im Wesentlichen eine Angelegenheit männlicher Jugendlicher war. Die Mädchen in diesem Umfeld kleideten sich zwar auch schick, trugen hohe Absätze und entweder weite, bunte Röcke oder aber hautenge Bleistiftröcke; sie wurden aber dennoch nicht als „Bewegung" wahrgenommen, und ihr Stil wurde nicht als gesellschaftliches Statement interpretiert. In diesem Rahmen blieben auch die Autoren der *Molodaja proza*, die ihren Mädchenfiguren die traditionellen Rollen zukommen lassen: entweder als „Belohnung" für den männlichen Protagonisten oder als unsichere Kantonistin in der Partnerschaft. Vergleichbare Modulationen und Differenzierungen wie bei den männlichen *stiljaga*-Figuren bleiben im Prinzip aus. In der *povest'* von Aksënov kann man zumindest einen Ansatz davon finden: Viktors Freundin Šura kommt in einem engen, roten Kleid zum Rendezvous, wobei Viktor ihren Kleidungsstil explizit als ‚geschmackvoll' bezeichnet, was in einem unausgesprochenen Gegensatz zu „modisch" steht. Und auch Galja tauscht nach allen Irrungen und Wirrungen in ihrem Verhältnis zu Dima, sozusagen Mode gegen Geschmack ein.

In „*Продолжение легенды*" kann Juna, die Freundin von Tolja, nicht mit dessen Läuterungsprozess mithalten, denn sie kann den Reizen des *stiljaga*-Vitja nicht widerstehen. Dabei ist sie jedoch kein verführtes Opfer, sondern hatte bereits die entsprechende Disposition, was aus ihren Kleidungs- und Lektürepräferenzen deutlich wird: Tolja erinnert sich daran, dass sie sich schon ab der siebten Klasse nach der letzten Mode kleidete und über Oscar Wilde, Theodore Dreiser und Ernest Hemingway – also über lauter ausländische Schriftsteller – parlierte (KUZNECOV 1990: 91).

Die wirklich hoffnungsvollen Mädchen werden jedoch erst gar nicht über ihre Kleidung charakterisiert, sondern bevorzugt über Gesicht und Augen, die ja seit der Romantik in der Literatur als Spiegel der Seele dienen. So blickt z. B. Alja, die neue Auserwählte von Viktor Podgurskij mit großen, etwas erstaunten Augen in die Welt, was explizit seinem weiblichen Ideal entspricht (GLADILIN 1989: 374). Außerdem ist sie Funktionärin im Komsomol und kümmert sich um vieles und viele – eine wichtige Zusatzqualifikation, die indiziert, dass sie ihre Zeit nicht mit Modefragen vertändelt, sondern bereits am richtigen Weg ist. Am deutlichsten wird das bei Tonja, einer fleißigen Arbeiterin, zu der sich Tolja auf der Baustelle in Sibirien hingezogen fühlt:

> „Она худенькая, крепкая и стройная. Лицо у нее узкое, нос острый. Глаза большие, широко расставленные; косы венком вокруг головы и очень красивые брови

– тонкие, густые, словно проведенные углем. Я про себя назвал ее «Тоня с соколиными бровями».“ (KUZNECOV 1990: 74)

Resümee

Die Autoren der *Molodaja proza* ‚Junge Prosa', die in der Tauwetterzeit der späten 1950er Jahre an einer literarischen Erneuerung mitwirkten, bedienten sich mit Vorliebe vestimentärer Codes, um ihre jugendlichen Protagonisten als Hoffnungsträger für das Neue, durch die Stalinzeit nicht Kontaminierte zu positionieren. Mit ihren Kleidungssignalen von farbenfrohen Jacketts, Röhrenhosen und Schuhen mit hoher Microporsohle begaben sich diese Autoren jedoch auf das ideologisch verminte Feld der *stiljagi* ‚Hipsters'. Im Kontext des Kalten Krieges war diese Gruppe nämlich bereits ab 1949, also noch während der Stalinzeit, eine willkommene Zielscheibe für antiwestliche Stimmungsmache und wurde in den entsprechenden Kampagnen als Unkraut, Parasiten, Giftpilze und Hohlköpfe bezeichnet und damit zu Feinden der Gesellschaft gestempelt. Als soziales Phänomen betrachtet, war der familiäre Hintergrund der *stiljagi* allerdings meist die Schicht der politischen Funktionäre, gegen deren Verfehlungen sich die Kritik der Tauwetteraktivisten ganz gezielt richtete. Das Spiel mit beiden Positionen – sowohl mit der Kampagne gegen die *stiljagi* seitens der Traditionalisten als auch mit der Kritik an der mittleren Führungsebene der Kommunistischen Partei seitens der Neuerer – nützten Autoren wie Vasilij Aksënov, Anatolij Gladilin und Anatolij Kuznecov, um das Bild von einer Jugend im Aufbruch zurechtzurücken und zugleich die Rückkehr zu den Leninschen Prinzipien als Ideal in ihre Erzählungen einfließen zu lassen. Das trifft jedoch nur auf die männlichen Protagonisten zu, denn die Mädchenfiguren spielen nur eine Nebenrolle und bleiben statisch – sei es als Belohnung für den Helden oder als Verräterin an der gemeinsamen Sache.

Summary

The authors of 'Young Prose', who were part of the literary renewal during the Thaw period in the late 1950s, preferably used dress code signals in order to position their youthful heroes as beacons of hope for a new age that was not contaminated by the Stalin era. Yet with their dress code signals of colourful jackets, tight drainpipe jeans, cowboy shirts and pointed shoes they ventured on the ideological minefield of the *stiliagi,* 'hipsters'. Within the context of the Cold War this group had already served as a welcome target for anti-Western propaganda since 1949: in those campaigns these youngsters were referred to as weed, parasites, and toadstools and thus labelled as enemies of society. Looked at as a social phenomenon, the family background of these *stiliagi* was mostly that of political functionaries, against whose misconduct the criticism by the activists of the thaw era was specifically directed. Writers such as Vasilii Aksënov, Anatolii Gladilin and Anatolii Kuznecov used both positions, the campaign against the *stiliagi* as well as the criticism of the intermediate level of party officials, in order to counter the negative image of a deviant young generation and to imply in the narrative at the same time that a return to Leninist principles would represent an ideal development. This, however, is only true of the male protagonists. The female characters play a minor role only and remain static – either as a reward for the hero or as a betrayer of the common cause.

Bibliographie

AKSËNOV, V. 1961. Zvëzdnyj bilet. In: *Junost'* 6/1961, 3–34; 7/1961, 33–66. Dass. in: *Ottepel': 1960–1962: Stranicy russkoj sovetskoj literatury.* Moskva 1990, 57–218. http://www.libok.net/writer/75/kniga/32014/aksenov_vasiliy_pavlovich/zvezdnyiy_bilet (24.10.2014).

BELJAEV, D. 1949. Stiljaga. In: *Krokodil* 7/1949, 10. http://smeshnye-istorii.ru/category/1949/ (24.10.2014).

DMITRIEVA, M. 2010. Jazz and Dress. Stilyagi in Soviet Russia and Beyond. In: Pickhan, G., Ritter, R. (eds.). *Jazz Behind the Iron Curtain.* Frankfurt a. M. 2010, 239–255.

ENGEL, C. 2011. Vom Tauwetter zur Perestrojka (1953–1990). In: Städtke, K. (ed.). *Russische Literaturgeschichte.* Stuttgart, Weimar 2011, 349–396.

FLAKER, A. 1975. *Modelle der Jeans Prosa: Zur literarischen Opposition bei Plenzdorf im osteuropäischen Romankontext.* Kronberg.

GLADILIN, A. 1956. Chronika vremen Viktora Podgurskogo: Sostavlena iz dnevnikov, letopisej, istoričeskich sobytij i vospominanij sovremennikov. In: *Junost'* 9/1956, 5–35. Dass. in: *Ottepel': 1953 –1956: Stranicy russkoj sovetskoj literatury.* Moskva 1989, 321–400. http://read24. ru/pdf/anatoliy-gladilin-hronika-vremen-viktora-podgurskogo.html (24.10.2014).

KOMSOMOL I ŠKOLA 1955. In: *Pravda* 29.11.1955.

KONONENKO, E. 1960. Okrylennye mečtoj: Pis'ma s „Trechjurki". In: *Pravda* 31.8.1960.

KOZLOV, A. 2009. *Proischoždenie slova „stiljaga" ili otkuda proizošlo slovo stiljaga.* http://www. koryazhma.ru/usefull/know/doc.asp?doc_id=121 (24.10.2014).

KUZNECOV, A. 1957. Prodolženie legendy: Zapiski molodogo čeloveka. In: *Junost'* 4/1957, 6–59. Dass. in: *Ottepel': 1957–1959: Stranicy russkoj sovetskoj literatury.* Moskva 1990, 30–173. http: //www.libros.am/book/read/id/158653/slug/prodolzhenie-legendy (24.10.2014).

LITVINOV, G. 2009. *Stiljagi. Kak ėto bylo. Dokumental'nyj roman.* Sankt Peterburg.

MOSKOVSKIJ BIT: Vsë o stiljach i ich kollegach. In: *Moskovsky bits Journal* [Blog seit 2011]. http:// moskovsky-bit.livejournal.com/2102.html (24.10.2014).

POMERANCEV, V. 1953. Ob iskrennosti v literature. In: *Novyj mir* 8/1953, 218–245. http://modernlib. ru/books/pomerancev_vladimir/ob_iskrennosti_v_literature/read/ (24.10.2014).

TIMOFEEV, B. 1959. Garri. In: *Krokodil* 15/1959. http://smeshnye-istorii.ru/garri/ (24.10.2014).

TIMOFEEV, B. 1960. Sornjaki. In: *Pravda* 30.10.1960.

VINKEN, B. 2013. *Angezogen: Das Geheimnis der Mode.* Stuttgart.

Abbildungen

Abbildung 10: BAŽENOV, A.: *Podražateli* (o.J.).
http://young.rzd.ru/dbmm/images/41/4080/8386167 (25.10.2014).
Abbbildung 11: GOROCHOVA, E.: Garri. In: *Krokodil* 15/1959.
http://lib.rus.ec/i/10/444510/i_010.jpg (25.10.2014).
Abbildung 12: KUKRYNIKSY: *Poganki.* Otkrytka izd-va. Sovetskij chudožnik: Moskva 1961.
http://maysurian.narod.ru/pics/poganki_yellow.jpg (25.10.2014).

ПОДПОЛЬНЫЙ ПОЭТ И ПОРТНОЙ
Дискурс моды в трилогии Эдуарда Лимонова «Русское»

ОЛЬГА КАСПЕРС, ЗАЛЬЦБУРГ

На первый взгляд скандального писателя и оппозиционного политика Эдуарда Лимонова связывает с миром моды немногое. При ближайшем рассмотрении его творчества становится ясно, что художественные тексты Лимонова являются пло-дотворным материалом как для изучения советской культуры повседневности, так и для их интерпретации в аспекте теории моды. Этот писатель являлся одним из немногих в Советском Союзе, кто был напрямую связан с модой. В 1970-е годы Лимонов вращается в кругах советской богемы, внимательно следящей за последними веяниями западной индустрии моды. Используя постоянный дефицит стильной одежды в СССР, а также связи среди стиляг и диссидентов, молодой поэт зарабатывает на жизнь, занимаясь пошивом на дому:

> «Я обшивал творческую Москву все семь лет, что прожил в ней. И скульптору Эрнсту Неизвестному сделал джинсы, и поэту Окуджаве, и ещё сотням, уже забытым мною «творческим работникам» и их подругам. Жене писателя Мам-леева, помню, сшил белые, в чёрт знает как далеко отстоящем от современ-ности году.» (Лимонов 2013)

Несмотря на положительные отзывы о поэзии Лимонова в литературных кругах Москвы, ни одна его строчка не была напечатана в советских изданиях. По словам самого Лимонова, его слава подпольного портного растет быстрее репутации поэта, так что основным источником дохода в это время остается все же пошив брюк для московской культурной элиты. Уже здесь глаголы ШИТЬ и ЖИТЬ в буквальном смысле слова связаны друг с другом. Тема шитья и писательства постоянно сосед-ствуют в текстах Лимонова. В «*Книге мертвых*» (2001) он так описывает свою жизнь конца шестидесятых: «Молодой поэт, я еле выживал в Москве... часто перемещался с квартиры на квартиру с двумя машинками: швейной и пишущей»(Лимонов 2000: 65). Во время эмиграции Лимонов публикует ряд автобиографических произведений, в которых постоянно фигурирует тема стиля и моды, чередующаяся с мотивом написания стихов. В парижской квартире писателя, где он работает над автобио-графической трилогией «*Русское*», швейная машинка стоит возле его письменного стола. После возвращения на родину Лимонов не перестает писать о моде. В 2008 г. в сборнике «*Дети гламурного рая*» Лимонов уже, по праву, позиционирует себя как знатока моды (Лимонов 2008: 315). Подтверждая свое амплуа эстета с непревзойденным вкусом и арбитра элегантности, Лимонов в последнее время ведет постоянную колонку в издании российской версии культового журнала *Vogue*, где публикует эссе на темы моды и стиля.

Лимонов является одним из немногих современных российских писателей, оценивших общественное значение моды и успешно применивших его как в конструи-ровании своего собственного имиджа, так и в выстраивании образов своих литератур-ных героев. Мода у Лимонова – это не просто одежда или вестиментарный знак, а формирующая составляющая его творчества. Одежда выполняет у него роль семиоти-ческого кода, целенаправленно применяемого писателем в художественных текстах, а мода является стратегией конструирования художественной/литературной идентич-ности.

В этой связи интересно высказывание украинского коллеги Лимонова, писателя Сергея Жадана, о его прозе как о «плотном и туго натянутом сукне» и о «только ему свойственном акцентировании на мелочах, разной, мягко говоря, бытовой фигне», постоянно трансформируемой им в эстетический материал (ЖАДАН 2003). Именно из кусков автобиографии Лимонов сооружает все еще творимую им легенду, мастерски пользуясь законами моды. На эту же особенность обхождения с бытовыми фактами как «податливым материалом в умелых закройщицких пальцах» и «непринужденным выкраиванием» художественных текстов Лимоновым указывает и литературовед Алек-сандр Гольдштейн:

> «Лимонов – чемпион по переводу типовой эмигрантской биографической заурядности в текст, исполненный поэтического вдохновения [...] Он владеет редчайшим искусством трансформации бытового сора и пепла, гигантских стоячих мусорных куч банально пережитого – в динамическую словесность, да так, что читателю мнится, будто автор параллельно литературе реализовал удивительно захватывающую, авантюрную и глубокую жизнь.» (ГОЛЬДШТЕЙН 1997: 340–342)

В рамках этой статьи представляется особенно интересным проследить соотношение аспектов портного ремесла и искусства стихосложения в жизни и творчестве писателя. Литературовед Ольга Матич обращает внимание на то, что в эмигрантских произведениях автора «*Мы – национальный герой*» и «*Это я – Эдичка*» поэзия и швейное дело буквально вплетены в ткань текста. А в одном из его лучших стихотворений – «*Я в мыслях поддержу другого человека*» (1969) – нарциссизм лирического героя проявляется среди прочего в повышенном внимании к одежде: «И вещь любую на себе я досконально рассмотрю/Рубашку/я до шовчиков изглажу» (МАТИЧ 2013). Далее исследовательница указывает и на тот факт, что шитье у Лимонова «метафора – чтобы не говорить «повествовательная нить» – конструирования своей литературной идентичности в «Мы – национальный герой» и напоминание об этой идентичности в «Это я – Эдичка» (МАТИЧ 2013). На мой взгляд, эта метафора представлена в т.н. харьковской трилогии писателя «*Русское*» еще в более развернутом виде, а поэзия в ней – это прежде всего ремесло, которому он обучается параллельно и по аналогии с шитьем брюк и костюмов. Поэтому с целью выделения базовых принципов функционирования феномена моды в текстах Лимонова, мне хотелось бы остановиться прежде всего на детальном анализе именно трилогии «*Русское*» (1982–1987).[1] На примере ее интер-претации я постараюсь показать продуктивность применения теории моды как для литературоведческого, так и для культурологического анализа творчества писателя.

В качестве теоретической базы для данной статьи мной была использована недавно опубликованная монография Джурджи Бартлетт «*Fashion East: Призрак, бродивший по Восточной Европе*» (2011), в которой исследовательница указывает на существование нескольких видов моды в СССР: социалистической, утопической и повседневной. Ключевым в аспекте нашей проблемы представляется противостояние социа-листической моды как своего рода идеологического конструкта, имевшего сугубо символическую репрезентацию, повседневной моде, включающей в себя неофициаль-ные индивидуальные практики, посредством которых социалистические страны усваивали и адаптировали тенденции западной моды (БАРТЛЕТТ 2011: 15). Ярким представителем

---

[1] В 2004 году режиссер Александр Велединский снял по мотивам трилогии «*Русское*» художественный фильм под одноименным названием. На XX кинофестивале «*Окно в Европу*» в Выборге фильм получил второй приз в разделе игрового кино.

такого противостояния являлся Лимонов, практиковавший уже в 1950-е и 1960-е годы самопошив и кустарное производство одежды как тактику сопро-тивления власти, стремившейся в свою очередь дисциплинировать советских граждан.

Кроме того, в работе были использованы сочинения немецкого философа и социолога Георга Зиммеля (“*Philosophie der Mode*” (1905) и “*Lebensanschauung. Vier metaphysische Kapitel*” (1918), определяющего моду как диалектику имитации ‚*Imitation*‘ и дистинкции ‚*Distinktion*‘ (SIMMEL 1905: 7-37). Этот тезис Зиммеля представляется мне особо важным в контексте интерпретации жизнетворчества писателя и анализа литературного бренда «Лимонов».

Трилогия «*Русское*» в хронологическом порядке повествует о становлении Лимонова как поэта андеграунда и подпольного портного в СССР. Перед читателем поочередно предстают картины повседневной культуры сменяющих друг друга советских эпох: время правления Сталина и зарождение т.н. советского гламура, хрущевское время – время опошления вкуса, и брежневский период дефицита и блата.

Тема моды настолько доминирует в трилогии «*Русское*», что она по праву может считаться энциклопедией советской бытовой культуры 1950-ых – 1970-ых гг. В первой ее части – «*У нас была великая эпоха*» – автор описывает модные направления советской эстрады, дизайн жилых помещений (стиль коммуналок и служебных квартир для военных), культуру питания, совершения покупок (барахолка) и даже особую культуру похорон по-советски. Однако, главный акцент приходится на тему советской моды. Во втором романе трилогии «*Подросток Савенко*» речь идет о модных веяниях в среде молодежных субкультур: стиляг и блатных. В последней части трилогии Лимонов среди прочего повествует о моде и антимоде в кругах диссидентов родного города Харькова.

Так как же на самом деле выстраивается «советская часть» литературного бренда Лимонов?

«У нас была великая эпоха»

В первой части трилогии, в романе «*У нас была великая эпоха*», Лимонов прежде всего подчеркивает свое появление на свет именно в «великую эпоху» – эпоху победы СССР во Второй мировой войне, время правления Сталина и время зарождения монументального стиля социалистической моды, т.н. «советского гламура».[2] Мода сталинского времени выступает в романе как медиум, связывающий личность писателя с «великой» эпохой истории. Она становится инструментом для возвеличивания собственной личности, на фоне восславления которой, писатель творит собственный миф.

Выстраивание мифа начинается по традиции с родителей. Героическая эпоха, описываемая в романе, – время незаурядных личностей, и поэтому своего отца-военного Лимонов представляет «блистательным и неотразимым витязем в сияющих погонах», «таинственным чекистом», мифологизированным от сапог до шинели (ЛИМОНОВ 2010: 123,126).

В книге «*Денди: мода, литература и стиль жизни*» (ВАЙНШТЕЙН 2006) Ольга Вайнштейн указывает на основополагающие признаки дендизма: особое отношение к моде, к одежде, эпатаж, экстравагантность и самоинсценирование, а также культ тела и подчеркнутая маскулинность. Советский денди Вениамин Савенко, наделён всеми характерными особенностями этого типа:

---

[2]Лимонов подчеркнуто строит повествование как автобиографическое и скрывает присутствующие в нем элементы вымысла. Неразличение искусства и жизни является фирменным знаком Лимонова. На это указывали уже многие литературоведы, в том числе и Александр Гольдштейн (ГОЛЬДШТЕЙН 1997).

> «Фотографии конца сороковых годов демонстрируют обаятельного молодого лейтенанта в более или менее фривольных позах, обняв дерево, бедро отставлено, как во фламенко, кажется, озабоченного чем-то иным, а не своей военной карьерой. Военная форма сидит ловко, аккуратно, ушита, и, о, невероятно, Вениамин очень следил за своими красивыми руками и лишь в конце пятидесятых годов перестал покрывать ногти бесцветным лаком! Лейтенант Савенко был франт.» (Лимонов 2005: 31)

Далее в романе следует описание ухода лейтенанта за униформой, чистка сапог, пуговиц, пришивание погон и т.д. – ритуалы, которые можно сравнить с поведением французских или английских денди, тщательно следивших за своей одеждой и внешностью.

Для Лимонова униформа отца всегда оставалась предметом восхищения: она подчеркивала мужественность ее носителя, с одной стороны, а с другой, являлась подтверждением принадлежности к элите нового советского общества. Ее описание занимает в романе целые главы. Отдельно и подробно описываются ее составные части: сапоги, брюки-галифе, гимнастерка, фуражка и шинель. Описание униформы содержит массу отсылок и скрытых кодов. Оно начинается с ассоциации по запаху а ля Марсель Пруст и заканчивается уже прямым упоминанием этого автора, известного французского денди. Имя французского писателя всплывает в этом контексте, конечно же, не случайно. Пруст одним из первых в литературе модерна придает феномену моды должное значение и задается вопросом о психологических пружинах моды и ее роли в светских салонах предместья Сен-Жермен. Пруст использует в своих произведениях моду как механизм производства текста и образа. Подражая французскому писателю, Лимонов создает свои харьковские тексты.

И, конечно же, это описание униформы не могло обойтись без упоминания гоголевской шинели. Лимонов указывает на традицию русского классика украинского происхождения как на своего литературного предшественника. Намекая на высказывание «Все мы вышли из «*Шинели*» Гоголя» (цитата, часто приписываемая Достоевскому), Лимонов вписывает свое имя в русский литературный классический канон.

Фигура отца является в романе, несомненно, ключевой. Так, например, отец писателя уже выбором имени в честь «революционного поэта-романтика Эдуарда Багрицкого» как бы предвосхищает судьбу сына. Знаменательны здесь все три определения личности и творчества Багрицкого: будущий *поэт* Лимонов намеренно занимается жизнетворчеством, как впервые это стали делать такие представители *романтизма* как Байрон или Оскар Уайльд. А в 1990е годы Лимонов станет основателем НБП – экстремистской партии, ориентирующейся на идеалы револю-ционеров-*большевиков*.

Свою мать Раису Лимонов характеризует как первую модницу харьковских окраин и подробно описывает ее стиль одежды. Интересно, что описывая советскую женскую моду послевоенного времени, писатель подчеркивает прежде всего ее вторичность по отношению к западной. При этом он указывает на две основные тенденции этого времени: новые платья советские женщины шьют обычно сами, перелицовывая их из военных униформ. При этом они внимательно следят за новыми веяниями западной моды и копируют не только модели одежды, обуви и головных уборов, но также прически и макияж голливудских звезд:

> «Глядя на голливудских девушек и суровых гангстеров в двубортных костюмах и шляпах, запоминала русская молодежь модели одежды. Если военная мода в стране, только что выигравшей войну, подавила гражданскую мужскую моду полностью, то Рая и ее подружки – жены лейтенантов – выглядели бы нормально

> и на берлинском или парижском фоне, перенеси их судьба вдруг туда с сурового фона харьковских развалин.» (Лимонов 2005: 48)

Мать Эдички Раиса не отстает от моды и носит завитки и беретик а-ля Марлен Дитрих:

> «Мама Раиса запечатлена на фотографиях того времени обыкновенно в беретике. Из-под беретика на татарское скуластое личико мамы выбивается кокетливо несколько завитков. […] Отправляясь с Вениамином на офицерские вечера, мать чаще всего надевала платье серо-голубого шелка, узкое в талии и с накладными большими плечами. На ногах мамы так называемые «танкетки» – лаковые туфли со множеством ремешков, на крупном квадратном каблуке. Танкетки – модная обувь тех лет — изготовлялись частными сапожниками и стоили дорого.» (Лимонов 2005: 119, 46–47)

Значима в этом описании прежде всего семиотика головного убора. Раиса носит не косынку или платок, как это делали рабочие или крестьяне, а берет, что еще раз подчеркивает ее принадлежность к советской элите. Интересны также и туфли, которые, как известно, являются индикатором социального положения носящего. Раиса надевает к наряду дорогие лаковые танкетки на крупном квадратном каблуке, которые характеризуют мать автора как личность, уверенную в себе, и намекают на ее амбиции на социальный рост. Описание гардероба матери Лимонов заканчивает в легком ироническом стиле упоминанием фетиша того времени – модных нейлоновых колго-ток. Колготки, были таким дорогим и дефицитным товаром, что некоторые женщины имитировали их наличие, рисуя на ноге карандашом линию. Раиса Савенко могла позволить себе покупку колготок, но дыры на них оплакивала трагически.

Значимым является и тот факт, что свою мать Раису писатель представляет не только как первую модницу, но и как весьма «начитанную домохозяйку», имеющую в доме обширную библиотеку, и впервые знакомящую будущего писателя с миром литературы и театра:

> «Вокруг были книги. Всегда. […] Материны книги были пухлые, желтые и старые. Каждая как взбитая подушка. […] Мать брала свои странные книги у девушки Розы. Почему странные? Потому что пухлые и старые. У отца, например, книги были совсем другие: крепкие, хорошо стянутые переплетами, на каждой странице был или рисунок, изображающий военного с оружием в различных позах, заряжающего оружие или выполняющего какую-нибудь команду, или на целую страницу была помещена карта местности, или схема, или летящий снаряд и пунктирный путь, по которому летит снаряд… […] У книг [матери] были не нормальные не наши названия. Одна под названием «Консуэло» произвела на мать очень большое впечатление, отец говорил, что после «Консуэло» мать «стала спать на ходу, ударилась в мистику». Что значит «удариться в мистику», он так и не понял тогда и решил, что, может быть, это синоним «спать на ходу». (Лимонов 2005: 97–98)

Описывая детские годы жизни, писатель обращает внимание не только на моду этого поколения, но и на литературные одежды эпохи. Таким образом, он не только в деталях описывает модные тенденции сталинского времени, углубляясь в подробности, но и связывает текст и «текстиль», наполняя роман интертекстуальными отсылками разного плана.

Не обходит вниманием писатель и детскую моду послевоенного времени. Эксперт в области моды Лимонов со знанием дела описывает фасон и материал детской одежды, подчеркивая элегантность своих детских костюмов. С присущей автору любовью к эпатажу, он называет эти трофейные костюмчики «хорошим пинком в зад русской моде того времени»:

> «Ваш покорный слуга, камрады, имел удовольствие быть обладателем пары немецких костюмчиков. С особенным удовольствием вспоминается один: комплект темно-синего строгого габардина, прорезанного на солидных расстояниях директорской слабо видимой белой полосой. Элегантный пиджачок в талию и брючки выше колен. Костюмчик принадлежал ребенку с большим вкусом, может быть, сыну директора «ИГ-фарбэн» или ребенку семейства Круппов. К костюмчику надевались чулки. Чулки пристегивались к поясу (как девочки, приличные мальчики носили тогда пояса) резинками.» (Лимонов 2005: 49)

Описание этого костюма на метауровне связано с описанием детской одежды хрущевского времени в следующем романе трилогии «*Подросток Савенко*». Сравнивая описание детской одежды двух эпох, легко проследить негативное отношение писателя ко времени правления Хрущева.

«Подросток Савенко»

Во второй части трилогии главным действующим персонажем является уже 15-ти летний Эди, поэт и хулиган. Действие романа, большего по объему, чем первая часть, разворачивается на рабочей окраине Харькова. Оно занимает всего два дня и начи-нается 7 ноября – в День Октябрьской революции, в самый советский из всех празд-ников. В этот день подросток Савенко решает пригласить свою подружку Светку на модную вечеринку, на что ему нужно 250 рублей. Деньги он сначала пытается занять у друзей и знакомых, потом выпросить у родителей и, в конце концов, совершает ограбление магазина. Все эти попытки достать заветную сумму заканчиваются в фи-нале неудачей.

Интересно, что уже на первой странице романа встречаем описание одежды представителей советского среднего класса, которые не просто ходят, а именно дефилируют по главной площади Харькова, как на показе мод. Политика формовки и дисциплинирования советского тела и духа уже дала плоды, и активные строители социализма – советский средний класс – облачились в практичные, скромные (просто, удобно, прилично) одежды:

> «Сегодня Седьмое ноября, в прохладный полдень мимо Эди дефилируют наряженные граждане, или козье племя, как он их называет. [...] Глава семьи напялил тяжелое пальто, и черный или темно-синий пиджак, и галстук, и новые туфли, которые причиняют ему невероятную боль при каждом шаге. Нарядные дети, одетые под взрослых в большие нелепые костюмы, жрут неизменное мороженое, и каждый волокет за собой по нескольку шаров на нитках. [...] Платье супруги и ее пальто наверняка воняют невыдохшимся нафталином — они берегут свои вещи. Эди-бэби морщится.
> Эди-бэби не такой, как они. Потому он и стоит тут в рваных и мятых польских вельветовых брюках и желтой куртке с капюшоном, стоит этаким Гамлетом Салтовского поселка и сплевывает независимо.» (Лимонов 2005: 131–132)

На примере этого отрывка можно показать, какие вестиментарные функции выполняет одежда в текстах Лимонова и как конструируется образ главного героя в дискурсе моды. Данное описание одежды содержит целый ряд оппозиций: первое, что обращает на себя внимание, это противопоставление поэта и толпы. Одежда поэта подчеркивает его особое положение по отношению к массе, выделяет его из толпы по вестиментарному принципу. Инаковость героя подчеркивается не только его статусом поэта, но и стилем одежды. Наряжая молодого поэта, автор продумывает каждую деталь его туалета. Так, например, желтая куртка и привычка сплевывать являются прямой отсылкой к образу Владимира Маяковского, желтая кофта которого являлась отличительным знаком поэта-авангардиста. Желтая куртка поэта Лимонова как бы вписывает его в традицию и демонстрирует его связь с предшественниками.

Значим также и тот момент, что уже в подростковом возрасте в биографии Эди намечается типичный конфликт поэта и государства. Надевая яркую необычную одежду, он пытается прежде всего выделиться из серой массы плохо одетых сограждан.

Узкие брюки и обувь на плотной высокой подошве, выражают потребность не только подчеркнуть свою индивидуальность, но и демонстрируют попытку протеста против навязываемого сверху стиля одежды. Создавая своей манерой одеваться оппозицию официальной моде, он протестует против государства, насаждающего своим гражданам скромный и безликий вкус, и жестко регламентирующего их дресс-код. Уже в это время Эди-бэби не только подражает в выборе одежды западным образцам, но и проявляет индивидуализм и креативность в ее изготовлении:

> «Удобная вещь – желтая куртка, а все потому, что модель снята с австрийского альпийского пальто. [...] Кадик привез пальто с фестиваля. Конечно, такой материи, из которой сшито альпийское пальто, они не смогли найти в харьковских магазинах, пришлось купить обивочный желтый материал – такой употребляют на обивку кресел и диванов. В дождь материал чуть промокает, но ничего, зато подкладку выбрали толстую. Кадик даже предложил вставить под плечи и в капюшон полиэтиленовые прокладки, чтоб не промокали плечи и голова, но Эди не захотел – полиэтилен будет шелестеть.» (Лимонов 2005: 164)

Кроме того, в одежде героя скрыт и бунт против обывательского вкуса семьи поэта. Втайне от матери Эди ушивает брюки так, чтобы они обтягивали тело, подчеркивая фигуру. А вельветовые польские брюки Эди носит до тех пор, пока они окончательно не разваливаются, демонстративно игнорируя одежду отечественных производителей.[3]

Значимые вестиментарные знаки в романе можно обнаружить буквально на каждой странице. Лимонов подробно освещает тему стиля молодежных субкультур: стиляг и блатных и модели их социального поведения. Обе группы имеют т.н. дресс-код и общаются друг с другом посредством манеры одеваться. Так, например, друг Эди-бэби, Кадик, являющийся типичным представителем стиляг, носит брюки-дудочки и широкий пиджак, слушает джаз, и занимается фарцовкой – перепродает пластинки запрещенных исполнителей, поступающих из Прибалтики. Эди-бэби и Кадик не только подражают в одежде западным образцам, но и пытаются проявлять свою индивидуальность, занимаясь кустарным производством обуви:

---

[3] Протагонист продолжает носить эти брюки еще и по другой причине: «Польские брюки кое-где разорваны и зашиты самим Эди-бэби, но Эди упорно продолжает их носить, так как Ася однажды сказала ему, что в этих брюках и белой рубашке Эди-бэби очень похож на недавно умершего американского актера Джеймса Дина, и показала ему книгу с фотографиями. Действительно, этот парень-актер был очень похож на Эди-бэби, только он был старше. Прическа у Эди-бэби чуть короче, чем у Джеймса, а в остальном – разительное сходство. Славный парень был, жаль, что он умер, разбился на мотоцикле. Эди-бэби спросил, в каких фильмах снимался Джеймс, но Ася с сожалением сказала, что фильмы эти в Советском Союзе не показывают, Хрущев их не купил. Хотя Хрущев купил немало американских фильмов, но они не с Джеймсом Дином». (Лимонов 2005: 237–238)

> «Кадик уходит, жестко стуча подкованными туфлями по асфальту. Такие же туфли и у Эди-бэби, вернее, такие же огромные, почти лошадиные подковы привинчены к его туфлям тоже. Это их совместное изобретение. Подковы сдела-ны из особой твердейшей стали. Чтобы просверлить в каждой из них три дыры для шурупов, бедный Эдька Додонов сломал несколько победитовых сверл. Зато Кадик и Эди-бэби щеголяют своими подковами и узнают по ним друг друга в темноте – дело в том, что если слегка возить каблуками по асфальту при ходьбе, то за туфлями тянутся длинные красно-желтые искры – дуги. Посмотришь – искры на другой стороне темного Салтовского шоссе, значит, Кадик идет, кто еще?» (Лимонов 2005: 155)

Другие приятели Эди, Кот и Тузик, представители субкультуры блатных, уделяют своему внешнему виду меньше внимания, но зато культивируют употребление ненормативной лексики и ношение холодного оружия. В этой среде бытуют свободные «нравы по понятиям», но им присуща и любовь к сентиментальной лирике. Обе субкультуры достаточно мирно сосуществуют друг с другом, но отказ от дресс-кода, попытки обособления строго наказываются как с одной, так и с другой стороны.

Романтические приключения подростка Савенко заканчиваются неудачным побегом в город-порт Новороссийск, где он с приятелем собирался заняться фарцовкой. Значимым является эпилог романа, повествующий о судьбах приятелей Эди (стиляг и блатных). Именно на этом фоне и открывается второй сюжетный пласт романа: формирование облика поэта, состоящее из трех фаз, и заканчивающееся поэтическим триумфом Эди – получением главной литературной премии молодых стихотворцев.

В этой сюжетной линии романа герой знакомится с творчеством Александра Блока, воспринимая ее вначале только на примитивном уровне – идентифицируя себя с лирическим героем стихотворения:

> «Эди-бэби повезло со стихами. Первые стихи, прочитанные им в жизни, [...] были «Юношеские стихи Александра Блока» с нарисованной на обложке веткой сирени. Стихи Блока Эди-бэби открыл в мае, в саду у Витьки Фоменко, как раз цвела именно сирень. [...] Эди, ужасаясь и поражаясь, захлебываясь, читал, сидя на бревнах, спрятавшись от соучеников в угол сада:
> «Снится, снова я мальчик и снова любовник,/ И — овраг, и в овраге колючий шиповник.../ Старый дом глянет в сердце мое, / Розовея от края до края,/ И окош-ко твое... Этот голос — он твой,/ И его непонятному звуку/Жизнь и горе от-дам...»/ «Хоть во сне, твою прежнюю милую руку/ Прижимая к губам» — и от этих слов Эди хотелось умереть, умереть от любви к Светке, с которой он только на Первое мая познакомился.» (Лимонов 2005: 135)

Следующей фазой этой событийной линии становится написание стихов в подражание Блоку, Есенину и другим поэтам, с лирикой которых знакомится подросток Савенко:

> «А Раиса Федоровна утверждает, что стихи Эди-бэби – бред и похожи на тех поэтов, которых он только что прочел. Прочел Блока – похожи на Блока, прочел Брюсова – Эди-бэби немедленно пишет стихи, похожие на стихи Брюсова, прочел Есенина – пишет под Есенина...» (Лимонов 2005: 216–217)

Значимо, что уже на этой подражательной стадии Эди-бэби в отличие от своих приятелей осознает фикциональность лирики. Эди-бэби читает своему товарищу Гришке только что написанные стихи о милицейском автомобиле, в котором поэта везут в тюрьму и на расстрел. Закончить Эди-бэби не успевает, потому что Гришка останавливает его вопросом:

> «– Кто сука, начальник или Светка? – спрашивает Гришка ехидно.
> – При чем здесь Светка? — говорит Эди. – Это же стихи.
> – Нужно выражаться яснее, – поучительно выдавливает из себя Гришка.» (Лимонов 2005: 249)

Заканчивается роман повествованием о самом большом триумфе в жизни молодого поэта. На конкурсе юных чтецов, прочитав собственное стихотворение «*Наташа*», молодой поэт выигрывает первую премию:

> «Когда Эди выпаливает им все двенадцать строф и заканчивает той же самой первой строфой-рефреном […] вся площадь разражается аплодисментами, ревом, и Эди понимает, что, что бы ни произошло, какие бы после него ни читались стихи – первый приз ему достанется. Поэтому он читает еще два стихотворения и, несмотря на возгласы «Браво!» и «Еще!», «Еще!», уходит от микрофона.» (Лимонов 2005: 283–285)

Любопытно, что собираясь на поэтический конкурс, Эди-бэби прежде всего занят выбором подходящей одежды:

> «Эди-бэби одевается не так, как он оделся бы к Сашке Плотникову, но все же надевает свои праздничные туфли, предварительно завернув голую ногу в газету, а потом уже натянув носок. Газеты – испытанный способ. Заворачивать ноги в газеты, чтоб не мерзли, научил его Славка Цыган, когда прошлой зимой в жестокие морозы они ходили на танцы в легких туфлях на коже. Эди надевает также свои праздничные, очень узкие брюки, белую рубашку, сверху натягивает куртку с капюшоном, а бабочку сует в карман, на всякий случай. Может быть, он наденет бабочку перед выступлением.» (Лимонов 2005: 277)

Таким образом, в финале романа «*Подросток Савенко*» становится ясно, что карьера молодого бандита (роман назывался первоначально «*Автопортрет бандита в отрочестве*») не складывается, зато начинается формирование ПОЭТА.[4]

Итак, в подростковом возрасте Эди-бэби читает и пишет первые стишки и делает первые стежки. Автор демонстрирует, как его герой становится поэтом и портным, обучается одновременно портному ремеслу и искусству стихосложения. Чтение полулегальных поэтов Полонского, Брюсова и Блока и создание стихотворений в подражание им идет параллельно с первым опытом портного – ушиванием брюк и копированием выкроек для соседей из журналов мод. Переход от слепого следования образцам к их планомерной переработке и созданию собственного стиля как в модной, так и поэтической области, совершится в следующей части трилогии.

[4] Юрий Мамлеев назовет впоследствии поэзию Эдуарда Лимонова – «шедевром, который идет от глубокой русской традиции, в которой сочетается и глубокая традиция и авангард. Авангард не вызывающий, авангард мягкий, нежный, лирический» (Мамлеев 2013).

«Молодой негодяй»

Выстраивая образ повзрослевшего alter ego, Лимонов прибегает к механизмам действия моды, точно описанным Зиммелем как диалектика имитации и дистинкции. Весь роман пронизан этой диалектикой. Сначала молодым поэтом движет желание выделиться из массы шпаны с окраины, заявить о своей индивидуальности. Затем, попав в круги харьковской богемы, он подражает ей во всем – одежде, вкусам, образу жизни в целом, а в конце повествования, добившись успеха и признания, покидает провинциальный город в поиске перемен и новых экспериментов.

Важно обратить внимание на тот факт, что в последнем романе трилогии Лимонов демонстративно позиционирует себя как поэта и кутюрье. Единство поэта и портного-творца подчеркивается в самом начале романа:

> «Вынув из книжного шкафа, нижняя часть которого переделана в шифоньер, свою гордость – костюм цвета какао, с золотой искрой, пробивающейся по ткани, юноша спешно натягивает брюки, розовую рубашку и пиджак. В изголовье кровати стоит ломберный стол, а на нем в беспорядке карандаши, ручки, бумаги, недопитая бутылка вина, раскрытая тетрадь. С некоторым сожалением поглядев на недописанное стихотворение, юноша закрывает самодельную тетрадку [...]» (Лимонов 2005: 325–326)

Символично, что в начале романа Эди выходит из квартиры-мастерской, оставляя в ней недописанные стихи и недошитые брюки. В «*Молодом негодяе*» Лимонов особенно наглядно указывает на параллели между ремеслом портного и творчеством поэта. Глагол «строчить» – означающий в русском языке не только быстро писать, но и шить (на машинке) – подчеркивает связь между работой поэта и писателя и как бы помогает осуществить плавный переход из области создания модной одежды в область стихосложения.

Текстильная метафорика наполняет текст романа. Материал становится материей произведения, текстиль превращается в текст. В романе лейтмотив «кройки и шитья» постоянно чередуется с мотивом написания стихов. Интересным в этом отношении является описание того, как Эд Лимонов начинает заниматься пошивом одежды:

> «Прежде всего он в сотне точек измерил свои собственные расклешенные брюки и перенес размеры на бумагу. Получился чертеж брюк. [...] Конечно, он никогда не шил брюк, но иголку держать в руках умел. Несколько лет практики – подпольного, втайне от матери, зауживания штанин, сделали его вполне сносным передельщиком брюк. Еще у него был явный прирожденный талант чертежника, он хорошо понимал геометрию. Вооруженный этими начальными навыками и здравым смыслом, затратив на свое предприятие сорок восемь часов (особенно трудно оказалось понять устройство карманов), он соорудил брюки. [...] Так он стал портным.» (Лимонов 2005: 364-366)

Практически на этой же странице находим описание того, как Лимонов становится поэтом:

> «Всю весну и лето 1965 года он просидел взаперти и писал стихи. Извел две пачки грубой серой бумаги по пятьсот листов каждая. [...] Лето было жаркое, нечем было дышать, а тщеславный юноша все выводил строчки на серой бумаге... [...] Может, год он упорно писал плохие стихи, пока однажды, воз-мутившись собой, вдруг сумел вытащить из самой глубины себя мелодию, которая, хотя и вырази-

лась в смутных и плохо организованных словах, была его мелодией, и Эд почувствовал это.» (Лимонов 2005: 367)

Характерно также, что именно в этом тексте Эдуард Савенко получает свой литературный псевдоним «Лимонов», символизирующий переход из одного состояние в другое, т.о. смена идентичности, появление иной персоны, подтверждается и на уровне смены имени.

Превращение работяги с завода и мальчика с окраины в поэта андеграунда демонстрируется особенно выразительно на вестиментарном уровне:

> «Брусиловский с сомнением оглядел худенького поэта, одетого в наряд, усугубляющий впечатление хрупкости, – черные брюки, черный жилет и белая рубашка. Следует отметить, что став поэтом, рабочий парень утерял многие килограммы рабочего веса и за пару лет общения с умными книгами и нервных бесед с поэтами, художниками и интеллектуалами лицо его необыкновенным образом утончилось.» (Лимонов 2005: 373)

Становление Лимонова как писателя развивается параллельно с его ремесленным ростом. Лимонов трактует поэзию как ремесло. У него это не божественный дар, не внезапное вдохновение, которое находит на избранного, а повседневный труд.

Умение шить позволяет Лимонову избегать трудности с одеждой в униформированном советском обществе и проявлять свою индивидуальность в одежде собственного покроя. Кроме того, профессия портного дает ему финансовую свободу и возможность заниматься поэзией. Благодаря мастерству кройки и шитья, он попадает в круги интеллектуальной харьковской богемы.

Как при написании стихов, так и при создании моделей одежды на начальной стадии важную роль играет фактор подражания. Эдичка открывает для себя мир поэзии русских символистов, акмеистов и авангардистов и пишет стихи, подражая им, но внося собственные нюансы. Позже он становится самобытным, как сказал о нем Евтушенко, ни на кого не похожим автором (Евтушенко 1995: 883). И если вначале романа он шьет брюки по образцам западных журналов или по выкройкам настоящих портных, то в его завершении Эди начинает моделировать одежду сам. В сшитых им моделях этого времени фундаментальное подражание в крое сочетается с индивиду-альностью деталей. В ярких моделях собственного изготовления Лимонов фланирует с приятелями по улицам Харькова, демонстрируя модели собственного пошива и декламируя свои оригинальные стихи. Трилогия заканчивается тем, что Лимонов поки-дает провинциальный город и уезжает завоевывать столицу.

Заключение

Подводя итог, нужно отметить, что ремесло портного и постоянный контакт с миром моды воспитал у Лимонова определенный вкус, в том числе и литературный, сделал его восприимчивым к воспроизведению самых мелких различий в стиле, научил быстро воспринимать и принимать новые формы, получать удовольствие от деталей. Мода не только моделировала вкус писателя и придавала ему изысканность, но также оттачивала эстетическую чувствительность. Она формировала механизм наблюдения за самим собой (самолюбование), образующий вектор в сторону нарциссической индивидуализации, распространения культа собственного «Я». Все эти факторы способствовали формированию Лимонова как самобытного поэта, быстро снискавшего себе славу сначала в харьковских, а потом и в московских кругах литературной богемы.

Совершенно очевидно, что Лимонов при конструировании своей художественной идентичности ориентируется именно на моду как систему, позволяющую ему эстетизировать свое жизненное пространство, самовыражаться, создавать собственный стиль *haute couture*, отличающий его от других как в поэтическом, так и идеологическом плане. Культура советского быта сталинской, хрущевской и бреж-невской эпохи становится при этом материалом, из которого Лимонов выбирает подходящее, чтобы смастерить собственный образ, сшить свои поэтические одежды.

Показательна в этом отношении фотография, сделанная в 1974-ом году непосредственно перед эмиграцией писателя. На ней Лимонов позирует в барочном костюме, сшитом им самим из 114 частей. Поэт выступает здесь в роли портного, облачающего себя в костюм «национального героя». На фотографии визуально оформлено то, что Лимонов пытался выразить в текстах автобиографической трилогии «*Русское*»: именно самопошив являлся единственным способом индивидуализации и самоидентификации в тоталитарном советском обществе.

Любопытно также, что в 1960-е и 1970-е годы Лимонов подрабатывает тем, что перепечатывает на машинке запрещенных поэтов, вручную переплетает обложки ситцем и продает их. Не имея возможности публиковаться в СССР, он также поступает со своими собственными сборниками. Это значит, что Лимонов занимался в СССР не только самопошивом, но и самиздатом. Таким образом, феномен советского государства с его постоянным дефицитом на товары и жесточайшей идеологической цензурой способствует созданию такого ЛИТЕРАТУРНОГО БРЕНДА как ЛИМОНОВ. Мода, самостоятельное изготовление одежды и самиздат становятся важными аспектами создания собственного литературного бренда (SELF-FASHION) и Лимонов может по, праву, считаться писателем SELF-MADE.

На мой взгляд, исследование творчества Лимонова в аспекте теории моды является перспективным и плодотворным, т.к. оно дает ключ к адекватному восприятию и пониманию его художественных текстов. В этой статье мною была предпринята попытка применения теории моды к анализу (жизне)творчества Лимонова. Такая постановка вопроса открывает перспективы для дальнейших исследований.

Summary

In this article I analyse the autobiographical trilogy "Russian" by Eduard Limonov from the perspective of the fashion theory. I will draw a connection between the trade of a tailor and the art of a poet. It is instructive to find out how fashion influences the shaping of the main character in Limonov's trilogy as well as Limonov's literary brand as a whole.

Библиография

БАРТЛЕТТ, Д. 2011. *Fashion East: Призрак, бродивший по Восточной Европе.* Москва.

ВАЙНШТЕЙН, О. 2006. *Денди, мода, стиль жизни.* Москва.

ГОЛЬДШТЕЙН, А. 1997. Эдуард Великолепный. In: Гольдштейн, А. *Расставание с Нарциссом. Опыты поминальной риторики.* Москва 1997, 328–348.

ЕВТУШЕНКО, Е. 1995. *Строфы века. Антология русской поэзии.* Минск, Москва.

ЖАДАН, С. 2003. *Народ против Эдуарда Лимонова. Только настоящий писатель может встречать 60-летие за решеткой.* http://www.limonow.de/others/others.html (02.07.2014).

ЛИМОНОВ, Э. 2000. *Книга мертвых*, Санкт-Петербург.

ЛИМОНОВ, Э. 2005. У нас была великая эпоха. In: Лимонов, Э. *Русское.* Москва 2005, 11–128.

ЛИМОНОВ, Э. 2005. Подросток Савенко. In: Лимонов, Э. *Русское.* Москва 2005, 131–322.

ЛИМОНОВ, Э. 2005. Молодой негодяй. In: Лимонов, Э. *Русское.* Москва 2005, 325–543.

ЛИМОНОВ, Э. 2008. *Дети гламурного рая.* Москва.

ЛИМОНОВ, Э. 2010. *Книга мёртвых-2. Некрологи.* Санкт-Петербург, Москва.

ЛИМОНОВ, Э. *Задолго до Китая. Как я шил джинсы.* http://svpressa.ru/culture/article/68517 (25.05.2013).

МАМЛЕЕВ, Ю. 2003. *Истинно русское слово.* http://www.limonow.de/others/others.html (02.07. 2014).

МАТИЧ, О. 2013. *Эдуард Лимонов. История автора и его персонажа.* http://magazines.russ.ru/october/2013/11/32m.html (02.07.2014).

SIMMEL, G. 1905. Philosophie der Mode. In: Simmel, G. *Gesamtausgabe. Band 10.* Frankfurt am Main 1995, 7-37.

КИНО И МОДА В ЭПОХУ ОТТЕПЕЛИ

ОКСАНА БУЛГАКОВА, МАЙНЦ-БЕРЛИН

Моду – во всяком случае, ее существование в кино – невозможно воспринимать, оценивать и анализировать как статичную картинку. Она создается не столько сочетанием самих вещей, сколько существование в кино – невозможно воспринимать, оценивать и анализировать как сочетанием вещей с движущимся кино-телом, особой медиальной конструкцией. Кино моделировало это идеальное медиальное тело, чьи жесты, поведение, движения, манера одеваться и причесываится перенимались зрителями из темного зала кинотеатра в дневные пространства (БУЛГАКОВА 2005: 2010). Образ и динамика этого тела создавались при помощи раскадровки, света, движения камеры, ритма мизансцены и монтажа, расстановки акцентов в нарративе. Аффективное воздействие этого тела способствовало гораздо более эффективному утверждению или уничтожению моды. Фильм Фрэнка Капры «*Однажды ночью*» (1934) избавил несколько поколений мужчин от привычки носить майку под рубашкой, и это потрясение было вызвано проходной – для актера – сценой, эротичная двусмысленность которой целилась традиционно на женское тело. Сбежавшая дочь миллионера должна разделить комнату в мотеле со случайным знакомым. Дама при побеге не захватила с собой ночной рубашки, и мужчина одалживает ей свою пижаму. Разгороженная простыней комната видна зрителям, но их внимание перехватила не Клодетт Кольбер, переодевающаяся в пижаму, а Кларк Гейбл, снимающий рубашку. При этом потрясенные зрители обнаруживают, что он не носит майки! Покупка мужских маек упала настолько резко, что трикотажная промышленность не оправилась от этого шока до «реанимации» майки Калвином Клайном. Вряд ли футболка могла бы сделать такую карьеру в мире моды, если бы Марлон Брандо не появился в ней на экране в «*Трамвае желание*» в 1952-ом году. Сексуальная драма «*Трамвай желание*» была перенасыщена извращенной эротикой – гомосексуализм, педофилия, нимфомания, изнасилование, насилие в браке, комплексы старого мужчины под властью матери. Все герои фильма были либо сексуально одержимы, либо сексуально закомплексованы. Воплощением незакомплексованных желаний был молодой Брандо, который смог передать бушующую сексуальную энергию в затрапезной кухне бедной новоорлеанской квартиры, одетый (раздетый) в потную грязную футболку, и неприметные штаны пузырями. Художник по костюмам просила Брандо одеть эти штаны мокрыми на голое тело, чтобы скульптурнее вылепить его при помощи одежды. После экранизации «*Трамвая желания*» жена Брандо могла заявить в своей книге «*Брандо на завтрак*»: «Марлон [...] сделал для футболки то же, что Бардо для бикини» (BRANDO, STEIN 1979: 37). Фильм Элиа Казана получил 12 номинаций на Оскара. Брандо, как известно, награды не дали, но она досталась Люсинде Баллард – за костюмы, не только за пеньюары Вивьен Ли, но и за потную футболку Марлона. Также стали культовыми явлениями одежда и бессмысленные жесты Джеймса Дина, немедленно скопировавшего манеру Брандо раскованно двигаться и небрежно одеваться. Их воспроизводили и позже, забыв источник и смысл. Когда немецкая террористка Гудрун Энслин одела для своего первого процесса по поджогу универмага белую футболку и красную кожаную куртку, никто не вспомнил о прототипе. Недавно для рекламы Matsuba (Vogue International, Homme Hors Serie 1994) фотограф, очевидно, заставил воспроизвести свою модель культовый жест Дина из «*Бунтаря без причины*». Там, возвращаясь после пробы мужества, на которой погиб, сорвавшись в пропасть, его соперник, Дин достал из холодильника бутылку молока и прижимал к ней свой разгоряченный лоб. Сегодня эта бутылка молока в руке модели, может быть, помнилась фотографу, но уже не критику, недоумевающего по поводу сочетания анорексичного тела и здоровой жидкости.[1] Память культовых поз, если ее не закреплять, стирается. Поза ушла. Футболка осталась.

Взаимодействие кино и моды, сложные отношения между созданной медиальной картиной тела и ее наполнением (смыслом, фантазиями, желанием, тайной) тематизировали европейские режиссеры шестидесятых годов, сделав фотографов и моделей фигурами знаменитых фильмов: «*Дарлинг*» (1965) Джона Шлезингера, «*Блоу ап*» Микельанджело Антониони (1966), «*Плей герл*» Вилла Тремпера (1966) и «*Кто Вы, Поли Магу*» (1966) фотографа «*Вог*» Уильма Клайна. Рефлексия о взаимодействии моды и тела стала одной из сюжетных линий недавнего сериала «*Оттепель*» (2013) и более давнего мюзикла «*Стиляги*» (2008) Валерия Тодоровского. Неслучайно режиссер отослал этот сюжет в оттепельное время, наиболее любопытную в этом отношении советскую эпоху. Хотя историкам моды легко заметить отставание одежды советских киногероев от западной моды того времени (рискованные мини, голубые и розовые колготки, мотивы Мондриана появляются на советском экране гораздо позже), фильмы этого времени утверждают новое тело, новые техники тела (манеру ходить, сидеть, стоять) и новые жесты, которые становятся первым шагом к эмансипации инди-видуального поведения, особождают «советское» тело из зажима дисциплинированной «культурности» и подготовливают его к ношению новой моды.

Прозрачный занавес

Изменения в искусстве периода оттепели чаще всего связывают с ослаблением цензуры и открытием железного занавеса, объясняя из этих двух обстоятельств новую программатику: правдиво говорить о настоящем, вернуть из забвения прошлое, вступить в диалог с современной западной культурой. Открытие железного занавеса означало не только встречу с абстрактным экспрессионизмом, атональной музыкой и современным дизайном, но и колебание норм «общинности» иным физиогномическим опытом до вербализации. Этот опыт повлиял даже на бытовую моторику – на манеру ходить и сидеть, резко отделив молодое поколение, воспитываемое не на советских фильмах тридцатых годов, а на трофейных, западных, от мира их отцов.

> «И я утверждаю, что одни только четыре серии «*Тарзана*» способствовали десталинизации больше, чем все речи Хрущева на XX съезде и впоследствии. Нужно помнить про наши широты, наши наглухо застегнутые, жесткие, зажатые, диктуемые зимней психологией нормы публичного и частного поведения, чтобы оценить впечатление от голого длинноволосого одиночки, преследующего блондинку в гуще тропических джунглей, с шимпанзе в качестве Санчо Пансы и лианами в качестве средств передвижения. Прибавьте к этому вид Нью-Йорка (в последней из серий, которые шли в России), когда Тарзан прыгает с Бруклинского моста, и вам станет понятно, почему чуть ли не целое поколение социально самоустранилось» (BRODSKY 1995: 8–9).

Иосиф Бродский начинает с раскованности суставов, положившей начало раскованности мышления, но моторика была частью более широкого слома. Невербальные

[1] «Поражает контраст: белое питательное молоко и истощенное тело, потухший взгляд. Он держит бутылку с молоком, но, похоже, отнюдь не торопится сделать глоток и утолить жажду», пишет Катарина Уоллерстайн, анализируя эстетику отверженности в современной модной рекламе (УОЛЛЕРСТАЙН 2006: 124).

искусства этого периода меняют парадигму восприятия – и зрительную, и акустическую, и фильм становится одним из самых мощных проводников нового опыта. Если в книге Вайля и Гениса (1996) кино выпадает из «мира советского человека», Бродский передал опыт своего поколения по-другому:

> «Подозреваю, что мое поколение составляло самую внимательную аудиторию для всех этих до- и послевоенных продуктов фабрики снов. Некоторые из нас на какое-то время стали завзятыми киноманами, но, вероятно, по другим причинам, нежели наши ровесники на Западе. Для нас кино было единственным способом увидеть Запад. Начисто забывая про сюжет, мы старались рассмотреть все, что появлялось на экране, – улицу или квартиру, приборную панель в машине героя, одежду, которую носила героиня, ощутить место, структуру пространства» (Brodsky 1995: 13).

Ему вторит много лет спустя Эдуард Лимонов:

> «Глядя на голливудских девушек и суровых гангстеров в двубортных костюмах и шляпах, запоминала русская молодежь модели одежды [...] Эди-бэби [...] воспитывает в себе мужской характер. В данном случае он подражает персонажу одного из нескольких ковбойских фильмов, которые Хрущев привез из Америки и разрешил показывать населению» (Лимонов 2005: 48, 152).

Американский абстрактный экспрессионизм могли увидеть посетители американской выставке в Сокольниках, к которым принадлежали далеко не все жители Москвы. Звуки модернисткой музыки Шенберга, Волконского и Шнитке были достоянием закрытых групп, посещавших концерты в доме композиторов. Фильм «*Америка глазами француза*» Франсуа Райшенбаха (*L'Amérique insolite*, 1958) увидели, а музыку Джованни Фуско из фильма Антониони «*Затмение*» (*L'Eclisse*, 1962) услышали несколько миллионов. Кино было доступно всем слоям населения, оно формирует манеру видеть, слышать, двигаться; оно часть процесса универсализации восприятия и воображения, на которые реагируют журналисты, писатели, социологи и антропологи.

В конце пятидесятых годов французские философы замечают, что визуальная информация и коммуникация способна провоцировать социальный и психологический дисбаланс. С включением в повседневный визуально-акустический опыт и телеизображения, перемежающего рекламу, серии, старые фильмы и новости, начинается еще более интенсивный процесс порабощения воображения человека визуальной информацией. Воспринимая вербальную информацию, субъект продолжает оставаться в своем мире. Визуальная информация, внедряясь в его воображение, переструктурирует его восприятие и становится частью его реальности, вернее, субъект видит себя частью этого воображаемого мира (Cohen-Séat 1959). Одним из первых в советской среде обратил внимание на феномен подобного психологического разлада Хрущев в своей тайной речи, замечая, что Сталин судил о реальности по картинам, предлагаемым им советским кино, и перенимал поведенческие модели управления закрытой группой из американских гангстерских фильмов (Talbott 1971: 578).

Фильмы оттепели освежили нарративы «романа воспитания», принятые в сталинском кино, в другом визуальном стиле. Литературные синопсисы сюжетов и еще более рецензии на фильмы в критике того времени поражают сегодня их близостью к риторике до-оттепельного периода.[2] Параллельно этой вербальной и нарративной

---

[2] Валерий Фомин издал важные документы, позволяющие проследить за историей запрета известных фильмов этого времени в обсуждениях, внутренних рецензиях, доносах (Фомин 1992; 1993; 1998).

стабильности меняются, однако, все физиогномические критерии фильма – свет, акустическое пространство, лица, телесное поведение и аффективный костюм героев, их голоса, их предметное окружение. Яркая солнечная погода, сияющий свет или глубокие тени, насыщенные локальные краски поздних сталинских фильмов (пылающий красный, пронзительная синька, яркая зелень и желтизна «*Падения Берлина*» Михаила Чиаурели, 1949, или «*Щедрого лета*» Бориса Барнета, 1950) сменяется серой гаммой черно-белых фильмов, пастельными красками цветных фильмов и обильными дождями, заливающими советский экран не только у Тарковского. Эти потоки воды вызваны не привязанностью к «оттепельной» метафорике. В это время дождь распространен и у итальянцев, французов и немцев, отсылающих эту климатическую особенность к моде на японское кино.[3] Дождь в «*Деле Румянцева*» (1956) мотивирован драматически (из-за дождя шофер не может затормозить и ранит девушку; грязью преступник замывазывает номер машины), но одновременно он меняет и визуальные параметры. Дождь по-иному рассеивает свет и смягчает краски. Слякоть и грязь, мокрая темная одежда, «лепящая тело», слипшиеся волосы и небритые лица создают сознательно воспринимаемый новый стиль, определенный как «документальный», и невоспринимаемую сознательно визуальную атмосферность, которая резко меняет «температуру кино».

В течение пяти лет производство фильмов возрастает в десять раз, от 9 картин в 1951-ом году до 104 в 1956-ом году. Также резко меняется прокатная политика, резко расширяя иностранный опыт советского зрителя. В 1949-ом году он смог впервые после затяжной паузы увидеть зарубежные фильмы, сначала трофейные, американские, итальянские, немецкие, привезенные из Германии, потом купленные для проката, и новые ленты, представленные на возобновленном после 24летней паузы в 1959-ом году Московском кинофестивале или на неделях зарубежного кино.[4] В 1956-ом году в Москве прошла неделя итальянского, в 1957-ом году – китайского и корейского, в 1958-ом году – французского кино. Освобождение кино из зажимов общего канона, расширение проката и рост сети кинотеатров привело к тому, что число зрителей за 10 лет удваивается.[5] В 1955-ом году советский человек в среднем ходил 12,5 раз в кино, в 1966-ом году – 18,5 и в 1967-ом году – 19,1 раз (Фомин 1998: 90; *Ежегодник кино* 1957: 73, *Экран* 1968: 73).

Экономическая политика студий с установкой на недорогие фильмы поддерживает новый стиль, в котором советское кино следует *интернациональной* моде на анонимную реальность без интерпретации. Эта программа определяет документальную эстетику авторского кино Франции и Англии – free cinema, cinéma verité, nouvelle vague, кино новой волны в Польше или Чехословакии, которые следуют опыту итальянского

Виталий Трояновский руководил изданием двух томов (Трояновский 1996: 2002), в которых подробно проанализированы новые нарративы, новые герои и их восприятие современной критикой. Это стоит в центре внимания и американского исследования: Josephine Woll (Woll 2000). Очень ценны и публикация документов из архива ЦК (Афанасьева, Афиани 2001). В совокупности эти книги следуют тайной, частной и явной истории кинооттепели. Лишь в немногих статьях анализируются невербальные критерии, как например анализ Ирины Изволой пространственных деформаций в кино оттепели (Изволова 1998).

[3] Об этом говорит Клод Соте в своем предсмертном 15-часовом интервью с N. T. Binh и Dominique Raburdin в фильме «*Claude Sautet La magie invisible*», France 2002.

[4] Если в 1949 в кинотеатрах шли 19 зарубежных фильмов, в 1956 г. их число возрасло до 79 картин ихз Индии, Мексики, Италии, Австрии, ГДР, Японии, ФРГ, Бельгии, Греции (*Ежегодник кино* 1957: 73–128). С 1969 г. в прокате стабильно поддерживалось чилсо 99 иностранных фильмов, половина из них из стран Восточной Европы.

[5] В 1956 г. было продано 2 812 000 миллиардов билетов, в 1966 г. – 4 192 000 и в 1968 г. – 4 717 000 (данные по Народное хозяйство СССР 1971: 677). Этот рост посещений ведет к росту доходов от кино, даже при низких ценах на билеты. (Народное хозяйство СССР 1986: 529).

неорелизма. Признаками новой объективности становятся теперь натуральный солнечный свет вместо искуственного, улицы и оригинальные интерьеры вместо кино-ателье и построенных декораций, дедраматизация вместо интриги, черно-белое изо-бражение с грубым зерном вместо цветного, типажи вместо актеров, небрежная прическа и отсутствие грима на лицах и тех и других, который до этого полностью сглаживал фактуру кожи и у мужчин и у женщин, стирая следы возраста, болезни, бес-соницы, социального состояния. Камера снимается со штатива и свободно движется, наблюдает за молчащими протагонистами, не отличимыми от случайных прохожих, ухватывает случайности потока жизни, не артикулированные настроения. Камера наб-людает и регистрирует изменения в облике города и людей, в их формах коммуникации, в их манере двигаться и интонировать фразы, что становится интерес-нее, нежели традиционные кинофабулы. В документальном кино становится модным прием скрытой камеры, следующей за покупателями, посетителями театра или музея. Если интерьеры сталинских фильмов определялись цехом, актовым залом, бюро и большой («помпезной») квартирой, то в конце 1950-х годов действие (включая об-суждение производственных проблем) переносится в маленькую комнату или спальню общежития, которые доминируют над публичными пространствами. Зрители ста-новятся свидетелями подсмотренной чужой интимной жизни, в которой они узнают детали своей.

> «Нас долго пичкали в искусстве плакатными образами людей, парадной действительностью. Кадры ставились «точкой на фасад». Сегодня некоторые фильмы сворачивают с проспектов в переулки, точка зрения камеры и художника захватывает задворки, где не все еще расчищено, где есть мусор, хлам, старье. В после зрения попадет человек, снявший костюм, в котором он ходит в театр»,

пишут Хуциев и Миронер после завершения съемок фильма «*Весна на Заречной улице*» (Хуциев, Миронер 1957: 128). Московская студия имени Горького становится адвокатом этого «*переулочного*» реализма.

Фильмы пользуются массой субкодов, которые имеют мало отношения к развитию сюжета (остающего в рамках принятого нарратива – покорение природы и социализация индивидуума), но дающим нам представление о том, чем завтракают (сигаретой, консервами или манной кашей), на какой диете сидят, где покупают одежду и какую, какими духами душатся «роскошные» женщины, какие подарки делают девушке (часы-браслет) и сколько они стоят, сколько зарабатывает повар, директор сберкассы и лесоруб, какие салаты готовят для вечеринки, под какие пластинки танцуют, на какие фильмы ходят в кино, какие прически модны, каким видом спорта занимаются (машинистка перепечатывает на машинке руководство по йоге, бухгалтер делает в бюро зарядку под радио, молодой стиляга ходит в студию бокса), куда едут в отпуск (в Гагру или на Ладогу), что едят во время обеденного перерыва в столовой (лесорубы – щи и гречневую кашу, однако без мяса, рабочие – кефир с батоном, младшие научные сотрудники – просто кефир, а замдиректора сберкассой – рыбные палочки), что делать, когда кончаются деньги, сколько зарабатывает шофер такси, сколько стоит участок под Москвой, за сколько лет можно накопить на свою машину, столько стоит межугородний разговор и слово в телеграмме, билет на самолет, какая жилая норма принята при распределении квартир, где наконец можно (скорее невозможно) переспать с любимой (Михаил Калик показывает в «*Любить*» (1968), как тщетны усилия мужчины и женщины найти место для удовлетворения спонтанного эротического желания и как они пытаются снять номер в гостинице, пристроиться на скамейке в парке, заднем сидении в такси, на опушке в осеннем лесу или в подъезде). Подобные детали не засоряли сюжетов фильмов 1930-х и 1950-х годов. Тем нео-жиданнее кажется скачок в моделях *быто-*

вого поведения киногероев, если мы отстранимся от сюжета, между «*Люди на мосту*» (1959) и «*Иду на грозу*» (1964). В первом внебрачные отношения должны быть узаконены браком, у героев на экране нет свободного от работы времени (и чувства юмора), они не обладают почти никакими личными вещами и не отвлекаются на «частное». Во втором героиня, о профессии которой мы ничего не узнаем, ездит на своем мотоцикле, ходит на йогу, копирует при-чески актрис из киножурналов, загорает на набережной у Петропавловской крепости. Герои мобильны и движутся между Москвой, Ленинградом, Новосибирском, Ладогой, Марселем и Кавказом. Они целуются не только на пустынной улице, но в пере-полненном автобусе, дурачат милицию и не спешат идти в загс. В «*Високосном годе*» (1961) желание героя отдыхать в Гаграх, обедать в ресторане, выиграть в лотерею одновременно с нежеланием жениться на забеременевшей девушке вызывает недо-умение у его родителей и криминализируется в сюжете, в «*Июльском дожде*» (1966) это принятое поведение среднего научного сотрудника.

Вещи в интерьере и платья, рубашки, плащи, прически, бусы становятся свидетелями времени и хранителями памяти и открывают заметные социальные и индивидуальные ньюансы. Имитируя скрытую камеру, Хуциев наблюдает за манерой курить, сидеть, слушать музыку, обмениваться асемантичными жестами, устанавливающими контакт. Это мотивируется тем, что герои в фильме становятся наблюдателями документальной жизнь вокруг них. Юноша наблюдает в троллейбусе за девушкой, сидящей напротив («*Мне 20 лет*», 1961/64), которая читает и не замечает наблюдателя-камеру, начинающую преследовать ее и подмечать, как она поправляет волосы, смеется, пьет кофе в уличном кафе, разговаривает по телефону из будки, рассматривает афиши, едет в метро, идет по улице. Так попадают в кадр вечеринки, кухни, транспорт, танцы в подворотне, выпивка на детской площадке, пение у костра, кофе из бумажных стаканчиков, вино, которое пьют из бутылки, и макароны, которые едят из кастрюли, спонтанная пирушка с консервами, которых едят с ножа. Это антропологическое внимание к физической стороне быта ведет к желанию ехать в деревню и снимать фильмы среди крестьян как Флаерти среди эскимосов или полинезийцев, наблюдая за рабочими или крестьянами, как это делает Кира и Александр Муратовы в «*Наш честный хлеб*» (1964) или Андрей Михалков-Кончаловский в «*Истории Аси Клячиной*» (1966).

Сюжет перевоспитания, столь характерный для сталинского кино, смягчается жанром комедии («*Высота*», 1956, «*Весна на Заречной улице*», 1956, «*Неподдаю-щиеся*», 1959, «*Девчата*», 1961). Работница курит и вульгарна («*Высота*»), рабочий не понимает классической музыки и не владеет грамматикой («*Весна на Заречной улице*»). Пара из «*Падения Берлина*» – сталевар, не знающий Пушкина, и учительница, декла-мирующая стихи, чей неравный брак благославляется Сталиным, – преобразуется здесь в screwball комедию о борьбе и примирении неравных полов, о браке барышни, которая любит Блока, и неграмотного хулигана. Эти простые корректуры мифо-логизиро-ванного советским кино гегемона истории пролетариата воспринимаются как знак обновления и индивидуализации.

То, что лица актеров небриты, потны, усталы, одежда грязна и поношена, домашняя обстановка бедна, в физиогномике ощущаются национальные различия (рядом со стандартным украинским шутником и обаятельным грузином появляется вдруг еврейская девушка на выданье), на улицах слякоть и грязь, воспринимается как знак «правды» и придают схематическому действию «*Весны на Заречной улице*», мало отличающемуся от прежних нарративов перевоспитания, бытовую достоверность.

Ни один из этих фильмов не стал фаворитом проката. Директор Мосфильма Иван Пырьев нашел на студии документальных фильмов (!) молодого выпускника ВГИКа Эльдара Рязанова и предложил ему поставить комедию в цвете. Не «*Летят журавли*» был прокатным чемпионом 1957-ом году (фильм попал на десятое место, собрав 28,3 миллионов зрителей), а комедия ошибок «*Девушка без адреса*» Рязанова, которую увидели 36,4 милионов.[6] В «*Карнавальной ночи*» (1958) Рязанов предложил музыкальный фильм с советской Диной Дурбин, Людмилой Гурченко, объем талии которой (47 см) стал предметом обсуждения и восхищения, состоявший наполовину из новогоднего ревю и обновивший сюжет о бюрократе, поставленным управлять самодеятельным искусством. В 1962-ом году зрители предпочли не «*Чистое небо*» или «*Девять дней одного года*» с оттепельными сюжетами и героями (реабилитированный летчик и атомный физик), которые получили главные призы социалистических кинофестивалей в Москве и Карловых Варах, a science-fiction-мелодрама «*Человек-амфибия*» (1961). Фильм собрал небывалое доселе, рекордное число зрителей 65,4 миллионов.[7] Нежный юноша Ихтиандр в исполнении Владимира Коренева, получеловек-полурыба, обитает как свободное существо на дне моря. Человек-амфибия был продуктом сознательного научного эксперимента, благородным прекрасным Франкештейном, любимым прелестной девушкой, исполняемой юной Анастасией Вертинской. Его движения поражают неземной грациозностью, он ведет себя как Робин Гуд, помогая бедным ловцам жемчуга, он живет в чистой природе как герой Руссо, не знает деформаций социального устройства и становится объектом охоты алчных преступников. Экзотическая атмосфера средиземногоморского города, стильные западные интерьеры с современным дизайном, эффектные подводные съемки сделали «*Человека-амфибию*» самым успешным фильмом *всего* оттепельного времени.[8] Картина настолько смутила начальство, что режиссер Владимир Чеботарев не под-пускался к подобным сюжетам, а Коренев, ставшей иконой советской гомосексуальной общины, исчез с экрана. «Ихтиандр? Какой там Ихтиандр! Тарзан с жабрами!», возмутилась *Литературная газета*, предвосхищая панегрик Тарзану Иосифа Бродского (*Литературная газета*, 20 января 1962).

Киноначальство боится популярности Ихтиандра, но общество не знает страха не перед чем, даже ни перед новой неконтрулируемой социальной группой – молодежью, которая криминализирована в Америке («*The Wild One*», 1953; «*The Black Board Jungle*», 1955) и в Европе («*Avant le déluge*», 1954, «*Les tricheurs*», 1958, во Франции, «*The Damned*», 1963, в Англии, «*Die Halbstarken*», 1956, в ФРГ, «*Berlin Ecke Schönhauser*», 1956, и «*Glatzkopfbande*», 1960, в ГДР), вместе с роком, мотоциклами, новой модой и новыми раскрепощенными движениями.

Физиогномика героя

В это время в западном кино намечена резкая смена гендерных ролей. Слишком сильные женщины, обретшие во время войны самостоятельность, и ставшие слабыми импотентные невротичные андрогинные мужчины смущают обычный фабульный порядок. Подростки – Джеймс Дин, Бриджит Бардо – занимают места первого любовника и фамм фаталь. Американские и европейские подростки копируют жесты и манеру одеваться Джеймса Дина, Вайда делает Збигнева Цибульского его польской вариацией. Стиль Элвиса Пресли и новых западных танцев раскрепостил колени, бедра, плечи, руки, шею. Походка американских актеров, выбрасывающих ногу от бедра, как

---

[6] Эти цифры печатались в *Искусстве кино* и в *Советском экране*, сейчас эт данные по статистике советского проката собраны и опубликованы Сергеем Кудрявцевым в мультимедиальной Энциклопедии кино (Кудрявцев 2003).

[7] Подобного количества зрителей не мог собрать до этого ни один советский фильм. В предыдущие пять лет 32–35 миллионов считались самой высокой цифрой.

[8] Только в 1966 г. на исходе кинооттепели «*Операция «Ы» и другие приключения Шурика*» побила этот рекорд, собрав 69,6 миллионов зрителей.

манекенщицы, перенимается советскими молодыми людьми. Мода на высокие тонкие каблуки-шпильки меняет походку женщин. Вызывающая телесность поддерживается модой – ноги подчеркнуты узкими брюками и постепенно укорачивающимися юбками, рубашки расстегнуты и открывают грудь. Карикатуры в «*Крокодиле*» на наркоманов, танцующих буги-вуги и рок-энд-ролл, рейды народных дружин, которые вылавливали стиляг, разрезая слишком узкие брюки, не могли остановить эту новую моду и в советском быту. На экране они появляются поздно – в оперетте Шостаковича « *Черемушки*» (1964) Американизация техник тела и коммуникативных жестов, форм приветствия и прощания, манеры сидеть и ходить, становится глобальным процессом, значимым не только для России, но и для всей Европы; она формирует молодежную неформальную культуру.[9] До студенческих волнений и сексуальной революции еще далеко, но подростки, исполнителям которых по шестнадцать-семнадцать лет, представлены на экране в основном через конфликты с взрослыми. Контраст их худых, гибких, хрупких тел с корпулентными и атлетическими телами старшего поколения еще более оттеняет их другой телесный язык. В реальности для них нет помещений (ни диско, ни клубов, ни кафе), поэтому полем их действия становится город. Их телесные техники приспособлены к городскому ландшафту, но одновременно представлены как «стихийные», «природные».

Бриджит Бардо вводит этот новый тип в европейском кино, который поначалу смягчается жанром комедии. Провокация воспринимается гораздо острее в мелодраме «*И Бог создал женщину*» (1956). Она, дитя природы, трудно воспитываемый ребенок, выросший без родителей и надзора, с друзьями-животными, обладает повышенной сенсуальностью и чувством собственного тела. Все ее позы «непринужденно анимальны». У нее ритмичная пружинистая походка манекенщицы и танцовщицы, но ходит она босиком по асфальту, сидит с ногами на столе, ложится во время чинной коктейльной вечеринки взрослых на пол, ест руками, облизывает пальцы, катается по песку. Все ее движения и телесные навыки воспринимаются как вызывающе эротичные: езда на велосипеде, манера танцевать, сидеть, лежать. Также поразительна пластика Джеймса Дина, его кошачья походка, его опасные трюки. Его прыжок с поезда на полном ходу кажется таким легким, но стоит подражающему Дину Збигневу Цыбульскому – жизни.

Фильмы с Джеймсом Дином и мелодрамы с Бардо не шли в советском прокате. Бардо была знакома лишь по комедии Кристиана-Жака «*Бабетта идет на войну*» (1959) и по фотографиям в «*Искусстве кино*». Но эту новую манеру двигаться, танцевать и одеваться вопроизводят популярные в советском прокате иностранные тела Збигнева Цибульского («*Пепел и алмаз*», 1958, «*Поезд*», в советском прокате «*Загадочный пассажир*», 1959, «*Как быть любимой*», 1962) и др.) и Сильваны Мангано («*Горький рис*», 1949). Беспокойное тело Цибульского было постоянно в движении. В его опасных прыжках (на идущий поезд), пританцовывающих пируэтах, манере ходить и сидеть — на полу, на земле, на столе, на всем том, что не придумано для сидения, – была элегантная небрежность. Руки в карманах, поднятые плечи, шаркающие ноги: потерянность, ранимость послевоенного молодого поколения грациозно изживалась в новой субъективности, сделавшей возможным для мужчин плакать и отчаиваться. Сильвана Мангано дебютировала в эротической крестьянской мелодраме, демон-стрируя на экране элементарные физические действия – еду, сон, неприхотливый туа-лет, тяжелую

[9] Неслучайно именно в это время позникает огромное количество исследований жестового поведения и невербальной коммуникации. Антрополг Ray L. Birdwhistell вводит новую дисциплину кинетику (Introduction to kinesics: an anotation system for analysis of body motion and gesture, 1952). Edward T. Hall обосновывает проксемику (The Hidden Dimension, 1966), а америкаснкий социаолог Erwin Goffman публикает свое исследование «*The Presentation of Self in Everyday Life*» (1956).

работу. В ее юном теле, которое появлилось на экране в разорванных чулках, мужской рубашке, и коротких щортах вибрировала энергия и эротика. Это тело было введено в действие в новом американском – неприличном, расрепощенном – танце буги-вуги, также как тело Бардо достигало полной свободы в эстатичной эротичной самбе. Мангано бешено вертела бедрами, плечами, руками, и ее движения восхищали женщин и мужчин. Расрепощение суставов было перенято в быт, в синкопичные ритмы с резкой переменой от быстрого, импульсивного движения к замедленному эстетизировали ее простые физические действия. Мангано играла своеноравную, дерзкую девчонку, не знающую деликатных манер, но заразительную в телесной свободе.

Новые телесные техники вербализрованы в переведенном Ритой Райт-Ковалевой культовом романе «*Над пропастью во ржи*» (1951; русс. 1960). Роман очень физический, и его действие происходит в душевых, спальнях, туалетах. Там стригут ногти, причесываются, почесываются, вытирают носы, моются, хихикают, напиваются. Герой Селинджера обучен многим телесным техникам, которые сегодня не так уж приняты (он умеет фехтовать, играть в гольф, он любит танцевать) но в остальном он проваливается везде: его бьют, он падает, спотыкается, плачет, рыдает. Он идет по Пятой авеню без галстука (!), бежит сломя голову, скатывается с лестницы. Он обладает подвижностью ребенка, которой он восхищается в своей сестренке Фиби. Примечательно то, что советская молодежная литература этого времени, чувствуя раскрепощение суставов, вводит массу жаргонных слов, чтобы описать элементарные телесные техники – походку, сидение, жесты приветствия, и этот сленг передает новое «развинчивание» суставов (не ходить, а хилять).

И в России молодые киногерои перестают следовать установленному в тридцатые годы на экране коду «культурного» и «приличного» поведения. Чтобы понять это, стоит взглянуть, как воспитывался код новой походки на советском экране – при помощи привлекательных тел советских звезд – Любови Орловой, Сергея Столярова.

Тренированная, ритмически организованная походка или маршировка в советских фильмах двадцатых годов была атрибутом угнетателей. Идеальная синхронность и ритмичность их ног была кодирована как часть бездушной машины подавления. Однако в середине двадцатых годов зарождается новая мода. Фильмы – и документальные и художественные – показывают, как дети и пионеры обучаются маршировке – то есть ритмичному синхронному осознанному шагу. А с тридцатых годов маршируют все. В хронике первых парадов 1918 года видно, что солдаты не умеют держать строй, их спины не упруги. Но в 1936 году парад выглядит по-другому. И актеры (в фильме «*Цирк*»), и непрофессиональные участники демонстраций (в документальной картине «*Цветущая молодость*») достигли необходимой синхронности движений и военной выправки. Маршировка, первая базисная техника тела, помогает научиться пружинистой, спортивной походке. Так движутся советские кинотела мужчины и женщины в рабочем цеху, на параде, на сцене, на свидании. Чтобы подчеркнуть, какой походкой овладела в процессе «цивилизации» неуклюжая крестьянка Любови Орловой из «*Светлого пути*» (1941), режиссер вклеивает в финале фильма длинный эпизод ее прохода черным силуэтом на фоне сияющего светлого фона, чтобы зрители смогли разглядеть движение ноги с вытянутым носком, выпрямленную спину, разворот корпуса, постановку головы. В советском кино офицер может стоять расслабленно, но традиционно военная выправка (стойка смирно или вольно) перенимается в быт – и мужчинами и женщинами. Эта военизированная походка пародируется в Голливуде, и трансформация походки красного комиссара Ниночки Греты Гарбо идет от маршировки к вальсирующему, танцевальному шагу.

В шестидесятые годы по сравнению с инсценированными красавицами Голливуда и подражающими им дамами «нимфетки» нового европейского кино кажутся вызывающе «природными». Брижжит Бардо ходит босиком, но строит походку как профессиональная балерина. Раскрепощению ног и бедер помогают новые танцы. Так же в конце пятидесятых годоа раскрепощается походка и советских киногероинь – в фильме «*Высота*» при помощи чечетки.

В этом фильме раскрепощение телесного языка молодых рабочих, Николая Рыбникова и Инны Макаровой, мотивировано в сюжете двумя обстоятельствами: они выросли в детских домах (как Бардо) и ведут кочевую жизнь вне установленных форм семейного порядка. Однако эта «беспризорная» свобода от «норм» воспринимается как непринужденная естественность. Герои по профессии монтажники-высотники, поэтому их рабочие движения отличает легкость и лихость, их телам придана акробатическая ловкость (в «производственный фильм» вводится тело героев мюзикла или циркового представления). Они исполняют опасные трюки при монтаже на высоте, карабкаются по отвесным плоскостям, отбивают чечетку на узкой дощечке, съезжают по канату, спускаются с балкона на веревке. И в быту их жесты отличаются от демонстрируемой в начале пятидесятых годов сдержанной нормы культурного поведения. Рабочие едят лежа, сидят развалившись, открывают бутылку пива зубами, дерутся. Их грубость и вульгарность, тем не менее, не подается как физиологически отвратительная (как это делало, например, кино 1930-х годов, воспитывая население). В интимном разговоре между друзьями появляются иные жесты, с более подвижной кистью и ладонью, отличающие их от ораторов пятидесятых годов, над которыми в кино уже смеются. Девушка Катя Инны Макаровой перенимает манеры хулиганистого подростка, курит, приветствует парня широким ударом по открытой ладони, свистит как мальчишка и взбирается к кому-то на закорки, но эта травестия манер подана теперь как кокетливая вызывающая эротичность, осознанная режиссером и провоцирующая фиктивного героя. Она вызывающе танцует, обнажает ногу, чтобы снять чулок, ходит по городскому парку босиком, правда с иной мотивировкой, нежели Бардо, «естественной» грации которой мешает стесняющая обувь, здесь девушка ходит босиком, чтобы беречь туфли. Эти раскрепощенные манеры меняются к концу фильма, потому что герои перевоспитываются и становятся похожими на сдержанных интеллигентов, мужчину-инженера и женщину-врача, их учителей. Сдерживание «жестов» идет параллельно убиранию «красок»: герой Рыбникова движется в конце на костылях после аварии, а его подруга Катя меняет красно-зеленую одежду на пастельную гамму и белый халат медсестры, перестает курить, учится сервировать стол и начинает пить кефир из стакана, а не из бутылки. Фильм демонстрирует, несмотря на традиционный сюжет дисциплинирования анархичного хулиганского тела, что понятия невоспитанности и развязности меняются. Они теперь оцениваются не как вульгарность, а как «открытость», а раннее так высоко ценимые приличие и воспитанность (ноги сжаты, руки сложены или прижаты к телу, тело напряжено) в этом контексте воспринимается как «закрытость», скованность, закомплексованность. И этот пример был заразителен, как вспоминает актриса о своей Кате:

> «Как лихо она носится по высотным сооружениям, и, как над бездной, на огромной высоте отплясывает свой залихватский танец, и как отправляется в ресторан – погулять! [...] Знаете, такая вот внешняя бравада была очень популярна тогда, в пятидесятые годы. Многие девушки старались вести себя так «эмансипированно», как моя Катя» (Макарова 1977: 192).

В «*Девчатах*» (1961) появляется неуклюжий подросток, тоже сирота без манер из детского дома, мальчик-девочка, без груди и без бедер, с крысиными косичками. Актриса Надежда Румянцева ориентируется на клоунессу Джульетту Мазину, поразившую воображение советских кинематографистов в феллиниевской «*Дороге*»

(1959). В Румянцевой нет «старой женственности», она не умеет кокетничать и целоваться, она дерется подушками, скачет, и как клоун носит слишком большие валенки, падает и спотыкается. Мужская бригада в фильме наделена шиком приблатненных «апашей». Эти традиционные киномаски – клоунессы и апаша – кодируются также как аутентичность и спонтанность. Николай Рыбников использует этот телесный костюм в каждом фильме. В «*Весне на Заречной улице*» его герой сталевар, одетый в кожаное пальто, спрыгивает с едущей машины, как Джеймс Дин с поезда. Хуциев сталкивает два тела – окультуренное и сырое, которые становятся физиогномической основой сюжета перевоспитания. Рабочие ходят без галстуков и пиджаков, приличный «дресс код» закрепляется за инженером. В конце апаш превращается в атлета с легкой походкой, без развалки, с ритмично движущимися руками.

Также мотивировано выпадание из пластики в «*Карьере Димы Горина*» – монтажники-высотники ходят по проводам как канатоходцы. Герой Александра Демьяненко, тоже, кстати, сирота, играет, как и Джерри Льюис, асексуального «переростка-подростка», переполненного бушующими гормонами, который влюбляется, как и Джерри Льюис в «*Художники и модели*» (1955) в девушку из «комикса». Он склеивает свою идеальную красавицу из фотографий «Советского экрана», составляя ее из Элизабет Тейлор (лоб и прическа), Аллы Ларионовой (рот и подбородок) и носа Всеволода Пудовкина в роли юродивого из «*Ивана Грозного*». Получается Татьяна Конюхова, которую Демьяненко находит на стройке в Сибири.

Повести Василия Аксенова и Анатолия Гладилина, пьесы Виктора Розова и Алексея Арбузова вводят этих новых героев: «звездных» мальчиков, «младших братьев», сбежавших из дома студентов и подростков, разбивающих саблей времен гражданской войны полированную мебель родителей.[10] Но физиогномика и моторика этих новых героев формируется в кино. Целый ряд фильмов регистрирует новые техники тела молодежи, и сюжетом многих фильмов становятся шатания по Москве, поэтому ходьба – основная характеристика героя. Герои «*Мне двадцать лет*» (1961/64) созданы Валентином Поповым, Николаем Губенко, Станиславом Любшиным походкой. С прогулок на рассвете по абсолютно пустому городу начинается «*Летят журавли*». Никита Михалков в «*Я шагаю по Москве*» (1964) вводит походку шестнадцатилетнего фланера – вразвалку, глазея, не спеша. У подростков сутулые спины и длинные болтающиеся руки. Также расслаблено и «открыто» их сидение – расставив колени, сгорбившись, опираясь на локти. Даже солдаты ходят вразвалку, и их шаг ничем не отличается от ходьбы штатских. Не маршируют и на демонстрации первого мая («*Мне двадцать лет*»), она совсем расхлябанно-растрепанная – все бегут и смеются, никто не умеет и не собирается держать шаг и ряд. Походка «тематизируется», осваивается, дифференцируется. Марлен Хуциев показывает в «*Мне двадцать лет*», как ходит профессиональная манекенщица (но снабжает ее в сюжете фильма деревенскими корнями). Герои его «*Июльского дождя*» (1966) наблюдают, как сидят, выскакивают из машин и ходят как иностранные дипломаты. Походки и осанки документальных москвичей ненамного отличаются от поведения фиктивных персонажей. Юноша и девушка (Александр Белявский, Евгения Уралова) ходят теперь не чинно, под руку, а в обнимку. Фильм регистрирует новую стремительность. Герои летят по лестнице вниз и

[10] Эти повести и пьесы экранизируются: Александр Зархи ставит «*Мой младший брат*» по «*Звездному билету*» (1962), Алексей Сахаров экранизирует «*Коллеги*» (1962) Аксенова, Анатолий Эфрос и Георгий Натансон переносит на экран пьесу Розова «*Шумный день*» (1961). Но не фильмы становятся наиболее яркими выражениями молодежной культуры, а фильмы по оригинальным сценариям Геннадия Шпаликова, Евгения Григорьева, Анатолия Гребнева: «*Мне двадцать лет*» (1961/64), «*Я шагаю по Москве*» (1964) и «*Три дня Виктора Чернышева*» (1968)

вверх («*Летят журавли*», «*Мне двадцать лет*»). Странные жестовые «фортеля» «смягчают» язык пожилых функционеров.

Бег становится знаком юности (витальности, энергии, переполняющих тело эмоций). Герои владеют разными темпами. После стремительного полета по лестнице – замедленное приближение друг к другу. Походка становится подпрыгивающей, шутовской. На бегу успеть забить футбольный мяч в ворота или вскочить на ходу в троллейбус – особый шик. Это развивается в восьмидесятые и девяностые годы до опасных трюков городского «сервинга» на идущих электричках: открывания двери на полном ходу, висения над шпалами и мостами (ср. «*Метро*» Люка Бессонна, 1985).

Код «хороших манер», усвоенных крестьянами в советских фильмах тридцатых годов, сбивается. Выпрямленность спины, сжатые колени, неподвижные руки теперь оцениваются как знак «зажатости» и «формальности». Если раньше сдержанный язык начальника – знак его более высокой сознательности, то в фильмах шестидесятых это признак окостенелости или маски. Культ неформальности утверждается не агрессивно, как в двадцатые годы, а как освобождение из мускульного зажима. Все знаки раскрепощения – размахивание руками, жевание на ходу, стояние, прислонившись к стене или косяку двери, сидение развалившись, на ручке кресла, болтая ногами, повернув спинку стула к себе или распластавшись на полу – передаются теперь юным, гибким и тонким телам, не напряженным и не натренированным. Это придает техникам тела, которые могут восприниматься и как «неокультуренные» и вульгарные – грациозность, непринужденность, легкость. Спортивные игры на экране отличаются не мускульным напряжением и тяжелой нагрузкой, а шутливо-игровым началом. В фильмах устанавливается деление между профессиональным спортом, часто хоккеем, зрителями которого– на стадионе или по телевизору– становятся герои («*Ты и я*», 1971). Сами же они только на ходу гоняют мяч во дворе вместе с мальчишками, не озабоченные напряжением победы, как это было во «*Вратаре*» (1936).

Советские кинотела позволяют себе держаться раскованнее и в публичном пространстве. Напряженные мускулы освобождаются из-под строгого контроля. Раскованные позы и сутулые спины становятся знаком антиавторитарного поведения, неформальной культуры.

Наряду с этим заметны и другие перемены: исчезают с экрана параллельные и дугообразные жесты. Фольклорные крестьяне появляются только в фильмах-сказках. Из молодежного языка исчезают ораторские жесты: ритмичные подчеркивания слов скандирующей рукой, удары кулаком. В «*Летят журавли*» две молодые комсомолки приходят от имени фабкома прощаться с героем, уходящим на фронт, и, скандируя слова прощания, сопровождают свою речь ритмизирующими жестами трибуна – агрессивными взмахами кулака от локтя. Отец героя, старый хирург, останавливает их, передразнивает эти ораторские взмахи кулаком, и предлагает им перейти к другим формам общения – застолью – и поднять руки в тосте.

Возвращается дифференциация «профессиональных» движений, военного / штатского, женского/мужского, взрослого/ детского, молодого/старого и разграничение интимной и публичной сферы. В фильмах появляются документально заснятые диспуты, спектакли, выступления поэтов, вернисажи. Их трибунная публичность отделена от «интимности», сохраняемой в публике. Во время слушания стихов в Политехническом музее герои «*Мне двадцать лет*» обмениваются только им заметными и понятными жестами, спрятанными от посторонних взоров и вынесенными на крупный план.

Даже если эта молодежь танцует на улице, то в этом открытом пространстве инсценируется интимность. Они новые городские беспризорники. В публичном пространстве культуры – в библиотеке или в музее – они обязаны поддаваться «запрету» на движение и шум. Поэтому они обживают как «свое» пространство подворотню, где устраиваются танцы; детскую площадку, на которой три друга в рассветных сумерках обсуждают отношения. Публичное превращается в интимное – иначе, чем в двадцатые годы. Улицы, бульвары, троллейбусы, почтамты, поезда, вокзалы, аэропорты и кафе обживаются опять как пространство для эротично окрашенной коммуникации, знакомств с девушками, флирта, свиданий. Сергей встречает свою прекрасную незнакомку в троллейбусе, Николай Губенко встречает и теряет ее в трамвае. Сюжет знакомства в поезде или на улице (как ни странно, не такой частый в советском кино – «*Девушка с коробкой*», 1927, «*Девушка с характером*», 1939, «*Поезд идет на восток*», 1949) актуализируется.

Молодежью перенимаются формы приветствия из других культур (двойной французский поцелуй) или архаичные формы куртуазности (целование руки). В фильмах появляется много сцен неформального общения – вместо ранее возможных митингов, собраний и торжественных пиров. В «*Мне двадцать лет*» и «*Июльском дожде*» общество распадается на интимные группы и каждый уходит в свой «контакт».

Сохраняются телесные формы контакта между друзьями (встряхивать руку, похлопывать по плечу или по спине), но они исчезают из иерархического общения, которое восстанавливается в фильмах (чего не было на экране пятидесятых). Начальников в фильмах Хуциева отличают сдержанные жесты, даже резкий диспут героя с отцом девушки, высоким начальником, сопровождается крайне сдержанной жестикуляцией. Его руки спрятаны за спиной, дочь стоит, сложив руки на груди, молодой герой вообще не двигается. Если же отец пытается употребить язык оратора в интимной среде, это вызывает сочувственную жалость.

Телесный контакт в общении между полами также переориентирован. Не только объятиям, поцелуям, танцам, но и прикосновениям между мужчиной и женщиной на экране возвращается эротический оттенок. Также возвращается эротичность еде. Флирт возможен не только в ресторане, но и в рабочей столовой – за шпротами и кефиром (у Хуциева, у Муратовой). Отсутствие столовых манер (вне сервированного стола) воспринимается как непринужденность. Бутерброды на улице, кофе из бумажных стаканчиков, вино из бутылки, макароны из кастрюли, спонтанная пирушка с консервами, которые едят с ножа, еда руками не только у костра, но и на вечеринке…

Любопытно, однако, что в то время, как экран раскрепощают зажим «культурности», начинают печататься в довольно внушительном количестве русские и переводные книги о манерах и «эстетике поведения». В книгах по домоводству появляются отделы о манерах за столом и правилах поведения со старыми узнаваемыми запретами (не смеяться громко, не махать руками, не хватить еду руками) и четкими градациями «мужского», «женского», «детского» поведения. Писатели вспоминают в автобиографиях, что их учили манерам бывшие воспитанницы института благородных девиц, и появляются переводные книги по этикету – с эстонского, немецкого, польского. Оппозиция «вульгарности – интеллигентности» заменяет понятие «культурности», над которым уже смеется Джеймс Бонд в «*Из России с любовью*» (1963).

Одновременно преобразуется выражение аффектов. Кира Муратова подолгу наблюдает за автоматическими, ошибочными, бессознательными жестами своих героев и документальных, «случайно» забредших в кадр персонажей, среди которых много непрофессионалов и провинциалов с особым стилем поведения, выбивающимся из «нормы» («*Короткие встречи*», 1966). Амплитуда жеста резко сокращается – теперь действует не рука и даже не кисть, а только пальцы, которые барабанят по столу, играют с карандашом, крошат бисквит, теребят карты, рисуют линии на тарелке, стене. Внимание к этим симптоматическим жестам, выражениям инстинктивного бессознательного, сочетается с вниманием к искалеченному телу: безногие, безрукие, слепые, уродливые, неуклюжие люди движутся по-иному. Эротика, насилие, агрессия стирается в меланхолии. Аффекты не переводятся в язык тела.

Инцестуозные либидональные энергии оправдывается в советском кино по-иному, чем на западе. На сломе 50-х и 60-х годов здесь непрпопорционально большую роль занимают герои-дети – и не в детском, а во взрослом кино. Этот выбор оправдан и производственно (молодые режиссеры дебютируют в жанре детского фильма с малым бюджетом), и концепционно. В рамках новой субъективной апроприации коллективной истории наиболее «удобным» героем становится ребенок, не обладающий тяжелой исторической памятью. Он не связан с виной и ошибками мира отцов, за которые он не может нести отвественности, да и большинство детей и подростков на экране – сироты. Дети появляются на экране как паллиативная реакция на начинающийся Gender Trouble, в котором исключена инцестуозная эротика. В английских фильмах эти неуправляемые подростки социализируются в постелях взрослых женщин, в советском варианте социализация происходит без эротики. Эксцентрическая парабола Климова «*Добро пожаловать или постронним вход воспрещен*» (1964) оживляет узор замятинской антиутопии «*Мы*», которая переносится режиссером в пионерский летний лагерь и заканчивается восстанием детей против диктатора в белых брюках, отца всех детей, с сельскохозяйственной фамилией Дынин и початком кукурузы в руке. Комбайн сметает аллею гипсовых героев, и дети прорывают вместо железного занавеса деревянный забор, ведущий в стихийную природу. Роль охраны в лагере перенимается не строгими мужчинами, а толстыми бесформенными матронами-уборщицами. Дети пародируют конфликты взрослых с властью (инакомыслие, бунт в подполье). Слишком толстые или слишком худые взрослые превращаются в фигуры комиксов, и камера разрезает эти фигуры на огромнейший разверстый рот, издающий сигнал сирены, или гигантское подслушивающее ухо. Климов включил в свою комедии элементы немого слэпстика и менял скорость съемки, которая подчеркивала другую моторику. Раскрепощение этой спонтанной моторики и новое «дикое» грациозное тело на экране было частью изменения физиогномического строя советского кино. Климовские «Тарзанчики», чья нагота минус эротика была допустима, смягчали «западные» образцы нового телесного языка, на который ориентировалась молодежь оттепели.

Наконец, интеллигент впервые появляется на экране не как отрицательный герой, и утверждение его на главную роль полностью вытесняет телесный язык простолюдина. Жестовая «интеллигентная» сдержанность становится на экране признаком всех социальных слоев во все времена: Гамлет, русский князь, провинциальный учитель, крестьянин, солдат и столичный физик обладают одним и тем же телесным языком – Иннокентия Смоктуновского.

Первыми цензурными казусами оттепели стали фильмы о молодых людях, вступающих в жизнь, – «*Тугой узел*» Михаила Швейцера (1956) и «*Застава Ильча*» Хуциева, вызвавшим возмущение Хрущева, которое он формулирует в речи 8 марта 1963 г.:

> «Даже наиболее положительные из персонажей фильма – трое рабочих парней – не являются олицетворением нашей замечательной молодежи. Они показаны так, что не знают, как им жить и к чему стремиться […] Нет, на таких людей общество не может положиться – они не борцы и не преобразователи мира. Это – морально хилые, состарившиеся в юности люди, лишенные высоких целей и призваний в жизни. […] Свое намерение осудить праздных людей, тунеядцев постановщики фильма не сумели осуществить. У них не хватило гражданского мужества и гнева заклеймить, пригвоздить к позорному столбу подобных выродков и отщепенцев». (Фомин 1998: 163).

Хуциев работал после этого два года над поправками и в 1964-ом году выпустил сокращенную версию фильма под названием «*Мне двадцать лет*», показанную в Венеции. Западные критики не смогли понять, что в этом фильме было субверсивно или провокативно. Этот вопрос остался и после того, как Хуциев в 1987/88 восстановил первоначальную версию фильма и представил ее на фестивале в Локарно. Конфликт молодого инженера со своим начальником, дискуссии молодого героя с отцом своей возлюбленной, понятые режиссером как конфронтации со «сталинистами», были настолько смутными, что открывались лишь инсайдерам. Подростки и молодые люди в еропейском кино угоняли машину, стреляли в полицейских, перевозили наркотики. В московском варианте они ходили на работу и были бравыми молодыми людьми, наполненными лишь тоской по непонятному, которую они и сами не могли артикулировать. Но нерваблизованный физиогномический слом героя и появление в бытовом фильме метафизической тоски было ново, хотя и не переведено в нарратив или поступок. Именно на эти «физиогномические» отклонения, которые и маркируют неуловимое «другое», остро реалигировали при обсуждении фильма режиссеры старого поколения, Сергей Герасимов и Марк Донской:

> «Здесь беда состоит, как мне кажется, не в том, что герой несимпатичный, как здесь говорили, а в *лексике, в фонетике, в пластическом поведении.* […] *Шагают* все-таки *шалопаи* […]. Они *даже курят шалопайски.* Пожалуйста, пусть они *ходят*, пусть не знают, что с собой делать, но пусть умеют гневаться и радоваться. [...] А у тебя не гневается, не радуется. Он *ходит*, он *курит*, он *смотрит*. [...] А что это за унылость? Ты можешь обижаться на меня, но считаю, что и людей ты подобрал благодаря твоему видению – ты плохо видишь! Ты взял Тарковского, *худосочного* – кажется, плюнь на него, и он упадет, – ты и Вознесенского специально подобрал. Ты подобрал даже не фрондирующих молодых людей... Шалопаи ходят. И не один я об этом говорю. И публично говорят. И уже в международном плане. Вы должны сказать: «Эй вы, мальчики, жалеющие меня, удалитесь от меня, я сам знаю, что делать! Убирайтесь от меня! Я понял вместе с товарищами, педагогами, председателем объединения и партийной организацией!» (Курсив мой – ОБ).[11]

Кода

В начале двадцатого века новые медиа был использован в советском обществе как своеобразный антропологический эксперимент. Фотография, плакат и кино (художественое и научно-популярное) должны были ускорить модернизацию аграрной страны и научить ее крестьянское население двигаться – ходить, переходить улицу, пользоваться трамваем – городском пространстве, мыться под душем, чистить зубы, пользоваться молотком, ножом и вилкой и не плевать на пол. В пятидесятые годы Советские Союз переживает, так же как и страны старой Европы, мощное влияние глобализации (называемой в этот период американизацией), которая осваивается как медиальный опыт. Иностранные фильмы приносят в советский быт новые манеры поведения и новую моду, и молодежь реагирует на это подвижнее поколения отцов.

Когда-то для освобождения от канона кодифицированного жеста в поисках «естественных» способов проявления эмоций режиссеры натуралистического театра обра-

[11] Выступление Марка Донского на заседании партбюро киностудии имени Горького совместно с комиссией содействия органам партийно- государственного контроля, 13 мая 1963 г. Цит. по опубликованной стенограмме ДЕМЕНОК 1988: 114.

щались к телесной выразительности животных, детей и дикарей (Тарзанов), то есть существ, не обученных культуре и не зажатых в дисциплинарные нормы цивилизации. Европейцу пятидесятых годов таким дикарем кажется американец, который кладет ноги на стол, сидит развалившись, танцует неприличные танцы и постоянно жует жвачку. В американских фильмах слом в моделях поведения мотивирован трудными подростками, которые заброшены родителями и воспитателями. В английском кино непоспитанность молодых героев мотивируется их пролетарским происхождением. В немецких фильмах – и западных и восточных – это сироты, выросшие без отцов на улице. Их непринужденный телесный язык взрывает код принятых приличия, но молодые тела актеров – Джеймса Дина, Хорста Буххольца, Лорана Терзиева, Жан-Поля Бельмондо – настолько привлекательны, что их «вульгарные», «неприличные» движения становятся образцами для подражания вопреки нарративам, в которых герои перевоспитываются – или погибают. Эти же социальные и возрастные группы служат и в советском кино поначалу мотивировкой непринужденного телесного языка. Раскрепощение походки демонстрирует, какой телесный язык способно создать тело, освобожденное от предписываемого социализацией стандарта.

Новые тела появляются на экране не в искусно сшитых сложных костюмах, но в джинсах, футболках и кожаных куртках, в рабочих халатиках, комбинезонах, туфлях без каблуков или босиком – в простой дешевой одежде, которая подчеркивает «несложное» отношение к собственному телу. Эта небрежность следует тому же принципу, что и дешевая детская одежда, в которой появилась на экране Бардо. Франция «заработала на недорогих молодых звездах и еще более дешевой моды так же много, как и на экспорте fois gras», остроумно заметила британская исследовательница (VINCENDEAU 2000: 83). Раскрепощенные движения и физическое обаяние актеров сделало возможным освобождение советского мужского тела от обязательного костюма и галстука. На работе, представленной на экране, он мог теперь проявиться в узких брюках, в рубашке с открытым воротом и джемпере. Элегантная небрежность женской одежды была на экране гораздо более проблематична. Но замена тела тяжелой славянской красавицы грациозной нимфеткой приблизила и советских кинозвезд интернациональному стандарту.

Кино оттепели началось с отталкивания от аллегорий сталинского кино, визуализирующего видение будущего, и увердило потную прозу обыденного и галлюцинации-сны о потерянном прошлом. Множество невербализованных деталей, физиогномически уловленных этими фильмами, предложили внутри старых нарративов, корректуру социальных ролей и снабдили героев техниками «частных практик», подготавливая советские тела к смене ролей, моделей поведения и новой моде. Они показали, какая мощная взрывная сила лежит в легких отклонениях от ожидаемого стандарта поведения и это стало основанием неформальной (молодежной) субкультуры. Эти атмосферные перемены происходят на протяжении одного деся-тилетия, в котором фильмы второй половины 1950-х годов резко отличаются от фильмов начала 1960-х. Радикальные перемены происходят, однако, в конце 1950-х, и последующее развитие кино – реакция на них. Пока старый нарратив обрабатывается в рамках нового визуального опыта, это провоцировало дискуссию и критику. В тот момент, когда новый физиогномический опыт переводится в нарратив, целая плеяда фильмов запрещается, что совпадает с концом кинооттепели.

Джек Керуак подвел гораздо более оптимистичный итог движению битников на западе:

> „Слово битник значило раньше […] бродяга, бездомный, ночующий в метро […] Теперь оно распространено на людей, не ночующих в метро, но отличающихся

другими манерами [...] Битник стало этикетом революции в поведения [...] и в результате не только стулья исчезнут из гостиных, но и появится битник-минист иностранных дел» (Kerouac 1979: 363, 366).

Summary

Fashion in Film does not exist as a static image. Films function as complex behavioral texts and create models that influence the motor and fashion behavior of its spectators in the everyday life. In the 1920s a Soviet society modeled a new type on the screen in order to ensure the success of industrialization and to educate the population of an agrarian country to the conditions of industrial and urban society. In the late 1950s we can observe a radical change of bodily behavior. These changes are happening in the context of an increasingly global image circulation. The foreign films penetrated the hermetically sealed off Soviet system, and Soviet films of this period visualized and simulated new types on the screen adapting a changing multicultural modernity to Soviet conditions. In the films of the 1930s an athletic military gait with the wide steps and the decisive swinging of hands was attributed to female and male protagonists in each situation (during the parade but also on a date). But in the 1960s even the rally in Red Square (like in Khutsiev's "*I am 20 years old*") is represented as an informal, relaxed walk. In the manner of walking of the generation from the 1960s we can recognize the manner of walking of American actors from the 1950s – where the motion of the foot starts from the hip and the back is relaxed. The cramped movements of the stift Soviet bodies were loosening up by new dances, new way of walking and sitting, preparing them for wearing new non-formal clothes.

Литература

Brodsky, J. 1995. *On Grief and Reason.* New York.

Brando, K., Stein, E. 1979. *Brando for Breakfast.* New York.

Cohen-Séat, G. 1959. *Problèmes actuels du cinéma et de l'information visuelle.* Paris.

Kerouac, J. 1979. *On the Road.* New York.

Krumrey, H.-V. 1984. *Entwicklungsstrukturen von Verhaltensstandarden: eine soziologische Prozenssanalyse auf der Grundlage deutscher Anstands- und Manierenbücher von 1870 bis 1970.* Frankfurt am Main.

Talbott, S. (ed) 1971. *Chruschtschow erinnert sich.* Reinbek.

Vincendeau, G. 2000. *Stars and Stardom in French Cinema.* London, New York.

Woll, J. 2000. *Real Images: Soviet Cinema and the Thaw.* London.

Афанасьева, Е., Афиани В. (ed.) 2001. *Аппарат ЦК и культура: 1953–1957. Документы.* Москва.

Бродский, И. 1995. Трофейное. In: Бродский И. *Собр. Соч. в 4 т.* СПб 1995, Том 4.

Булгакова, О. 2005. *Фабрика жестов.* Москва.

Булгакова, О. 2010. *Советский слухоглаз: кино и его органы чувств.* Москва.

Вайль, П., Генис, А. 1996. *60-е. Мир советского человека.* Москва.

Деменок, А. 1988. «Застава Ильича» - урок истории. In: *Искусство кино* 6, 101–120.

Ежегодник кино 1957. Москва.

Изволова, И. 1998. «Другое пространство». In: Трояновский В. (ed.) *Кинематограф оттепели. Книга первая.* Москва 1998, 77–98.

Лимонов, Э. 2005. *У нас была великая эпоха. Русское.* Москва.

Кудрявцев, С. 2003. *Энциклопедии кино Кирилла и Мефодия.* СД.

Макарова, И. 1977. Связь времен связь поколений. In: *Искусство кино* 11, 187–197.

Народное хозяйство СССР 1971. *Статистический ежегодник.* Москва.

Народное хозяйство СССР 1986. *Статистический ежегодник.* Москва.

Советские художественные фильмы 1961. *Аннотированный каталог.* Том 3. Москва.

Трояновский, В. 1996. *Кинематограф оттепели.* Книга первая. Москва.

Трояновский, В. 2002. *Кинематограф оттепели.* Книга вторая. Москва.

Уоллерстайн, К. 2006. Худоба и эстетика отверженности в современной модной рекламе. In: *Теория моды: одежда, тело, культура* 1. 115–138.

Фомин, В. 1992. *Полка. Документы, свидетельства. Комментарии.* Москва.

ФОМИН, В. 1993. *Запрещенные фильмы. Документы, свидетельства, комментарии.* Выпуск 2. Москва.
ФОМИН, В. 1998. *Кинематограф оттепели. Документы и свидетельства.* Москва.
ХУЦИЕВ, М., МИРОНЕР, Ф. 1957. Облик героя. In: *Искусство кино* 1, 128.
ЭКРАН. 1968. Москва.

Die Welt der Slaven

Sammelbände • Сборники

Herausgegeben von Peter Rehder und Igor Smirnov

Bd. 1: **Anton P. Čechov – Philosophische und religiöse Dimensionen im Leben und im Werk. Vorträge des Zweiten Internationalen Čechov-Symposiums, Badenweiler 20.-24. Oktober 1994.** Herausgegeben von Vladimir Kataev, Rolf-Dieter Kluge, Regine Nohejl.
1997. Hardcover. XXII, 641 S. 72.00 €. (3-87690-675-X)

Bd. 2 / 4 / 8 / 12 / 15 / 20 / 22 / 24 / 27 / 29 / 33 / 37 / 40 / 43 / 46 / 49 / 53: **Beiträge der Europäischen Slavistischen Linguistik (Polyslav).** Band 1–16. Herausgegeben u.a. von M. Bayer, M. Betsch, R. Blankenhorn, J. Błaszczak, B. Brehmer, K. Böttger, S. Dönninghaus, M. Giger, E. Graf, K.B. Karl, E. Kislova, K. Knapik-Gawin, G. Krumbholz, E. Kubicka, M. Lazar, J. Rabiega-Wiśniewska, K. Szafraniec, N. Thielemann, M. Tomancová, S. Ulrich, B. Wiemer, V. Ždanova, R. Zimny.

Bd. 1:	1998.	Hardcover. X, 212 S.	44.00 €	(ISBN 3-87690-705-5)
Bd. 2:	1999.	Hardcover. VIII, 320 S.	57.00 €	(ISBN 3-87690-738-1)
Bd. 3:	2000.	Hardcover. X, 232 S.	48.00 €	(ISBN 3-87690-773-X)
Bd. 4:	2001.	Hardcover. VIII, 292 S.	50.00 €	(ISBN 3-87690-803-5)
Bd. 5:	2002.	Hardcover. X, 303 S.	54.00 €	(ISBN 3-87690-825-6)
Bd. 6:	2003.	Hardcover. X, 281 S.	53.00 €	(ISBN 3-87690-852-3)
Bd. 7:	2004.	Hardcover. X, 251 S.	48.00 €	(ISBN 3-87690-882-5)
Bd. 8:	2005.	Hardcover. X, 252 S.	48.00 €	(ISBN 3-87690-924-4)
Bd. 9:	2006.	Hardcover. VIII, 168 S.	36.00 €	(ISBN 3-87690-969-1)
Bd. 10:	2007.	Hardcover. VIII, 208 S.	38.00 €	(ISBN 3-87690-988-2)
Bd. 11:	2008.	Hardcover. VIII, 297 S.	64.00 €	(ISBN 3-86688-008-5)
Bd. 12:	2009.	Hardcover. VIII, 223 S.	46.00 €	(ISBN 3-86688-055-9)
Bd. 13:	2010.	Hardcover. X, 312 S.	58.00 €	(ISBN 3-86688-084-9)
Bd. 14:	2011.	Hardcover. VIII, 269 S.	46.00 €	(ISBN 3-86688-137-2)
Bd. 15:	2012.	Hardcover. X, 328 S.	48.00 €	(ISBN 3-86688-236-2)
Bd. 16:	2013.	Hardcover. X, 272 S.	44.00 €	(ISBN 3-86688-361-1)
Bd. 17:	2014.	Hardcover. VIII, 252 S.	42.00 €	(ISBN 3-86688-467-0)

Bd. 16: **Itinera Slavica. Studien zu Literatur und Kultur der Slaven. Festschrift für Rolf-Dieter Kluge zum 65. Geburtstag.** Herausgegeben von Heide Willich-Lederbogen, Regine Nohejl, Michaela Fischer, Heinz Setzer.
2002. Hardcover. 308 S. 60.- €. (ISBN 3-87690-824-8)

Bd. 17: **Bühne und Öffentlichkeit. Drama und Theater im Spät- und Postsozialismus (1983-1993).** Herausgegeben von Norbert Franz und Herta Schmid.
2002. Hardcover. 200 S. 46.- €. (ISBN 3-87690-833-7)

Bd. 19: **Rusistika • Slavistika • Lingvistika. Festschrift für Werner Lehfeldt zum 60. Geburtstag.** Herausgegeben von Sebastian Kempgen, Ulrich Schweier, Tilman Berger.
2003. Hardcover. 532 S. 90.- €. (ISBN 3-87690-837-5)

Bd. 21: **Germano-Slavistische Beiträge. Festschrift für Peter Rehder zum 65. Geburtstag.** Herausgegeben von Miloš Okuka und Ulrich Schweier.
2004. Hardcover. 568 S. 90.- €. (ISBN 3-87690-874-4)

Bd. 23: **Der Text und seine Spielarten im polnischen Barock. Bausteine zu einer Epochenanalyse.** Herausgegeben von Herta Schmid unter Mitwirkung von Holt Meyer und Bernhard Hartmann.
2005. Hardcover. 208 S. 44.- €. (ISBN 3-87690-925-2)

Bd. 25: **Čechovs Einakter Tatjana Repina. Analyse und Umfeld eines verkannten Meisterwerks.** Herausgegeben von Jenny Stelleman und Herta Schmid unter Mitwirkung von Ursula Hanuš.
2006. Hardcover. 351 S. 64.- €. (ISBN 3-87690-929-5)

Bd. 26: **Exklusion. Chronotopoi der Ausgrenzung in der russischen und polnischen Literatur.** Herausgegeben von Wolfgang Stephan Kissel und Franziska Thun-Hohenstein.
2006. Hardcover. 303 S. 44.- €. (ISBN 3-87690-931-7)

Bd. 28: **Iter philologicum. Festschrift für Helmut Keipert zum 65. Geburtstag.** Herausgegeben von Daniel Bunčić und Nikolaos Trunte.
2006. Hardcover. 342 S. 68.- €. (ISBN 978-3-87690-971-4)

Bd. 30: **Wortkunst • Erzählkunst • Bildkunst. Festschrift für Aage A. Hansen-Löve.** Herausgegeben von Rainer Grübel und Wolf Schmid.
2008. Hardcover. 326 S. 68.- €. (ISBN 978-3-86688-005-4)

Bd. 32: **Deutsche Beiträge zum 14. Internationalen Slavistenkongress Ohrid 2008.** Herausgegeben von Sebastian Kempgen, Karl Gutschmidt, Ulrike Jekutsch, Ludger Udolph.
2008. Hardcover, 532 S. 98.- €. (ISBN 978-3-86688-007-8)

Bd. 34: **Die slavischen Grenzen Mitteleuropas. Festschrift für Sergio Bonazza.** Herausgegeben von Stefano Aloe.
2008. Hardcover. 202 S. 38.- €. (ISBN 978-3-86688-036-8)

Bd. 35: **Kapitel aus der Poetik. Die zehner Jahre in der tschechischen Literatur zwischen Symbolismus und Avantgarde.** Herausgegeben von Birgit Krehl und Herta Schmid.
2008. Hardcover, 299 S. 38.- €. (ISBN 978-3-86688-043-6)

Bd. 36: **Proceedings of the Second International *Perspectives on Slavistics* Conference, Regensburg 2006.** Edited by Sandra Birzer, Miriam Finkelstein, Imke Mendoza.
2009. Hardcover, VIII, 318 S. 68.- €. (ISBN 978-3-86688-045-0)+

Bd. 39: **Text – Sprache – Grammatik. Slavisches Schrifttum der Vormoderne. Festschrift für Eckhard Weiher.** Herausgegeben von Juliane Besters-Dilger und Achim Rabus.
2009. Hardcover, 416 S. 74.- €. (ISBN 978-3-86688-081-8)

Bd. 42: **Studien zu Sprache, Literatur und Kultur bei den Slaven. Gedenkschrift für George Y. Shevelov aus Anlass seines 100. Geburtstages und 10. Todestages.** Herausgegeben von Andrii Danylenko und Serhii Vakulenko.
2012. Hardcover, XLIV, 520 S. 64.- €. (ISBN 978-3-86688-205-8)

Bd. 44: **Anton P. Čechov – der Dramatiker. Drittes internationales Čechov-Symposium Badenweiler im Oktober 2004.** Herausgegeben von Regine Nohejl und Heinz Setzer.
2012. Hardcover, 642 S. 36.- €. (ISBN 978-3-86688-267-6, e-Book: 978-3-86688-268-3)

Bd. 45: **»Isochimenen«. Kultur und Raum im Werk von Isidora Sekulić.** Herausgegeben von Tatjana Petzer und Angela Richter.
2012. Hardcover, 281 S. 69.80 €. (ISBN 978-3-86688-230-0, e-Book: 978-3-86688-231-7)

Bd. 47: **Slavisches Drama und Theater in Vergangenheit und Gegenwart. Beiträge zur Jubiläumstagung anlässlich des 65. Geburtstages von Herta Schmid an der Universität Potsdam.** Herausgegeben von Birgit Krehl.
2012. Hardcover, 239 S. 38,- €. (ISBN 978-3-86688-273-7, e-Book: 978-3-86688-274-4)

Bd. 48: **Lermontov neu bewertet neue bewertet. Lermontov Revisited. Dramen – Epik – Lyrik – Übersetzung.** Herausgegeben von Herta Schmid und Jenny Stelleman
2013. Hardcover, 571 S. 64,- €. (ISBN 978-3-86688-324-6, e-Book: 978-3-86688-325-3)

Bd. 50: **Deutsche Beiträge zum 15. Internationalen Slavistenkongress Minsk 2013.** Herausgegeben von Sebastian Kempgen, Monika Wingender, Norbert Franz, Miranda Jakiša.
2013. Hardcover, 442 S. 68,- €. (ISBN 978-3-86688-359-8, e-Book: 978-3-86688-360-4)

Bd. 51: **Genderdiskurse und nationale Identität in Russland – Sowjetische und postsowjetische Zeit.** Herausgegeben von Regine Nohejl, Olga Gorfinkel, Friederike Carl und Elisabeth Cheauré.
2013. Hardcover. 333 S. 42.- €. (ISBN 978-3-86688-365-9, e-Book: 978-3-86688-366-6)

Bd. 52: **Osteuropäisch-jüdische Literaturen im 20. und 21. Jahrhundert: Identität und Poetik.** Eastern European Jewish Literature of the 20th and 21st Centuries: Identity and Poetics. Herausgegeben von / Edited by Klavdia Smola.
2013. Hardcover. 440 S. 58.- €. (ISBN 978-3-86688-383-3, e-Book: 978-3-86688-384-0)